ELEMENTS OF CRITICISM

VOLUME 2

NATURAL LAW AND
ENLIGHTENMENT CLASSICS

Knud Haakonssen
General Editor

Henry Home, Lord Kames

NATURAL LAW AND
ENLIGHTENMENT CLASSICS

Elements

of

Criticism

VOLUME 2

Henry Home, Lord Kames

The Sixth Edition

Edited and with an Introduction by Peter Jones

Major Works of Henry Home, Lord Kames

LIBERTY FUND

Indianapolis

This book is published by Liberty Fund, Inc., a foundation established to encourage study of the ideal of a society of free and responsible individuals.

𒂼𒄀

The cuneiform inscription that serves as our logo and as the design motif for our endpapers is the earliest-known written appearance of the word "freedom" (*amagi*), or "liberty." It is taken from a clay document written about 2300 B.C. in the Sumerian city-state of Lagash.

09 08 07 06 05 c 5 4 3 2 1
09 08 07 06 05 p 5 4 3 2 1

Frontispiece and cover (detail): Portrait of Henry Home, Lord Kames, by David Martin. Reproduced with permission of the National Galleries of Scotland.

Library of Congress Cataloging-in-Publication Data
Kames, Henry Home, Lord, 1696–1782.
Elements of criticism / Henry Home, Lord Kames;
edited and with an introduction by Peter Jones.
p. cm.—(Major works of Henry Home, Lord Kames)
(Natural law and enlightenment classics)
Originally published: 6th ed. Edinburgh: J. Bell and W. Creech;
London: T. Cadell and G. Robinson, 1785.
Includes bibliographical references.
ISBN 0-86597-466-7 (set: alk. paper)   ISBN 0-86597-469-1 (set: soft: alk. paper)
ISBN 0-86597-467-5 (v. 1: alk. paper)   ISBN 0-86597-470-5 (v. 1: sc: alk. paper)
1. Criticism.   2. Style, Literary.
I. Jones, Peter (Peter H.), 1935–   . II. Title. III. Series.
PN81.K3 2005
801′.95—DC22   2004063389
ISBN 0-86597-468-3 (v. 2: alk. paper)   ISBN 0-86597-471-3 (v. 2: sc: alk. paper)

LIBERTY FUND, INC.
8335 Allison Pointe Trail, Suite 300
Indianapolis, Indiana 46250-1684

CONTENTS

ELEMENTS

OF

CRITICISM.

The SIXTH EDITION.

WITH THE

AUTHOR'S LAST CORRECTIONS
AND ADDITIONS.

VOLUME II

EDINBURGH:
Printed for JOHN BELL and WILLIAM CREECH,
And for T. CADELL and G. ROBINSON, *London.*

M,DCC,LXXXV.

CONTENTS[1]

1. The original page numbers from the sixth edition are retained here.

ELEMENTS
OF
CRITICISM.

⋈ CHAPTER XVIII ⋈

Beauty of Language[1]

Of all the fine arts, painting only and sculpture are in their nature imitative. An ornamented field is not a copy or imitation of nature, but nature itself embellished. Architecture is productive of originals, and copies not from nature. Sound and motion may in some measure be imitated by music; but for the most part music, like architecture, is productive of originals. Language copies not from nature, more than music or architecture; unless where, like music, it is imitative of sound or motion. Thus, in the description of particular sounds, language sometimes furnisheth words, which, beside their customary power of <4> exciting ideas, resemble by their softness or harshness the sounds described; and there are words which, by the celerity or slowness of pronunciation, have some resemblance to the motion they signify. The imitative power of words goes one step farther: the loftiness of some words makes them proper symbols of lofty ideas; a rough subject is imitated by harsh-sounding words; and words of many syllables pronounced slow and smooth, are expressive of grief and melancholy.

---

1. Kames added many new quotations to the text of this central chapter in editions after the first.

Words have a separate effect on the mind, abstracting from their signification and from their imitative power: they are more or less agreeable to the ear, by the fulness, sweetness, faintness, or roughness of their tones.

These are but faint beauties, being known to those only who have more than ordinary acuteness of perception. Language possesseth a beauty superior greatly in degree, of which we are eminently sensible when a thought is communicated with perspicuity and sprightliness. This beauty of language, arising from its power of expressing thought, is apt to be confounded with the beauty of the thought itself: the beauty of thought, transferred to the expression, makes it appear more beautiful.* But these beauties, if we wish to <5> think accurately, must be distinguished from each other. They are in reality so distinct, that we sometimes are conscious of the highest pleasure language can afford, when the subject expressed is disagreeable: a thing that is loathsome, or a scene of horror to make one's hair stand on end, may be described in a manner so lively, as that the disagreeableness of the subject shall not even obscure the agreeableness of the description. The causes of the original beauty of language, considered as significant, which is a branch of the present subject, will be explained in their order. I shall only at present observe, that this beauty is the beauty of means fitted to an end, that of communicating thought: and hence it evidently appears, that of several expressions all conveying the same thought, the most beautiful, in the sense now mentioned, is that which in the most perfect manner answers its end.

The several beauties of language above mentioned, being of different kinds, ought to be handled separately. I shall begin with those beauties of language that arise from sound; after which will follow the beauties of language considered as significant: this order appears natural; for the <6> sound of a word is attended to, before we consider its signification. In a third section come those singular beauties of language that are derived from

---

* Chap. 2. part 1. sect. 5. Demetrius Phalereus (of Elocution, sect. 75.) makes the same observation. We are apt, says that author, to confound the language with the subject; and if the latter be nervous, we judge the same of the former. But they are clearly distinguishable; and it is not uncommon to find subjects of great dignity dressed in mean language. Theopompus is celebrated for the force of his diction; but erroneously: his subject indeed has great force, but his style very little.

a resemblance between sound and signification. The beauties of verse are handled in the last section: for though the foregoing beauties are found in verse as well as in prose, yet verse has many peculiar beauties, which for the sake of connection must be brought under one view; and versification, at any rate, is a subject of so great importance, as to deserve a place by itself.

SECTION I

Beauty of Language with respect to Sound.

This subject requires the following order. The sounds of the different letters come first: next, these sounds as united in syllables: third, syllables united in words: fourth, words united in a period: and in the last place, periods united in a discourse.

With respect to the first article, every vowel is sounded with a single expiration of air from the wind-pipe, through the cavity of the mouth. By varying this cavity, the different vowels are sounded: for the air in passing through cavities differing in size, produceth various sounds, some high or <7> sharp, some low or flat; a small cavity occasions a high sound, a large cavity a low sound. The five vowels accordingly, pronounced with the same extension of the wind-pipe, but with different openings of the mouth, form a regular series of sounds, descending from high to low, in the following order, *i, e, a, o, u.** Each of these sounds is agreeable to the ear: and if it be required which of them is the most agreeable, it is perhaps safest to hold, that those vowels which are the farthest removed from the extremes, will be the most relished. This is all I have to remark upon the first article: for consonants being letters that of themselves have no sound, serve only in conjunction with vowels to form articulate sounds; and as every articulate sound makes a syllable, consonants come naturally under the second article; to which we proceed.

A consonant is pronounced with a less cavity than any vowel; and con-

---

* In this scale of sounds, the letter *i* must be pronounced as in the word *interest,* and as in other words beginning with the syllable *in;* the letter *e* as in *persuasion;* the letter *a* as in *hat;* and the letter *u* as in *number.*

sequently every syllable into which a consonant enters, must have more than one sound, though pronounced with one expiration of air, or with one breath as commonly expressed: for however readily two sounds may unite, yet where they differ in tone, both of them must <8> be heard if neither of them be suppressed. For the same reason, every syllable must be composed of as many sounds as there are letters, supposing every letter to be distinctly pronounced.

We next enquire, how far syllables are agreeable to the ear. Few tongues are so polished, as entirely to have rejected sounds that are pronounced with difficulty; and it is a noted observation, That such sounds are to the ear harsh and disagreeable. But with respect to agreeable sounds, it appears, that a double sound is always more agreeable than a single sound: every one who has an ear must be sensible, that the dipththong *oi* or *ai* is more agreeable than any of these vowels pronounced singly: the same holds where a consonant enters into the double sound; the syllable *le* has a more agreeable sound than the vowel *e,* or than any vowel. And in support of experience, a satisfactory argument may be drawn from the wisdom of Providence: speech is bestowed on man, to qualify him for society; and his provision of articulate sounds is proportioned to the use he hath for them: but if sounds that are agreeable singly were not also agreeable in conjunction, the necessity of a painful selection would render language intricate and difficult to be attained in any perfection; and this selection, at the same time, would abridge the number of useful sounds, so as perhaps not to leave sufficient for answering the different ends of language. <9>

In this view, the harmony of pronunciation differs widely from that of music properly so called. In the latter are discovered many sounds singly agreeable, which in conjunction are extremely disagreeable; none but what are called *concordant sounds* having a good effect in conjunction. In the former, all sounds, singly agreeable, are in conjunction concordant; and ought to be, in order to fulfil the purposes of language.

Having discussed syllables, we proceed to words; which make the third article. Monosyllables belong to the former head: polysyllables open a different scene. In a cursory view, one would imagine, that the agreeableness or disagreeableness of a word with respect to its sound, should depend upon the agreeableness or disagreeableness of its component syllables: which is true in part, but not entirely; for we must also take under consideration, the effect of syllables in succession. In the first place, syllables in immediate succession, pronounced, each of them, with the same or nearly the same aperture of the mouth, produce a succession of weak and feeble sounds; witness the French words *dit-il, pathetique:* on the other hand, a syllable of the greatest aperture succeeding one of the smallest, or the contrary, makes a succession, which, because of its remarkable disagreeableness, is distinguished by a proper name, *hiatus.* The most agreeable succession is, where the cavity is increased and diminished alternately <10> within moderate limits. Examples, *alternative, longevity, pusillanimous.* Secondly, words consisting wholly of syllables pronounced slow, or of syllables pronounced quick, commonly called *long* and *short syllables,* have little melody in them; witness the words *petitioner, fruiterer, dizziness:* on the other hand, the intermixture of long and short syllables is remarkably agreeable; for example, *degree, repent, wonderful, altitude, rapidity, independent, impetuosity.* The cause will be explained afterward, in treating of versification.

Distinguishable from the beauties above mentioned, there is a beauty of some words which arises from their signification: when the emotion raised by the length or shortness, the roughness or smoothness, of the sound, resembles in any degree what is raised by the sense, we feel a very remarkable pleasure. But this subject belongs to the third section.

The foregoing observations afford a standard to every nation, for estimating, pretty accurately, the comparative merit of the words that enter into <11> their own language: but they are not equally useful in comparing the words of different languages; which will thus appear. Different nations judge differently of the harshness or smoothness of articulate sounds; a sound, for example, harsh and disagreeable to an Italian, may be abundantly smooth to a northern ear: here every nation must judge for itself; nor can there be any solid ground for a preference, when there is no common standard to which we can appeal. The case is precisely the same as in behaviour

---

* Italian words, like those of Latin and Greek, have this property almost universally: English and French words are generally deficient. In the former, the long syllable is removed from the end as far as the sound will permit; and in the latter, the last syllable is generally long. For example, Sēnator in English, Senātor in Latin, and Senatēur in French.

and manners: plain-dealing and sincerity, liberty in words and actions, form
the character of one people; politeness, reserve, and a total disguise of every
sentiment that can give offence, form the character of another people: to
each the manners of the other are disagreeable. An effeminate mind cannot
bear the least of that roughness and severity, which is generally esteemed
manly when exerted upon proper occasions: neither can an effeminate ear
bear the harshness of certain words, that are deemed nervous and sounding
by those accustomed to a rougher tone of speech. Must we then relinquish
all thoughts of comparing languages in point of roughness and smoothness, as a fruitless inquiry? Not altogether; for we may proceed a certain
length, tho' without hope of an ultimate decision. A language pronounced
with difficulty even by natives, must yield to a smoother language: and
supposing two languages pronounced with equal <12> facility by natives,
the rougher language, in my judgment, ought to be preferred, provided it
be also stored with a competent share of more mellow sounds; which will
be evident from attending to the different effects that articulate sound hath
on the mind. A smooth gliding sound is agreeable, by calming the mind,
and lulling it to rest: a rough bold sound, on the contrary, animates the
mind; the effort perceived in pronouncing, is communicated to the hearers,
who feel in their own minds a similar effort, rousing their attention, and
disposing them to action. I add another consideration: the agreeableness
of contrast in the rougher language, for which the great variety of sounds
gives ample opportunity, must, even in an effeminate ear, prevail over the
more uniform sounds of the smoother language.* This appears all that can
be safely determined upon the present point. With respect to the other
circumstances that constitute the beauty of words, the standard above mentioned is infallible when apply'd to foreign languages as well as to our own:
for every man, whatever be his mother-tongue, is equally capable to judge
of the length or shortness of words, of the alternate opening and closing
of the mouth in speaking, and of the relation that the <13> sound bears to

* That the Italian tongue is too smooth, seems probable from considering, that in
versification vowels are frequently suppressed in order to produce a rougher and bolder
tone.

the sense: in these particulars, the judgment is susceptible of no prejudice from custom, at least of no invincible prejudice.

That the English tongue, originally harsh, is at present much softened by dropping in the pronunciation many redundant consonants, is undoubtedly true: that it is not capable of being further mellowed without suffering in its force and energy, will scarce be thought by any one who possesses an ear; and yet such in Britain is the propensity for dispatch, that, overlooking the majesty of words composed of many syllables aptly connected, the prevailing taste is to shorten words, even at the expence of making them disagreeable to the ear, and harsh in the pronunciation. But I have no occasion to insist upon this article, being prevented by an excellent writer, who possessed, if any man ever did, the true genius of the English tongue.* I cannot however forbear urging one observation, borrowed from that author: several tenses of our verbs are formed by adding the final syllable *ed,* which, being a weak sound, has remarkably the worse effect by possessing the most conspicuous place in the word; upon which account, the vowel in common speech is generally suppressed, and the consonant added to the foregoing syllable; whence the following rugged sounds, <14> *drudg'd, disturb'd, rebuk'd, fledg'd.* It is still less excusable to follow this practice in writing; for the hurry of speaking may excuse what would be altogether improper in composition: the syllable *ed,* it is true, sounds poorly at the end of a word; but rather that defect, than multiply the number of harsh words, which, after all, bear an over-proportion in our tongue. The author above-mentioned, by showing a good example, did all in his power to restore that syllable; and he well deserves to be imitated. Some exceptions however I would make. A word that signifies labour or any thing harsh or rugged, ought not to be smooth; therefore *forc'd,* with an apostrophe, is better than *forced,* without it. Another exception is where the penult syllable ends with a vowel; in that case the final syllable *ed* may be apostrophized without making the word harsh: examples, *betray'd, carry'd, destroy'd, employ'd.*

* See Swift's proposal for correcting the English tongue, in a letter to the Earl of Oxford. [*A Proposal for correcting, improving and ascertaining the English tongue, in a letter to the Earl of Oxford,* 1712.]

The article next in order, is the music of words as united in a period. And as the arrangement of words in succession so as to afford the greatest pleasure to the ear, depends on principles remote from common view, it will be necessary to premise some general observations upon the appearance that objects make when placed in an increasing or decreasing series. Where the objects vary by small differences so as to have a mutual resemblance, we in ascending conceive <15> the second object of no greater size than the first, the third of no greater size than the second, and so of the rest; which diminisheth in appearance the size of every object except the first: but when, beginning at the greatest object, we proceed gradually to the least, resemblance makes us imagine the second as great as the first, and the third as great as the second; which in appearance magnifies every object except the first. On the other hand, in a series varying by large differences, where contrast prevails, the effects are directly opposite: a great object succeeding a small one of the same kind, appears greater than usual; and a little object succeeding one that is great, appears less than usual.* Hence a remarkable pleasure in viewing a series ascending by large differences; directly opposite to what we feel when the differences are small. The least object of a series ascending by large differences has the same effect upon the mind as if it stood single without making a part of the series: but the second object, by means of contrast, appears greater than when view'd singly and apart; and the same effect is perceived in ascending progressively, till we arrive at the last object. The opposite effect is produced in descending; for in this direction, every object, except the first, appears less than when view'd separately and independent of the series. We may <16> then assume as a maxim, which will hold in the composition of language as well as of other subjects, That a strong impulse succeeding a weak, makes double impression on the mind; and that a weak impulse succeeding a strong, makes scarce any impression.

After establishing this maxim, we can be at no loss about its application to the subject in hand. The following rule is laid down by Diomedes.† "In verbis observandum est, ne a majoribus ad minora descendat oratio; melius

---

* See the reason, chap. 8.
† De structura perfectae orationis, l. 2.

enim dicitur, *Vir est optimus,* quam, *Vir optimus est.*" This rule is also applicable to entire members of a period, which, according to our author's expression, ought not, more than single words, to proceed from the greater to the less, but from the less to the greater.* In arranging the members of a period, no writer equals Cicero: the beauty of the following examples out of many, will not suffer me to slur them over by a reference.

> Quicum quaestor fueram,
> Quicum me sors consuetudoque majorum,
> Quicum me deorum hominumque judicium conjunxerat.[2]

Again:

> Habet honorem quem petimus,
> Habet spem quam praepositam nobis habemus, <17>
> Habet existimationem, multo sudore, labore, vigiliisque,
>   collectam.[3]

Again:

> Eripite nos ex miseriis,
> Eripite nos ex faucibus eorum,
> Quorum crudelitas nostro sanguine non potest expleri.
>
> *De oratore, l.* I. § 52.[4]

This order of words or members gradually increasing in length, may, as far as concerns the pleasure of sound, be denominated *a climax in sound.*

The last article is the music of periods as united in a discourse; which shall be dispatched in a very few words. By no other human means is it possible to present to the mind, such a number of objects and in so swift a succession, as by speaking or writing: and for that reason, variety ought more to be studied in these, than in any other sort of composition. Hence

---

* See Demetrius Phalereus of Elocution, sect. 18.

2. "With whom I had been quaestor, with whom chance and tradition, with whom the decision of the gods and men had joined . . ."

3. Cicero, *Against Quintus Caecilius Niger* 22.72: "The office to which I seek election; the ambition that I cherish in my heart; the reputation for which I have risen early and toiled in the heat to gain."

4. *De Oratore* 1.52: "Deliver us out of our woes, deliver us out of the jaws of those whose ferocity cannot get its fill of blood."

a rule for arranging the members of different periods with relation to each
other, That to avoid a tedious uniformity of sound and cadence, the arrangement, the cadence, and the length of the members, ought to be diversified as much as possible: and if the members of different periods be
sufficiently diversified, the periods themselves will be equally so. <18>

SECTION II

Beauty of Language with respect to Signification.

It is well said by a noted writer,* "That by means of speech we can divert
our sorrows, mingle our mirth, impart our secrets, communicate our coun-
sels, and make mutual compacts and agreements to supply and assist each
other." Considering speech as contributing to so many good purposes,
words that convey clear and distinct ideas, must be one of its capital beauties. This cause of beauty, is too extensive to be handled as a branch of any
other subject: for to ascertain with accuracy even the proper meaning of
words, not to talk of their figurative power, would require a large volume;
an useful work indeed, but not to be attempted without a large stock of
time, study, and reflection. This branch therefore of the subject I humbly
decline. Nor do I propose to exhaust all the other beauties of language that
relate to signification: the reader, in a work like the present, cannot fairly
expect more than a slight sketch of those that make the greatest figure. This
task is the more to my taste, as being connected with certain natural principles; and the <19> rules I shall have occasion to lay down, will, if I judge
rightly, be agreeable illustrations of these principles. Every subject must be
of importance that tends to unfold the human heart; for what other science
is of greater use to human beings?

The present subject is too extensive to be discussed without dividing it
into parts; and what follows suggests a division into two parts. In every
period, two things are to be regarded: first, the words of which it is composed; next, the arrangement of these words; the former resembling the
stones that compose a building, and the latter resembling the order in which

* Scot's Christian life. [J. Scott, *The Christian Life, from Its Beginnings,* 1694–98.]

they are placed. Hence the beauties of language with respect to signification, may not improperly be distinguished into two kinds: first, the beauties
that arise from a right choice of words or materials for constructing the
period; and next, the beauties that arise from a due arrangement of these
words or materials. I begin with rules that direct us to a right choice of
words, and then proceed to rules that concern their arrangement.

And with respect to the former, communication of thought being the
chief end of language, it is a rule, That perspicuity ought not to be sacrificed
to any other beauty whatever: if it should be doubted whether perspicuity
be a positive beauty, it cannot be doubted that the want of it is the greatest
defect. Nothing therefore in language ought more to be studied, than to
prevent all ob-<20>scurity in the expression; for to have no meaning, is but
one degree worse, than to have a meaning that is not understood. Want of
perspicuity from a wrong arrangement, belongs to the next branch. I shall
here give a few examples where the obscurity arises from a wrong choice of
words; and as this defect is too common in the ordinary herd of writers to
make examples from them necessary, I confine myself to the most celebrated authors.

Livy, speaking of a rout after a battle,

Multique in ruina *majore* quam fuga oppressi obtruncatique.

L. 4. § 46.[5]

This author is frequently obscure by expressing but part of his thought,
leaving it to be completed by his reader. His description of the sea-fight,
l. 28. *cap.* 30. is extremely perplexed.

Unde tibi reditum *certo subtemine* Parcae
Rupere.   *Horace, epod.* xiii. 22.[6]

---

5. "Many of them, as they tumbled over rather than retreated, were overtaken and
put to the sword."
6. "Whence the Fates by fixed decree have cut off thy return."

Qui persaepe cava testudine flevit amorem,
Non elaboratum ad pedem.   *Horace, epod.* xiv. 11.[7]

Me fabulosae Vulture in Appulo,
Altricis extra limen Apuliae,
    Ludo, fatigatumque *somno,* <21>
    Fronde nova puerum palumbes
Texere.   *Horace, Carm. l.* 3. *ode.* 4.[8]

Purae rivus aquae, silvaque jugerum
Paucorum, et segetis certa fides meae,
Fulgentum imperio fertilis Africae
    Fallit sorte beatior.   *Horace, Carm. l.* 3. *ode* 16.[9]

Cum fas atque nefas exiguo *fine* libidinum
Discernunt avidi.   *Horace, Carm. l.* 1. *ode* 18.[10]

Ac spem fronte serenat.   *Aeneid.* iv. 477.[11]

I am in greater pain about the foregoing passages than about any I have ventured to criticise, being aware that a vague or obscure expression, is apt to gain favour with those who neglect to examine it with a critical eye. To some it carries the sense that they relish the most; and by suggesting various meanings at once, it is admired by others as concise and comprehensive: which by the way fairly accounts for the opinion generally entertained with respect to most languages in their infant state, of expressing much in few

---

7. "Who on his shallow shell sang full oft his plaintive strains of love in simple measure."

8. "In childhood's days, on trackless Vultur, beyond the borders of old nurse Apulia, when I was tired with play and overcome with sleep, the doves of story covered me o'er with freshly fallen leaves."

9. "My stream of pure water, my woodland of few acres, and sure trust in my crop of corn bring me more blessing than the lot of the dazzling lord of fertile Africa, though he know it not."

10. "When, furious with desire, they distinguish right and wrong only by the narrow line their passions draw."

11. "On her brow the calm of hope."

words. This observation may be illustrated by a passage from Quintilian, quoted in the first volume for a different purpose. <22>

> At quae Polycleto defuerunt, Phidiae atque Alcameni dantur. Phidias tamen diis quam hominibus efficiendis melior artifex traditur: in ebore vero, longe citra aemulum, vel si nihil nisi Minervam Athenis, aut Olympium in Elide Jovem fecisset, *cujus pulchritudo adjecisse aliquid etiam receptae religioni videtur; adeo majestas operis Deum aequavit.* [12]

The sentence in the Italic characters appeared to me abundantly perspicuous, before I gave it peculiar attention. And yet to examine it independent of the context, its proper meaning is not what is intended: the words naturally import, that the beauty of the statues mentioned, appears to add some new tenet or rite to the established religion, or appears to add new dignity to it; and we must consult the context before we can gather the true meaning; which is, that the Greeks were confirmed in the belief of their established religion by these majestic statues, so like real divinities.

There may be a defect in perspicuity proceeding even from the slightest ambiguity in construction; as where the period commences with a member conceived to be in the nominative case, which afterward is found to be in the accusative. Example: "Some emotions more peculiarly connected with the fine arts, I propose to handle in separate chapters."* Better thus: "Some <23> emotions more peculiarly connected with the fine arts, are proposed to be handled in separate chapters."

I add another error against perspicuity; which I mention the rather because with some writers it passes for a beauty. It is the giving different names to the same object, mentioned oftener than once in the same period. Example: Speaking of the English adventurers who first attempted the conquest of Ireland, "and instead of reclaiming the natives from their uncultivated manners, they were gradually assimilated to the ancient inhabitants,

---

* *Elements of Criticism,* vol. 1. p. 43. edit. 1.

12. [Bk.12.10] "But the qualities lacking in Polyclitus are allowed to have been possessed by Phidias and Alcamanes. In the other hand Phidias is regarded as more gifted in his representation of gods than of men, and indeed for chryselephantine statues he is without peer, as he would in truth be, even if he had produced nothing in this material beyond his Minerva at Athens and his Jupiter at Olympia in Elis, whose beauty is said to have added something even to the awe with which the god was already regarded."

and degenerated from the customs of their own nation." From this mode of expression, one would think the author meant to distinguish *the ancient inhabitants* from *the natives;* and we cannot discover otherwise than from the sense, that these are only different names given to the same object for the sake of variety. But perspicuity ought never to be sacrificed to any other beauty, which leads me to think that the passage may be improved as follows: "and degenerating from the customs of their own nation, they were gradually assimilated to the natives, instead of reclaiming them from their uncultivated manners."

The next rule in order, because next in importance, is, That the language ought to correspond to the subject: heroic actions or sentiments re-<24>quire elevated language; tender sentiments ought to be expressed in words soft and flowing; and plain language void of ornament, is adapted to subjects grave and didactic. Language may be considered as the dress of thought; and where the one is not suited to the other, we are sensible of incongruity, in the same manner as where a judge is dressed like a fop, or a peasant like a man of quality. Where the impression made by the words resembles the impression made by the thought, the similar emotions mix sweetly in the mind, and double the pleasure;* but where the impressions made by the thought and the words are dissimilar, the unnatural union they are forced into is disagreeable.†

This concordance between the thought and the words has been observed by every critic, and is so well understood as not to require any illustration. But there is a concordance of a peculiar kind that has scarcely been touched in works of criticism, though it contributes to neatness of composition. It is what follows. In a thought of any extent, we commonly find some parts intimately united, some slightly, some disjoined, and some directly opposed to each other. To find these conjunctions and disjunctions imitated in the expression, is a beauty; because such imitation makes the words concordant with the sense. <25> This doctrine may be illustrated by a familiar example. When we have occasion to mention the intimate connection that the soul

* Chap. 2. part 4.
† Ibid.

hath with the body, the expression ought to be, *the soul and body;* because the particle *the,* relative to both, makes a connection in the expression, resembling in some degree the connection in the thought: but when the soul is distinguished from the body, it is better to say *the soul and the body;* because the disjunction in the words resembles the disjunction in the thought. I proceed to other examples, beginning with conjunctions.

Constituit agmen; et expedire tela animosque, equitibus jussis, *&c.*

Livy, l. 38. § 25.[13]

Here the words that express the connected ideas are artificially connected by subjecting them both to the regimen of one verb. And the two following are of the same kind.

Quum ex paucis quotidie aliqui eorum caderent aut vulnerarentur, et qui superarent, fessi et corporibus et animis essent, *&c.*

Livy, l. 38. § 29.[14]

Post acer Mnestheus adducto constitit arcu,
Alta petens, pariterque oculos telumque tetendit.

Aeneid, v. 507.[15]

But to justify this artificial connection among the <26> words, the ideas they express ought to be intimately connected; for otherwise that concordance which is required between the sense and the expression will be impaired. In that view, a passage from Tacitus is exceptionable; where words that signify ideas very little connected, are however forc'd into an artificial union. Here is the passage:

13. "He halted his column, and, ordering the troopers to prepare arms, and minds, for battle."
14. "Since every day some of their small number were killed or wounded and those who remained were wearied in both body and mind."
15. "Next valiant Mnestheus took his stand with bow bent, aiming aloft, and eyes and shaft levelled alike."

Germania omnis a Galliis, Rhaetiisque, et Pannoniis, Rheno et Danubio
fluminibus; a Sarmatis Dacisque, mutuo metu aut montibus separatur.
De moribus Germanorum.[16]

Upon the same account, I esteem the following passage equally exceptionable.

———— The fiend look'd up, and knew
His mounted scale aloft; nor more, but fled
Murm'ring, and with him fled the shades of night.
Paradise Lost, b. 4. at the end.

There is no natural connection between a person's flying or retiring, and
the succession of day-light to darkness; and therefore to connect artificially
the terms that signify these things cannot have a sweet effect.

Two members of a thought connected by their relation to the same action, will naturally be expressed by two members of the period governed
by the same verb; in which case these members, <27> in order to improve
their connection, ought to be constructed in the same manner. This beauty
is so common among good writers, as to have been little attended to; but
the neglect of it is remarkably disagreeable: For example, "He did not mention Leonora, nor that her father was dead." Better thus: "He did not
mention Leonora, nor her father's death."

Where two ideas are so connected as to require but a copulative, it is
pleasant to find a connection in the words that express these ideas, were it
even so slight as where both begin with the same letter:

The peacock, in all his pride, does not display half the colour that appears
in the garments of a British lady, when she is either dressed for a ball or a
birth-day.   *Spectator,* No. 265.

---

16. Tacitus, *De Moribus Germanorum* (A.D. 98). Translated as *A Treatise on the Situation, Manners, and People of Germany,* by Arthur Murphy, 1793: "The whole vast
country of Germany is separated from Gaul, from Rhaetia, and Panonia, by the Rhine
and the Danube; from Dacia and Sarmatia, by a chain of mountains."

Had not my dog of a steward run away as he did, without making up his accounts, I had still been immersed in sin and sea-coal.

Ibid. No. 530.

My life's companion, and my bosom-friend,
One faith, one fame, one fate shall both attend.

Dryden, Translation of Aeneid.

There is sensibly a defect in neatness when uniformity in this case is totally neglected;* witness the following example, where the construction of <28> two members connected by a copulative is unnecessarily varied.

For it is confidently reported, that two young gentlemen of real hopes, bright wit, and profound judgement, who upon a thorough examination of causes and effects, and by the mere force of natural abilities, without the least tincture of learning, have made a discovery that there was no God, and *generously communicating* their thoughts for the good of the public, were some time ago, by an unparalleled severity, and upon I know not what obsolete law, broke for blasphemy.† [Better thus]:—having made a discovery that there was no God, and having generously communicated their thoughts for the good of the public, were some time ago, *&c.*

He had been guilty of a fault, for which his master would have put him to death, had he not found an opportunity to escape out of his hands, and *fled* into the deserts of Numidia. *Guardian,* No. 139.[17]

If all the ends of the revolution are already obtained, it is not only impertinent to argue for obtaining any of them, but *factious designs might be*

---

* See Girard's French Grammar, discourse 12. [G. Girard, *Les vraies principes de la langue françoise,* 1747.]

† An argument against abolishing Christianity. *Swift.* [In Swift, *Miscellanies,* 1711.]

17. Addison, *Guardian,* No. 139. The journal was started by Steele, but several eminent writers contributed to it, including Addison, Berkeley, Pope, and Gay.

imputed, and the name of incendiary be applied with some colour, perhaps, to any one who should persist in pressing this point.

Dissertation upon parties, Dedication. [18] <29>

Next as to examples of disjunction and opposition in the parts of the thought, imitated in the expression; an imitation that is distinguished by the name of *antithesis.*

Speaking of Coriolanus soliciting the people to be made consul:

> With a proud heart he wore his humble weeds.
>
> *Coriolanus.*

> Had you rather Caesar were living, and die all slaves,
> than that Caesar were dead, to live all free men?
>
> *Julius Caesar.*

> He hath cool'd my friends and heated mine enemies.
>
> *Shakespear.*[19]

An artificial connection among the words, is undoubtedly a beauty when it represents any peculiar connection among the constituent parts of the thought; but where there is no such connection, it is a positive deformity, as above observed, because it makes a discordance between the thought and expression. For the same reason, we ought also to avoid every artificial opposition of words where there is none in the thought. This last, termed *verbal antithesis,* is studied by low writers, because of a certain degree of liveliness in it. They do not consider how incongruous it is, in a grave composition, to cheat the reader, and to <30> make him expect a contrast in the thought, which upon examination is not found there.

> A *light* wife doth make a *heavy* husband.
>
> *Merchant of Venice.*

---

18. Bolingbroke, *Dissertation upon Parties,* 1735. Henry St. John, Lord Bolingbroke (1678–1751), was a Tory statesman and a friend of Pope and Swift.

19. *Coriolanus,* act 2, sc. 3; *Julius Caesar,* act 3, sc. 2; *Merchant of Venice,* act 3, sc. 1.

Here is a studied opposition in the words, not only without any opposition in the sense, but even where there is a very intimate connection, that of cause and effect; for it is the levity of the wife that torments the husband.

> ———— Will maintain
> Upon his *bad* life to make all this *good.*
> > *King Richard* II. *act* 1. *sc.* 3.

> *Lucetta.* What, shall these papers lie like tell-tales here?
> *Julia.* If thou respect them, best to take them up.
> *Lucetta.* Nay, I was *taken up* for *laying them down.*
> > *Two Gentlemen of Verona, act* 1. *sc.* 3.[20]

A fault directly opposite to that last mentioned, is to conjoin artificially words that express ideas opposed to each other. This is a fault too gross to be in common practice; and yet writers are guilty of it in some degree, when they conjoin by a copulative things transacted at different periods of time. Hence a want of neatness in the following expression.

> The nobility too, whom the King had no means of retaining by suitable offices and preferments, had been <31> seized with the general discontent, and unwarily threw themselves into the scale which began already too much to preponderate.   *History of G. Britain, vol.* 1. *p.* 250.[21]

In periods of this kind, it appears more neat to express the past time by the participle passive, thus:

> The nobility having been seized with the general discontent, unwarily threw themselves, *&c.* (or), The nobility, who had been seized, *&c.* unwarily threw themselves, *&c.*

It is unpleasant to find even a negative and affirmative proposition connected by a copulative:

---

20. *Merchant of Venice,* act 5, sc. 1; *Richard II,* act 1, sc. 3; *Two Gentlemen of Verona,* act 1, sc. 2.

21. David Hume, *History of Great Britain,* ch. 55 [1770 ed. 6.402].

Nec excitatur classico miles truci,
Nec horret iratum mare;
Forumque vitat, et superba civium
Potentiorum limina.   *Horace, Epod. 2. l. 5.*[22]

If it appear not plain, and prove untrue,
Deadly divorce step between me and you.   *Shakespear.*[23]

In mirth and drollery it may have a good effect to connect verbally things that are opposite to each other in the thought. Example: Henry the Fourth of France introducing the Mareschal Biron to some of his friends, "Here, Gentlemen," says he, "is the Mareschal Biron, whom I freely present both to my friends and enemies." <32>

This rule of studying uniformity between the thought and expression, may be extended to the construction of sentences or periods. A sentence or period ought to express one entire thought or mental proposition; and different thoughts ought to be separated in the expression by placing them in different sentences or periods. It is therefore offending against neatness, to crowd into one period entire thoughts requiring more than one; which is joining in language things that are separated in reality. Of errors against this rule take the following examples.

Behold, thou art fair, my beloved, yea pleasant; also our bed is green.[24]

Caesar, describing the Suevi:

Atque in eam se consuetudinem adduxerunt, ut locis frigidissimis, neque vestitus, praeter pelles, habeant quidquam, quarum propter exiguitatem, magna est corporis pars aperta, et laventur in fluminibus.

Commentaria, l. 4. prin.[25]

22. "Who is not, as a soldier, roused by the wild clarion, nor dreads the angry sea; he avoids the Forum and proud thresholds of more powerful citizens."

23. *All's Well That Ends Well,* act 5, sc. 3.

24. *The Song of Solomon,* 1.16.

25. Gaius Julius Caesar (100–44 B.C.): born into a patrician Roman family, military leader on numerous successful overseas expeditions. Caesar initially obtained political

Burnet, in the history of his own times, giving Lord Sunderland's character, says,

His own notions were always good; but he was a man of great expence.[26]

I have seen a woman's face break out in heats, as she has been talking against a great lord, whom she had ne-<33>ver seen in her life; and indeed never knew a party-woman that kept her beauty for a twelvemonth.

Spectator, No. 57.

Lord Bolingbroke, speaking of Strada:

I single him out among the moderns, because he had the foolish presumption to censure Tacitus, and to write history himself; and your Lordship will forgive this short excursion in honour of a favourite writer.

Letters on history, vol. 1. *let.* 5.[27]

It seems to me, that in order to maintain the moral system of the world at a certain point, far below that of ideal perfection, (for we are made capable of conceiving what we are incapable of attaining), but however sufficient upon the whole to constitute a state easy and happy, or at the worst tolerable: I say, it seems to me, that the Author of nature has thought fit to mingle from time to time, among the societies of men, a few, and but a few, of those on whom he is graciously pleased to bestow a larger

---

power by bribery, becoming perpetual dictator in 44. He published his own version of the civil wars, and of the Gallic wars. From *Commentaria* 4.1:

Custom has render'd 'em so hardy that they wash themselves in their Rivers, and wear no Cloaths even in the coldest Weather, except small Skins, which hardly ever cover one half of their Bodies, while the rest is expos'd to the Weather.
(*Commentaries on His Wars in Gaul,* 3rd ed., trans. M. Bladen, 1719)

26. Gilbert Burnet (1643–1715), *History of His Own Time,* 1724–34, vol. 1, bk. 3, p. 458.
27. *Letters on the Study and Use of History,* 1752.

proportion of the etherial spirit than is given in the ordinary course of his
providence to the sons of men.

Bolingbroke, on the spirit of patriotism, let. 1.

To crowd into a single member of a period different subjects, is still worse
than to crowd them into one period:

——— Trojam, genitore Adamasto
Paupere (mansissetque utinam fortuna) profectus.

Aeneid. iii. 614.[28] <34>

From conjunctions and disjunctions in general, we proceed to comparisons, which make one species of them, beginning with similies. And here
also, the intimate connection that words have with their meaning requires,
that in describing two resembling objects a resemblance in the two members
of the period ought to be studied. To illustrate the rule in this case, I shall
give various examples of deviations from it; beginning with resemblances
expressed in words that have no resemblance.

I have observed of late, the style of some great *ministers* very much to
exceed that of any other *productions.*

Letter to the Lord High Treasurer. Swift.

This, instead of studying the resemblance of words in a period that expresses a comparison, is going out of one's road to avoid it. Instead of
productions, which resemble not ministers great nor small, the proper word
is *writers* or *authors.*

If men of eminence are exposed to censure on the one hand, they are as
much liable to flattery on the other. If they receive reproaches which are
not due to them, they likewise receive praises which they do not deserve.

Spectator.[29]

28. "Since my father Adamastus was poor—and would to heaven that fortune has so
stayed!—[I set out] for Troy."

29. Joseph Addison, *Spectator,* no. 101 (1711).

Here the subject plainly demands uniformity in expression instead of variety; and therefore it is submitted, whether the period would not do better in the following manner: <35>

> If men of eminence be exposed to censure on the one hand, they are as much exposed to flattery on the other. If they receive reproaches that are not due, they likewise receive praises that are not due.

> I cannot but fancy, however, that this imitation, which passes so currently with *other judgements,* must at some time or other have stuck a little with your *Lordship.** [Better thus]: I cannot but fancy, however, that this imitation, which passes so currently with *others,* must at some time or other have stuck a little with your *Lordship.*

> A glutton or mere sensualist is as ridiculous as the other two characters.
> *Shaftesbury, vol.* 1. *p.* 129.

> They wisely prefer *the generous efforts of goodwill and affection,* to the reluctant compliances *of such as* obey by force.
> *Remarks on the history of England, letter* 5. *Bolingbroke.*

Titus Livius, mentioning a demand made by the people of Enna of the keys from the Roman governor, makes him say,

> Quas simul tradiderimus, Carthaginiensium extemplo Enna erit, foediusque hic trucidabimur, quam Murgantiae praesidium interfectum est.
> *l.* 24. § 38.[30] <36>

Quintus Curtius, speaking of Porus mounted on an elephant, and leading his army to battle:

---

* Letter concerning enthusiasm. Shaftesbury. [In *Characteristics,* 1711.]

30. "And the moment we surrender to them, Henna will be in the hands of the Carthaginians, and we shall be more cruelly slaughtered here than was the garrison slain at Murgantia."

Magnitudini Pori adjicere videbatur bellua qua vehebatur, tantum inter
caeteras eminens, quanto aliis ipse praestabat.   *l. 8. cap.* 14.[31]

It is still a greater deviation from congruity, to affect not only variety in
the words, but also in the construction. Describing Thermopylae, Titus
Livius says,

Id jugum, sicut Apennini dorso Italia dividitur, ita mediam Graeciam
diremit.   *l.* 36. § 15.[32]

Speaking of Shakespear:

There may remain a suspicion that we over-rate the greatness of his genius,
in the same manner as bodies appear more gigantic on account of their
being disproportioned and mishapen.

History of G. Britain, vol. 1. *p.* 138.[33]

This is studying variety in a period where the beauty lies in uniformity.
Better thus:

There may remain a suspicion that we over-rate the greatness of his genius,
in the same manner as we overrate the greatness of bodies that are disproportioned and mishapen. <37>

Next as to the length of the members that signify the resembling objects.
To produce a resemblance between such members, they ought not only to
be constructed in the same manner, but as nearly as possible be equal in
length. By neglecting this circumstance, the following example is defective
in neatness.

As the performance of all other religious duties will not avail in the sight
of God, *without charity;* so neither will the discharge of all other minis-

---

31. "[Porus himself was of almost superhuman size.] The elephant which he was
riding seemed to increase this size, for it stood above the other animals by as much as
Porus towered over the Indians." (*The History of Alexander,* trans. John Yardley)

32. "This ridge, just as Italy is cut in two by the backbone of the Apennines, divides
Greece."

33. In his edition of 1770, Hume modified the text: 6.213.

terial duties avail in the sight of men, *without a faithful discharge of this principal duty.* *Dissertation upon parties, Dedication.*

In the following passage are accumulated all the errors that a period expressing a resemblance can well admit.

Ministers are answerable for every thing done to the prejudice of the constitution, in the same proportion as the preservation of the constitution in its purity and vigour, or the perverting and weakening it, are of greater consequence to the nation, than any other instances of good or bad government. *Dissertation upon parties, Dedication.*

Next of a comparison where things are opposed to each other. And here it must be obvious, that if resemblance ought to be studied in the words which express two resembling objects, there is equal reason for studying opposition in the words which express contrasted objects. This rule will <38> be best illustrated by examples of deviations from it:

A friend exaggerates a man's virtues, an enemy inflames his crimes.
Spectator, No. 399.

Here the opposition in the thought is neglected in the words, which at first view seem to import, that the friend and the enemy are employ'd in different matters, without any relation to each other, whether of resemblance or of opposition. And therefore the contrast or opposition will be better marked by expressing the thought as follows.

A friend exaggerates a man's virtues, an enemy his crimes.

The following are examples of the same kind.

The wise man is happy when he gains his own approbation; the fool when he recommends himself to the applause of those about him.
Ibid. No. 73.

Better:

The wise man is happy when he gains his own approbation; the fool when he gains that of others.

Sicut in frugibus pecudibusque, non tantum semina ad servandum indolem valent, quantum terrae proprietas coelique, sub quo aluntur, mutat.

Livy, lib. 38. § 17.[34] <39>

We proceed to a rule of a different kind. During the course of a period, the scene ought to be continued without variation: the changing from person to person, from subject to subject, or from person to subject, within the bounds of a single period, distracts the mind, and affords no time for a solid impression. I illustrate this rule by giving examples of deviations from it.

Honos alit artes, *omnesque* incenduntur ad studia gloriâ; jacentque *ea* semper quae apud quosque improbantur.

Cicero, Tuscul. quaest. l. 1.[35]

Speaking of the distemper contracted by Alexander bathing in the river Cydnus, and of the cure offered by Philip the physician:

Inter hac à Parmenione fidissimo purpuratorum, literas *accipit,* quibus ei *denunciabat,* ne salutem suam Philippo committeret.

Quintus Curtius, l. 3. *cap.* 6.[36]

Hook, in his Roman history,[37] speaking of Eumenes, who had been beat to the ground with a stone, says,

After a short time *he* came to himself; and the next day, *they* put him on board his ship, *which* conveyed him first to Corinth, and thence to the island of Aegina.

I give another example of a period which is unpleasant, even by a very slight deviation from the rule: <40>

34. "Just as, in the case of plants and animals, the seeds have less power to maintain their natural quality than the character of the soil and the climate in which they live has power to change it."

35. "Public esteem is the nurse of the arts, and all men are fired to application by fame, whilst those pursuits which meet with general disapproval, always lie neglected."

36. "Meanwhile he received a letter from the most faithful of his officers, Parmenion, in which he was told not to trust his life to Philip." (*The History of Alexander*)

37. N. Hooke, *The Roman History,* 1738–71.

That sort of instruction which is acquired by inculcating an important moral truth, &c.

This expression includes two persons, one acquiring, and one inculcating; and the scene is changed without necessity. To avoid this blemish, the thought may be expressed thus:

That sort of instruction which is afforded by inculcating, &c.

The bad effect of such change of person is remarkable in the following passage.

The *Britons,* daily harassed by cruel inroads from the Picts, were forced to call in the Saxons for their defence, *who* consequently reduced the greatest part of the island to their own power, drove the Britons into the most remote and mountainous parts, and *the rest of the country,* in customs, religion, and language, became wholly Saxons.

Letter to the Lord High Treasurer. Swift.[38]

The following passage has a change from subject to person.

This prostitution of praise is not only a deceit upon the gross of mankind, who take their notion of characters from the learned; but also *the better sort* must by this means lose some part at least of that desire of fame which is the incentive to generous actions, when they find it promiscuously bestowed on the meritorious and undeserving.

Guardian, No. 4.[39] <41>

Even so slight a change as to vary the construction in the same period, is unpleasant:

Annibal luce prima, Balearibus levique alia armatura praemissa, transgressus flumen, ut quosque traduxerat, ita in acie locabat; Gallos Hispanosque equites prope ripam laevo in cornu adversus Romanum equitatum; dextrum cornu Numidis equitibus datum. *Tit. Liv. l.* 22. § 46.[40]

---

38. 1712.

39. 1713.

40. "Hannibal crossed the river at break of day, after sending ahead of him the Baliares and the other light-armed troops, and posted each corps in line of battle, in the order in which he had brought it over. The Gallic and Spanish horse were next to the river, on

Speaking of Hannibal's elephants drove back by the enemy upon his own army:

> Eo magis ruere in suos belluae, tantoque majorem stragem edere quam inter hostes ediderant, quanto acrius pavor consternatam agit, quam insidentis magistri imperio regitur.
>
> *Liv. l. 27. § 14.*[41]

This passage is also faulty in a different respect, that there is no resemblance between the members of the sentence, though they express a simile.

The present head, which relates to the choice of materials, shall be closed with a rule concerning the use of copulatives. Longinus observes, that it animates a period to drop the copulatives; and he gives the following example from Xenophon.

> Closing their shields together, they were push'd, they fought, they slew, they were slain.   *Treatise of the Sublime, cap.* 16.[42]

The reason I take to be what follows. A conti-<42>nued sound, if not loud, tends to lay us asleep: an interrupted sound rouses and animates by its repeated impulses. Thus feet composed of syllables, being pronounced with a sensible interval between each, make more lively impressions than can be made by a continued sound. A period of which the members are connected by copulatives, produceth an effect upon the mind approaching to that of a continued sound; and therefore the suppressing copulatives must animate a description. It produces a different effect akin to that mentioned: the members of a period connected by proper copulatives, glide smoothly and gently along; and are a proof of sedateness and leisure in the speaker: on the other hand, one in the hurry of passion, neglecting copulatives and other particles, expresses the principal image only; and for that reason, hurry or quick action is best expressed without copulatives:

---

the left wing, facing the Roman cavalry; the right wing was assigned to the Numidian horse."

41. "All the more did the brutes dash among their own men and cause a greater slaughter than they had done among the enemy, in proportion as the frightened beast is urged on more fiercely by terror than when under the control of a driver on its back."

42. Chapter 19.

Veni, vidi, vici.[43]

————— ————— Ite:
Ferte citi flammas, date vela, impellite remos.

Aeneid. iv. 593.[44]

Quis globus, O cives, caligine volvitur atra?
Ferte citi ferrum, dete tela, scandite muros.
Hostis adest, eja. *Aeneid.* ix. 37.[45]

In this view Longinus* justly compares copula-<43>tives in a period to strait tying, which in a race obstructs the freedom of motion.

It follows, that a plurality of copulatives in the same period ought to be avoided: for if the laying aside copulatives give force and liveliness, a redundancy of them must render the period languid. I appeal to the following instance, though there are but two copulatives.

Upon looking over the letters of my female correspondents, I find several from women complaining of jealous husbands; and at the same time protesting their own innocence, and desiring my advice upon this occasion.

Spectator, No. 170.

I except the case where the words are intended to express the coldness of the speaker; for there the redundancy of copulatives is a beauty:

Dining one day at an alderman's in the city, Peter observed him expatiating after the manner of his brethren, in the praises of his sirloin of beef. "Beef," said the sage magistrate, "is the king of meat: Beef comprehends in it the quintessence of partridge, and quail, and venison, and pheasant, and plum-pudding, and custard." *Tale of a Tub,* § 4.

* Treatise of the Sublime, cap. 16.

43. "I came, I saw, I conquered." Suetonius, *Divus Julius* (Caesar), xxxvii.2, reports the saying as an inscription displayed during Caesar's Pontic triumph, but Plutarch bk. 2 ascribes it to a letter written by Caesar announcing the victory of Zela, which concluded the Pontic campaign.

44. "Go, fetch fire in haste, serve weapons, ply the oars!"

45. "What mass, my countrymen, rolls onwards in murky gloom? Quick with the sword! Serve weapons, climb the walls. The enemy is upon us, ho!"

And the author shows great delicacy of taste by varying the expression in the mouth of Peter, who is represented more animated:

> "Bread," says he, "dear brothers, is the staff of life; in which bread is contained, *inclusivè*, the quint-<44>essence of beef, mutton, veal, venison, partridges, plum-pudding, and custard."

Another case must also be excepted: copulatives have a good effect where the intention is to give an impression of a great multitude consisting of many divisions; for example: "The army was composed of Grecians, and Carians, and Lycians, and Pamphylians, and Phrygians." The reason is, that a leisurely survey, which is expressed by the copulatives, makes the parts appear more numerous than they would do by a hasty survey: in the latter case the army appears in one group; in the former, we take as it were an accurate survey of each nation, and of each division.*

We proceed to the second kind of beauty; which consists in a due arrangement of the words or materials. This branch of the subject is no less nice than extensive; and I despair of setting it in a clear light, except to those who are well acquainted with the general principles that govern the structure or composition of language.

In a thought, generally speaking, there is at least one capital object considered as acting or as suffering. This object is expressed by a substantive noun: its action is expressed by an active verb; and the thing affected by the action is expressed by another substantive noun: its suffering <45> or passive state is expressed by a passive verb; and the thing that acts upon it, by a substantive noun. Beside these, which are the capital parts of a sentence or period, there are generally under-parts; each of the substantives as well as the verb, may be qualified: time, place, purpose, motive, means, instrument, and a thousand other circumstances, may be necessary to complete the thought. And in what manner these several parts are connected in the expression, will appear from what follows.

In a complete thought or mental proposition, all the members and parts are mutually related, some slightly, some intimately. To put such a thought in words, it is not sufficient that the component ideas be clearly expressed;

---

* See Demetrius Phalereus of Elocution, sect. 63.

it is also necessary, that all the relations contained in the thought be expressed according to their different degrees of intimacy. To annex a certain meaning to a certain sound or word, requires no art: the great nicety in all languages is, to express the various relations that connect the parts of the thought. Could we suppose this branch of language to be still a secret, it would puzzle, I am apt to think, the acutest grammarian, to invent an expeditious method: and yet, by the guidance merely of nature, the rude and illiterate have been led to a method so perfect, as to appear not susceptible of any improvement; and the next step in our progress shall be to explain that method. <46>

Words that import a relation, must be distinguished from such as do not. Substantives commonly imply no relation; such as *animal, man, tree, river.* Adjectives, verbs, and adverbs, imply a relation: the adjective *good* must relate to some being possessed of that quality: the verb *write* is applied to some person who writes; and the adverbs *moderately, diligently,* have plainly a reference to some action which they modify. When a relative word is introduced, it must be signified by the expression to what word it relates, without which the sense is not complete. For answering that purpose, I observe in Greek and Latin two different methods. Adjectives are declined as well as substantives; and declension serves to ascertain their connection: If the word that expresses the subject be, for example, in the nominative case, so also must the word be that expresses its quality; example, *vir bonus:* again, verbs are related, on the one hand, to the agent, and, on the other, to the subject upon which the action is exerted: and a contrivance similar to that now mentioned, serves to express the double relation; the nominative case is appropriated to the agent, the accusative to the passive subject; and the verb is put in the first, second, or third person, to intimate its connection with the word that signifies the agent: examples, *Ego amo Tulliam; tu amas Semproniam; Brutus amat Portiam.*[46] The other method is by juxtaposition, which is ne-<47>cessary with respect to such words only as are not declined, adverbs, for example, articles, prepositions, and conjunctions. In the English language there are few declensions; and therefore juxtapo-

---

46. "I myself love Tully; you love Sempronius; Brutus loves Portia."

sition is our chief resource: adjectives accompany their substantives;* an adverb accompanies the word it qualifies; and the verb occupies the middle place between the active and passive subjects to which it relates.

It must be obvious, that those terms which have nothing relative in their signification, cannot be connected in so easy a manner. When two substantives happen to be connected, as cause and effect, as principal and accessory, or in any other manner, such connection cannot be expressed by contiguity solely; for words must often in a period be placed together which are not thus related: the relation between substantives, therefore, cannot otherwise be expressed but by particles denoting the relation. Latin indeed and Greek, by their declensions, go a certain length to express <48> such relations, without the aid of particles. The relation of property, for example, between Caesar and his horse, is expressed by putting the latter in the nominative case, the former in the genitive; *equus Caesaris:* the same is also expressed in English without the aid of a particle, *Caesar's horse.* But in other instances, declensions not being used in the English language, relations of this kind are commonly expressed by prepositions. Examples: That wine came *from* Cyprus. He is going *to* Paris. The sun is *below* the horizon.

This form of connecting by prepositions, is not confined to substantives. Qualities, attributes, manner of existing or acting, and all other circumstances, may in the same manner be connected with the substances to which they relate. This is done artificially by converting the circumstance into a substantive; in which condition it is qualified to be connected with the principal subject by a preposition, in the manner above describ'd. For example, the adjective *wise* being converted into the substantive *wisdom,* gives opportunity for the expression "a man *of* wisdom," instead of the more simple expression *a wise man:* this variety in the expression, enriches language. I observe, beside, that the using a preposition in this case, is not

---

* Taking advantage of a declension to separate an adjective from its substantive, as is commonly practised in Latin, though it detract not from perspicuity, is certainly less neat than the English method of juxtaposition. Contiguity is more expressive of an intimate relation, than resemblance merely of the final syllables. Latin indeed has evidently the advantage when the adjective and substantive happen to be connected by contiguity, as well as by resemblance of the final syllables.

always a matter of choice: it is indispensable with respect to every circumstance that cannot be expressed by a single adjective or adverb.

To pave the way for the rules of arrangement, <49> one other preliminary is necessary; which is, to explain the difference between a natural style, and that where transposition or inversion prevails. There are, it is true, no precise boundaries between them, for they run into each other like the shades of different colours. No person, however, is at a loss to distinguish them in their extremes: and it is necessary to make the distinction; because tho' some of the rules I shall have occasion to mention are common to both, yet each hath rules peculiar to itself. In a natural style, relative words are by juxtaposition connected with those to which they relate, going before or after, according to the peculiar genius of the language. Again, a circumstance connected by a preposition, follows naturally the word with which it is connected. But this arrangement may be varied, when a different order is more beautiful: a circumstance may be placed before the word with which it is connected by a preposition; and may be interjected even between a relative word and that to which it relates. When such liberties are frequently taken, the style becomes inverted or transposed.

But as the liberty of inversion is a capital point in the present subject, it will be necessary to examine it more narrowly, and in particular to trace the several degrees in which an inverted style recedes more and more from that which is natural. And first, as to the placing a circumstance before <50> the word with which it is connected, I observe, that it is the easiest of all inversion, even so easy as to be consistent with a style that is properly termed natural: witness the following examples.

In the sincerity of my heart, I profess, &c.

By our own ill management, we are brought to so low an ebb of wealth and credit, that, &c.

On Thursday morning there was little or nothing transacted in Change-alley.

At St. Bride's church in Fleetstreet, Mr. Woolston, (who writ against the miracles of our Saviour), in the utmost terrors of conscience, made a public recantation.

The interjecting a circumstance between a relative word and that to which it relates, is more properly termed inversion; because, by a disjunction of words intimately connected, it recedes farther from a natural style. But this licence has degrees; for the disjunction is more violent in some instances than in others. And to give a just notion of the difference, there is a necessity to enter a little more into an abstract subject, than would otherwise be my inclination.

In nature, tho' a subject cannot exist without its qualities, nor a quality without a subject; yet in our conception of these, a material difference may be remarked. I cannot conceive a quality <51> but as belonging to some subject: it makes indeed a part of the idea which is formed of the subject. But the opposite holds not; for tho' I cannot form a conception of a subject void of all qualities, a partial conception may be formed of it, abstracting from any particular quality: I can, for example, form the idea of a fine Arabian horse without regard to his colour, or of a white horse without regard to his size. Such partial conception of a subject, is still more easy with respect to action or motion; which is an occasional attribute only, and has not the same permanency with colour or figure: I cannot form an idea of motion independent of a body; but there is nothing more easy than to form an idea of a body at rest. Hence it appears, that the degree of inversion depends greatly on the order in which the related words are placed: when a substantive occupies the first place, the idea it suggests must subsist in the mind at least for a moment, independent of the relative words afterward introduced; and that moment may without difficulty be prolonged by interjecting a circumstance between the substantive and its connections. This liberty, therefore, however frequent, will scarce alone be sufficient to denominate a style inverted. The case is very different, where the word that occupies the first place denotes a quality or an action; for as these cannot be conceived without a subject, they cannot without greater violence be separated from the subject that follows; <52> and for that reason, every such separation by means of an interjected circumstance belongs to an inverted style.

To illustrate this doctrine, examples are necessary; and I shall begin with those where the word first introduced does not imply a relation:

>   ———— Nor Eve to iterate
> Her former trespass fear'd.

——— Hunger and thirst at once,
Powerful persuaders, quicken'd at the scent
Of that alluring fruit, urg'd me so keen.

Moon that now meet'st the orient sun, now fli'st
With the fix'd stars, fix'd in their orb that flies,
And ye five other wand'ring fires that move
In mystic dance not without song, resound
His praise.

In the following examples, where the word first introduced imports a relation, the disjunction will be found more violent.

Of man's first disobedience, and the fruit
Of that forbidden tree, whose mortal taste
Brought death into the world, and all our wo,
With loss of Eden, till one greater man
Restore us, and regain the blissful seat,
Sing heav'nly muse.

——— Upon the firm opacous globe
Of this round world, whose first convex divides <53>
The luminous inferior orbs, inclos'd
From chaos and th' inroad of darkness old,
Satan alighted walks.

——— On a sudden open fly
With impetuous recoil and jarring sound,
Th' infernal doors.

——— Wherein remain'd,
For what could else? to our almighty foe
Clear victory, to our part loss and rout.

——— Forth rush'd, with whirlwind sound,
The chariot of paternal Deity.[47]

47. *Paradise Lost:* IX.1006; IX.586; V.178; I.1; III.418; II.880; II.770; VI.749.

Language would have no great power, were it confined to the natural order of ideas. I shall soon have opportunity to make it evident, that by inversion a thousand beauties may be compassed, which must be relinquished in a natural arrangement. In the mean time, it ought not to escape observation, that the mind of man is happily so constituted as to relish inversion, tho' in one respect unnatural; and to relish it so much, as in many cases to admit a separation between words the most intimately connected. It can scarce be said that inversion has any limits; tho' I may venture to pronounce, that the disjunction of articles, conjunctions, or prepositions, from the words to which they belong, has very seldom a good effect. The following example with relation to a preposition, is perhaps as tolerable as any of the kind: <54>

> He would neither separate *from,* nor act against *them.*

I give notice to the reader, that I am now ready to enter on the rules of arrangement; beginning with a natural style, and proceeding gradually to what is the most inverted. And in the arrangement of a period, as well as in a right choice of words, the first and great object being perspicuity, the rule above laid down, that perspicuity ought not to be sacrificed to any other beauty, holds equally in both. Ambiguities occasioned by a wrong arrangement are of two sorts; one where the arrangement leads to a wrong sense, and one where the sense is left doubtful. The first, being the more culpable, shall take the lead, beginning with examples of words put in a wrong place.

> How much the imagination of such a presence must exalt a genius, we
> may observe *merely* from the influence which an ordinary presence has
> over men.   *Characteristicks, vol.* i. *p.* 7.

This arrangement leads to a wrong sense: the adverb *merely* seems by its position to affect the preceding word; whereas it is intended to affect the following words, *an ordinary presence;* and therefore the arrangement ought to be thus:

> How much the imagination of such a presence must exalt a genius, we
> may observe from the influence which an ordinary presence merely has
> over men. [Or, better],—which even an ordinary presence has over men.
> <55>

The time of the election of a poet-laureat being now at hand, it may be proper to give some account of the rites and ceremonies anciently used at that solemnity, and *only* discontinued through the neglect and degeneracy of later times.   *Guardian.*

The term *only* is intended to qualify the noun *degeneracy*, and not the participle *discontinued;* and therefore the arrangement ought to be as follows:

———— and discontinued through the neglect and degeneracy only, of later times.

Sixtus the Fourth was, if I mistake not, a great collector of books at least.
                              Letters on History, vol. 1. let. 6. Bolingbroke.

The expression here leads evidently to a wrong sense; the adverb *at least,* ought not to be connected with the substantive *books,* but with *collector* thus:

Sixtus the Fourth was a great collector at least, of books.

Speaking of Lewis XIV.

If he was not the greatest king, he was the best actor of majesty at least, that ever filled a throne.   *Ibid. letter 7.* <56>

Better thus:

If he was not the greatest king, he was at least the best actor of majesty, &c.

This arrangement removes the wrong sense occasioned by the juxtaposition of *majesty* and *at least.*

The following examples are of a wrong arrangement of members.

I have confined myself to those methods for the advancement of piety, which are in the power of a prince limited like ours by a strict execution of the laws.   *A project for the advancement of religion. Swift.*[48]

48. 1709.

The structure of this period leads to a meaning which is not the author's, *viz.* power limited by a strict execution of the laws. That wrong sense is removed by the following arrangement:

> I have confined myself to those methods for the advancement of piety, which, by a strict execution of the laws, are in the power of a prince limited like ours.

> This morning, when one of Lady Lizard's daughters was looking over some hoods and ribands brought by her tirewoman, with great care and diligence, I employ'd no less in examining the box which contained them.
>
> *Guardian,* No. 4. <57>

The wrong sense occasioned by this arrangement, may be easily prevented by varying it thus:

> This morning when, with great care and diligence, one of Lady Lizard's daughters was looking over some hoods and ribands, &c.

> A great stone that I happened to find after a long search by the sea-shore, served me for an anchor.   *Gulliver's Travels, part* 1. *chap.* 8.[49]

One would think that the search was confined to the sea-shore; but as the meaning is, that the great stone was found by the sea-shore, the period ought to be arranged thus:

> A great stone, that, after a long search, I happened to find by the sea-shore, served me for an anchor.

Next of a wrong arrangement where the sense is left doubtful; beginning, as in the former sort, with examples of wrong arrangement of words in a member:

> These forms of conversation *by degrees* multiplied and grew troublesome.
>
> *Spectator,* No. 119.

49. 1726.

Here it is left doubtful whether the modification *by degrees* relates to the preceding member or to what follows: it should be,

These forms of conversation multiplied by degrees. <58>

Nor does this false modesty expose us *only* to such actions as are indiscreet, but very often to such as are highly criminal.

Spectator, No. 458.

The ambiguity is removed by the following arrangement:

Nor does this false modesty expose us to such actions only as are indiscreet, &c.

The empire of Blefuscu is an island situated to the north-east side of Lilliput, from whence it is parted *only* by a channel of 800 yards wide.

Gulliver's Travels, part I. *chap.* 5.

The ambiguity may be removed thus:

———— from whence it is parted by a channel of 800 yards wide only.

In the following examples the sense is left doubtful by wrong arrangement of members.

The minister who grows less by his elevation, *like a little statue placed on a mighty pedestal,* will always have his jealousy strong about him.

Dissertation upon parties, Dedication. Bolingbroke.

Here, as far as can be gathered from the arrangement, it is doubtful, whether the object introduced by way of simile, relate to what goes before or <59> to what follows: the ambiguity is removed by the following arrangement:

The minister, who, like a little statue placed on a mighty pedestal, grows less by his elevation, will always, &c.

Since this is too much to ask of freemen, nay of slaves, *if his expectation be not answered,* shall he form a lasting division upon such transient motives? *Ibid.*

Better thus:

> Since this is too much to ask of freemen, nay of slaves, shall he, if his
> expectations be not answered, form, *&c.*

Speaking of the superstitious practice of locking up the room where a person of distinction dies:

> The knight, seeing his habitation reduced to so small a compass, and himself in a manner shut out of his own house, *upon the death of his mother,* ordered all the apartments to be flung open, and exorcised by his chaplain.
>
> *Spectator,* No. 110.

Better thus:

> The knight, seeing his habitation reduced to so small a compass, and himself in a manner shut out of his own house, ordered, upon the death of his mother, all the apartments to be flung open.

Speaking of some indecencies in conversation: <60>

> As it is impossible for such an irrational way of conversation to last long among a people that make any profession of religion, or show of modesty, *if the country gentlemen get into it,* they will certainly be left in the lurch.
>
> *Spectator,* No. 119.

The ambiguity vanishes in the following arrangement:

> ———— the country gentlemen, if they get into it, will certainly be left in
> the lurch.

Speaking of a discovery in natural philosophy, that colour is not a quality of matter:

> As this is a truth which has been proved incontestably by many modern philosophers, and is indeed one of the finest speculations in that science, *if the English reader would see the notion explained at large,* he may find it in the eighth chapter of the second book of Mr. Locke's essay on human understanding.   *Spectator,* No. 413.

Better thus:

As this is a truth, *&c.* the English reader, if he would see the notion ex-plained at large, may find it, *&c.*

A woman seldom asks advice before she has bought her wedding-cloaths. When she has made her own choice, *for form's sake* she sends a *conge d'elire* to her friends.   *Ibid.* No. 475. <61>

Better thus:

———— she sends, for form's sake, a *conge d'elire to* her friends.

And since it is necessary that there should be a perpetual intercourse of buying and selling, and dealing upon credit, *where fraud is permitted or connived at, or hath no law to punish it,* the honest dealer is always undone, and the knave gets the advantage.

Gulliver's Travels, part 1. *chap.* 6.

Better thus:

And since it is necessary that there should be a perpetual intercourse of buying and selling, and dealing upon credit, the honest dealer, where fraud is permitted or connived at, or hath no law to punish it, is always undone, and the knave gets the advantage.

From these examples, the following observation will occur, that a cir-cumstance ought never to be placed between two capital members of a period; for by such situation it must always be doubtful, as far as we gather from the arrangement, to which of the two members it belongs: where it is interjected, as it ought to be, between parts of the member to which it belongs, the ambiguity is removed, and the capital members are kept dis-tinct, which is a great beauty in composition. In general, to preserve mem-bers distinct that signify things distinguished in the thought, the best method is, <62> to place first in the consequent member, some word that cannot connect with what precedes it.

If it shall be thought, that the objections here are too scrupulous, and that the defect of perspicuity is easily supplied by accurate punctuation; the answer is, That punctuation may remove an ambiguity, but will never produce that peculiar beauty which is perceived when the sense comes out clearly and distinctly by means of a happy arrangement. Such influence has this beauty, that by a natural transition of perception, it is communicated to the very sound of the words, so as in appearance to improve the music of the period. But as this curious subject comes in more properly afterward, it is sufficient at present to appeal to experience, that a period so arranged as to bring out the sense clear, seems always more musical than where the sense is left in any degree doubtful.

A rule deservedly occupying the second place, is, That words expressing things connected in the thought, ought to be placed as near together as possible. This rule is derived immediately from human nature, prone in every instance to place together things in any manner connected:* where things are arranged according to their connections, we have a sense of order; otherwise we have a sense of disorder, as of things placed by chance: and we naturally place words in the same order in <63> which we would place the things they signify. The bad effect of a violent separation of words or members thus intimately connected, will appear from the following examples.

> For the English are naturally fanciful, and very often disposed, by that gloominess and melancholy of temper which is so frequent in our nation, to many wild notions and visions, to which others are not so liable.
>
> *Spectator,* No. 419.

Here the verb or assertion is, by a pretty long circumstance, violently separated from the subject to which it refers: this makes a harsh arrangement; the less excusable that the fault is easily prevented by placing the circumstance before the verb, after the following manner:

> For the English are naturally fanciful, and, by that gloominess and melancholy of temper which is so frequent in our nation, are often disposed to many wild notions, &c.

> For as no moral author, in the ordinary fate and vicissitude of things, knows to what use his works may, some time or other, be apply'd, &c.
>
> *Spectator,* No. 85.

---

* See chap. 1.

Better thus:

> For as, in the ordinary fate and vicissitude of things, no mortal author
> knows to what use, some time or other, his works may be apply'd, &c.
> <64>

> From whence we may date likewise the rivalship of the house of France,
> for we may reckon that of Valois and that of Bourbon as one upon this
> occasion, and the house of Austria, that continues at this day, and has oft
> cost so much blood and so much treasure in the course of it.
> *Letters on history, vol.* 1. *let.* 6. *Bolingbroke.*

> It cannot be impertinent or ridiculous therefore in such a country, what-
> ever it might be in the Abbot of St. Real's, which was Savoy I think; or
> in Peru, under the Incas, where Garcilasso de la Vega says it was lawful for
> none but the nobility to study—for men of all degrees to instruct them-
> selves, in those affairs wherein they may be actors, or judges of those that
> act, or controllers of those that judge.
> *Letters on history, vol.* 1. *let.* 5. *Bolingbroke.*

> If Scipio, who was naturally given to women, for which anecdote we have,
> if I mistake not, the authority of Polybius, as well as some verses of Nevius
> preserved by Aulus Gellius, had been educated by Olympias at the court
> of Philip, it is improbable that he would have restored the beautiful
> Spaniard.   *Ibid. let.* 3.

If any one have a curiosity for more specimens of this kind, they will be
found without number in the works of the same author.

A pronoun, which saves the naming a person or thing a second time,
ought to be placed as near as possible to the name of that person or thing.
This is a branch of the foregoing rule; and with the <65> reason there given,
another concurs, *viz.* That if other ideas intervene, it is difficult to recal
the person or thing by reference:

> If I had leave to print the Latin letters transmitted to me from foreign
> parts, they would fill a volume, and be a full defence against all that Mr.
> Partridge, or his accomplices of the Portugal inquisition, will be ever able

to object; *who,* by the way, are the only enemies my predictions have ever met with at home or abroad.

Better thus:

———— and be a full defence against all that can be objected by Mr. Partridge, or his accomplices of the Portugal inquisition; who, by the way, are, *&c.*

There being a round million of creatures in human figure, throughout this kingdom, *whose* whole subsistence, *&c.*

A modest proposal, &c. *Swift.*[50]

Better,

There being, throughout this kingdom, a round million of creatures in human figure, whose whole subsistence, *&c.*

Tom is a lively impudent clown, and has wit enough to have made him a pleasant companion, had *it* been polished and rectified by good manners.

Guardian, No. 162.

It is the custom of the Mahometans, if they see any <66> printed or written paper upon the ground, to take it up, and lay it aside carefully, as not knowing but it may contain some piece of their Alcoran.

Spectator, No. 85.

The arrangement here leads to a wrong sense, as if the ground were taken up, not the paper.—Better thus:

It is the custom of the Mahometans, if they see upon the ground any printed or written paper, to take it up, *&c.*

The following rule depends on the communication of emotions to related objects; a principle in human nature that hath an extensive operation: and we find this operation, even where the objects are not otherwise related

50. 1729.

than by juxtaposition of the words that express them. Hence, to elevate or depress an object, one method is, to join it in the expression with another that is naturally high or low: witness the following speech of Eumenes to the Roman senate.

> Causam veniendi sibi Roman fuisse, praeter cupiditatem visendi *deos ho-*
> *minesque,* quorum beneficio in ea fortuna esset, supra quam ne optare
> quidem auderet, etiam ut coram moneret senatum ut Persei conatus
> obviam iret. *Livy, l. 42. cap.* 11.[51]

To join the Romans with the gods in the same enunciation, is an artful stroke of flattery, because it tacitly puts them on a level. On the other <67> hand, the degrading or vilifying an object, is done successfully by ranking it with one that is really low:

> I hope to have this entertainment in a readiness for the next winter; and
> doubt not but it will please more than the opera or puppet-show.
> *Spectator,* No. 28.

> Manifold have been the judgements which Heaven from time to time, for
> the chastisement of a sinful people, has inflicted upon whole nations. For
> when the degeneracy becomes common, 'tis but just the punishment
> should be general. Of this kind, in our own unfortunate country, was that
> destructive pestilence, whose mortality was so fatal as to sweep away, if Sir
> William Petty may be believed, five millions of Christian souls, besides
> women and Jews. *God's revenge against punning. Arbuthnot.*[52]

> Such also was that dreadful conflagration ensuing in this famous metrop-
> olis of London, which consumed, according to the computation of Sir
> Samuel Moreland, 100,000 houses, not to mention churches and stables.
> *Ibid.*

51. "He said the reason for his coming to Rome, in addition to his desire to see the gods and men by whose kindness he enjoyed a fortune beyond which he did not venture even to wish for anything, had been to give public warning to the senate that they should take measures against the designs of Perseus."

52. 1716.

But on condition it might pass into a law, I would gladly exempt both lawyers of all ages, subaltern and field officers, young heirs, dancing-masters, pick-pockets, and players.

An infalliable scheme to pay the public debts. Swift.[53]

Sooner let earth, air, sea, to chaos fall,
Men, monkeys, lap-dogs, parrots, perish all.

Rape of the Lock. <68>

Circumstances in a period resemble small stones in a building, employ'd to fill up vacuities among those of a larger size. In the arrangement of a period, such under-parts crowded together make a poor figure; and never are graceful but when interspersed among the capital parts. I illustrate this rule by the following example.

It is likewise urged, that there are, by computation, in this kingdom, above 10,000 parsons, whose revenues, added to those of my Lords the bishops, would suffice to maintain, &c.

Argument against abolishing Christianity. Swift.

Here two circumstances, *viz. by computation* and *in this kingdom,* are crowded together unnecessarily: they make a better appearance separated in the following manner:

It is likewise urged, that in this kingdom there are, by computation, above 10,000 parsons, &c.

If there be room for a choice, the sooner a circumstance is introduced, the better; because circumstances are proper for that coolness of mind, with which we begin a period as well as a volume: in the progress, the mind warms, and has a greater relish for matters of importance. When a circumstance is placed at the beginning of the period, or near the beginning, the transition from it to the principal subject is agreeable: it is like a-<69>scending, or going upward. On the other hand, to place it late in the period has a bad effect; for after being engaged in the principal subject,

53. 1731.

one is with reluctance brought down to give attention to a circumstance. Hence evidently the preference of the following arrangement,

> Whether in any country a choice altogether unexceptionable has been made, seems doubtful.

Before this other,

> Whether a choice altogether unexceptionable has in any country been made, &c.

For this reason the following period is exceptionable in point of arrangement.

> I have considered formerly, with a good deal of attention, the subject upon which you command me to communicate my thoughts to you.
> *Bolingbroke of the study of history, letter* 1.

which, with a slight alteration, may be improved thus:

> I have formerly, with a good deal of attention, considered the subject, &c.

Swift speaking of a virtuous and learned education:

> And although they may be, and too often are drawn, by the temptations of youth, and the opportunities of <70> a large fortune, into some irregularities, *when they come forward into the great world;* it is ever with reluctance and compunction of mind, because their bias to virtue still continues. *The Intelligencer,* No. 9.[54]

Better,

> And although, *when they come forward into the great world,* they may be, and too often, &c.

The bad effect of placing a circumstance last or late in a period, will appear from the following examples.

> Let us endeavour to establish to ourselves an interest in him who holds the reins of the whole creation in his hand. *Spectator,* No. 12.

---

54. Swift, 1728.

Better thus:

> Let us endeavour to establish to ourselves an interest in him, who, in his
> hand, holds the reins of the whole creation.

> Virgil, who has cast the whole system of Platonic philosophy, so far as it
> relates to the soul of man, into beautiful allegories, *in the sixth book of his
> Aeneid,* gives us the punishment, *&c.*   *Spectator,* No. 90.

Better thus:

> Virgil, who in the sixth book of his Aeneid, has cast, *&c.* <71>

> And Philip the Fourth was obliged at last to conclude a peace, on terms
> repugnant to his inclination, to that of his people, to the interest of Spain,
> and to that of all Europe, in the Pyrenean treaty.
>   *Letters on history, vol.* 1. *letter 6. Bolingbroke.*

Better thus:

> And at last, in the Pyrenean treaty, Philip the Fourth was obliged to con-
> clude a peace, *&c.*

In arranging a period, it is of importance to determine in what part of
it a word makes the greatest figure; whether at the beginning, during the
course, or at the close. The breaking silence rouses the attention, and prepares for a deep impression at the beginning: the beginning, however, must
yield to the close; which being succeeded by a pause, affords time for a word
to make its deepest impression.* Hence the following rule, That to give the
utmost force to a period, it ought if possible to be closed with that word
which makes the greatest figure. The opportunity of a pause should not be
thrown away upon accessories, <72> but reserved for the principal object,
in order that it may make a full impression: which is an additional reason
against closing a period with a circumstance. There are however periods
that admit not such a structure; and in that case, the capital word ought,

---

* To give force or elevation to a period, it ought to begin and end with a long syllable.
For a long syllable makes naturally the strongest impression; and of all the syllables in a
period, we are chiefly moved with the first and last.
                    Demetrius Phalereus of Elocution, sect. 39.

if possible, to be placed in the front, which next to the close is the most advantageous for making an impression. Hence, in directing our discourse to a man of figure, we ought to begin with his name; and one will be sensible of a degradation, when this rule is neglected, as it frequently is for the sake of verse. I give the following examples.

> Integer vitae, scelerisque purus,
> Non eget Mauri jaculis, neque arcu,
> Nec venenatis gravidâ sagittis,
>   Fusce, pharetrâ.   *Horat. Carm. l. 1. ode 22.*[55]

Je crains Dieu, cher Abner, et n'ai point d'autre crainte.

In these examples, the name of the person addressed to, makes a mean figure, being like a circumstance slipt into a corner. That this criticism is well founded, we need no other proof than Addison's translation of the last example:

O Abner! I fear my God, and I fear none but him.
>   *Guardian,* No. 117.[56] <73>

> O father, what intends thy hand, she cry'd,
> Against thy only son? What fury, O son,
> Possesses thee to bend that mortal dart
> Against thy father's head?   *Paradise lost, book 2. l. 727.*

Every one must be sensible of a dignity in the invocation at the beginning, which is not attained by that in the middle. I mean not however to censure this passage: on the contrary, it appears beautiful, by distinguishing the respect that is due to a father from that which is due to a son.

The substance of what is said in this and the foregoing section, upon the method of arranging words in a period, so as to make the deepest im-

---

55. "He who is upright in his way of life and unstained by guilt, needs not Moorish darts nor bow nor quiver loaded with poisoned arrows, Fuscus."
56. The quotation Addison translates is from Racine, *Athalie,* act 1, sc. 1.

pression with respect to sound as well as signification, is comprehended in the following observation: That order of words in a period will always be the most agreeable, where, without obscuring the sense, the most important images, the most sonorous words, and the longest members, bring up the rear.

Hitherto of arranging single words, single members, and single circumstances. But the enumeration of many particulars in the same period is often necessary; and the question is, In what order they should be placed? It does not seem easy, at first view, to bring a subject apparently so loose under any general rule: but luckily, reflecting <74> upon what is said in the first chapter about order, we find rules laid down to our hand, which leave us no task but that of applying them to the present question. And, first, with respect to the enumerating particulars of equal rank, it is laid down in the place quoted, that as there is no cause for preferring any one before the rest, it is indifferent to the mind in what order they be viewed. And it is only necessary to be added here, that for the same reason, it is indifferent in what order they be named. 2dly, If a number of objects of the same kind, differing only in size, are to be ranged along a straight line, the most agreeable order to the eye is that of an increasing series. In surveying a number of such objects, beginning at the least, and proceeding to greater and greater, the mind swells gradually with the successive objects, and in its progress has a very sensible pleasure. Precisely for the same reason, words expressive of such objects ought to be placed in the same order. The beauty of this figure, which may be termed *a climax in sense,* has escaped lord Bolingbroke in the first member of the following period:

> Let but one great, brave, disinterested, active man arise, and he will be received, followed, and almost adored.

The following arrangement has sensibly a better effect: <75>

> Let but one brave, great, active, disinterested man arise, &c.

Whether the same rule ought to be followed in enumerating men of different ranks, seems doubtful: on the one hand, a number of persons presented to the eye in form of an increasing series, is undoubtedly the most agreeable order: on the other hand, in every list of names, we set the person of the greatest dignity at the top, and descend gradually through his inferiors. Where the purpose is to honour the persons named according to their rank, the latter order ought to be followed; but every one who regards himself only, or his reader, will choose the former order. 3dly, As the sense of order directs the eye to descend from the principal to its greatest accessory, and from the whole to its greatest part, and in the same order through all the parts and accessories till we arrive at the minutest; the same order ought to be followed in the enumeration of such particulars. I shall give one familiar example. Talking of the parts of a column, the base, the shaft, the capital, these are capable of six different arrangements, and the question is, Which is the best? When we have in view the erecting a column, we are naturally led to express the parts in the order above mentioned; which at the same time is agreeable by ascending. But considering the column as it stands, without reference to its erec-<76>tion, the sense of order, as observed above, requires the chief part to be named first: for that reason we begin with the shaft; and the base comes next in order, that we may ascend from it to the capital. Lastly, In tracing the particulars of any natural operation, order requires that we follow the course of nature: historical facts are related in the order of time: we begin at the founder of a family, and proceed from him to his descendants: but in describing a lofty oak, we begin with the trunk, and ascend to the branches.

When force and liveliness of expression are demanded, the rule is, to suspend the thought as long as possible, and to bring it out full and entire at the close: which cannot be done but by inverting the natural arrangement. By introducing a word or member before its time, curiosity is raised about what is to follow; and it is agreeable to have our curiosity gratified at the close of the period: the pleasure we feel resembles that of seeing a stroke exerted upon a body by the whole collected force of the agent. On the other hand, where a period is so constructed as to admit more than one complete close in the sense, the curiosity of the reader is exhausted at the first close, and what follows appears languid or superfluous: his disappointment contributes also to that appearance, when he finds, contrary to expectation, that the period is not yet finished. Cicero, and after him Quintilian, recommend the verb to the last place. <77> This method evidently tends to suspend the sense till the close of the period; for without the verb the sense cannot be complete: and when the verb happens to be the capital word, which it frequently is, it ought at any rate to be the last, according to another rule, above laid down. I proceed as usual to illustrate this rule by examples. The following period is placed in its natural order.

> Were instruction an essential circumstance in epic poetry, I doubt whether a single instance could be given of this species of composition, in any language.

The period thus arranged admits a full close upon the word *composition;* after which it goes on languidly, and closes without force. This blemish will be avoided by the following arrangement:

> Were instruction an essential circumstance in epic poetry, I doubt whether, in any language, a single instance could be given of this species of composition.

> Some of our most eminent divines have made use of this Platonic notion, as far as it regards the subsistence of our passions after death, with great beauty and strength of reason.   *Spectator,* No. 90.

Better thus:

> Some of our most eminent divines have, with great beauty and strength of reason, made use of this Platonic notion, *&c.* <78>

> Men of the best sense have been touched, more or less, with these groundless horrors and presages of futurity, upon surveying the most indifferent works of nature.   *Spectator,* No. 505.

Better,

> Upon surveying the most indifferent works of nature, men of the best sense, *&c.*

> She soon informed him of the place he was in, which, notwithstanding all its horrors, appeared to him more sweet than the bower of Mahomet, in the company of his Balsora.   *Guardian,* No. 167.

Better,

> She soon, &c. appeared to him, in the company of his Balsora, more sweet, &c.

> The Emperor was so intent on the establishment of his absolute power in Hungary, that he exposed the Empire doubly to desolation and ruin for the sake of it.   *Letters on history, vol. 1. let. 7. Bolingbroke.*

Better,

> —— that for the sake of it he exposed the Empire doubly to desolation and ruin.

None of the rules for the composition of periods are more liable to be abused, than those last mentioned; witness many Latin writers, among the <79> moderns especially, whose style, by inversions too violent, is rendered harsh and obscure. Suspension of the thought till the close of the period, ought never to be preferred before perspicuity. Neither ought such suspension to be attempted in a long period; because in that case the mind is bewildered amidst a profusion of words: a traveller, while he is puzzled about the road, relishes not the finest prospect:

> All the rich presents which Astyages had given him at parting, keeping only some Median horses, in order to propagate the breed of them in Persia, he distributed among his friends whom he left at the court of Ecbatana.   *Travels of Cyrus, book 1.*[57]

The foregoing rules concern the arrangement of a single period: I add one rule more concerning the distribution of a discourse into different periods. A short period is lively and familiar: a long period, requiring more attention, makes an impression grave and solemn.* In general, a writer ought to study a mixture of long and short periods, which prevent an irk-

---

* Demetrius Phalereus (of Elocution, sect. 44.) observes, that long members in a period make an impression of gravity and importance. The same observation is applicable to periods.

57. Andrew Michael Ramsay (1686–1743): disciple of Fénelon and tutor to Prince Charles Edward Stuart and his brother Henry, author of *Travels of Cyrus*, 1727.

some uniformity, and entertain the mind with variety of impressions. In particular, long periods ought to be avoided till the <80> reader's attention be thoroughly engaged; and therefore a discourse, especially of the familiar kind, ought never to be introduced with a long period. For that reason, the commencement of a letter to a very young lady on her marriage is faulty:

> Madam, The hurry and impertinence of receiving and paying visits on account of your marriage, being now over, you are beginning to enter into a course of life, where you will want much advice to divert you from falling into many errors, fopperies, and follies, to which your sex is subject.
>
> *Swift*.[58]

See another example, still more faulty, in the commencement of Cicero's oration, *Pro Archia poeta*.

Before proceeding farther, it may be proper to review the rules laid down in this and the preceding section, in order to make some general observations. That order of the words and members of a period is justly termed natural, which corresponds to the natural order of the ideas that compose the thought. The tendency of many of the foregoing rules is to substitute an artificial arrangement, in order to catch some beauty either of sound or meaning for which there is no place in the natural order. But seldom it happens, that in the same period there is place for a plurality of <81> these rules: if one beauty can be retained, another must be relinquished; and the only question is, Which ought to be preferred? This question cannot be resolved by any general rule: if the natural order be not relished, a few trials will discover that artificial order which has the best effect; and this exercise, supported by a good taste, will in time make the choice easy. All that can be said in general is, that in making a choice, sound ought to yield to signification.

The transposing words and members out of their natural order, so remarkable in the learned languages, has been the subject of much speculation. It is agreed on all hands, that such transposition or inversion bestows upon a period a very sensible degree of force and elevation; and yet writers

---

58. *A Letter to a Very Young Lady on Her Marriage,* 1727.

seem to be at a loss how to account for this effect. Cerceau* ascribes so much power to inversion, as to make it the characteristic of French verse, and the single circumstance which in that language distinguishes verse from prose: and yet he pretends not to say, that it hath any other effect but to raise surprise; he must mean curiosity, which is done by suspending the thought during the period, and bringing it out entire at the close. This indeed is one effect of inversion; but neither its sole effect, nor even that which is the most remarkable, as is made evident above. But waving <82> censure, which is not an agreeable task, I enter into the matter; and begin with observing, that if conformity between words and their meaning be agreeable, it must of course be agreeable to find the same order or arrangement in both. Hence the beauty of a plain or natural style, where the order of the words corresponds precisely to the order of the ideas. Nor is this the single beauty of a natural style: it is also agreeable by its simplicity and perspicuity. This observation throws light upon the subject: for if a natural style be in itself agreeable, a transposed style cannot be so; and therefore its agreeableness must arise from admitting some positive beauty that is excluded in a natural style. To be confirmed in this opinion, we need but reflect upon some of the foregoing rules, which make it evident, that language, by means of inversion, is susceptible of many beauties that are totally excluded in a natural arrangement. From these premises it clearly follows, that inversion ought not to be indulged, unless in order to reach some beauty superior to those of a natural style. It may with great certainty be pronounced, that every inversion which is not governed by this rule, will appear harsh and strained, and be disrelished by every one of taste. Hence the beauty of inversion when happily conducted; the beauty, not of an end, but of means, as furnishing opportunity for numberless ornaments that find no place in a natural style: hence the force, the elevation, <83> the harmony, the cadence, of some compositions: hence the manifold beauties of the Greek and Roman tongues, of which living languages afford but faint imitations.

* *Reflections sur la poesie Françoise.* [J. A. Du Cerceau (1670–1730), *Réflexions sur la poésie française*, 1718.]

SECTION III

Beauty of Language from a resemblance between
Sound and Signification.

A Resemblance between the sound of certain words and their signification, is a beauty that has escaped no critical writer, and yet is not handled with accuracy by any of them. They have probably been of opinion, that a beauty so obvious to the feeling, requires no explanation. This is an error; and to avoid it, I shall give examples of the various resemblances between sound and signification, accompanied with an endeavour to explain why such resemblances are beautiful. I begin with examples where the resemblance between the sound and signification is the most entire; and next examples where the resemblance is less and less so.

There being frequently a strong resemblance of one sound to another, it will not be surprising to find an articulate sound resembling one that is not articulate: thus the sound of a bow-string is imitated by the words that express it: <84>

> ———— ———— The string let fly,
> *Twang'd short and sharp,* like the shrill swallow's cry.
>   *Odyssey,* xxi. 449.

The sound of felling trees in a wood:

> Loud sounds the ax, redoubling strokes on strokes,
> On all sides round the forest hurls her oaks
> Headlong. Deep echoing groan the thickets brown,
> Then *rustling, crackling, crashing,* thunder down.
>   *Iliad,* xxiii. 144.

> But when loud surges lash the sounding shore,
> The hoarse rough verse should like the torrent roar.
>   *Pope's Essay on Criticism,* 369.

Dire Scylla there a scene of horror forms,
And here Charybdis fills the deep with storms:
When the tide rushes from her rumbling caves,
The rough rock roars; tumultuous boil the waves.

Pope.[59]

No person can be at a loss about the cause of this beauty: it is obviously that of imitation.

That there is any other natural resemblance of sound to signification, must not be taken for granted. There is no resemblance of sound to motion, nor of sound to sentiment. We are however apt to be deceived by artful pronunciation: the same passage may be pronounced in many different tones, elevated or humble, sweet or harsh, brisk or melancholy, so as to accord with the thought <85> or sentiment: such concord must be distinguished from that concord between sound and sense, which is perceived in some expressions independent of artful pronunciation: the latter is the poet's work; the former must be attributed to the reader. Another thing contributes still more to the deceit: in language, sound and sense being intimately connected, the properties of the one are readily communicated to the other; for example, the quality of grandeur, of sweetness, or of melancholy, tho belonging to the thought solely, is transferred to the words, which by that means resemble in appearance the thought that is expressed by them.* I have great reason to recommend these observations to the reader, considering how inaccurately the present subject is handled by critics: not one of them distinguishes the natural resemblance of sound and signification, from the artificial resemblances now described; witness Vida in particular, who in a very long passage has given very few examples but what are of the latter kind.†

That there may be a resemblance of articulate sounds to some that are not articulate, is self-evident; and that in fact there exist such resemblances successfully employed by writers of genius, is clear from the foregoing ex-

* See chap. 2. part 1. sect. 5.
† Poet. L. 3. l. 365–454.
59. *Odyssey* 12.290.

amples, and from many others that might be given. But we may safe-<86>ly pronounce, that this natural resemblance can be carried no farther: the objects of the different senses, differ so widely from each other, as to exclude any resemblance: sound in particular, whether articulate or inarticulate, resembles not in any degree taste, smell, nor motion; and as little can it resemble any internal sentiment, feeling, or emotion. But must we then admit, that nothing but sound can be imitated by sound? Taking imitation in its proper sense, as importing a resemblance between two objects, the proposition must be admitted: and yet in many passages that are not descriptive of sound, every one must be sensible of a peculiar concord between the sound of the words and their meaning. As there can be no doubt of the fact, what remains is to inquire into its cause.

Resembling causes may produce effects that have no resemblance; and causes that have no resemblance may produce resembling effects.[60] A magnificent building, for example, resembles not in any degree an heroic action; and yet the emotions they produce, are concordant, and bear a resemblance to each other. We are still more sensible of this resemblance in a song, when the music is properly adapted to the sentiment: there is no resemblance between thought and sound; but there is the strongest resemblance between the emotion raised by music tender and pathetic, and that raised by the complaint of an unsuccessful lover. Ap-<87>plying this observation to the present subject, it appears, that in some instances, the sound even of a single word makes an impression resembling that which is made by the thing it signifies: witness the word *running*, composed of two short syllables; and more remarkably the words *rapidity, impetuosity, precipitation.* Brutal manners produce in the spectator an emotion not unlike what is produced by a harsh and rough sound; and hence the beauty of the figurative expression, *rugged* manners. Again, the word *little*, being pronounced with a very small aperture of the mouth, has a weak and faint sound, which makes an impression resembling that made by a diminutive object. This resemblance of effects is still more remarkable where a number of words are connected in a period: words pronounced in succession make often a strong impression; and when this impression happens to accord with that made by the

60. This intentionally contradicts one of David Hume's central tenets.

sense, we are sensible of a complex emotion, peculiarly pleasant; one proceeding from the sentiment, and one from the melody or sound of the
words. But the chief pleasure proceeds from having these two concordant
emotions combined in perfect harmony, and carried on in the mind to a
full close.* Except in the single case where sound is described, all the examples given by critics of sense being imitated in sound, resolve into a
resemblance of <88> effects: emotions raised by sound and signification
may have a resemblance; but sound itself cannot have a resemblance to any
thing but sound.

Proceeding now to particulars, and beginning with those cases where the
emotions have the strongest resemblance, I observe, first, That by a number
of syllables in succession, an emotion is sometimes raised, extremely similar
to that raised by successive motion; which may be evident even to those
who are defective in taste, from the following fact, that the term *movement*
in all languages is equally apply'd to both. In this manner, successive motion, such as walking, running, galloping, can be imitated by a succession
of long or short syllables, or by a due mixture of both. For example, slow
motion may be justly imitated in a verse where long syllables prevail; especially when aided by a slow pronunciation:

> Illi inter sese magnâ vi brachia tollunt.   *Georg.* iv. 174.[61]

On the other hand, swift motion is imitated by a succession of short
syllables:

> Quadrupedante putrem sonitu quatit ungula campum.[62]

Again:

> Radit iter liquidum, celeres neque commovet alas.[63]

Thirdly, A line composed of monosyllables, <89> makes an impression,
by the frequency of its pauses, similar to what is made by laborious interrupted motion:

---

* See chap. 2. part 4.
61. "They with mighty force, now one, now another, raise their arms."
62. *Aeneid* 8.596: "With galloping tramp the horse-hoof shakes the crumbling plain."
63. *Aeneid* 5.217: "She skims her liquid way and stirs not her swift pinions."

With many a weary step, and many a groan,
Up the high hill he heaves a huge round stone.

Odyssey, xi. 736.

First march the heavy mules securely slow;
O'er hills, o'er dales, o'er craggs, o'er rocks they go.

Iliad, xxiii. 138.

Fourthly, The impression made by rough sounds in succession, resembles that made by rough or tumultuous motion: on the other hand, the impression of smooth sounds resembles that of gentle motion. The following is an example of both.

Two craggy rocks projecting to the main,
The roaring wind's tempestuous rage restrain;
Within, the waves in softer murmurs glide,
And ships secure without their haulsers ride.

Odyssey, iii. 118.

Another example of the latter:

Soft is the strain when Zephyr gently blows,
And the smooth stream in smoother numbers flows.

Essay on Crit. 366.

Fifthly, Prolonged motion is expressed in an Alexandrine line. The first example shall be of slow motion prolonged. <90>

A needless Alexandrine ends the song;
That, like a wounded snake, drags its slow length along,

Essay on Crit. 356.

The next example is of forcible motion prolonged:

The waves behind impel the waves before,
Wide-rolling, foaming high, and tumbling to the shore.

Iliad, xiii. 1004.

The last shall be of rapid motion prolonged:

> Not so when swift Camilla scours the plain,
> Flies o'er th' unbending corn, and skims along the main.
>
> *Essay on Crit.* 373.

Again, speaking of a rock torn from the brow of a mountain:

> Still gath'ring force, it smokes, and urg'd amain,
> Whirls, leaps, and thunders down, impetuous to the plain.
>
> *Iliad,* xiii. 197.

Sixthly, A period consisting mostly of long syllables, that is, of syllables pronounced slow, produceth an emotion resembling faintly that which is produced by gravity and solemnity. Hence the beauty of the following verse:

> Olli sedato respondit corde Latinus.[64]

It resembles equally an object that is insipid and uninteresting. <91>

> Taedet quotidianarum harum formarum.
>
> *Terence, Eunuchus, act* 2. *sc.* 3.[65]

Seventhly, A slow succession of ideas is a circumstance that belongs equally to settled melancholy, and to a period composed of polysyllables pronounced slow; and hence, by similarity of emotions, the latter is imitative of the former:

> In those deep solitudes, and awful cells,
> Where heav'nly-pensive Contemplation dwells,
> And ever-musing Melancholy reigns.
>
> *Pope, Eloisa to Abelard.*

Eighthly, A long syllable made short, or a short syllable made long, raises, by the difficulty of pronouncing contrary to custom, a feeling similar to that of hard labour:

---

64. *Aeneid* 12.18: "To him Latinus with unruffled soul replied."
65. Terence, *The Eunuch,* act 2, sc. 3: "I've had enough of these everyday beauties."

When Ajax strives some rock's *vast* weight to throw,
The line too labours, and the words move slow.

Essay on Crit. 370.

Ninthly, Harsh or rough words pronounced with difficulty, excite a feeling similar to that which proceeds from the labour of thought to a dull writer:

Just writes to make his barrenness appear,
And strains from hard-bound brains eight lines a-year.

Pope's epistle to Dr. Arbuthnot, l. 181.

I shall close with one example more, which of <92> all makes the finest figure. In the first section mention is made of a climax in sound; and in the second, of a climax in sense. It belongs to the present subject to observe, that when these coincide in the same passage, the concordance of sound and sense is delightful: the reader is conscious not only of pleasure from the two climaxes separately, but of an additional pleasure from their concordance, and from finding the sense so justly imitated by the sound. In this respect, no periods are more perfect than those borrowed from Cicero in the first section.

The concord between sense and sound is no less agreeable in what may be termed an *anticlimax,* where the progress is from great to little; for this has the effect to make diminutive objects appear still more diminutive. Horace affords a striking example:

Parturiunt montes, nascetur ridiculus mus.[66]

The arrangement here is singularly artful: the first place is occupied by the verb, which is the capital word by its sense as well as sound: the close is reserved for the word that is the meanest in sense as well as in sound. And it must not be overlooked, that the resembling sounds of the two last syllables give a ludicrous air to the whole.

Reviewing the foregoing examples, it appears to me, contrary to expectation, that in passing from the strongest resemblances to those that are

---

66. Horace, *Ars Poetica* 139: "Mountains will labour, to birth will come a single laughable little mouse."

<93> fainter, every step affords additional pleasure. Renewing the experiment again and again, I feel no wavering, but the greatest pleasure constantly from the faintest resemblances. And yet how can this be? for if the pleasure lie in imitation, must not the strongest resemblance afford the greatest pleasure? From this vexing dilemma I am happily relieved, by reflecting on a doctrine established in the chapter of resemblance and contrast, that the pleasure of resemblance is the greatest, where it is least expected, and where the objects compared are in their capital circumstances widely different. Nor will this appear surprising, when we descend to familiar examples. It raiseth no degree of wonder to find the most perfect resemblance between two eggs of the same bird: it is more rare to find such resemblance between two human faces; and upon that account such an appearance raises some degree of wonder: but this emotion rises to a still greater height, when we find in a pebble, an agate, or other natural production, any resemblance to a tree or to any organised body. We cannot hesitate a moment, in applying these observations to the present subject: what occasion of wonder can it be to find one sound resembling another, where both are of the same kind? it is not so common to find a resemblance between an articulate sound and one not articulate; which accordingly affords some slight pleasure. But the pleasure swells greatly, when we employ sound to imitate <94> things it resembles not otherwise than by the effects produced in the mind.

I have had occasion to observe, that to complete the resemblance between sound and sense, artful pronunciation contributes not a little. Pronunciation therefore may be considered as a branch of the present subject; and with some observations upon it the section shall be concluded.

In order to give a just idea of pronunciation, it must be distinguished from singing. The latter is carried on by notes, requiring each of them a different aperture of the windpipe: the notes properly belonging to the former, are expressed by different apertures of the mouth, without varying the aperture of the windpipe. This however doth not hinder pronunciation to borrow from singing, as one sometimes is naturally led to do, in expressing a vehement passion.

In reading, as in singing, there is a key-note: above this note the voice is frequently elevated, to make the sound correspond to the elevation of the subject: but the mind in an elevated state, is disposed to action; therefore, in order to a rest, it must be brought down to the key-note. Hence the term *cadence.*

The only general rule that can be given for directing the pronunciation, is, To sound the words in such a manner as to imitate the things they signify. In pronouncing words signifying what is elevated, the voice ought to be raised above its ordi-<95>nary tone; and words signifying dejection of mind, ought to be pronounced in a low note. To imitate a stern and impetuous passion, the words ought to be pronounced rough and loud; a sweet and kindly passion, on the contrary, ought to be imitated by a soft and melodious tone of voice: in Dryden's ode of *Alexander's feast,* the line, *Faln, faln, faln, faln,* represents a gradual sinking of the mind; and therefore is pronounced with a falling voice by every one of taste, without instruction. In general, words that make the greatest figure ought to be marked with a peculiar emphasis. Another circumstance contributes to the resemblance between sense and sound, which is slow or quick pronunciation: for though the length or shortness of the syllables with relation to each other, be in prose ascertained in some measure, and in verse accurately; yet taking a whole line or period together, it may be pronounced slow or fast. A period accordingly ought to be pronounced slow, when it expresses what is solemn or deliberate; and ought to be pronounced quick, when it expresses what is brisk, lively, or impetuous.

The art of pronouncing with propriety and grace, being intended to make the sound an echo to the sense, scarce admits of any other general rule than that above mentioned. It may indeed be branched out into many particular rules and observations: but without much success; because no language furnisheth words to signify the diffe-<96>rent degrees of high and low, loud and soft, fast and slow. Before these differences can be made the subject of regular instruction, notes must be invented, resembling those employ'd in music. We have reason to believe, that in Greece every tragedy was accompanied with such notes, in order to ascertain the pronunciation; but the moderns hitherto have not thought of this refinement. Cicero indeed,* without the help of notes, pretends to give rules for ascertaining the various tones of voice that are proper in expressing the different passions;

---

* *De oratore,* 1. 3. cap. 58.

and it must be acknowledged, that in this attempt he hath exhausted the whole power of language. At the same time, every person of discernment will perceive, that these rules avail little in point of instruction: the very words he employs, are not intelligible, except to those who beforehand are acquainted with the subject.

To vary the scene a little, I propose to close with a slight comparison between singing and pronouncing. In this comparison, the five following circumstances relative to articulate sound, must be kept in view. 1st, A sound or syllable is harsh or smooth. 2d, It is long or short. 3d, It is pronounced high or low. 4th, It is pronounced loud or soft. And, lastly, A number of words in succession, constituting a period or member of a period, are pronounced slow or quick. Of these <97> five the first depending on the component letters, and the second being ascertained by custom, admit not any variety in pronouncing. The three last are arbitrary, depending on the will of the person who pronounces; and it is chiefly in the artful management of these that just pronunciation consists. With respect to the first circumstance, music has evidently the advantage; for all its notes are agreeable to the ear; which is not always the case of articulate sounds. With respect to the second, long and short syllables variously combined, produce a great variety of feet; yet far inferior to the variety that is found in the multiplied combinations of musical notes. With respect to high and low notes, pronunciation is still more inferior to singing; for it is observed by Dionysius of Halicarnassus,* that in pronouncing, *i.e.* without altering the aperture of the windpipe, the voice is confined within three notes and a half: singing has a much greater compass. With respect to the two last circumstances, pronunciation equals singing.

In this chapter, I have mentioned none of the beauties of language but what arise from words taken in their proper sense. Beauties that depend on the metaphorical and figurative power of words, are reserved to be treated chap. 20. <98>

---

* De structura orationis, sect. 2.

SECTION IV

Versification.

The music of verse, though handled by every grammarian, merits more attention than it has been honoured with. It is a subject intimately connected with human nature; and to explain it thoroughly, several nice and delicate feelings must be employ'd. But before entering upon it, we must see what verse is, or, in other words, by what mark it is distinguished from prose; a point not so easy as may at first be apprehended. It is true, that the construction of verse is governed by precise rules; whereas prose is more loose, and scarce subjected to any rules. But are the many who have no rules, left without means to make the distinction? and even with respect to the learned, must they apply the rule before they can with certainty pronounce whether the composition be prose or verse? This will hardly be maintained; and therefore, instead of rules, the ear must be appealed to as the proper judge. But by what mark does the ear distinguish verse from prose? The proper and satisfactory answer is, That these <99> make different impressions upon every one who hath an ear. This advances us one step in our inquiry.

Taking it then for granted, that verse and prose make upon the ear different impressions; nothing remains but to explain this difference, and to assign its cause. To this end, I call to my aid an observation made above upon the sound of words, that they are more agreeable to the ear when composed of long and short syllables, than when all the syllables are of the same sort: a continued sound in the same tone, makes not a musical impression: the same note successively renewed by intervals, is more agreeable; but still makes not a musical impression. To produce that impression, variety is necessary as well as number: the successive sounds or syllables, must be some of them long, some of them short; and if also high and low, the music is the more perfect. The musical impression made by a period consisting of long and short syllables arranged in a certain order, is what the Greeks call *rhythmus,* the Latins *numerus,* and we *melody* or *measure.* Cicero justly observes, that in one continued sound there is no melody: "Numerus in continuatione nullus est." But in what follows he is wide of the truth, if by *numerus* he mean melody or musical measure: "Distinctio, et aequalium et saepe variorum intervallorum percussio, numerum conficit; quem in cadentibus guttis, quod intervallis distin-<100>guuntur, notare possumus."[67] Falling drops, whether with equal or unequal intervals, are certainly not music: we are not sensible of a musical impression but in a succession of long and short notes. And this also was probably the opinion of the author cited, tho' his expression be a little unguarded.*

It will probably occur, that melody, if it depend on long and short syllables combined in a sentence, may be found in prose as well as in verse; considering especially, that in both, particular words are accented or pronounced in a higher tone than the rest; and therefore that verse cannot be distinguished from prose by melody merely. The observation is just; and it follows, that the distinction between them, since it depends not singly on melody, must arise from the difference of the melody: which is precisely the case; tho' that difference cannot with any accuracy be explained in words; all that can be said is, that verse is more musical than prose, and its melody more perfect. The difference between verse and <101> prose, resembles the difference, in music properly so called, between the song and the recitative: and the resemblance is not the less complete, that these differences, like the shades of colours, approximate sometimes so nearly as scarce to be discernible: the melody of a recitative approaches sometimes to that of a song; which, on the other hand, degenerates sometimes to that of a recitative. Nothing is more distinguishable from prose, than the bulk of Virgil's Hexameters: many of those composed by Horace, are very little

---

* From this passage, however, we discover the etymology of the Latin term for musical impression. Every one being sensible that there is no music in a continued sound; the first inquiries were probably carried no farther than to discover, that to produce a musical impression a number of sounds is necessary; and musical impression obtained the name of *numerus,* before it was clearly ascertained, that variety is necessary as well as number.

67. [*De Oratore* III.48] "In a continuous flow there is no rhythm; rhythm is the product of a dividing up, that is of a beat marking equal and also frequently varying intervals, the rhythm that we can notice in falling drops of water."

removed from prose: Sapphic verse has a very sensible melody: that, on the other hand, of an Iambic, is extremely faint.*

This more perfect melody of articulate sounds, is what distinguisheth verse from prose. Verse is subjected to certain inflexible laws; the number and variety of the component syllables being ascertained, and in some measure the order of succession. Such restraint makes it a matter of difficulty to compose in verse; a difficulty that is not to be surmounted but by a peculiar genius. Useful lessons convey'd to us in verse, are agreeable by the union of music with instruction: but are <102> we for that reason to reject knowledge offered in a plainer dress? That would be ridiculous: for knowledge is of intrinsic merit, independent of the means of acquisition; and there are many, not less capable than willing to instruct us, who have no genius for verse. Hence the use of prose; which, for the reason now given, is not confined to precise rules. There belongs to it, a certain melody of an inferior kind, which ought to be the aim of every writer; but for succeeding in it, practice is necessary more than genius. Nor do we rigidly insist for melodious prose: provided the work convey instruction, its chief end, we are the less solicitous about its dress.

Having ascertained the nature and limits of our subject, I proceed to the laws by which it is regulated. These would be endless, were verse of all different kinds to be taken under consideration. I propose therefore to confine the inquiry, to Latin or Greek Hexameter, and to French and English Heroic verse; which perhaps may carry me farther than the reader will choose to follow. The observations I shall have occasion to make, will at any rate be sufficient for a specimen; and these, with proper variations, may easily be transferred to the composition of other sorts of verse.

Before I enter upon particulars, it must be premised in general, that to verse of every kind, five things are of importance. 1st, The number of syllables that compose a verse line. 2d, The dif-<103>ferent lengths of syllables, *i.e.* the difference of time taken in pronouncing. 3d, The arrangement of these syllables combined in words. 4th, The pauses or stops in pro-

---

* Music, properly so called, is analysed into melody and harmony. A succession of sounds so as to be agreeable to the ear, constitutes melody: harmony arises from coexisting sounds. Verse therefore can only reach melody, and not harmony.

nouncing. 5th, The pronouncing syllables in a high or a low tone. The three first mentioned are obviously essential to verse: if any of them be wanting, there cannot be that higher degree of melody which distinguisheth verse from prose. To give a just notion of the fourth, it must be observed, that pauses are necessary for three different purposes: one, to separate periods, and members of the same period, according to the sense; another, to improve the melody of verse; and the last, to afford opportunity for drawing breath in reading. A pause of the first kind is variable, being long or short, frequent or less frequent, as the sense requires. A pause of the second kind, being determined by the melody, is in no degree arbitrary. The last sort is in a measure arbitrary, depending on the reader's command of breath. But as one cannot read with grace, unless, for drawing breath, opportunity be taken of a pause in the sense or in the melody, this pause ought never to be distinguished from the others; and for that reason shall be laid aside. With respect then to the pauses of sense and of melody, it may be affirmed without hesitation, that their coincidence in verse is a capital beauty: but as it cannot be expected, in a long work especially, that every line should be so per-<104>fect; we shall afterward have occasion to see, that the pause necessary for the sense must often, in some degree, be sacrificed to the verse-pause, and the latter sometimes to the former.

The pronouncing syllables in a high or low tone, contributes also to melody. In reading whether verse or prose, a certain tone is assumed, which may be called *the key-note;* and in that tone the bulk of the words are sounded. Sometimes to humour the sense, and sometimes the melody, a particular syllable is sounded in a higher tone; and this is termed *accenting a syllable,* or gracing it with an accent. Opposed to the accent, is the cadence, which I have not mentioned as one of the requisites of verse, because it is entirely regulated by the sense, and hath no peculiar relation to verse. The cadence is a falling of the voice below the key-note at the close of every period; and so little is it essential to verse, that in correct reading the final syllable of every line is accented, that syllable only excepted which closes the period, where the sense requires a cadence. The reader may be satisfied of this by experiments; and for that purpose I recommend to him the *Rape of the Lock,* which, in point of versification, is the most complete performance in the English language. Let him consult in a particular period canto 2. beginning at line 47. and closed line 52. with the word *gay*, which only of the whole final syllables is pronounced with a cadence. He may also exa-<105>mine another period in the 5th canto which runs from line 45. to line 52.

Tho' the five requisites above mentioned, enter the composition of every species of verse, they are however governed by different rules, peculiar to each species. Upon quantity only, one general observation may be premised, because it is applicable to every species of verse, That syllables, with respect to the time taken in pronouncing, are long or short; two short syllables, with respect to time, being precisely equal to a long one. These two lengths are essential to verse of all kinds; and to no verse, as far as I know, is a greater variety of time necessary in pronouncing syllables. The voice indeed is frequently made to rest longer than usual, upon a word that bears an important signification; but this is done to humour the sense, and is not necessary for melody. A thing not more necessary for melody occurs with respect to accenting, similar to that now mentioned: A word signifying any thing humble, low, or dejected, is naturally, in prose as well as in verse, pronounced in a tone below the key-note.

We are now sufficiently prepared for particulars; beginning with Latin or Greek Hexameter, which are the same. What I have to observe upon this species of verse, will come under the four following heads; number, arrangement, pause, and accent: for as to quantity, what is observed above may suffice. <106>

Hexameter lines, as to time, are all of the same length; being equivalent to the time taken in pronouncing twelve long syllables or twenty-four short. An Hexameter line may consist of seventeen syllables; and when regular and not Spondaic, it never has fewer than thirteen: whence it follows, that where the syllables are many, the plurality must be short; where few, the plurality must be long.

This line is susceptible of much variety as to the succession of long and short syllables. It is however subjected to laws that confine its variety within certain limits: and for ascertaining these limits, grammarians have invented a rule by Dactyles and Spondees, which they denominate *feet*. One at first view is led to think, that these feet are also intended to regulate the pronunciation: which is far from being the case; for were one to pronounce according to these feet, the melody of a Hexameter line would be destroyed, or at best be much inferior to what it is when properly pronounced.* These feet must be confined to regu-<107>late the arrangement, for they serve no other purpose. They are withal so artificial and complex, that I am tempted to substitute in their stead, other rules more simple and of more easy ap-

---

* After giving some attention to this subject, and weighing deliberately every circumstance, I was necessarily led to the foregoing conclusion, That the Dactyle and Spondee are no other than artificial measures invented for trying the accuracy of composition. Repeated experiments have convinced me, that though the sense should be neglected, an Hexameter line read by Dactyles and Spondees will not be melodious. And the composition of an Hexameter line demonstrates this to be true, without necessity of an experiment; for, as will appear afterward, there must always, in this line, be a capital pause at the end of the fifth long syllable, reckoning, as above, two short for one long; and when we measure this line by Dactyles and Spondees, the pause now mentioned divides always a Dactyle, or a Spondee, without once falling in after either of these feet. Hence it is evident, that if a line be pronounced as it is scanned, by Dactyles and Spondees, the pause must utterly be neglected; which destroys the melody, because this pause is essential to the melody of an Hexameter verse. If, on the other hand, the melody be preserved by making that pause, the pronouncing by Dactyles or Spondees must be abandoned.

What has led grammarians into the use of Dactyles and Spondees, seems not beyond the reach of conjecture. To produce melody, the Dactyle and the Spondee, which close every Hexameter line, must be distinctly expressed in the pronunciation. This discovery, joined with another, that the foregoing part of the verse could be measured by the same feet, probably led grammarians to adopt these artificial measures, and perhaps rashly to conclude, that the pronunciation is directed by these feet as the composition is: the Dactyle and the Spondee at the close, serve indeed to regulate the pronunciation as well as the composition; but in the foregoing part of the line, they regulate the composition only, not the pronunciation.

If we must have feet in verse to regulate the pronunciation and consequently the melody, these feet must be determined by the pauses. All the syllables interjected between two pauses ought to be deemed one musical foot; because, to preserve the melody, they must all be pronounced together, without any stop. And therefore, whatever number there are of pauses in a Hexameter line, the parts into which it is divided by these pauses, make just so many musical feet.

Connection obliges me here to anticipate, and to observe, that the same doctrine is applicable to English heroic verse. Considering its composition merely, it is of two kinds; one composed of five Iambi; and one of a Trochaeus followed by four Iambi: but these feet afford no rule for pronouncing; the musical feet being obviously those parts of the line that are interjected between two pauses. To bring out the melody, these feet must be expressed in the pronunciation; or, which comes to the same, the pronunciation must be directed by the pauses, without regard to the Iambus or Trochaeus.

plication; for example, the following. 1st, The line must always commence with a long syllable, and <108> close with two long preceded by two short. 2d, More than two short can never be found together, nor fewer than two. And, 3d, Two long syllables which have been preceded by two short, cannot also be followed by two short. These few rules fulfil all the conditions of a Hexameter line, with relation to order or arrangement. To these again a single rule may be substituted, for which I have a still greater relish, as it regulates more affirmatively the construction of every part. That I may put this rule into words with perspicuity, I take a hint from the twelve long syllables that compose <109> an Hexameter line, to divide it into twelve equal parts or portions, being each of them one long syllable or two short. A portion being thus defined, I proceed to the rule. The 1st, 3d, 5th, 7th, 9th, 11th, and 12th portions, must each of them be one long syllable; the 10th must always be two short syllables; the 2d, 4th, 6th, and 8th, may either be one long or two short. Or to express the thing still more curtly, The 2d, 4th, 6th, and 8th portions may be one long syllable or two short; the 10th must be two short syllables; all the rest must consist each of one long syllable. This fulfils all the conditions of an Hexameter line, and comprehends all the combinations of Dactyles and Spondees that this line admits.

Next in order comes the pause. At the end of every Hexameter line, every one must be sensible of a complete close or full pause; the cause of which follows. The two long syllables preceded by two short, which always close an Hexameter line, are a fine preparation for a pause: for long syllables, or syllables pronounced slow, resembling a slow and languid motion, tending to rest, naturally incline the mind to rest, or to pause; and to this inclination the two preceding short syllables contribute, which, by contrast, make the slow pronunciation of the final syllables the more conspicuous. Beside this complete close or full pause at the end, others are also re-<110>quisite for the sake of melody; of which I discover two clearly, and perhaps there may be more. The longest and most remarkable, succeeds the 5th portion: the other, which, being shorter and more faint, may be called *the semipause*, succeeds the 8th portion. So striking is the pause first mentioned, as to be distinguished even by the rudest ear: the monkish rhymes are evidently built upon it; in which, by an invariable rule, the final word always chimes with that which immediately precedes the said pause:

> De planctu cudo ‖ metrum cum carmine nudo[68]

> Mingere cum bumbis ‖ res est saluberrima lumbis.[69]

The difference of time in the pause and semipause, occasions another difference no less remarkable; that it is lawful to divide a word by a semipause, but never by a pause, the bad effect of which is sensibly felt in the following examples:

> Effusus labor, at ‖ que inmitis rupta Tyranni

Again:

> Observans nido im ‖ plumes detraxit; at illa[70]

Again,

> Loricam quam De ‖ moleo detraxerat ipse[71] <III>

The dividing a word by a semipause has not the same bad effect:

> Jamque pedem referens ‖ casus e|vaserat omnes.

Again:

> Qualis populea ‖ moerens Philo|mela sub umbra[72]

Again:

> Ludere que vellem ‖ calamo per|misit agresti.

Lines, however, where words are left entire, without being divided even by a semipause, run by that means much the more sweetly.

---

68. Ascribed to Andrew Baston, bard and fourteenth-century Carmelite monk: the opening of "a monkish rhyme, consisting of barbarous jingle," in William Nimmo, *The History of Stirlingshire,* 1777, ch. 10.
69. Roman proverb: "Piss and fart. Sound at heart."
70. *Georgics* 4.492, 513.
71. *Aeneid* 5.260.
72. *Georgics* 4.485, 511.

> Nec gemere aërea ‖ cessabit | turtur ab ulmo.[73]

Again:

> Quadrupedante putrem ‖ sonitu quatit | ungula campum.[74]

Again:

> Eurydicen toto ‖ referebant | flumine ripae.[75]

The reason of these observations will be evident upon the slightest reflection. Between things so intimately connected in reading aloud, as are sense and sound, every degree of discord is unpleasant: and for that reason, it is a matter of importance, to make the musical pauses coincide as <112> much as possible with those of sense; which is requisite, more especially, with respect to the pause, a deviation from the rule being less remarkable in a semipause. Considering the matter as to melody solely, it is indifferent whether the pauses be at the end of words or in the middle; but when we carry the sense along, it is disagreeable to find a word split into two by a pause, as if there were really two words: and though the disagreeableness here be connected with the sense only, it is by an easy transition of perceptions transferred to the sound; by which means, we conceive a line to be harsh and grating to the ear, when in reality it is only so to the understanding.*

To the rule that fixes the pause after the fifth portion, there is one exception, and no more: If the syllable succeeding the 5th portion be short, the pause is sometimes postponed to it.

> Pupillis quos dura ‖ premit custodia matrum[76]

Again,

> In terras oppressa ‖ gravi sub religione[77]

---

* See chap. 2. part 1. sect. 5.
73. *Eclogues* 1.10, 58.
74. *Aeneid* 8.596: "with galloping tramp the horse-hoof shakes the crumbling plain."
75. *Georgics* 4.527.
76. Horace, *Epistles* 1.22.
77. Lucretius, *De Rerum Natura* 1.63.

Again:

> Et quorum pars magna ‖ fui; quis talia fando[78]

This contributes to diversify the melody; and <113> where the words are smooth and liquid, is not ungraceful; as in the following examples:

> Formosam resonare ‖ doces Amaryllida sylvas[79]

Again:

> Agricolas, quibus ipsa ‖ procul discordibus armis[80]

If this pause, placed as aforesaid after the short syllable, happen also to divide a word, the melody by these circumstances is totally annihilated. Witness the following line of Ennius, which is plain prose:

> Romae moenia terru ‖ it impiger | Hannibal armis.

Hitherto the arrangement of the long and short syllables of an Hexameter line and its different pauses, have been considered with respect to melody: but to have a just notion of Hexameter verse, these particulars must also be considered with respect to sense. There is not perhaps in any other sort of verse, such latitude in the long and short syllables; a circumstance that contributes greatly to that richness of melody which is remarkable in Hexameter verse, and which made Aristotle pronounce, that an epic poem in any other verse would not succeed.* One defect, however, must not be dissembled, that the same means <114> which contribute to the richness of the melody, render it less fit than several other sorts for a narrative poem. There cannot be a more artful contrivance, as above observed, than to close an Hexameter line with two long syllables preceded by two short: but unhappily this construction proves a great embarrassment to the sense; which will thus be evident. As in general, there ought to be a strict concordance between a thought and the words in which it is dressed; so in particular, every close in the sense ought to be accompanied with a close in

---

* *Poet.* cap. 25.
78. *Aeneid* 2.6.
79. *Eclogues* 1.5.
80. *Georgics* 2.459.

the sound. In prose, this law may be strictly observed; but in verse, the same strictness would occasion insuperable difficulties. Willing to sacrifice to the melody of verse, some share of the concordance between thought and expression, we freely excuse the separation of the musical pause from that of the sense, during the course of a line; but the close of an Hexameter line is too conspicuous to admit this liberty: for which reason there ought always to be some pause in the sense at the end of every Hexameter line, were it but such a pause as is marked with a comma; and for the same reason, there ought never to be a full close in the sense but at the end of a line, because there the melody is closed. An Hexameter line, to preserve its melody, cannot well admit any greater relaxation; and yet in a narrative poem, it is extremely difficult to adhere strictly to the rule even with these indulgences. Virgil, the <115> chief of poets for versification, is forc'd often to end a line without any close in the sense, and as often to close the sense during the running of a line; tho' a close in the melody during the movement of the thought, or a close in the thought during the movement of the melody, cannot be agreeable.

The accent, to which we proceed, is no less essential than the other circumstances above handled. By a good ear it will be discerned, that in every line there is one syllable distinguishable from the rest by a capital accent: that syllable, being the 7th portion, is invariably long.

> Nec bene promeritis ‖ capitûr nec | tangitur ira.[81]

Again:

> Non sibi sed toto ‖ genitûm se | credere mundo.[82]

Again:

> Qualis spelunca ‖ subitô com|mota columba.[83]

In these examples, the accent is laid upon the last syllable of a word; which is favourable to the melody in the following respect, that the pause,

81. Lucretius, *De Rerum Natura* 1.49.
82. Lucan, *Pharsalia* 2.383.
83. *Aeneid* 5.213.

which for the sake of reading distinctly must follow every word, gives opportunity to prolong the accent. And for that reason, a line thus accented, <116> has a more spirited air, than when the accent is placed on any other syllable. Compare the foregoing lines with the following:

> Alba neque Assyrio ‖ fucâtur | lana veneno.[84]

Again:

> Panditur interea ‖ domus ômnipo|tentis Olympi.

Again:

> Olli sedato ‖ respôndit | corde Latinus.

In lines where the pause comes after the short syllable succeeding the 5th portion, the accent is displaced, and rendered less sensible: it seems to be split into two, and to be laid partly on the 5th portion, and partly on the 7th, its usual place; as in

> Nuda genu, nodôque ‖ sinûs col|lecta fluentes[85]

Again:

> Formosam resonâre ‖ docês Amar|yllida sylvas[86]

Beside this capital accent, slighter accents are laid upon other portions; particularly upon the 4th, unless where it consists of two short syllables; upon the 9th, which is always a long syllable; <117> and upon the 11th, where the line concludes with a monosyllable. Such conclusion, by the by, impairs the melody, and for that reason is not to be indulged unless where it is expressive of the sense. The following lines are marked with all the accents.

> Ludere quae vêllem calamô permîsit agresti.

---

84. *Georgics* 2.465.
85. *Aeneid* 10.1; 12.18; 1.320.
86. *Eclogues* 1.5.

Again:

> Et durae quêrcus sudâbunt rôscida mella.[87]

Again:

> Parturiunt môntes, nascêtur rîdiculûs mus.[88]

Reflecting upon the melody of Hexameter verse, we find, that order or arrangement doth not constitute the whole of it; for when we compare different lines, equally regular as to the succession of long and short syllables, the melody is found in very different degrees of perfection; which is not occasioned by any particular combination of Dactyles and Spondees, or of long and short syllables, because we find lines where Dactyles prevail, and lines where Spondees prevail, equally melodious. Of the former take the following instance:

> Aeneadum genitrix hominum divumque voluptas.[89] <118>

Of the latter:

> Molli paulatim flavescet campus arista.[90]

What can be more different as to melody than the two following lines, which, however, as to the succession of long and short syllables, are constructed precisely in the same manner?

> Spond. Dact. Spond. Spond. Dact.   Spond.
> Ad talos stola dimissa et circumdata palla.   *Hor.*[91]

> Spond. Dact. Spond. Spond.   Dact.   Spond.
> Placatumque nitet diffuso lumine coelum.   *Lucret.*

In the former, the pause falls in the middle of a word, which is a great blemish, and the accent is disturbed by a harsh elision of the vowel *a* upon

---

87. *Eclogues* 1.10; 4.30.
88. *Ars Poetica* 139.
89. Lucretius, *De Rerum Natura* 1.1.
90. *Eclogues* 4.28.
91. *Satires* 1.2.99.

the particle *et.* In the latter, the pauses and the accent are all of them distinct and full: there is no elision; and the words are more liquid and sounding. In these particulars consists the beauty of an Hexameter line with respect to melody: and by neglecting these, many lines in the Satires and Epistles of Horace are less agreeable than plain prose; for they are neither the one nor the other in perfection. To draw melody from these lines, they must be pronounced without relation to the sense: it must not be regarded, that words are divided by pauses, nor that harsh elisions are multiplied. To add to the account, prosaic low-sounding words are introduced; and which is still worse, <119> accents are laid on them. Of such faulty lines take the following instances.[92]

Candida rectaque sit, munda hactenus sit neque longa.

Jupiter exclamat simul atque audirit; at in se

Custodes, lectica, ciniflones, parasitae

Optimus est modulator, ut Alfenus Vafer omni

Nunc illud tantum quaeram, meritone tibi sit.

Next in order comes English Heroic verse, which shall be examined under the whole five heads, of number, quantity, arrangement, pause, and accent. This verse is of two kinds; one named *rhyme* or *metre,* and one *blank verse.* In the former, the lines are connected two and two by similarity of sound in the final syllables; and two lines so connected are termed a *couplet:* similarity of sound being avoided in the latter, couplets are banished. These two sorts must be handled separately, because there are many peculiarities in each. Beginning with rhyme or metre, the first article shall be discussed in a few words. Every line consists of ten syllables, five short and five long; from which there are but two exceptions, both of them rare. The first is, where each line of a couplet is made eleven syllables, by an additional syllable at the end:

92. Horace, *Satires:* 1.2.123; 1.2.18; 1.2.98; 1.3.130; 1.1.64.

> There heroes' wits are kept in pond'rous vases,
> And beaus' in snuff-boxes and tweezer-cases. <120>
>
> The piece, you think, is incorrect? Why, take it;
> I'm all submission; what you'd have it, make it.

This licence is sufferable in a single couplet; but if frequent, would give disgust.

The other exception concerns the second line of a couplet, which is sometimes stretched out to twelve syllables, termed an *Alexandrine line:*

> A needless Alexandrine ends the song,
> That, like a wounded snake, drags its slow length along.[93]

It doth extremely well when employ'd to close a period with a certain pomp and solemnity, where the subject makes that tone proper.

With regard to quantity, it is unnecessary to mention a second time, that the quantities employ'd in verse are but two, the one double of the other; that every syllable is reducible to one or other of these standards; and that a syllable of the larger quantity is termed *long,* and of the lesser quantity *short.* It belongs more to the present article, to examine what peculiarities there may be in the English language as to long and short syllables. Every language has syllables that may be pronounced long or short at pleasure; but the English above all abounds in syllables of that kind: in words of three or more syllables, the quantity for the most part is invariable: the exceptions are more frequent in dissyllables: but as to monosyl-<121>lables, they may, without many exceptions, be pronounced either long or short; nor is the ear hurt by a liberty that is rendered familiar by custom. This shows, that the melody of English verse must depend less upon quantity, than upon other circumstances: in which it differs widely from Latin verse, where every syllable, having but one sound, strikes the ear uniformly with its acustomed impression; and a reader must be delighted to find a number of such syllables, disposed so artfully as to be highly melodious. Syllables variable in quantity cannot possess this power: for tho' custom may render

---

93. *Rape of the Lock,* V.116; *Essay on Criticism,* 356.

familiar, both a long and a short pronunciation of the same word; yet the mind wavering between the two sounds, cannot be so much affected as where every syllable has one fixed sound. What I have further to say upon quantity, will come more properly under the following head, of arrangement.

And with respect to arrangement, which may be brought within a narrow compass, the English Heroic line is commonly Iambic, the first syllable short, the second long, and so on alternately through the whole line. One exception there is, pretty frequent, of lines commencing with a Trochaeus, *i.e.* a long and a short syllable: but this affects not the order of the following syllables, which go on alternately as usual, one short and one long. The following couplet affords an example of each kind. <122>

> Sōme ĭn thĕ fields ŏf pūrĕst ēthĕr plāy,
> Ănd bāsk ănd whītĕn īn thĕ blāze ŏf dāy.[94]

It is a great imperfection in English verse, that it excludes the bulk of polysyllables, which are the most sounding words in our language; for very few of them have such alternation of long and short syllables as to correspond to either of the arrangements mentioned. English verse accordingly is almost totally reduced to dissyllables and monosyllables: *magnanimity* is a sounding word totally excluded: *impetuosity* is still a finer word, by the resemblance of the sound and sense; and yet a negative is put upon it, as well as upon numberless words of the same kind. Polysyllables composed of syllables long and short alternately, make a good figure in verse; for example, *observance, opponent, ostensive, pindaric, productive, prolific,* and such others of three syllables. *Imitation, imperfection, misdemeanor, mitigation, moderation, observator, ornamental, regulator,* and others similar of four syllables, beginning with two short syllables, the third long, and the fourth short, may find a place in a line commencing with a Trochaeus. I know not if there be any of five syllables. One I know of six, *viz. misinterpretation:* but words so composed are not frequent in our language.

One would not imagine without trial, how uncouth false quantity appears in verse; not less than <123> a provincial tone or idiom. The article

---

94. *Rape of the Lock,* II.77.

the is one of the few monosyllables that is invariably short: observe how harsh it makes a line where it must be pronounced long;

> Thĭs nȳmph, tō thē dĕstrūctiŏn ōf mănkīnd.

Again,

> Th' ădvēnt'rŏus bārŏn thē brĭght lōcks ădmīr'd.[95]

Let it be pronounced short, and it reduces the melody almost to nothing: better so however than false quantity. In the following examples we perceive the same defect:

> And old impertinence ‖ expel by new

> With varying vanities ‖ from ev'ry part

> Love in these labyrinths ‖ his slaves detains

> New stratagems ‖ the radiant lock to gain

> Her eyes half languishing ‖ half drown'd in tears

> Roar'd for the handkerchief ‖ that caus'd his pain[96]

> Passions like elements ‖ though born to fight.[97]

The great variety of melody conspicuous in English verse, arises chiefly from the pauses and accents; which are of greater importance than is commonly thought. There is a degree of intricacy in this branch of our subject, and it will be dif-<124>ficult to give a distinct view of it; but it is too late to think of difficulties after we are engaged. The pause, which paves the way to the accent, offers itself first to our examination; and from a very short trial, the following facts will be verified. 1st, A line admits but one capital pause. 2d, In different lines, we find this pause after the fourth syl-

---

95. *Rape of the Lock:* II.19; II.29.
96. *Rape of the Lock:* I.94; I.99; II.23; III.120; IV.144; V.106.
97. *Essay on Man,* II.111.

lable, after the fifth, after the sixth, and after the seventh. These four places of the pause lay a solid foundation for dividing English Heroic lines into four kinds; and I warn the reader beforehand, that unless he attend to this distinction, he cannot have any just notion of the richness and variety of English versification. Each kind or order hath a melody peculiar to itself, readily distinguishable by a good ear: and I am not without hopes to make the cause of this peculiarity sufficiently evident. It must be observed, at the same time, that the pause cannot be made indifferently at any of the places mentioned: it is the sense that regulates the pause, as will be seen afterward; and consequently, it is the sense that determines of what order every line must be: there can be but one capital musical pause in a line; and that pause ought to coincide, if possible, with a pause in the sense, in order that the sound may accord with the sense.

What is said shall be illustrated by examples of each sort or order. And first of the pause after the fourth syllable: <125>

> Back through the paths ‖ of pleasing sense I ran.[98]

Again,

> Profuse of bliss ‖ and pregnant with delight.[99]

After the 5th:

> So when an angel ‖ by divine command,
> With rising tempests ‖ shakes a guilty land.[100]

After the 6th:

> Speed the soft intercourse ‖ from soul to soul.[101]

Again,

> Then from his closing eyes ‖ thy form shall part.[102]

---

98. *Eloise to Abelard,* 69.

99. Addison, *A Letter from Italy to The Right Honourable Charles Lord Halifax in the Year MDCCI,* line 120.

100. Addison, "The Campaign" (1705).

101. *Eloise to Abelard,* 57.

102. *Elegy to the Memory of an Unfortunate Lady,* 79.

After the 7th:

> And taught the doubtful battle ‖ where to rage.[103]

Again,

> And in the smooth description ‖ murmur still.[104]

Beside the capital pause now mentioned, inferior pauses will be discovered by a nice ear. Of these there are commonly two in each line: one before the capital pause, and one after it. The former comes invariably after the first long syllable, whether the line begin with a long syllable or a short. <126> The other in its variety imitates the capital pause: in some lines it comes after the 6th syllable, in some after the 7th, and in some after the 8th. Of these semipauses take the following examples.

1st and 8th:

> Led | through a sad ‖ variety | of wo.

1st and 7th:

> Still | on that breast ‖ enamour'd | let me lie.[105]

2d and 8th:

> From storms | a shelter ‖ and from heat | a shade.[106]

2d and 6th:

> Let wealth | let honour ‖ wait | the wedded dame.[107]

2d and 7th:

> Above | all pain ‖ all passion | and all pride.[108]

103. Addison, "The Campaign," st. 24.
104. Addison, *A Letter from Italy,* line 36.
105. *Eloise to Abelard,* 36, 121.
106. *Messiah,* 16.
107. *Eloise to Abelard,* 77.
108. *Epistle to Harley,* I.24.

Even from these few examples it appears, that the place of the last semi-pause, like that of the full pause, is directed in a good measure by the sense. Its proper place with respect to the melody is after the eighth syllable, so as to finish the line with an Iambus distinctly pronounced, which, by a long syllable after a short, is a preparation for rest: but < 127 > sometimes it comes after the 6th, and sometimes after the 7th syllable, in order to avoid a pause in the middle of a word, or between two words intimately connected; and so far melody is justly sacrificed to sense.

In discoursing of Hexameter verse, it was laid down as a rule, That a full pause ought never to divide a word: such licence deviates too far from the coincidence that ought to be between the pauses of sense and of melody. The same rule must obtain in an English line; and we shall support reason by experiments:

A noble super ‖ fluity it craves

Abhor, a perpe ‖ tuity should stand[109]

Are these lines distinguishable from prose? Scarcely, I think.

The same rule is not applicable to a semipause, which being short and faint, is not sensibly disagreeable when it divides a word:

Relent|less walls ‖ whose darksome round | contains

For her | white virgins ‖ hyme|neals sing

In these | deep solitudes ‖ and aw|ful cells.[110]

It must however be acknowledged, that the melody here suffers in some degree: a word ought to be pronounced without any rest between its com- < 128 >ponent syllables: a semipause that bends to this rule, is scarce perceived.

The capital pause is so essential to the melody, that one cannot be too nice in the choice of its place, in order to have it clear and distinct. It cannot

109. Pope, *Epistle* I.vi.91; *Epistle* II.ii.247.
110. *Eloise to Abelard,* 17; 220; 1.

be in better company than with a pause in the sense; and if the sense require but a comma after the fourth, fifth, sixth, or seventh syllable, it is sufficient for the musical pause. But to make such coincidence essential, would cramp versification too much; and we have experience for our authority, that there may be a pause in the melody where the sense requires none. We must not however imagine, that a musical pause may come after any word indifferently: some words, like syllables of the same word, are so intimately connected, as not to bear a separation even by a pause. The separating, for example, a substantive from its article would be harsh and unpleasant: witness the following line, which cannot be pronounced with a pause as marked,

    If Delia smile, the ‖ flow'rs begin to spring.[111]

But ought to be pronounced in the following manner,

    If Delia smile, ‖ the flow'rs begin to spring.

If then it be not a matter of indifference where to make the pause, there ought to be rules for deter-<129>mining what words may be separated by a pause, and what are incapable of such separation. I shall endeavour to ascertain these rules; not chiefly for their utility, but in order to unfold some latent principles, that tend to regulate our taste even where we are scarce sensible of them: and to that end, the method that appears the most promising, is to run over the verbal relations, beginning with the most intimate. The first that presents itself, is that of adjective and substantive, being the relation of subject and quality, the most intimate of all: and with respect to such intimate companions, the question is, Whether they can bear to be separated by a pause. What occurs is, that a quality cannot exist independent of a subject; nor are they separable even in imagination, because they make parts of the same idea: and for that reason, with respect to melody as well as sense, it must be disagreeable, to bestow upon the adjective a sort of independent existence, by interjecting a pause between it and its substantive. I cannot therefore approve the following lines, nor any of the sort; for to my taste they are harsh and unpleasant.

111. Pope, *Spring,* 71.

Of thousand bright ‖ inhabitants of air

The sprites of fiery ‖ termagants inflame

The rest, his many-colour'd ‖ robe conceal'd

The same, his ancient ‖ personage to deck[112] <130>

Ev'n here, where frozen ‖ Chastity retires[113]

I sit, with sad ‖ civility, I read[114]

Back to my native ‖ moderation slide

Or shall we ev'ry ‖ decency confound

Time was, a sober ‖ Englishman would knock

And place, on good ‖ security, his gold

Taste, that eternal ‖ wanderer, which flies[115]

But ere the tenth ‖ revolving day was run

First let the just ‖ equivalent be paid.

Go, threat thy earth-born ‖ Myrmidons; but here

Haste to the fierce ‖ Achilles' tent (he cries)

All but the ever-wakeful ‖ eyes of Jove

Your own resistless ‖ eloquence employ[116]

112. *Rape of the Lock:* I.28; I.59; III.58; V.89.
113. *Eloise to Abelard,* 181.
114. *An Epistle from Mr. Pope to Dr. Arbuthnot,* 37.
115. Pope, *Epistle* I.i.33; *Epistle* I.vi.118; *Epistle* II.i.161, 168, 312.
116. *Iliad* 1.73, 172, 239, 422; 2.4, 217.

I have upon this article multiplied examples, that in a case where I have the misfortune to dislike what passes current in practice, every man upon the spot may judge by his own taste. And to taste I appeal; for tho' the foregoing reasoning appears to me just, it is however too subtile to afford conviction in opposition to taste.

Considering this matter superficially, one might be apt to imagine, that it must be the same, whether the adjective go first, which is the natural order, or the substantive, which is indulged by the laws of inversion. But we soon discover this to be a mistake: colour, for example, cannot be con-<131>ceived independent of the surface coloured; but a tree may be conceived, as growing in a certain spot, as of a certain kind, and as spreading its extended branches all around, without ever thinking of its colour. In a word, a subject may be considered with some of its qualities independent of others; though we cannot form an image of any single quality independent of the subject. Thus then, though an adjective named first be inseparable from the substantive, the proposition does not reciprocate: an image can be formed of the substantive independent of the adjective; and for that reason, they may be separated by a pause, when the substantive takes the lead.

> For thee the fates ‖ severely kind ordain
>
> And curs'd with hearts ‖ unknowing how to yield.[117]

The verb and adverb are precisely in the same condition with the substantive and adjective. An adverb, which modifies the action expressed by the verb, is not separable from the verb even in imagination; and therefore I must also give up the following lines:

> And which it much ‖ becomes you to forget
>
> 'Tis one thing madly ‖ to disperse my store.[118]

---

117. *Eloise to Abelard*, 249; *Unfortunate Lady*, 42.
118. Pope, *Epistle* I.vi.94; *Epistle* II.ii.292.

But an action may be conceived with some of its modifications, leaving out others; precisely as a <132> subject may be conceived with some of its qualities, leaving out others: and therefore, when by inversion the verb is first introduced, it has no bad effect to interject a pause between it and the adverb that follows. This may be done at the close of a line, where the pause is at least as full as that is which divides the line:

> While yet he spoke, the Prince advancing drew
> Nigh to the lodge, &c.[119]

The agent and its action come next, expressed in grammar by the active substantive and its verb. Between these, placed in their natural order, there is no difficulty of interjecting a pause: an active being is not always in motion, and therefore it is easily separable in idea from its action: when in a sentence the substantive takes the lead, we know not that action is to follow; and as rest must precede the commencement of motion, this interval is a proper opportunity for a pause.

But when by inversion the verb is placed first, is it lawful to separate it by a pause from the active substantive? I answer, No; because an action is not in idea separable from the agent, more than a quality from the subject to which it belongs. Two lines of the first rate for beauty, have always appeared to me exceptionable, upon account of the pause thus interjected between the verb and the consequent substantive; and I have now discovered a reason to support my taste: <133>

> In these deep solitudes and awful cells,
> Where heav'nly-pensive ‖ Contemplation dwells,
> And ever-musing ‖ Melancholy reigns.[120]

The point of the greatest delicacy regards the active verb and the passive substantive placed in their natural order. On the one hand, it will be observed, that these words signify things which are not separable in idea. Killing cannot be conceived without a being that is put to death, nor painting without a surface upon which the colours are spread. On the other hand, an action and the thing on which it is exerted, are not, like subject and

---

119. *Odyssey* 16.11.
120. *Eloise to Abelard*, 3.

quality, united in one individual object: the active substantive is perfectly distinct from that which is passive; and they are connected by one circumstance only, that the action of the former is exerted upon the latter. This makes it possible to take the action to pieces, and to consider it first with relation to the agent, and next with relation to the patient. But after all, so intimately connected are the parts of the thought, that it requires an effort to make a separation even for a moment: the subtilising to such a degree is not agreeable, especially in works of imagination. The best poets, however, taking advantage of this subtilty, scruple not to separate by a pause an active verb from the thing upon which it is exerted. Such pauses in a long work may be indulged; but taken singly, they certainly are not agreeable; and I appeal to the following examples: <134>

> The peer now spreads ‖ the glitt'ring forfex wide

> As ever sully'd ‖ the fair face of light

> Repair'd to search ‖ the gloomy cave of Spleen[121]

> Nothing, to make ‖ Philosophy thy friend

> Shou'd chance to make ‖ the well-dress'd rabble stare

> Or cross, to plunder ‖ provinces, the main

> These madmen never hurt ‖ the church or state

> How shall we fill ‖ a library with wit

> What better teach ‖ a foreigner the tongue[122]

> Sure, if I spare ‖ the minister, no rules
> Of honour bind me, not to maul his tools.[123]

121. *Rape of the Lock:* III.147; IV.14; IV.16.
122. Pope, *Epistle* I.i.74, 111, and 127; *Epistle* II.i.190, 354, and 206.
123. Pope, *Epilogue to Satires,* II.146.

On the other hand, when the passive substantive is by inversion first named, there is no difficulty of interjecting a pause between it and the verb, more than when the active substantive is first named. The same reason holds in both, that though a verb cannot be separated in idea from the substantive which governs it, and scarcely from the substantive it governs; yet a substantive may always be conceived independent of the verb: when the passive substantive is introduced before the verb, we know not that an action is to be exerted upon it; therefore we may rest till the action commences. For the sake of illustration take the following examples: <135>

Shrines! where their vigils ‖ pale-ey'd virgins keep

Soon as thy letters ‖ trembling I unclose

No happier task ‖ these faded eyes pursue.[124]

What is said about the pause, leads to a general observation, That the natural order of placing the active substantive and its verb, is more friendly to a pause than the inverted order; but that in all the other connections, inversion affords a far better opportunity for a pause. And hence one great advantage of blank verse over rhyme; its privilege of inversion giving it a much greater choice of pauses than can be had in the natural order of arrangement.

We now proceed to the slighter connections, which shall be discussed in one general article. Words connected by conjunctions and prepositions admit freely a pause between them, which will be clear from the following instances:

Assume what sexes ‖ and what shape they please

The light militia ‖ of the lower sky[125]

124. *Eloise to Abelard,* 21; 29; 47.
125. *Rape of the Lock:* I.70; I.42.

Connecting particles were invented to unite in a period two substances signifying things occasionally united in the thought, but which have no natural union: and between two things not only separable in idea, but really distinct, the mind, for <136> the sake of melody, cheerfully admits by a pause a momentary disjunction of their occasional union.

One capital branch of the subject is still upon hand, to which I am directed by what is just now said. It concerns those parts of speech which singly represent no idea, and which become not significant till they be joined to other words. I mean conjunctions, prepositions, articles, and such like accessories, passing under the name of *particles*. Upon these the question occurs, Whether they can be separated by a pause from the words that make them significant? Whether, for example, in the following lines, the separation of the accessory preposition from the principal substantive be according to rule?

The goddess with ‖ a discontented air

And heighten'd by ‖ the diamond's circling rays[126]

When victims at ‖ yon altar's foot we lay[127]

So take it in ‖ the very words of Creech[128]

An ensign of ‖ the delegates of Jove

Two ages o'er ‖ his native realm he reign'd[129]

While angels, with ‖ their silver wings o'ershade.[130]

126. *Rape of the Lock:* IV.79; IV.115.
127. *Eloise to Abelard,* 108.
128. Pope, *Epistle* I.vi. 4.
129. *Iliad* 1.314, 335.
130. *Unfortunate Lady,* 67.

Or the separation of the conjunction from the word that is connected by it with the antecedent word:

> Talthybius and ‖ Eurybates the good[131] <137>

It will be obvious at the first glance, that the foregoing reasoning upon objects naturally connected, is not applicable to words which of themselves are mere ciphers: we must therefore have recourse to some other principle for solving the present question. These particles out of their place are totally insignificant: to give them a meaning, they must be joined to certain words; and the necessity of this junction, together with custom, forms an artificial connection that has a strong influence upon the mind: it cannot bear even a momentary separation, which destroys the sense, and is at the same time contradictory to practice. Another circumstance tends still more to make this separation disagreeable in lines of the first and third order, that it bars the accent, which will be explained afterward in treating of the accent.

Hitherto upon that pause only which divides the line. We proceed to the pause that concludes the line; and the question is, Whether the same rules be applicable to both? This must be answered by making a distinction. In the first line of a couplet, the concluding pause differs little, if at all, from the pause that divides the line; and for that reason, the rules are applicable to both equally. The concluding pause of the couplet is in a different condition: it resembles greatly the concluding pause in an Hexameter line. Both of them indeed are so remarkable, that they <138> never can be graceful, unless where they accompany a pause in the sense. Hence it follows, that a couplet ought always to be finished with some close in the sense; if not a point, at least a comma. The truth is, that this rule is seldom transgressed. In Pope's works, I find very few deviations from the rule. Take the following instances:

> Nothing is foreign: parts relate to whole;
> One all-extending, all-preserving soul
> Connects each being ———[132]

131. *Iliad* 1.421.
132. *Essay on Man*, III.21.

Another:

> To draw fresh colours from the vernal flow'rs,
> To steal from rainbows ere they drop in show'rs
> A brighter wash ——[133]

I add, with respect to pauses in general, that supposing the connection to be so slender as to admit a pause, it follows not that a pause may in every such case be admitted. There is one rule to which every other ought to bend, That the sense must never be wounded or obscured by the music; and upon that account I condemn the following lines:

> Ulysses, first ‖ in public cares, she found[134]

And,

> Who rising, high ‖ th' imperial sceptre rais'd. <139>

With respect to inversion, it appears, both from reason and experiments, that many words which cannot bear a separation in their natural order, admit a pause when inverted. And it may be added, that when two words, or two members of a sentence, in their natural order, can be separated by a pause, such separation can never be amiss in an inverted order. An inverted period, which deviates from the natural train of ideas, requires to be marked in some measure even by pauses in the sense, that the parts may be distinctly known. Take the following examples:

> As with cold lips ‖ I kiss'd the sacred veil

> With other beauties ‖ charm my partial eyes

> Full in my view ‖ set all the bright abode[135]

> With words like these ‖ the troops Ulysses rul'd

133. *Rape of the Lock,* II.95.
134. *Iliad* 2.205.
135. *Eloise to Abelard,* 111, 126, 127.

Back to th'assembly roll ‖ the thronging train

Not for their grief ‖ the Grecian host I blame.[136]

The same where the separation is made at the close of the first line of the couplet:

> For spirits, freed from mortal laws, with ease,
> Assume what sexes and what shapes they please.[137]

The pause is tolerable even at the close of the couplet, for the reason just now suggested, that inverted members require some slight pause in the sense: <140>

> 'Twas where the plane-tree spreads its shades around
> The altars heav'd; and from the crumbling ground
> A mighty dragon shot.[138]

Thus a train of reasoning hath insensibly led us to conclusions with regard to the musical pause, very different from those in the first section, concerning the separating by a circumstance words intimately connected. One would conjecture, that where-ever words are separable by interjecting a circumstance, they should be equally separable by interjecting a pause: but, upon a more narrow inspection, the appearance of analogy vanisheth. This will be evident from considering, that a pause in the sense distinguishes the different members of a period from each other; whereas, when two words of the same member are separated by a circumstance, all the three make still but one member; and therefore that words may be separated by an interjected circumstance, tho' these words are not separated by a pause in the sense. This sets the matter in a clear light; for, as observed above, a musical pause is intimately connected with a pause in the sense, and ought, as far as possible, to be governed by it: particularly a musical pause ought never to be placed where a pause is excluded by the sense; as, for example, between the adjective and following substantive, which make parts of the

---

136. *Iliad* 2.245, 247, 362.
137. *Rape of the Lock,* I.69.
138. *Iliad* 2.370.

same idea; and still less between a particle and the word that makes it significant. <141>

Abstracting at present from the peculiarity of melody arising from the different pauses, it cannot fail to be observed in general, that they introduce into our verse no slight degree of variety. A number of uniform lines having all the same pause, are extremely fatiguing; which is remarkable in French versification. This imperfection will be discerned by a fine ear even in the shortest succession, and becomes intolerable in a long poem. Pope excels in the variety of his melody; which, if different kinds can be compared, is indeed no less perfect than that of Virgil.

From what is last said, there ought to be one exception. Uniformity in the members of a thought demands equal uniformity in the verbal members which express that thought. When therefore resembling objects or things are expressed in a plurality of verse-lines, these lines in their structure ought to be as uniform as possible; and the pauses in particular ought all of them to have the same place. Take the following examples:

> By foreign hands ‖ thy dying eyes were clos'd,
> By foreign hands ‖ thy decent limbs compos'd,
> By foreign hands ‖ thy humble grave adorn'd.[139]

Again:

> Bright as the sun ‖ her eyes the gazers strike;
> And, like the sun, ‖ they shine on all alike.[140] <142>

Speaking of Nature, or the God of Nature:

> Warms in the sun ‖ refreshes in the breeze,
> Glows in the stars ‖ and blossoms in the trees;
> Lives through all life ‖ extends through all extent,
> Spreads undivided ‖ operates unspent.[141]

Pauses will detain us longer than was foreseen; for the subject is not yet exhausted. It is laid down above, that English Heroic verse admits no more

139. *Unfortunate Lady,* 51.
140. *Rape of the Lock,* II.13.
141. *Essay on Man,* I.271.

but four capital pauses; and that the capital pause of every line is determined by the sense to be after the fourth, the fifth, the sixth, or seventh syllable. That this doctrine holds true as far as melody alone is concerned, will be testified by every good ear. At the same time, I admit, that this rule may be varied where the sense or expression requires a variation, and that so far the melody may justly be sacrificed. Examples accordingly are not unfrequent, in Milton especially, of the capital pause being after the first, the second, or the third syllable. And that this licence may be taken, even gracefully, when it adds vigour to the expression, will be clear from the following example. Pope, in his translation of Homer, describes a rock broke off from a mountain, and hurling to the plain, in the following words:

> From steep to steep the rolling ruin bounds;
> At every shock the crackling wood resounds; <143>
> Still gath'ring force, it smokes; and urg'd amain,
> Whirls, leaps, and thunders down, impetuous to the plain:
> There stops ‖ So Hector. Their whole force he prov'd,
> Resistless when he rag'd; and when he stopt, unmov'd.[142]

In the penult line, the proper place of the musical pause is at the end of the fifth syllable; but it enlivens the expression by its coincidence with that of the sense at the end of the second syllable: the stopping short before the usual pause in the melody, aids the impression that is made by the description of the stone's stopping short; and what is lost to the melody by this artifice, is more than compensated by the force that is added to the description. Milton makes a happy use of this licence: witness the following examples from his *Paradise Lost*.

> ———— Thus with the year
> Seasons return, but not to me returns
> Day ‖ or the sweet approach of even or morn.

> Celestial voices to the midnight-air
> Sole ‖ or responsive each to others note.

142. *Iliad* 13.195.

And over them triumphant Death his dart
Shook ‖ but delay'd to strike.

——— And wild uproar
Stood rul'd ‖ stood vast infinitude confin'd.

——— And hard'ning in his strength
Glories ‖ for never since created man
Met such embodied force.[143] <144>

From his slack hand the garland wreath'd for Eve
Down dropp'd ‖ and all the faded roses shed.

Of unessential night, receives him next,
Wide gaping ‖ and with utter loss of being,
Threatens him, &c.

——— For now the thought
Both of lost happiness and lasting pain
Torments him ‖ round he throws his baleful eyes, &c.[144]

If we consider the foregoing passages with respect to melody singly, the pauses are undoubtedly out of their proper place; but being united with those of the sense, they enforce the expression, and enliven it greatly; for, as has been more than once observed, the beauty of expression is communicated to the sound, which, by a natural deception, makes even the melody appear more perfect than if the musical pauses were regular.

To explain the rules of accenting, two general observations must be premised. The first is, That accents have a double effect: they contribute to the melody, by giving it air and spirit: they contribute no less to the sense, by distinguishing important words from others.* These two effects never can be separated, without impairing the <145> concord that ought to subsist

---

* An accent considered with respect to sense is termed *emphasis*.
143. *Paradise Lost*: 3.42; 4.682; 11.491; 3.711; 1.574.
144. *Paradise Lost*: 9.892; 2.439; 1.55.

between the thought and the melody: an accent, for example, placed on a low word, has the effect to burlesque it, by giving it an unnatural elevation; and the injury thus done to the sense does not rest there, for it seems also to injure the melody. Let us only reflect what a ridiculous figure a particle must make with an accent or emphasis put upon it, a particle that of itself has no meaning, and that serves only, like cement, to unite words significant. The other general observation is, That a word of whatever number of syllables, is not accented upon more than one of them. The reason is, that the object is set in its best light by a single accent, so as to make more than one unnecessary for the sense: and if another be added, it must be for the sound merely; which would be a transgression of the foregoing rule, by separating a musical accent from that which is requisite for the sense.

Keeping in view the foregoing observations, the doctrine of accenting English Heroic verse is extremely simple. In the first place, accenting is confined to the long syllables; for a short syllable is not capable of an accent. In the next place, as the melody is enriched in proportion to the number of accents, every word that has a long syllable may be accented; unless the sense interpose, which rejects the accenting a word that makes no figure by its signification. According to this rule, <146> a line may admit five accents; a case by no means rare.

But supposing every long syllable to be accented, there is, in every line, one accent that makes a greater figure than the rest, being that which precedes the capital pause. It is distinguished into two kinds; one that is immediately before the pause, and one that is divided from the pause by a short syllable. The former belongs to lines of the first and third order; the latter to those of the second and fourth. Examples of the first kind:

> Smooth flow the wâves ‖ the zephyrs gently play,
> Belinda smîl'd ‖ and all the world was gay.

> He rais'd his azure wând ‖ and thus began.

Examples of the other kind:

> There lay three gârters ‖ half a pair of gloves,
> And all the trôphies ‖ of his former loves.

Our humble prôvince ‖ is to tend the fair,
Not a less plêasing ‖ though less glorious care.

And hew triumphal ârches ‖ to the ground.[145]

These accents make different impressions on the mind, which will be the
subject of a following speculation. In the mean time, it may be safely pronounced a capital defect in the composition of verse, to put a low word,
incapable of an accent, <147> in the place where this accent should be: this
bars the accent altogether; than which I know no fault more subversive of
the melody, if it be not the barring a pause altogether. I may add affirmatively, that no single circumstance contributes more to the energy of verse,
than to put an important word where the accent should be, a word that
merits a peculiar emphasis. To show the bad effect of excluding the capital
accent, I refer the reader to some instances given above,* where particles
are separated by a pause from the capital words that make them significant;
and which particles ought, for the sake of melody, to be accented, were they
capable of an accent. Add to these the following instances from the Essay
on Criticism.

Of leaving what ‖ is natural and fit   *line* 448.

Not yet purg'd off, ‖ of spleen and sour disdain   *l.* 528.

No pardon vile ‖ obscenity should find   *l.* 531.

When love was all ‖ an easy monarch's care   *l.* 537.

For 'tis but half ‖ a judge's task, to know   *l.* 562. <148>

'Tis not enough, ‖ taste, judgement, learning, join.   *l.* 563.

That only makes ‖ superior sense belov'd   *l.* 578.

---

* Page 136.
145. *Rape of the Lock:* II.51; II.72; II.39; II.91; III.176.

Whose right it is, ‖ uncensur'd, to be dull   *l.* 590.

'Tis best sometimes ‖ your censure to restrain.   *l.* 597.

When this fault is at the end of a line that closes a couplet, it leaves not the slightest trace of melody:

> But of this frame the bearings, and the ties,
> The strong connections, nice dependencies.[146]

In a line expressive of what is humble or dejected, it improves the resemblance between the sound and sense to exclude the capital accent. This, to my taste, is a beauty in the following lines.

> In thêse deep sôlitudes ‖ and aŵful cells[147]

> The pôor inhâbitant ‖ behôlds in vain.[148]

To conclude this article, the accents are not, like the syllables, confined to a certain number: some lines have no fewer than five, and there are lines that admit not above one. This variety, as <149> we have seen, depends entirely on the different powers of the component words: particles, even where they are long by position, cannot be accented; and polysyllables, whatever space they occupy, admit but one accent. Polysyllables have another defect, that they generally exclude the full pause. It is shown above, that few polysyllables can find place in the construction of English verse; and here are reasons for excluding them, could they find place.

I am now ready to fulfil a promise concerning the four sorts of lines that enter into English Heroic verse. That these have, each of them, a peculiar melody distinguishable by a good ear, I ventured to suggest, and promised to account for: and tho' the subject is extremely delicate, I am not without hopes of making good my engagement. But first, by way of precaution, I warn the candid reader not to expect this peculiarity of modulation in every

146. *Essay on Man,* I.30.
147. *Eloise to Abelard,* 1.
148. Addison, *A Letter from Italy,* 113.

instance. The reason why it is not always perceptible has been mentioned more than once, that the thought and expression have a great influence upon the melody; so great, as in many instances to make the poorest melody pass for rich and spirited. This consideration makes me insist upon a concession or two that will not be thought unreasonable: first, That the experiment be tried upon lines equal with respect to the thought and expression; for otherwise one may <150> easily be misled in judging of the melody: and next, That these lines be regularly accented before the pause; for upon a matter abundantly refined in itself, I would not willingly be embarrassed with faulty and irregular lines.

These preliminaries adjusted, I begin with some general observations, that will save repeating the same thing over and over upon every example. And, first, an accent succeeded by a pause, as in lines of the first and third order, makes a much greater figure than where the voice goes on without a stop. The fact is so certain, that no person who has an ear can be at a loss to distinguish that accent from others. Nor have we far to seek for the efficient cause: the elevation of an accenting tone produceth in the mind a similar elevation, which continues during the pause;* but where the pause is separated from the accent by a short syllable, as in lines of the second and fourth order, the impression made by the accent is more <151> slight when there is no stop, and the elevation of the accent is gone in a moment by the falling of the voice in pronouncing the short syllable that follows. The pause also is sensibly affected by the position of the accent. In lines of the first and third order, the close conjunction of the accent and pause, occasions a sudden stop without preparation, which rouses the mind, and bestows on the melody a spirited air. When, on the other hand, the pause is separated from the accent by a short syllable, which always happens in lines of the second and fourth order, the pause is soft and gentle: for this short unaccented syllable, succeeding one that is accented, must of course

---

* Hence the liveliness of the French language as to sound, above the English; the last syllable in the former being generally long and accented, the long syllable in the latter being generally as far back in the word as possible, and often without an accent. For this difference I find no cause so probable as temperament and disposition; the French being brisk and lively, the English sedate and reserved: and this, if it hold, is a pregnant instance of a resemblance between the character of a people and that of their language.

be pronounced with a falling voice, which naturally prepares for a pause; and the mind falls gently from the accented syllable, and slides into rest as it were insensibly. Further, the lines themselves derive different powers from the position of the pause, which will thus appear. A pause after the fourth syllable divides the line into two unequal portions, of which the larger comes last: this circumstance resolving the line into an ascending series, makes an impression in pronouncing like that of ascending; and to this impression contribute the redoubled effort in pronouncing the larger portion, which is last in order. The mind has a different feeling when the pause succeeds the fifth syllable, which divides the line into two equal parts: these parts, pronounced with equal effort, are agreeable <152> by their uniformity. A line divided by a pause after the sixth syllable, makes an impression opposite to that first mentioned: being divided into two unequal portions, of which the shorter is last in order, it appears like a slow descending series; and the second portion being pronounced with less effort than the first, the diminished effort prepares the mind for rest. And this preparation for rest is still more sensibly felt where the pause is after the seventh syllable, as in lines of the fourth order.

To apply these observations is an easy task. A line of the first order is of all the most spirited and lively: the accent, being followed instantly by a pause, makes an illustrious figure: the elevated tone of the accent elevates the mind: the mind is supported in its elevation by the sudden unprepared pause, which rouses and animates: and the line itself, representing by its unequal division an ascending series, carries the mind still higher, making an impression similar to that of going upward. The second order has a modulation sensibly sweet, soft, and flowing; the accent is not so sprightly as in the former, because a short syllable intervenes between it and the pause: its elevation, by the same means, vanisheth instantaneously: the mind, by a falling voice, is gently prepared for a stop: and the pleasure of uniformity from the division of the line into two equal parts, is calm and sweet. The third order has a modulation not so easily ex-<153>pressed in words: it in part resembles the first order, by the liveliness of an accent succeeded instantly by a full pause: but then the elevation occasioned by this circumstance, is balanced in some degree by the remitted effort in pronouncing the second portion, which remitted effort has a tendency to rest. Another circumstance distinguisheth it remarkably: its capital accent comes late, being placed on the sixth syllable; and this circumstance bestows on it an air of gravity and solemnity. The last order resembles the second in the mildness of its accent, and softness of its pause; it is still more solemn than the third, by the lateness of its capital accent: it also possesses in a higher degree than the third, the tendency to rest; and by that circumstance is of all the best qualified for closing a period in the completest manner.

But these are not all the distinguishing characters of the different orders. Each order, also, is distinguished by its final accent and pause: the unequal division in the first order, makes an impression of ascending; and the mind at the close is in the highest elevation, which naturally prompts it to put a strong emphasis upon the concluding syllable, whether by raising the voice to a sharper tone, or by expressing the word in a fuller tone. This order accordingly is of all the least proper for concluding a period, where a cadence is proper, and not an accent. The second order, being destitute of the impression of ascent, cannot rival the <154> first order in the elevation of its concluding accent, nor consequently in the dignity of its concluding pause; for these have a mutual influence. This order, however, with respect to its close, maintains a superiority over the third and fourth orders: in these the close is more humble, being brought down by the impression of descent, and by the remitted effort in pronouncing; considerably in the third order, and still more considerably in the last. According to this description, the concluding accents and pauses of the four orders being reduced to a scale, will form a descending series probably in an arithmetical progression.

After what is said, will it be thought refining too much to suggest, that the different orders are qualified for different purposes, and that a poet of genius will naturally be led to make a choice accordingly? I cannot think this altogether chimerical. As it appears to me, the first order is proper for a sentiment that is bold, lively, or impetuous; the third order is proper for what is grave, solemn, or lofty; the second for what is tender, delicate, or melancholy, and in general for all the sympathetic emotions; and the last for subjects of the same kind, when tempered with any degree of solemnity. I do not contend, that any one order is fitted for no other task than that assigned it; for at that rate, no sort of melody would be left for accompanying thoughts that have nothing peculiar in them. I only venture to suggest, and I <155> do it with diffidence, that each of the orders is peculiarly adapted to certain subjects, and better qualified than the others for expressing them. The best way to judge is by experiment; and to avoid the imputation of a partial search, I shall confine my instances to a single poem, beginning with the

First order.

> On her white breast, a sparkling cross she wore,
> Which Jews might kiss, and infidels adore.
> Her lively looks a sprightly mind disclose,
> Quick as her eyes, and as unfix'd as those:
> Favours to none, to all she smiles extends;
> Oft she rejects, but never once offends.
> Bright as the sun, her eyes the gazers strike,
> And, like the sun, they shine on all alike.
> Yet graceful ease, and sweetness void of pride,
> Might hide her faults, if belles had faults to hide;
> If to her share some female errors fall,
> Look on her face, and you'll forget 'em all.

> *Rape of the Lock.*

In accounting for the remarkable liveliness of this passage, it will be acknowledged by every one who has an ear, that the melody must come in for a share. The lines, all of them, are of the first order; a very unusual circumstance in the author of this poem, so eminent for variety in his versification. Who can doubt, that he has been led by delicacy of taste to employ the first order preferably to the others? <156>

Second order.

> Our humble province is to tend the fair,
> Not a less pleasing, though less glorious care;
> To save the powder from too rude a gale,
> Nor let th' imprison'd essences exhale;
> To draw fresh colours from the vernal flow'rs;
> To steal from rainbows, ere they drop their show'rs,
> *&c.*

Again:

> Oh, thoughtless mortals! ever blind to fate,
> Too soon dejected, and too soon elate.
> Sudden, these honours shall be snatch'd away,
> And curs'd for ever this victorious day.

Third order.

> To fifty chosen sylphs, of special note,
> We trust th' important charge, the petticoat.

Again:

> Oh say what stranger cause, yet unexplor'd,
> Could make a gentle belle reject a lord?

A plurality of lines of the fourth order, would not have a good effect in succession; because, by a remarkable tendency to rest, their proper office is to close a period. The reader, therefore, must be satisfied with instances where this order is mixed with others. <157>

> Not louder shrieks to pitying Heav'n are cast,
> When husbands, or when lapdogs, breathe their last.

Again:

> Steel could the works of mortal pride confound,
> And hew triumphal arches to the ground.

Again:

> She sees, and trembles at th' approaching ill,
> Just in the jaws of ruin, and codille.

Again:

> With earnest eyes, and round unthinking face,
> He first the snuff-box open'd, then the case.

And this suggests another experiment, which is, to set the different orders more directly in opposition, by giving examples where they are mixed in the same passage.

First and second orders.

> Sol through white curtains shot a tim'rous ray,
> And ope'd those eyes that must eclipse the day.

Again:

> Not youthful kings in battle seiz'd alive,
> Not scornful virgins who their charms survive,
> Not ardent lovers robb'd of all their bliss,
> Not ancient ladies when refus'd a kiss, <158>
> Not tyrants fierce that unrepenting die,
> Not Cynthia when her mantua's pin'd awry,
> E'er felt such rage, resentment, and despair,
> As thou, sad virgin! for thy ravish'd hair.

First and third.

> Think what an equipage thou hast in air,
> And view with scorn two pages and a chair.

Again:

> What guards the purity of melting maids,
> In courtly balls, and midnight-masquerades,
> Safe from the treach'rous friend, the daring spark,
> The glance by day, the whisper in the dark?

Again:

> With tender billet-doux he lights the pyre,
> And breathes three am'rous sighs to raise the fire;
> Then prostrate falls, and begs, with ardent eyes,
> Soon to obtain, and long possess the prize.

Again:

> Jove's thunder roars, heav'n trembles all around,
> Blue Neptune storms, the bellowing deeps resound,
> Earth shakes her nodding tow'rs, the ground gives way,
> And the pale ghosts start at the flash of day! <159>

Second and third.

> Sunk in Thalestris' arms, the nymph he found,
> Her eyes dejected, and her hair unbound.

Again:

> On her heav'd bosom hung her drooping head,
> Which with a sigh she rais'd; and thus she said.

Musing on the foregoing subject, I begin to doubt whether all this while I have not been in a reverie, and whether the scene before me, full of objects new and singular, be not mere fairy-land. Is there any truth in the appearance, or is it wholly a work of imagination? We cannot doubt of its reality; and we may with assurance pronounce, that great is the merit of English Heroic verse: for though uniformity prevails in the arrangement, in the equality of the lines, and in the resemblance of the final sounds; variety is still more conspicuous in the pauses and in the accents, which are diversified in a surprising manner. Of the beauty that results from a due mixture of uniformity and variety,* many instances have already occurred, but none more illustrious than English versification; however rude it may be in the simplicity of its arrangement, it is highly melodious by its pauses and accents, so as already to rival the <160> most perfect species known in Greece or Rome; and it is no disagreeable prospect to find it susceptible of still greater refinement.

We proceed to blank verse, which hath so many circumstances in common with rhyme, that its peculiarities may be brought within a narrow compass. With respect to form, it differs from rhyme in rejecting the jingle of similar sounds, which purifies it from a childish pleasure. But this improvement is a trifle compared with what follows. Our verse is extremely cramped by rhyme; and the peculiar advantage of blank verse is, that it is at liberty to attend the imagination in its boldest flights. Rhyme necessarily divides verse into couplets; each couplet makes a complete musical period, the parts of which are divided by pauses, and the whole summed up by a

---

* See chap. 9.

full close at the end: the melody begins anew with the next couplet: and in this manner a composition in rhyme proceeds couplet after couplet. I have often had occasion to mention the correspondence and concord that ought to subsist between sound and sense; from which it is a plain inference, that if a couplet be a complete period with regard to melody, it ought regularly to be the same with regard to sense. As it is extremely difficult to support such strictness of composition, licences are indulged, as explained above; which, however, must be used with discretion, so as to preserve some degree of <161> concord between the sense and the music: there ought never to be a full close in the sense but at the end of a couplet; and there ought always to be some pause in the sense at the end of every couplet: the same period as to sense may be extended through several couplets; but each couplet ought to contain a distinct member, distinguished by a pause in the sense as well as in the sound; and the whole ought to be closed with a complete cadence.* Rules such as these, must confine rhyme within very narrow bounds: a thought of any extent, cannot be reduced within its compass; the sense must be curtailed and broken into parts, to make it square with the curtness of the melody; and beside, short periods afford no latitude for inversion.

I have examined this point with the stricter accuracy, in order to give a just notion of blank verse; and to show, that a slight difference in form may produce a great difference in substance. Blank verse has the same pauses and accents with rhyme, and a pause at the end of every line, like what concludes the first line of a couplet. In a <162> word, the rules of melody in blank verse, are the same that obtain with respect to the first line of a couplet; but being disengaged from rhyme, or from couplets, there is access to make every line run into another, precisely as to make the first line of a couplet run into the second. There must be a musical pause at the end of every line; but this pause is so slight as not to require a pause in the sense: and accordingly the sense may be carried on with or without pauses, till a period of the utmost extent be completed by a full close both in the sense

---

* This rule is quite neglected in French versification. Even Boileau makes no difficulty, to close one subject with the first line of a couplet, and to begin a new subject with the second. Such licence, however sanctified by practice, is unpleasant by the discordance between the pauses of the sense and of the melody.

and the sound: there is no restraint, other than that this full close be at the
end of a line; and this restraint is necessary, in order to preserve a coincidence between sense and sound, which ought to be aimed at in general,
and is indispensable in the case of a full close, because it has a striking effect.
Hence the fitness of blank verse for inversion: and consequently the lustre
of its pauses and accents; for which, as observed above, there is greater scope
in inversion, than when words run in their natural order.

In the second section of this chapter it is shown, that nothing contributes more than inversion to the force and elevation of language: the
couplets of rhyme confine inversion within narrow limits; nor would the
elevation of inversion, were there access for it in rhyme, readily accord
with the humbler tone of that sort of verse. It is universally agreed, that
the loftiness of Milton's style <163> supports admirably the sublimity of
his subject; and it is not less certain, that the loftiness of his style arises
chiefly from inversion. Shakespear deals little in inversion; but his blank
verse, being a sort of measured prose, is perfectly well adapted to the stage,
where laboured inversion is highly improper, because in dialogue it never
can be natural.

Hitherto I have considered that superior power of expression which
verse acquires by laying aside rhyme. But this is not the only ground for
preferring blank verse: it has another preferable quality not less signal; and
that is, a more extensive and more complete melody. Its music is not, like
that of rhyme, confined to a single couplet; but takes in a great compass,
so as in some measure to rival music properly so called. The interval between its cadences may be long or short at pleasure; and, by that means, its
melody, with respect both to richness and variety, is superior far to that of
rhyme, and superior even to that of the Greek and Latin Hexameter. Of
this observation no person can doubt who is acquainted with the *Paradise
Lost:* in which work there are indeed many careless lines; but at every turn
the richest melody as well as the sublimest sentiments are conspicuous. Take
the following specimen.

> Now Morn her rosy steps in th' eastern clime
> Advancing, sow'd the earth with orient pearl; <164>
> When Adam wak'd, so custom'd, for his sleep

Was aëry light from pure digestion bred
And temp'rate vapours bland, which th' only sound
Of leaves and fuming rills, Aurora's fan,
Lightly dispers'd, and the shrill matin song
Of birds on every bough; so much the more
His wonder was to find unwaken'd Eve
With tresses discompos'd, and glowing cheek,
As through unquiet rest: he on his side
Leaning half-rais'd, with looks of cordial love
Hung over her enamour'd, and beheld
Beauty, which, whether waking or asleep,
Shot forth peculiar graces; then with voice
Mild, as when Zephyrus on Flora breathes,
Her hand soft touching, whisper'd thus. Awake,
My fairest, my espous'd, my latest found,
Heaven's last best gift, my ever-new delight,
Awake; the morning shines, and the fresh field
Calls us: we lose the prime, to mark how spring
Our tended plants, how blows the citron grove,
What drops the myrrh, and what the balmy reed,
How nature paints her colours, how the bee
Sits on the bloom extracting liquid sweet.   *Book* 5. *l.* 1.

Comparing Latin Hexameter with English Heroic rhyme, the former has obviously the advantage in the following particulars. It is greatly preferable as to arrangement, by the latitude it admits in placing the long and short syllables. Secondly, the length of an Hexameter line hath a majestic air: ours, by its shortness, is indeed <165> more brisk and lively, but much less fitted for the sublime. And, thirdly, the long high-sounding words that Hexameter admits, add greatly to its majesty. To compensate these advantages, English rhyme possesses a greater number and greater variety both of pauses and of accents. These two sorts of verse stand indeed pretty much in opposition: in Hexameter, great variety of arrangement, none in the pauses nor accents; in English rhyme, great variety in the pauses and accents, very little in the arrangement.

In blank verse are united, in a good measure, the several properties of Latin Hexameter and English rhyme; and it possesses beside many signal properties of its own. It is not confined, like Hexameter, by a full close at the end of every line; nor, like rhyme, by a full close at the end of every couplet. Its construction, which admits the lines to run into each other, gives it a still greater majesty than arises from the length of a Hexameter line. By the same means, it admits inversion even beyond the Latin or Greek Hexameter; for these suffer some confinement by the regular closes at the end of every line. In its music it is illustrious above all: the melody of Hexameter verse is circumscribed to a line; and of English rhyme, to a couplet: the melody of blank verse is under no confinement, but enjoys the utmost privilege, of which melody of verse is susceptible; which is, to run hand in hand with <166> the sense. In a word, blank verse is superior to Hexameter in many articles; and inferior to it in none, save in the freedom of arrangement, and in the use of long words.

In French Heroic verse, there are found, on the contrary, all the defects of Latin Hexameter and English rhyme, without the beauties of either: subjected to the bondage of rhyme, and to the full close at the end of every couplet, it is also extremely fatiguing by uniformity in its pauses and accents: the line invariably is divided by the pause into two equal parts, and the accent is invariably placed before the pause.

> Jeune et vaillant herôs ‖ dont la haute sagesse
> N'est point la fruit tardif ‖ d'une lente vieillesse.[149]

Here every circumstance contributes to a tiresome uniformity: a constant return of the same pause and of the same accent, as well as an equal division of every line; which fatigue the ear without intermission or change. I cannot set this matter in a better light, than by presenting to the reader a French translation of the following passage of Milton:

> Two of far nobler shape, erect and tall,
> Godlike erect, with native honour clad,
> In naked majesty, seem'd lords of all:
> And worthy seem'd; for in their looks divine <167>
> The image of their glorious Maker shone

---

149. "Young and valiant heroes, whose wisdom is not the late fruit of a lingering old age."

> Truth, wisdom, sanctitude severe and pure;
> Severe, but in true filial freedom plac'd;
> Whence true authority in men: though both
> Not equal, as their sex not equal seem'd;
> For contemplation he and valour form'd,
> For softness she and sweet attractive grace;
> He for God only, she for God in him.

Were the pauses of the sense and sound in this passage but a little better assorted, nothing in verse could be more melodious. In general, the great defect of Milton's versification, in other respects admirable, is the want of coincidence between the pauses of the sense and sound.

The translation is in the following words:

> Ce lieux délicieux, ce paradis charmant,
> Reçoit deux objets son plus bel ornement;
> Leur port majestueux, et leur démarche altiere,
> Semble leur meriter sur la nature entiere
> Ce droit de commander que Dieu leur a donné,
> Sur leur auguste front de gloire couronné.
> Du souverain du cièl drille la resemblance:
> Dans leur simples regards éclatte l'innocence,
> L'adorable candeur, l'aimable vérité,
> La raison, la sagesse, et la sévérité,
> Qu' adoucit la prudence, et cet air de droiture
> Du visage des rois respectable parure.
> Ces deux objets divin n'ont pas les mêmes traits,
> Ils paroissent formés, quoique tous deux parfaits;
> L'un pour la majesté, la force, et la noblesse; <168>
> L'autre pour la douceur, la grace, et la tendresse;
> Celui-ci pour Dieu seul, l'autre pour l'homme encor.

Here the sense is fairly translated, the words are of equal power, and yet how inferior the melody!

Many attempts have been made to introduce Hexameter verse into the living languages, but without success. The English language, I am inclined to think, is not susceptible of this melody: and my reasons are these. First, the polysyllables in Latin and Greek are finely diversified by long and short syllables, a circumstance that qualifies them for the melody of Hexameter verse: ours are extremely ill qualified for that service, because they superabound in short syllables. Secondly, the bulk of our monosyllables are arbitrary with regard to length, which is an unlucky circumstance in Hexameter: for although custom, as observed above, may render familiar a long or a short pronunciation of the same word, yet the mind wavering between the two sounds, cannot be so much affected with either, as with a word that hath always the same sound; and for that reason, arbitrary sounds are ill fitted for a melody which is chiefly supported by quantity. In Latin and Greek Hexameter, invariable sounds direct and ascertain the melody. English Hexameter would be destitute of melody, unless by artful pronunciation; because of necessity the bulk of its sounds must be <169> arbitrary. The pronunciation is easy in a simple movement of alternate long and short syllables; but would be perplexing and unpleasant in the diversified movement of Hexameter verse.

Rhyme makes so great a figure in modern poetry, as to deserve a solemn trial. I have for that reason reserved it to be examined with deliberation; in order to discover, if I can, its peculiar beauties, and its degree of merit. The first view of this subject leads naturally to the following reflection: "That rhyme having no relation to sentiment, nor any effect upon the ear other than a mere jingle, ought to be banished all compositions of any dignity, as affording but a trifling and childish pleasure." It will also be observed, "that a jingle of words hath in some measure a ludicrous effect; witness the double rhymes of *Hudibras,* which contribute no small share to its drollery: that in a serious work this ludicrous effect would be equally remarkable, were it not obscured by the prevailing gravity of the subject: that having however a constant tendency to give a ludicrous air to the composition, more than ordinary fire is requisite to support the dignity of the sentiments against such an undermining antagonist."* <170>

* Vossius, *De poematum cantu,* p. 26. says, "Nihil aeque gravitati orationis afficit, quam in sono ludere syllabarum." ["Nothing affects the gravity of a speech more than a play on the sound of words."]

These arguments are specious, and have undoubtedly some weight. Yet, on the other hand, it ought to be considered, that in modern tongues rhyme has become universal among men as well as children; and that it cannot have such a currency without some foundation in human nature. In fact, it has been successfully employ'd by poets of genius, in their serious and grave compositions, as well as in those which are more light and airy. Here, in weighing authority against argument, the scales seem to be upon a level; and therefore, to come at any thing decisive, we must pierce a little deeper.

Music has great power over the soul; and may successfully be employed to inflame or soothe passions, if not actually to raise them. A single sound, however sweet, is not music; but a single sound repeated after intervals, may have the effect to rouse attention, and to keep the hearer awake: and a variety of similar sounds, succeeding each other after regular intervals, must have a still stronger effect. This consideration is applicable to rhyme, which connects two verse-lines by making them close with two words similar in sound. And considering attentively the musical effect of a couplet, we find, that it rouses the mind, and produceth an emotion moderately gay without dignity or elevation: like the murmuring of a brook gliding through pebbles, it calms the mind when perturbed, and gently raises it when sunk. These effects are scarce perceived when the whole poem is <171> in rhyme; but are extremely remarkable by contrast, in the couplets that close the several acts of our later tragedies: the tone of the mind is sensibly varied by them, from anguish, distress, or melancholy, to some degree of ease and alacrity. For the truth of this observation, I appeal to the speech of Jane Shore in the fourth act, when her doom was pronounced by Glo'ster; to the speech of Lady Jane Gray at the end of the first act; and to that of Calista, in the *Fair Penitent,* when she leaves the stage, about the middle of the third act. The speech of Alicia, at the close of the fourth act of *Jane Shore,* puts the matter beyond doubt: in a scene of deep distress, the rhymes which finish the act, produce a certain gaiety and cheerfulness, far from according with the tone of the passion:

> *Alicia.* For ever? Oh! For ever!
> Oh! who can bear to be a wretch for ever!
> My rival too! his last thoughts hung on her:

And, as he parted, left a blessing for her.
Shall she be bless'd, and I be curs'd, for ever!
No; since her fatal beauty was the cause
Of all my suff'rings, let her share my pains;
Let her, like me, of ev'ry joy forlorn,
Devote the hour when such a wretch was born:
Like me, to deserts and to darkness run,
Abhor the day, and curse the golden sun;
Cast ev'ry good and ev'ry hope behind;
Detest the works of nature, loathe mankind:
Like me with cries distracted fill the air,
Tear her poor bosom, and her frantic hair,
And prove the torments of the last despair. <172>

Having described, the best way I can, the impression that rhyme makes on the mind; I proceed to examine whether there be any subjects to which rhyme is peculiarly adapted, and for what subjects it is improper. Grand and lofty subjects, which have a powerful influence, claim precedence in this inquiry. In the chapter of Grandeur and Sublimity it is established, that a grand or sublime object, inspires a warm enthusiastic emotion disdaining strict regularity and order; which emotion is very different from that inspired by the moderately enlivening music of rhyme. Supposing then an elevated subject to be expressed in rhyme, what must be the effect? The intimate union of the music with the subject, produces an intimate union of their emotions; one inspired by the subject, which tends to elevate and expand the mind; and one inspired by the music, which, confining the mind within the narrow limits of regular cadence and similar sound, tends to prevent all elevation above its own pitch. Emotions so little concordant, cannot in union have a happy effect.

But it is scarce necessary to reason upon a case that never did, and probably never will happen, viz. an important subject clothed in rhyme, and yet supported in its utmost elevation. A happy thought or warm expression, may at times give a sudden bound upward; but it requires a genius greater than has hitherto existed, to support a poem of any length in a tone elevated much above <173> that of the melody. Tasso and Ariosto ought not to be made exceptions, and still less Voltaire. And after all, where the poet has the dead weight of rhyme constantly to struggle with, how can we expect an uniform elevation in a high pitch; when such elevation, with all the support it can receive from language, requires the utmost effort of the human genius?

But now, admitting rhyme to be an unfit dress for grand and lofty images; it has one advantage however, which is, to raise a low subject to its own degree of elevation. Addison* observes, "That rhyme, without any other assistance, throws the language off from prose, and very often makes an indifferent phrase pass unregarded; but where the verse is not built upon rhymes, there, pomp of sound and energy of expression are indispensably necessary, to support the style, and keep it from falling into the flatness of prose." This effect of rhyme is remarkable in French verse: which, being simple, and little qualified for inversion, readily sinks down to prose where not artificially supported: rhyme is therefore indispensable in French tragedy, and may be proper even in French comedy. Voltaire† assigns that very reason for adhering to <174> rhyme in these compositions. He indeed candidly owns, that, even with the support of rhyme, the tragedies of his country are little better than conversation-pieces; which seems to infer, that the French language is weak, and an improper dress for any grand subject. Voltaire was sensible of the imperfection; and yet Voltaire attempted an epic poem in that language.

The cheering and enlivening power of rhyme, is still more remarkable in poems of short lines, where the rhymes return upon the ear in a quick succession; for which reason, rhyme is perfectly well adapted to gay, light, and airy subjects. Witness the following:

> O the pleasing, pleasing anguish,
> When we love, and when we languish!
>   Wishes rising,
>   Thoughts surprising,
>   Pleasure courting,

---

* *Spectator,* No. 285.
† Preface to his *Oedipus,* and in his discourse upon tragedy, prefixed to the tragedy of *Brutus.*

Charms transporting,
Fancy viewing,
Joys ensuing,
O the pleasing, pleasing anguish!

Rosamond, act 1. *sc.* 2.[150]

For that reason, such frequent rhymes are very improper for any severe or serious passion: the dissonance between the subject and the melody is very sensibly felt. Witness the following: <175>

Ardito ti renda,
    T'accenda
    Di sdegno
    D'un figlio
    Il periglio
    D'un regno
    L'amor.
E'dolce ad un'alma
    Che aspetta
    Vendetta
Il perder la calma
Era l'ire del cor.   *Metastasio. Artaserse, act* 3. *sc.* 3.[151]

---

150. *Rosamond,* 1707, an opera by Addison, with music by Thomas Clayton (ca. 1670–ca. 1730): it was a failure, but a later setting in 1733 by Thomas Arne (1710–78) was a great success.

151. Pietro Bonaventura Trapassi, known as Metastasio (1698–1782): learned Roman poet and dramatist. Regarded as the preeminent librettist of the eighteenth century, he wrote texts for 27 three-act operas, including *Artaserse,* set to music by Thomas Arne (1710–78).

O let the Danger of a Son,
Excite vindictive Ire;
The Prospect of a Kingdom won,
Shou'd light Ambition's Fire.

To wounded Minds, Revenge is balm,
With Vigour they engage;
And sacrifice a Pleasing Calm
To a more pleasing Rage.
(*Artaxerxes,* trans. Thomas Arne, 1761)

Again:

> Now under hanging mountains,
> Beside the fall of fountains,
> Or where Hebrus wanders,
> Rolling in meanders,
>   All alone,
>   Unheard, unknown,
>   He makes his moan,
>   And calls her ghost,
> For ever, ever, ever lost;
>   Now with furies surrounded,
>   Despairing, confounded,
>   He trembles, he glows,
>   Amidst Rhodope's snows.
>
>   *Pope, Ode for Music, l. 97.*[152]

Rhyme is not less unfit for anguish or deep distress, than for subjects elevated and lofty; and <176> for that reason has been long disused in the English and Italian tragedy. In a work where the subject is serious though not elevated, rhyme has not a good effect; because the airiness of the melody agrees not with the gravity of the subject: the *Essay on Man,* which treats a subject great and important, would make a better figure in blank verse. Sportive love, mirth, gaiety, humour, and ridicule, are the province of rhyme. The boundaries assigned it by nature, were extended in barbarous and illiterate ages; and in its usurpations it has long been protected by custom: but taste in the fine arts, as well as in morals, improves daily; and makes a progress toward perfection, slow indeed but uniform; and there is no reason to doubt, that rhyme, in Britain, will in time be forc'd to abandon its unjust conquests, and to confine itself within its natural limits.

152. Although he claimed to be unmusical, Pope collaborated with three composers associated with Handel, in addition to Handel himself: Giovanni Bononcini (1670–1747), John Gay (1685–1732), and Maurice Greene (1696–1755) who, in 1730, set to music Pope's "Ode on St. Cecilia's Day" (1708). The music of all of them was popular in Edinburgh in Kames's day.

Having said what occurred upon rhyme, I close the section with a general observation, That the melody of verse so powerfully enchants the mind, as to draw a veil over very gross faults and imperfections. Of this power a stronger example cannot be given than the episode of Aristaeus, which closes the fourth book of the *Georgics*. To renew a stock of bees when the former is lost, Virgil asserts, that they may be produced in the entrails of a bullock, slain and managed in a certain manner. This leads him to say, how this strange <177> receit was invented; which is as follows. Aristaeus having lost his bees by disease and famine, never dreams of employing the ordinary means for obtaining a new stock; but, like a froward child, complains heavily to his mother Cyrene, a water-nymph. She advises him to consult Proteus, a sea-god, not how he was to obtain a new stock, but only by what fatality he had lost his former stock; adding, that violence was necessary, because Proteus would say nothing voluntarily. Aristaeus, satisfied with this advice, though it gave him no prospect of repairing his loss, proceeds to execution. Proteus is caught sleeping, bound with cords, and compelled to speak. He declares, that Aristaeus was punished with the loss of his bees, for attempting the chastity of Euridice the wife of Orpheus; she having been stung to death by a serpent in flying his embraces. Proteus, whose sullenness ought to have been converted into wrath by the rough treatment he met with, becomes on a sudden courteous and communicative. He gives the whole history of the expedition to hell which Orpheus undertook in order to recover his spouse; a very entertaining story, but without the least relation to what was in view. Aristaeus, returning to his mother, is advised to deprecate by sacrifices the wrath of Orpheus, who was now dead. A bullock is sacrificed, and out of the entrails spring miraculously a swarm of bees. Does it follow, that the same may be obtained without a miracle, as is supposed in the receit? <178>

A LIST of the different FEET, and of their NAMES.

1. PYRRHICHIUS, consists of two short syllables. Examples: *Deus, given, cannot, hillock, running.*

2. SPONDEUS, consists of two long syllables: *omnes, possess, forewarn, mankind, sometime.*

3. IAMBUS, composed of a short and a long: *pios, intent, degree, appear, consent, repent, demand, report, suspect, affront, event.*

4. TROCHAEUS, or CHOREUS, a long and short: *servat, whereby, after, legal, measure, burden, holy, lofty.*

5. TRIBRACHYS, three short: *melius, property.*

6. MOLOSSUS, three long: *delectant.*

7. ANAPAESTUS, two short and a long: *animos, condescend, apprehend, overheard, acquiesce, immature, overcharge, serenade, opportune.* <179>

8. DACTYLUS, a long and two short: *carmina, evident, excellence, estimate, wonderful, altitude, burdened, minister, tenement.*

9. BACCHIUS, a short and two long: *dolores.*

10. HYPPOBACCHIUS or ANTIBACCHIUS, two long and a short: *pelluntur.*

11. CRETICUS, or AMPHIMACER, a short syllable between two long: *insito, afternoon.*

12. AMPHIBRACHYS, a long syllable between two short: *honore, consider, imprudent, procedure, attended, proposed, respondent, concurrence, apprentice, respective, revenue.*

13. PROCELEUSMATICUS, four short syllables: *hominibus, necessary.*

14. DISPONDEUS, four long syllables: *infinitis.*

15. DIIAMBUS, composed of two Iambi: *severitas.*

16. DITROCHAEUS, of two Trochaei: *permanere, procurator.* <180>

17. IONICUS, two short syllables and two long: *properabant.*

18. Another foot passes under the same name, composed of two long syllables and two short: *calcaribus, possessory.*

19. CHORIAMBUS, two short syllables between two long: *nobilitas.*

20. ANTISPASTUS, two long syllables between two short: *Alexander.*

21. PAEON 1st, one long syllable and three short: *temporibus, ordinary, inventory, temperament.*

22. PAEON 2d, the second syllable long, and the other three short: *rapidity, solemnity, minority, considered, imprudently, extravagant, respectfully, accordingly.*

23. PAEON 3d, the third syllable long and the other three short: *animatus, independent, condescendence, sacerdotal, reimbursement, manufacture.*

24. PAEON 4th, the last syllable long and the other three short: *celeritas.* <181>

25. EPITRITUS 1st, the first syllable short and the other three long: *voluptates.*

26. EPITRITUS 2d, the second syllable short and the other three long: *paenitentes.*

27. EPITRITUS 3d, the third syllable short and the other three long: *discordias.*

28. EPITRITUS 4th, the last syllable short and the other three long: *fortunatus.*

29. A word of five syllables composed of a Pyrrhichius and Dactylus: *ministerial.*

30. A word of five syllables composed of a Trochaeus and Dactylus: *singularity.*

31. A word of five syllables composed of a Dactylus and Trochaeus: *precipitation, examination.*

32. A word of five syllables, the second only long: *significancy.*

33. A word of six syllables composed of two Dactyles: *impetuosity.*

34. A word of six syllables composed of a Tribrachys and Dactyle: *pusillanimity.* <182>

N.B. Every word may be considered as a prose foot, because every word is distinguished by a pause; and every foot in verse may be considered as a verse word, composed of syllables pronounced at once without a pause. <183>

CHAPTER XIX

Comparisons

Comparisons, as observed above,* serve two purposes: when addressed to the understanding, their purpose is to instruct; when to the heart, their purpose is to please. Various means contribute to the latter; first, the suggesting some unusual resemblance or contrast; second, the setting an object in the strongest light; third, the associating an object with others that are agreeable; fourth, the elevating an object; and, fifth, the depressing it. And that comparisons may give pleasure by these various means, appears from what is said in the chapter above cited; and will be made still more evident by examples, which shall be given after premising some general observations.

Objects of different senses cannot be compared together; for such objects, being entirely separated from each other, have no circumstance in common to admit either resemblance or contrast. Objects of hearing may be compared together, as also of taste, of smell, and of touch: but the chief fund <184> of comparison are objects of sight; because, in writing or speaking, things can only be compared in idea, and the ideas of sight are more distinct and lively than those of any other sense.

When a nation emerging out of barbarity begins to think of the fine arts,[1] the beauties of language cannot long lie concealed; and when discovered, they are generally, by the force of novelty, carried beyond moderation. Thus, in the early poems of every nation, we find metaphors and

---

* Chap. 8.

1. Kames added several additional quotations to the text after the first edition, most conspicuously from James Macpherson's *Fingal.*

similes founded on slight and distant resemblances, which, losing their grace with their novelty, wear gradually out of repute; and now, by the improvement of taste, none but correct metaphors and similes are admitted into any polite composition. To illustrate this observation, a specimen shall be given afterward of such metaphors as I have been describing: with respect to similes, take the following specimen.

> Behold, thou art fair, my love: thy hair is as a flock of goats that appear from Mount Gilead: thy teeth are like a flock of sheep from the washing, every one bearing twins: thy lips are like a thread of scarlet: thy neck like the tower of David built for an armoury, whereon hang a thousand shields of mighty men: thy two breasts like two young roes that are twins, which feed among the lilies: thy eyes like the fish-pools in Heshbon, by the gate of Bath-rabbim: thy nose like the tower of Lebanon, looking toward Damascus. *Song of Solomon.* <185>

> Thou art like snow on the heath; thy hair like the mist of Cromla, when it curls on the rocks and shines to the beam of the west: thy breasts are like two smooth rocks seen from Branno of the streams; thy arms like two white pillars in the hall of the mighty Fingal. *Fingal.*

It has no good effect to compare things by way of simile that are of the same kind; nor to compare by contrast things of different kinds. The reason is given in the chapter quoted above; and the reason shall be illustrated by examples. The first is a comparison built upon a resemblance so obvious as to make little or no impression.

> This just rebuke inflam'd the Lycian crew,
> They join, they thicken and th' assault renew:
> Unmov'd th' embody'd Greeks their fury dare,
> And fix'd support the weight of all the war;
> Nor could the Greeks repel the Lycian pow'rs,
> Nor the bold Lycians force the Grecian tow'rs.
> As on the confines of adjoining grounds,
> Two stubborn swains with blows dispute their bounds;
> They tugg, they sweat; but neither gain, nor yield,
> One foot, one inch, of the contended field:

Thus obstinate to death, they fight, they fall;
Nor these can keep, nor those can win the wall.

Iliad xii. 505.

Another, from Milton, lies open to the same objection. Speaking of the fallen angels searching for mines of gold: <186>

A numerous brigade hasten'd: as when bands
Of pioneers with spade and pick-ax arm'd,
Forerun the royal camp to trench a field
Or cast a rampart.[2]

The next shall be of things contrasted that are of different kinds.

Queen. What, is my Richard both in shape and mind
Transform'd and weak? Hath Bolingbroke depos'd
Thine intellect? Hath he been in thy heart!
The lion, thrusteth forth his paw,
And wounds the earth, if nothing else, with rage
To be o'erpower'd: and wilt thou, pupil-like,
Take thy correction mildly, kiss the rod,
And fawn on rage with base humility?

Richard II. *act* 5. *sc.* 1.[3]

This comparison has scarce any force: a man and a lion are of different species, and therefore are proper subjects for a simile; but there is no such resemblance between them in general, as to produce any strong effect by contrasting particular attributes or circumstances.

A third general observation is, That abstract terms can never be the subject of comparison, otherwise than by being personified. Shakespear compares adversity to a toad, and slander to the bite of a crocodile; but in such comparisons these abstract terms must be imagined sensible beings.

To have a just notion of comparisons, they <187> must be distinguished into two kinds; one common and familiar, as where a man is compared to

2. *Paradise Lost,* I.625.
3. Read "weaken'd" for "weak"; "lion dying" for "lion," and last line:

And fawn on rage with base humility
Which art a lion and a king of beasts?

a lion in courage, or to a horse in speed; the other more distant and refined, where two things that have in themselves no resemblance or opposition, are compared with respect to their effects. This sort of comparison is occasionally explained above;* and for further explanation take what follows. There is no resemblance between a flower-plot and a cheerful song; and yet they may be compared with respect to their effects, the emotions they produce being similar. There is as little resemblance between fraternal concord and precious ointment; and yet observe how successfully they are compared with respect to the impressions they make.

> Behold, how good and how pleasant it is for brethren to dwell together in unity. It is like the precious ointment upon the head, that ran down upon Aaron's beard, and descended to the skirts of his garment.
>
> *Psalm* 133.

For illustrating this sort of comparison, I add some more examples:

Delightful is thy presence, O Fingal! it is like the sun on Cromla, when the hunter mourns his absence for a season, and sees him between the clouds.

Did not Ossian hear a voice? or is it the sound of <188> days that are no more? Often, like the evening-sun, comes the memory of former times on my soul.

His countenance is settled from war; and is calm as the evening-beam, that from the cloud of the west looks on Cona's silent vale.

Sorrow, like a cloud on the sun, shades the soul of Clessammor.

The music was like the memory of joys that are past, pleasant and mournful to the soul.

Pleasant are the words of the song, said Cuchullin, and lovely are the tales of other times. They are like the calm dew of the morning on the hill of roes, when the sun is faint on its side, and the lake is settled and blue in the vale.

* p. 86.

These quotations are from the poems of Ossian, who abounds with comparisons of this delicate kind, and appears singularly happy in them.*

I proceed to illustrate by particular instances the different means by which comparisons, whether of the one sort or the other, can afford pleasure; and, in the order above established, I begin with such instances as are agreeable, by suggesting some unusual resemblance or contrast: <189>

> Sweet are the uses of Adversity,
> Which, like the toad, ugly and venomous,
> Wears yet a precious jewel in her head.
>
> *As you like it, act* 2. *sc.* 1.

> *Gardiner.* Bolingbroke hath seiz'd the wasteful King.
> What pity is't that he had not so trimm'd
> And dress'd his land, as we this garden dress,
> And wound the bark, the skin of our fruit-trees;
> Lest, being over proud with sap and blood,
> With too much riches it confound itself.
> Had he done so to great and growing men,
> They might have liv'd to bear, and he to taste
> Their fruits of duty. All superfluous branches
> We lop away, that bearing boughs may live:
> Had he done so, himself had borne the crown,
> Which waste and idle hours have quite thrown down.
>
> *Richard* II. *act* 3. *sc.* 7.[4]

---

* The nature and merit of Ossian's comparisons is fully illustrated, in a dissertation on the poems of that author, by Dr. Blair, professor of rhetoric in the college of Edinburgh; a delicious morsel of criticism. [Hugh Blair, *A Critical Dissertation on the Poems of Ossian, the Son of Fingal,* 1763.]

4. Act 3, sc. 4. Read opening lines as:

> . . . and Bolingbroke
> Hath seiz'd the wasteful king. O! what pity is it
> That he hath not so trimm'd and dress'd his land
> As we this garden. We at time of year
> Do wound the bark, the skin of our fruit-trees . . .

Delete "All" and "and" in lines 9 and 12.

See, how the Morning opes her golden gates,
And takes her farewell of the glorious Sun;
How well resembles it the prime of youth,
Trimm'd like a younker prancing to his love!

Second part Henry VI. *act* 2. *sc.* 1.[5]

Brutus. O Cassius, you are yoked with a lamb,
That carries anger as the flint bears fire:
Who, much enforced, shows a hasty spark,
And straight is cold again.   *Julius Caesar, act* 4. *sc.* 3.

Thus they their doubtful consultations dark
Ended, rejoicing in their matchless chief:
As when from mountain-tops, the dusky clouds
Ascending, while the North-wind sleeps, o'erspread <190>
Heav'n's cheerful face, the lowring element
Scowls o'er the darken'd landscape, snow, and show'r;
If chance the radiant sun with farewell sweet
Extends his ev'ning-beam, the fields revive,
The birds their notes renew, and bleating herds
Attest their joy, that hill and valley rings.

Paradise Lost, book 2.

As the bright stars, and milky way,
Show'd by the night, are hid by day:
So we in that accomplish'd mind,
Help'd by the night, new graces find,
Which, by the splendor of her view,
Dazzled before, we never knew.   *Waller.*[6]

The last exertion of courage compared to the blaze of a lamp before extinguishing, *Tasso Gierusalem, canto* 19. *st.* 22.

5. *Henry VI, Part 3,* act 2, sc. 1.
6. Edmund Waller, "The Night-piece or a Picture Drawn in the Dark."

None of the foregoing similes, as they appear to me, tend to illustrate the principal subject: and therefore the pleasure they afford must arise from suggesting resemblances that are not obvious: I mean the chief pleasure; for undoubtedly a beautiful subject introduced to form the simile affords a separate pleasure, which is felt in the similes mentioned, particularly in that cited from Milton.

The next effect of a comparison in the order mentioned, is to place an object in a strong point <191> of view; which effect is remarkable in the following similes:

> As when two scales are charg'd with doubtful loads,
> From side to side the trembling balance nods,
> (While some laborious matron, just and poor,
> With nice exactness weighs her woolly store),
> Till pois'd aloft, the resting beam suspends
> Each equal weight; nor this nor that descends:
> So stood the war, till Hector's matchless might,
> With fates prevailing, turn'd the scale of fight.
> Fierce as a whirlwind up the wall he flies,
> And fires his host with loud repeated cries.
>
> *Iliad, b.* xii. 521.

> Ut flos in septis secretis nascitur hortis,
> Ignotus pecori, nullo contusus aratro,
> Quem mulcent aurae, firmat sol, educat imber,
> Multi illum pueri, multae cupiere puellae;
> Idem, cum tenui carptus defloruit ungui,
> Nulli illum pueri, nullae cupiere puellae:
> Sic virgo, dum intacta manet, dum cara suis; sed
> Cum castum amisit, polluto corpore, florem,
> Nec pueris jucunda manet, nec cara puellis.   *Catullus.*[7]

7. Catullus, *Carmen nuptiale,* LX. 39–47:

   When withdrawn in some walled garden
   A rose blooms

The imitation of this beautiful simile by *Ariosto, canto* 1. *st.* 42. falls short of the original. It is also in part imitated by Pope.*

> *Lucetta.* I do not seek to quench your love's hot fire,
> But qualify the fire's extreme rage, <192>
> Lest it should burn above the bounds of reason.
>   *Julia.* The more thou damm'st it up, the more it burns:
> The current, that with gentle murmur glides,
> Thou know'st, being stopp'd, impatiently doth rage;
> But when his fair course is not hindered,
> He makes sweet music with th' enamel'd stones,
> Giving a gentle kiss to every sedge
> He overtaketh in his pilgrimage:
> And so by many winding nooks he strays
> With willing sport, to the wild ocean.
> Then let me go, and hinder not my course:
> I'll be as patient as a gentle stream,
> And make a pastime of each weary step,

> Safe from the farm plough
> From farm beasts
> Strong under the sun
> Fresh in light free air
> Sprouting in rain showers
> That rose is beauty's paragon for man or woman's pleasure,
> But once the bud has blown
> —when the thin stalk is left
> no paragon remains for man or woman's pleasure:
> so, intact
> a girl stays treasured of her sex
> but let her lose her maidenhead
> her close petals once polluted
> she cannot give the same delight again to men
> no longer be the cynosure of virgins
> Hymen Hymenaeus attend O Hymen!
>   (trans. Peter Whigham)

Kames departs from standard eighteenth-century texts: for "contusus" read "convulvus"; for both occurrences of "cupiere" read "optavere"; for "suis; sed" read "suis est;". Kames omits the last line: "Hymen o Hymenaee, Hymen ades o Hymenaee."

  * Dunciad, b. 4. l. 405.

Till the last step have brought me to my love;
And there I'll rest, as, after much turmoil,
A blessed soul doth in Elysium.

Two Gentlemen of Verona, act 2. *sc.* 10.[8]

——— She never told her love;
But let concealment, like a worm i' th' bud,
Feed on her damask cheek: she pin'd in thought;
And with a green and yellow melancholy,
She sat like Patience on a monument,
Smiling at Grief.   *Twelfth-Night, act* 2. *sc.* 6.[9]

York. Then, as I said, the Duke, great Bolingbroke,
Mounted upon a hot and fiery steed,
Which his aspiring rider seem'd to know,
With slow but stately pace, kept on his course:
While all tongues cry'd, God save thee, Bolingbroke.
   Duchess. Alas! poor Richard, where rides he the while! <193>
   York. As in a theatre, the eyes of men,
After a well grac'd actor leaves the stage,
Are idly bent on him that enters next,
Thinking his prattle to be tedious:
Even so, or with much more contempt, mens eyes
Did scowl on Richard; no man cry'd, God save him!
No joyful tongue gave him his welcome home;
But dust was thrown upon his sacred head:
Which with such gentle sorrow he shook off,
His face still combating with tears and smiles,
The badges of his grief and patience;
That had not God, for some strong purpose, steel'd
The hearts of men, they must perforce have melted,
And barbarism itself have pitied him.

Richard II. *act* 5. *sc.* 3.[10]

8. Act 2, sc. 7.
9. Act 2, sc. 4.
10. Act 5, sc. 2. Kames omits ten lines prior to the speech of the duchess.

Northumberland. How doth my son and brother?
Thou tremblest, and the whiteness in thy cheek
Is apter than thy tongue to tell thy errand.
Even such a man, so faint, so spiritless,
So dull, so dead in look, so wo-be-gone,
Drew Priam's curtain in the dead of night,
And would have told him, half his Troy was burn'd;
But Priam found the fire, ere he his tongue:
And I my Piercy's death, ere thou report'st it.

> *Second part, Henry* IV. *act* 1. *sc.* 3.[11]

Why, then I do but dream on sov'reignty,
Like one that stands upon a promontory,
And spies a far-off shore where he would tread,
Wishing his foot were equal with his eye,
And chides the sea that sunders him from thence,
Saying, he'll lave it dry to have his way:
So do I wish, the crown being so far off, <194>
And so I chide the means that keep me from it,
And so (I say) I'll cut the causes off,
Flatt'ring my mind with things impossible.

> *Third part, Henry* VI. *act* 3. *sc.* 3.[12]

———— Out, out, brief candle!
Life's but a walking shadow, a poor player,
That struts and frets his hour upon the stage,
And then is heard no more.   *Macbeth, act* 5. *sc.* 5.

O thou Goddess,
Thou divine Nature! how thyself thou blazon'st
In these two princely boys! they are as gentle
As zephyrs blowing below the violet,
Not wagging his sweet head; and yet as rough,
(Their royal blood inchaf'd) as the rudest wind,

11. Act 1, sc. 1.

12. Act 3, sc. 2: read "lade" for "lave" in line 6, and read last line as "Flatt'ring me with impossibilities."

That by the top doth take the mountain-pine,
And make him stoop to th' vale.

Cymbeline, act 4. sc. 4.[13]

Why did not I pass away in secret, like the flower of the rock that lifts its
fair head unseen, and strows its withered leaves on the blast?

Fingal.

There is a joy in grief when peace dwells with the sorrowful. But they are
wasted with mourning, O daughter of Toscar, and their days are few. They
fall away like the flower on which the sun looks in his strength, after the
mildew has passed over it, and its head is heavy with the drops of night.

Fingal. <195>

The sight obtained of the city of Jerusalem by the Christian army, compared to that of land discovered after a long voyage, Tasso's *Gierusalem,*
canto 3. *st.* 4. The fury of Rinaldo subsiding when not opposed, to that of
wind or water when it has a free passage, *canto* 20. *st.* 58.

As words convey but a faint and obscure notion of great numbers, a poet,
to give a lively notion of the object he describes with regard to number,
does well to compare it to what is familiar and commonly known. Thus
Homer* compares the Grecian army in point of number to a swarm of
bees: in another passage† he compares it to that profusion of leaves and
flowers which appear in the spring, or of insects in a summer's evening:
and Milton,

> ———— As when the potent rod
> Of Amram's son, in Egypt's evil day,
> Wav'd round the coast, up call'd a pitchy cloud
> Of locusts, warping on the eastern wind,
> That o'er the realm of impious Pharaoh hung
> Like night, and darken'd all the land of Nile:

---

* Book 2. l. iii.
† Book 2. l. 551.
13. Act 4, sc. 2.

> So numberless were those bad angels seen,
> Hovering on wing under the cope of hell,
> 'Twixt upper, nether, and surrounding fires.
>
> *Paradise Lost, book* I.

Such comparisons have, by some writers,* been <196> condemned for the lowness of the images introduced: but surely without reason; for, with regard to numbers, they put the principal subject in a strong light.

The foregoing comparisons operate by resemblance; others have the same effect by contrast.

> *York.* I am the last of Noble Edward's sons,
> Of whom thy father, Prince of Wales, was first;
> In war, was never lion rag'd more fierce;
> In peace, was never gentle lamb more mild;
> Than was that young and princely gentleman.
> His face thou hast, for even so look'd he,
> Accomplish'd with the number of thy hours.
> But when he frown'd, it was against the French,
> And not against his friends. His noble hand
> Did win what he did spend; and spent not that
> Which his triumphant father's hand had won.
> His hands were guilty of no kindred's blood,
> But bloody with the enemies of his kin.
> Oh, Richard! York is too far gone with grief,
> Or else he never would compare between.
>
> *Richard* II. *act* 2. *sc.* 3.[14]

Milton has a peculiar talent in embellishing the principal subject by associating it with others that are agreeable; which is the third end of a comparison. Similes of this kind have, beside, a separate effect: they diversify the narration by new images that are not strictly necessary to the compar-

---

* See Vidae Poetic. lib. 2. l. 282.
14. Act 2, sc. 1.

ison: they are short episodes, which, without <197> drawing us from the principal subject, afford great delight by their beauty and variety:

> He scarce had ceas'd, when the superior fiend
> Was moving toward the shore; his pond'rous shield,
> Ethereal temper, massy, large, and round,
> Behind him cast; the broad circumference
> Hung on his shoulders like the moon, whose orb
> Through optic glass the Tuscan artist views
> At ev'ning from the top of Fesole,
> Or in Valdarno, to descry new lands,
> Rivers, or mountains, in her spotty globe.   *Milton, b.* 1.

> ———— Thus far these, beyond
> Compare of mortal prowess, yet observ'd
> Their dread commander. He, above the rest
> In shape and gesture proudly eminent,
> Stood like a tow'r; his form had yet not lost
> All her original brightness, nor appear'd
> Less than archangel ruin'd, and th' excess
> Of glory obscur'd: as when the sun new-risen
> Looks through the horizontal misty air
> Shorn of his beams; or from behind the moon
> In dim eclipse, disastrous twilight sheds
> On half the nations, and with fear of change
> Perplexes monarchs.   *Milton, b.* 1.

> As when a vulture on Imaus bred,
> Whose snowy ridge the roving Tartar bounds,
> Dislodging from a region scarce of prey
> To gorge the flesh of lambs, or yeanling kids,
> On hills where flocks are fed, flies toward the springs <198>
> Of Ganges or Hydaspes, Indian streams,
> But in his way lights on the barren plains
> Of Sericana, where Chineses drive
> With sails and wind their cany waggons light:

So on this windy sea of land, the fiend
Walk'd up and down alone, bent on his prey.

Milton, b. 3.

———— Yet higher than their tops
The verdurous wall of paradise up sprung:
Which to our general fire gave prospect large
Into this nether empire neighbouring round.
And higher than that wall, a circling row
Of goodliest trees loaden with fairest fruit,
Blossoms and fruits at once of golden hue,
Appear'd, with gay enamel'd colours mix'd,
On which the sun more glad impress'd his beams
Than in fair evening cloud, or humid bow,
When God hath show'r'd the earth; so lovely seem'd
That landscape: and of pure now purer air
Meets his approach, and to the heart inspires
Vernal delight and joy, able to drive
All sadness but despair: now gentle gales
Fanning their odoriferous wings dispense
Native perfumes, and whisper whence they stole
Those balmy spoils. As when to them who sail
Beyond the Cape of Hope, and now are past
Mozambic, off at sea north-east winds blow
Sabean odour from the spicy shore
Of Araby the Blest; with such delay
Well-pleas'd they slack their course, and many a league,
Cheer'd with the grateful smell, old Ocean smiles.

Milton, b. 4.<199>

With regard to similes of this kind, it will readily occur to the reader, that when a resembling subject is once properly introduced in a simile, the mind is transitorily amused with the new object, and is not dissatisfied with the slight interruption. Thus, in fine weather, the momentary excursions of a traveller for agreeable prospects or elegant buildings, cheer his mind, relieve him from the languor of uniformity, and without much lengthening his journey in reality, shorten it greatly in appearance.

Next of comparisons that aggrandize or elevate. These affect us more than any other sort: the reason of which may be gathered from the chapter of Grandeur and Sublimity; and, without reasoning, will be evident from the following instances:

> As when a flame the winding valley fills,
> And runs on crackling shrubs between the hills,
> Then o'er the stubble, up the mountain flies,
> Fires the high woods, and blazes to the skies,
> This way and that, the spreading torrent roars;
> So sweeps the hero through the wasted shores.
> Around him wide, immense destruction pours,
> And earth is delug'd with the sanguine show'rs.
>
> *Iliad* xx. 569.

> Through blood, through death, Achilles still proceeds,
> O'er slaughter'd heroes, and o'er rolling steeds.
> As when avenging flames with fury driv'n
> On guilty towns exert the wrath of Heav'n, <200>
> The pale inhabitants, some fall, some fly,
> And the red vapours purple all the sky:
> So rag'd Achilles; Death, and dire dismay,
> And toils, and terrors, fill'd the dreadful day.
>
> *Iliad* xxi. 605.

> Methinks, King Richard and myself should meet
> With no less terror than the elements
> Of fire and water, when their thund'ring shock,
> At meeting, tears the cloudy cheeks of heav'n.
>
> *Richard* II. *act* 3. *sc.* 5.[15]

As rusheth a foamy stream from the dark shady steep of Cromla, when thunder is rolling above, and dark brown night rests on the hill: so fierce, so vast, so terrible, rush forward the sons of Erin. The chief, like a whale

---

15. Act 3, sc. 3.

of Ocean followed by all its billows, pours valour forth as a stream, rolling
its might along the shore.   *Fingal, b.* 1.

As roll a thousand waves to a rock, so Swaran's host came on; as meets a
rock a thousand waves, so Inisfail met Swaran.   *Ibid.*

I beg peculiar attention to the following simile, for a reason that shall be
mentioned:

> Thus breathing death, in terrible array,
> The close-compacted legions urg'd their way:
> Fierce they drove on, impatient to destroy;
> Troy charg'd the first, and Hector first of Troy.
> As from some mountain's craggy forehead torn,
> A rock's round fragment flies with fury borne, <201>
> (Which from the stubborn stone a torrent rends)
> Precipitate the pond'rous mass descends;
> From steep to steep the rolling ruin bounds:
> At every shock the crackling wood resounds;
> Still gath'ring force, it smokes; and, urg'd amain,
> Whirls, leaps, and thunders down, impetuous to the plain:
> There stops—So Hector. Their whole force he prov'd:
> Resistless when he rag'd; and when he stopt, unmov'd.
>   *Iliad* xiii. 187.

The image of a falling rock is certainly not elevating;* and yet undoubtedly
the foregoing simile fires and swells the mind: it is grand therefore, if not
sublime. And the following simile will afford additional evidence, that there
is a real, tho' nice, distinction between these two feelings:

> So saying, a noble stroke he lifted high,
> Which hung not, but so swift with tempest fell
> On the proud crest of Satan, that no sight,
> Nor motion of swift thought, less could his shield
> Such ruin intercept. Ten paces huge
> He back recoil'd; the tenth on bended knee
> His massy spear upstaid; as if on earth

* See chap. 4.

> Winds under ground or waters forcing way,
> Sidelong had push'd a mountain from his seat
> Half-sunk with all his pines.   *Milton, b. 6.*

A comparison by contrast may contribute to grandeur or elevation, no less than by resemblance; <202> of which the following comparison of Lucan is a remarkable instance:

> Victrix causa diis placuit, sed victa Catoni.[16]

Considering that the Heathen deities possessed a rank but one degree above that of mankind, I think it would not be easy by a single expression, to exalt more one of the human species, than is done in this comparison. I am sensible, at the same time, that such a comparison among Christians, who entertain more exalted notions of the Deity, would justly be reckoned extravagant and absurd.

The last article mentioned, is that of lessening or depressing a hated or disagreeable object; which is effectually done by resembling it to any thing low or despicable. Thus Milton, in his description of the rout of the rebel-angels, happily expresses their terror and dismay in the following simile:

> ———— As a herd
> Of goats or timorous flock together throng'd,
> Drove them before him thunder-struck, pursu'd
> With terrors and with furies to the bounds
> And crystal wall of heav'n, which op'ning wide,
> Rowl'd inward, and a spacious gap disclos'd
> Into the wasteful deep: the monstrous sight
> Struck them with horror backward, but far worse
> Urg'd them behind; headlong themselves they threw <203>
> Down from the verge of heav'n.   *Milton, b. 6.*

In the same view, Homer, I think, may be justified in comparing the shouts of the Trojans in battle to the noise of cranes,* and to the bleating of a

---

* Beginning of book 3.
16. Lucan 1.128: "for, if the victor had the gods on his side, the vanquished had Cato."

flock of sheep:* it is no objection that these are low images; for it was his intention to lessen the Trojans by opposing their noisy march to the silent and manly march of the Greeks. Addison,† describing the figure that men make in the sight of a superior being, takes opportunity to mortify their pride by comparing them to a swarm of pismires.[17]

A comparison that has none of the good effects mentioned in this discourse, but is built upon common and trifling circumstances, makes a mighty silly figure:

> Non sum nescius, grandia consilia a multis plerumque causis, ceu magna navigia a plurimis remis, impelli.   *Strada de bello Belgico.*[18]

By this time, I imagine, the different purposes of comparison, and the various impressions it makes on the mind, are sufficiently illustrated by proper examples. This was an easy task. It is more difficult to lay down rules about the proprie-<204>ty or impropriety of comparisons; in what circumstances they may be introduced, and in what circumstances they are out of place. It is evident, that a comparison is not proper on every occasion: a man when cool and sedate, is not disposed to poetical flights, nor to sacrifice truth and reality to imaginary beauties: far less is he so disposed, when oppressed with care, or interested in some important transaction that engrosses him totally. On the other hand, a man, when elevated or animated by passion, is disposed to elevate or animate all his objects: he avoids familiar names, exalts objects by circumlocution and metaphor, and gives even life and voluntary action to inanimate beings. In this heat of mind, the highest poetical flights are indulged, and the boldest similes and metaphors relished.‡ But without soaring so high, the mind is frequently in a tone to relish chaste and moderate ornament; such as comparisons that set

---

* Book 4. l. 498.

† *Guardian,* No. 153.

‡ It is accordingly observed by Longinus, in his Treatise of the Sublime, that the proper time for metaphor, is when the passions are so swelled as to hurry on like a torrent.

17. Ants.

18. Famiano Strada (1572–1649), *De bello Belgico decas prima,* 1632 (translated into English as *The History of the Low-Countrey Warres,* 1650). "I am not ignorant of the fact that great schemes are effected by many causes, just as large ships are impelled along by many oars."

the principal object in a strong point of view, or that embellish and diversify the narration. In general, when by any animating passion, whether pleasant or painful, an impulse is given to the imagination; we are in that condition disposed to every sort of figurative expression, and in particular to comparisons. This in a great measure <205> is evident from the comparisons already mentioned; and shall be further illustrated by other instances. Love, for example, in its infancy, rousing the imagination, prompts the heart to display itself in figurative language, and in similes:

> *Troilus.* Tell me, Apollo, for thy Daphne's love,
> What Cressid is, what Pandar, and what we?
> Her bed is India; there she lies, a pearl:
> Between our Ilium, and where she resides,
> Let it be call'd the wild and wandering flood;
> Ourself the merchant; and this sailing Pandar
> Our doubtful hope, our convoy, and our bark.
>
> *Troilus and Cressid, act* 1. *sc.* 1.

Again:

> Come, gentle Night; come, loving black-brow'd Night!
> Give me my Romeo; and, when he shall die,
> Take him, and cut him out in little stars,
> And he will make the face of Heav'n so fine,
> That all the world shall be in love with Night,
> And pay no worship to the garish Sun.
>
> *Romeo and Juliet, act* 3. *sc.* 4.[19]

The dread of a misfortune, however imminent, involving always some doubt and uncertainty, agitates the mind, and excites the imagination:

> *Wolsey.* ——— Nay, then, farewell;
> I've touch'd the highest point of all my greatness,
> And from that full meridian of my glory <206>
> I haste now to my setting. I shall fall,

19. Act 3, sc. 2.

> Like a bright exhalation in the evening,
> And no man see me more.   *Henry* VIII. *act* 3. *sc.* 4.[20]

But it will be a better illustration of the present head, to give examples where comparisons are improperly introduced. I have had already occasion to observe, that similes are not the language of a man in his ordinary state of mind, dispatching his daily and usual work. For that reason, the following speech of a gardener to his servants, is extremely improper:

> Go, bind thou up yon dangling apricots,
> Which, like unruly children, make their sire
> Stoop with oppression of their prodigal weight:
> Give some supportance to the bending twigs.
> Go thou; and, like an executioner,
> Cut off the heads of too-fast-growing sprays,
> That look too lofty in our commonwealth;
> All must be even in our government.
>   *Richard* II. *act* 3. *sc.* 7.[21]

The fertility of Shakespear's vein betrays him frequently into this error. There is the same impropriety in another simile of his:

> *Hero.* Good Margaret, run thee into the parlour;
> There shalt thou find my cousin Beatrice;
> Whisper her ear, and tell her, I and Ursula
> Walk in the orchard, and our whole discourse
> Is all of her; say, that thou overheard'st us: <207>
> And bid her steal into the pleached bower,
> Where honeysuckles, ripen'd by the sun,
> Forbid the sun to enter; like to favourites,
> Made proud by princes, that advance their pride
> Against that power that bred it.
>   *Much ado about Nothing, act* 3. *sc.* 1.

Rooted grief, deep anguish, terror, remorse, despair, and all the severe dispiriting passions, are declared enemies, perhaps not to figurative language

20. Act 3, sc. 2.
21. Act 3, sc. 4.

in general, but undoubtedly to the pomp and solemnity of comparison. Upon that account, the simile pronounced by young Rutland, under terror of death from an inveterate enemy, and praying mercy, is unnatural:

> So looks the pent-up lion o'er the wretch
> That trembles under his devouring paws;
> And so he walks insulting o'er his prey,
> And so he comes to rend his limbs asunder.
> Ah, gentle Clifford, kill me with thy sword,
> And not with such a cruel threat'ning look.
>
> *Third part Henry* VI. *act* 1. *sc.* 5.[22]

Nothing appears more out of place, nor more aukwardly introduced, than the following simile:

> *Lucia.* ——— Farewell, my Portius,
> Farewell, though death is in the word, *for-ever!*
>   *Portius.* Stay, Lucia, stay; what dost thou say? *for-ever?*
>   *Lucia.* Have I not sworn? If, Portius, thy success
> Must throw thy brother on his fate, farewell, <208>
> Oh, how shall I repeat the word, *for-ever!*
>   *Portius.* Thus, o'er the dying lamp th' unsteady flame
> Hangs quivering on a point, leaps off by fits,
> And falls again, as loath to quit its hold.*
> — Thou must not go, my soul still hovers o'er thee,
> And can't get loose.   *Cato, act* 3. *sc.* 2.[23]

Nor doth the simile which closes the first act of the same tragedy make a better appearance; the situation there represented being too dispiriting for a simile. A simile is improper for one who dreads the discovery of a secret machination:

> *Zara.* The mute not yet return'd! Ha! 'twas the King,
> The King that parted hence! frowning he went;
> His eyes like meteors roll'd, then darted down

---

* This simile would have a fine effect pronounced by the chorus in a Greek tragedy.
22. Act 1, sc. 3.
23. Joseph Addison, 1713.

Their red and angry beams; as if his sight
Would, like the raging Dog-star, scorch the earth,
And kindle ruin in its course.

Mourning Bride, act 5. sc. 3.

A man spent and dispirited after losing a battle, is not disposed to heighten
or illustrate his discourse by similes:

York. With this we charg'd again; but out, alas!
We bodg'd again; as I have seen a swan
With bootless labour swim against the tide, <209>
And spend her strength with over-matching waves.
Ah! hark, the fatal followers do pursue;
And I am faint and cannot fly their fury.
The sands are number'd that make up my life;
Here must I stay, and here my life must end.

Third part Henry VI. *act 1. sc. 6.*[24]

Far less is a man disposed to similes who is not only defeated in a pitch'd
battle, but lies at the point of death mortally wounded:

Warwick. ——— My mingled body shows,
My blood, my want of strength, my sick heart shows,
That I must yield my body to the earth,
And, by my fall, the conquest to my foe.
Thus yields the cedar to the ax's edge,
Whose arms gave shelter to the princely eagle;
Under whose shade the ramping lion slept,
Whose top-branch overpeer'd Jove's spreading tree,
And kept low shrubs from winter's pow'rful wind.

Third part Henry VI. *act 5. sc. 3.*[25]

Queen Katharine, deserted by the King, and in the deepest affliction on
her divorce, could not be disposed to any sallies of imagination: and for
that reason, the following simile, however beautiful in the mouth of a spectator, is scarce proper in her own:

24. Act 1, sc. 4.
25. Act 5, sc. 2: read "mangled" for "mingled."

I am the most unhappy woman living,
Shipwreck'd upon a kingdom, where no pity, <210>
No friends, no hope! no kindred weep for me!
Almost no grave allow'd me! like the lily,
That once was mistress of the field, and flourish'd,
I'll hang my head, and perish.

King Henry VIII. *act* 3. *sc.* 1.[26]

Similes thus unseasonably introduced, are finely ridiculed in the *Rehearsal.*

> *Bayes.* Now here she must make a simile.
> *Smith.* Where's the necessity of that, Mr. Bayes?
> *Bayes.* Because she's surprised; that's a general rule;
> You must ever make a simile when you are surprised;
> 'Tis a new way of writing.

A comparison is not always faultless even where it is properly introduced. I have endeavoured above to give a general view of the different ends to which a comparison may contribute: a comparison, like other human productions, may fall short of its aim; of which defect instances are not rare even among good writers; and to complete the present subject, it will be necessary to make some observations upon such faulty comparisons. I begin with observing, that nothing can be more erroneous than to institute a comparison too faint: a distant resemblance or contrast fatigues the mind with its obscurity, instead of amusing it; and tends not to fulfil any one end of a comparison. The following similes seem to labour under this defect. <211>

> Albus ut obscuro deterget nubila coelo
> Saepe Notus, neque parturit imbres
> Perpetuos: sic tu sapiens finire memento

---

26. Read first three lines as:

> I am the most unhappy woman living,
> Alas! Poor wenches, where are now your fortunes?
> Shipwreck'd upon a kingdom, where no pity . . .

Tristitiam, vitaeque labores,
Molli, Plance, mero. *Horat. Carm. l.* i. *ode* 7.[27]

———— Medio dux agmine Turnus
Vertitur arma tenens, et toto vertice supra est.
Ceu septem surgens sedatis amnibus altus
Per tacitum Ganges: aut pingui flumine Nilus
Cum refluit campis, et jam se condidit alveo.

Aeneid. ix. 28.[28]

Talibus orabat, talisque miserrima fletus
Fertque refertque soror: sed nullis ille movetur
Fletibus, aut voces ullas tractabilis audit.
Fata obstant: placidasque viri Deus obstruit auris.
Ac veluti annoso validam cum robore quercum
Alpini Boreae, nunc hinc, nunc flatibus illinc
Eruere inter se certant; it stridor, et alte
Consternunt terram concusso stipite frondes:
Ipsa haeret scopulis: et quantum vertice ad auras
Aethereas, tantum radice in Tartara tendit.
Haud secus assiduis hinc atque hinc vocibus heros
Tunditur, et magno persentit pectore curas:
Mens immota manet, lacrymae volvuntur inanes.

Aeneid. iv. 437.[29]

27. "As Notus is oft a clearing wind and dispels the clouds from darkened skies nor breeds perpetual showers, so do thou, O Plancus, remember wisely to end life's gloom and troubles with mellow wine."

28. "Turnus their captain in the centre of the line:—even as Ganges, rising high in silence with his seven peaceful streams, or Nile, when his rich flood ebbs from the fields, and at length he is sunk into his channel."

29. "Such was her prayer and such the tearful pleas the unhappy sister bears again and again. But by no tearful pleas is he moved, nor in yielding mood pays he heed to any words. Fate withstands and heaven seals his kindly, mortal ears. Even as when northern Alpine winds, blowing now hence, now thence, emulously strive to uproot an oak strong with the strength of years, there comes a roar, the stem quivers and the high leafage thickly strews the ground, but the oak clings to the crag, and as far it strikes its roots down towards hell—even so with ceaseless appeals, from this and from that, the hero is buffeted, and in his mighty heart feels the thrill of grief: steadfast stands his will; the tears fall in vain."

    K. Rich. Give me the crown.—Here, Cousin, seize the crown,
Here, on this side, my hand; on that side, thine.
Now is this golden crown like a deep well,
That owes two buckets, filling one another; <212>
The emptier ever dancing in the air,
The other down, unseen and full of water:
That bucket down, and full of tears, am I,
Drinking my griefs, whilst you mount up on high.

                              Richard II. *act* 4. *sc.* 3.[30]

    King John. Oh! Cousin, thou art come to set mine eye;
The tackle of my heart is crack'd and burnt;
And all the shrowds wherewith my life should fail,
Are turned to one thread, one little hair:
My heart hath one poor string to stay it by,
Which holds but till thy news be uttered.

                              King John, act. 5. *sc.* 10.[31]

    York. My uncles both are slain in rescuing me:
And all my followers, to the eager foe
Turn back, and fly like ships before the wind,
Or lambs pursu'd by hunger-starved wolves.

                          Third part Henry VI. *act* 1. *sc.* 6.[32]

The latter of the two similes is good: the former, by its faintness of resemblance, has no effect but to load the narration with an useless image.

    The next error I shall mention is a capital one. In an epic poem, or in a poem upon any elevated subject, a writer ought to avoid raising a simile on a low image, which never fails to bring down the principal subject. In general, it is a rule, That a grand object ought never to be resembled to one <213> that is diminutive, however delicate the resemblance may be: for it is the peculiar character of a grand object to fix the attention, and swell the

30. Act 4, sc. 1.
31. Act 5, sc. 7.
32. Act 1, sc. 4.

mind; in which state, to contract it to a minute object, is unpleasant. The resembling an object to one that is greater, has, on the contrary, a good effect, by raising or swelling the mind: for one passes with satisfaction from a small to a great object; but cannot be drawn down, without reluctance, from great to small. Hence the following similes are faulty.

> Meanwhile the troops beneath Patroclus' care,
> Invade the Trojans, and commence the war.
> As wasps, provok'd by children in their play,
> Pour from their mansions by the broad highway,
> In swarms the guiltless traveller engage,
> Whet all their stings, and call forth all their rage;
> All rise in arms, and with a general cry
> Assert their waxen domes, and buzzing progeny:
> Thus from the tents the fervent legion swarms,
> So loud their clamours, and so keen their arms.
>
> *Iliad* xvi. 312.

> So burns the vengeful hornet (soul all o'er)
> Repuls'd in vain, and thirsty still of gore;
> (Bold son of air and heat) on angry wings
> Untam'd, untir'd, he turns, attacks and stings.
> Fir'd with like ardour fierce Atrides flew,
> And sent his soul with ev'ry lance he threw.
>
> *Iliad* xvii. 642. <214>

> Instant ardentes Tyrii: pars ducere muros,
> Molirique arcem, et manibus subvolvere saxa;
> Pars aptare locum tecto, et concludere sulco.
> Jura magistratusque legunt, sanctumque senatum.
> Hic portus alii effodiunt: hic alta theatris
> Fundamenta locant alii, immanesque columnas
> Rupibus excidunt, scenis decora alta futuris.
> Qualis apes aestate nova per florea rura
> Exercet sub sole labor, cum gentis adultos
> Educunt foetus, aut cum liquentia mella
> Stipant, et dulci distendunt nectare cellas,

Aut onera accipiunt venientum, aut agmine facto
Ignavum fucos pecus a praesepibus arcent.
Fervet opus, redolentque thymo fragrantia mella.

Aeneid. i. 427.[33]

To describe bees gathering honey as resembling the builders of Carthage, would have a much better effect.*

Tum vero Teucri incumbunt, et littore celsas
Deducunt toto naves: natat uncta carina;
Frondentesque ferunt remos, et robora sylvis
Infabricata, fugae studio.
Migrantes cernas, totaque ex urbe ruentes.
Ac veluti ingentem formicae farris acervum
Cum populant, hyemis memores, tectoque reponunt:
It nigrum campis agmen, praedamque per herbas
Convectant calle angusto: pars grandia trudunt <215>
Obnixae frumenta humeris: pars agmina cogunt,
Castigantque moras: opere omnis semita fervet.

Aeneid. iv. 397.[34]

---

* And accordingly Demetrius Phalereus (of Elocution, sect. 85.) observes, that it has a better effect to compare small things to great than great things to small.

33. "Eagerly the Tyrians press on, some to build walls, to rear the citadel, and roll up stones by hand; some to choose the site for a dwelling and enclose it with a furrow. Laws and magistrates they ordain, and a holy senate. Here some are digging harbours, here others lay the deep foundations of their theatre and hew out of the cliffs vast columns, lofty adornments for the stage to be! Even as bees in early summer, amid flowery fields, ply their task in sunshine, when they lead forth the full-grown young of their race, or pack the fluid honey and strain their cells to bursting with sweet nectar, or receive the burdens of incomers, or in martial array drive from their folds the drones, a lazy herd; all aglow is the work and the fragrant honey is sweet with thyme." Read "Theatri" for "theatris"; "augmine" for "agmine."

34. "Then, indeed, the Teucrians fall to and all along the shore launch their tall ships. The keels, well-pitched, are set afloat; the sailors, eager for flight, bring from the woods leafy boughs for oars and logs unhewn. One could see them moving away and streaming forth from all the city. Even as when ants, mindful of winter, plunder a huge hap of corn and store it in their home; over the plain moves a black column, and through the grass they carry the spoil on a narrow track, some strain with their shoulders and heave on the huge grains, some close up the ranks and rebuke delay; all the path is aglow with work." Read "navis," "Frondetisque," "ruentis."

The following simile has not any one beauty to recommend it. The subject is Amata, the wife of King Latinus.

> Tum vero infelix, ingentibus excita monstris,
> Immensam sine more furit lymphata per urbem:
> Ceu quondam torto volitans sub verbere turbo,
> Quem pueri magno in gyro vacua atria circum
> Intenti ludo exercent. Ille actus habena
> Curvatis fertur spatiis: stupet inscia turba,
> Impubesque manus, mirata volubile buxum;
> Dant animos plagae. Non cursu segnior illo
> Per medias urbes agitur, populosque feroces.
>
> *Aeneid.* vii. 376.[35]

This simile seems to border upon the burlesque.

An error opposite to the former, is the introducing a resembling image, so elevated or great as to bear no proportion to the principal subject. Their remarkable disparity, seizing the mind, never fails to depress the principal subject by contrast, instead of raising it by resemblance: and if the disparity be very great, the simile degenerates into burlesque; nothing being more ridiculous than to force an object out of its proper rank in nature, by equalling it with one greatly superior or great-<216>ly inferior. This will be evident from the following comparisons.

> Fervet opus, redolentque thymo fragrantia mella,
> Ac veluti lentis Cyclopes fulmina massis
> Cum properant: alii taurinis follibus auras
> Accipiunt, redduntque: alii stridentia tingunt
> Aera lacu: gemit impositis incudibus Aetna:
> Illi inter sese magna vi brachia tollunt
> In numerum; versantque tenaci forcipe ferrum.

35. "Then, indeed, the luckless queen, stung by monstrous horrors, in wild frenzy rages from end to end of the city. As at times a top, spinning under the twisted lash, which boys intent on the game drive in a great circle through an empty court—urged by the whip it speeds on round after round; the puzzled, childish throng hang over it in wonder, marvelling at the whirling box-wood; the blows give it life: so, with course no slacker, is she driven through the midst of cities and proud peoples."

Non aliter (si parva licet componere magnis)
Cecropias innatus apes amor urget habendi,
Munere quamque suo. Grandaevis oppida curae,
Et munire favos, et Daedala fingere tecta.
At fessae multâ referunt se nocte minores,
Crura thymo plenae: pascuntur et arbuta passim,
Et glaucas salices, casiamque crocumque rubentem,
Et pinguem tiliam, et ferrugineos hyacinthos.
Omnibus una quies operum, labor omnibus unus.

Georgics, iv. 169.[36]

The Cyclopes make a better figure in the following simile:

———— The Thracian leader prest,
With eager courage, far before the rest;
Him Ajax met, inflam'd with equal rage:
Between the wond'ring hosts the chiefs engage;
Their weighty weapons round their heads they throw,
And swift, and heavy, falls each thund'ring blow.
As when in Aetna's caves the giant brood,
The one-ey'd servants of the Lemnian god,
In order round the burning anvil stand,
And forge, with weighty strokes, the forked brand; <217>
The shaking hills their fervid toils confess,
And echoes rattling through each dark recess:
So rag'd the fight.   *Epigoniad, b.* 8.

36. "All aglow is the work, and the fragrant honey is sweet with thyme. And as, when the Cyclopes in haste forge bolts from tough ore, some with ox-hide bellows make the blasts come and go, others dip the hissing brass in the lake, while Aetna groans under the anvils laid upon her; they, with mighty force, now one, now another, raise their arms in measured cadence, and turn the iron with gripping tongs—even so, if we may compare small things with great, an inborn love of gain spurs on the Attic bees, each after its own office. The aged have charge of the towns, the building of the hives, the fashioning of the cunningly wrought houses. But the young betake them home in weariness, late at night, their thighs freighted with thyme; far and wide they feed on arbutus, on pale-green willows, on cassia and ruddy crocus, on the rich linden, and the dusky hyacinth. All have one season to rest from labour, all one season to toil."

Tum Bitian ardentem oculis animisque frementem;
Non jaculo, neque enim jaculo vitam ille dedisset;
Sed magnum stridens contorta falarica venit
Fulminis acta modo, quam nec duo taurea terga,
Nec duplici squama lorica fidelis et auro
Sustinuit: collapsa ruunt immania membra:
Dat tellus gemitum, et clypeum super intonat ingens.
Qualis in Euboico Baiarum littore quondam
Saxea pila cadit, magnis quam molibus ante
Constructam jaciunt ponto: sic illa ruinam
Prona trahit, penitusque vadis illisa recumbit:
Miscent se maria, et nigrae attolluntur arenae:
Tum sonitu Prochyta alta tremit, durumque cubile
Inarime Jovis imperiis imposta Typhoëo.

> *Aeneid.* ix. 703.[37]

Loud as a bull makes hill and valley ring,
So roar'd the lock when it releas'd the spring.

> *Odyssey,* xxi. 51.

Such a simile upon the simplest of all actions, that of opening a door, is pure burlesque.

A writer of delicacy will avoid drawing his comparisons from any image that is nauseous, ugly, or remarkably disagreeable: for however strong the resemblance may be, more will be lost than gained <218> by such comparison. Therefore I cannot help condemning, though with some reluctance, the following simile, or rather metaphor.

---

37. "Then Bitias falls, fire in his eyes and rage in his hearts, yet not under a javelin—for not to a javelin had he given his life—but with a mighty hiss a whirled pike sped, driven by a thunderbolt. This not two bulls' hides, nor the trusty corslet with double scales of gold could withstand. The giant limbs totter and fall; earth groans, and the huge shield thunders over him. So on Euboic shore of Baiae falls at times a rocky mass, which, builded first of mighty blocks, men cast into the sea; so as it falls, it trails havoc, and crashing into the waters finds rest in the depths; the seas are in turmoil and the black sands mount upwards; then at the sound lofty Prochyta trembles, and Inarime's rugged bed, laid by Jove's command above Typhoeus."

O thou fond many! with what loud applause
Did'st thou beat heav'n with blessing Bolingbroke
Before he was what thou wou'dst have him be?
And now being trimm'd up in thine own desires,
Thou, beastly feeder, art so full of him,
That thou provok'st thyself to cast him up.
And so, thou common dog, didst thou disgorge
Thy glutton bosom of the royal Richard,
And now thou wou'st eat thy dead vomit up,
And howl'st to find it.

Second part, Henry IV. *act* 1. *sc.* 6.[38]

The strongest objection that can lie against a comparison is, that it consists in words only, not in sense. Such false coin, or bastard wit, does extremely well in burlesque; but is far below the dignity of the epic, or of any serious composition:

The noble sister of Poplicola,
The moon of Rome; chaste as the isicle
That's curled by the frost from purest snow,
And hangs on Dian's temple.   *Coriolanus, act* 5. *sc.* 3.[39]

There is evidently no resemblance between an isicle and a woman, chaste or unchaste: but chastity is cold in a metaphorical sense, and an isicle is cold in a proper sense: and this verbal resem-<219>blance, in the hurry and glow of composing, has been thought a sufficient foundation for the simile. Such phantom similes are mere witticisms, which ought to have no quarter, except where purposely introduced to provoke laughter. Lucian, in his dissertation upon history, talking of a certain author, makes the following comparison, which is verbal merely:

This author's descriptions are so cold, that they surpass the Caspian snow, and all the ice of the north.

38. Act 1, sc. 3.
39. Read "Publicola" for "Poplicola," "curdied" for "curled."

Virgil has not escaped this puerility:

> —————— Galathaea thymo mihi dulcior Hyblae.
>
> *Bucol.* vii. 37.

> —————— Ego Sardois videar tibi amarior herbis.   *Ibid.* 41.

> Gallo, cujus amor tantum mihi crescit in horas,
> Quantum vere novo viridis se subjicit alnus.
>
> *Bucol.* x. 37.[40]

Nor Tasso, in his *Aminta:*

> Picciola e' l' ape, e fa col picciol morso
> Pur gravi, e pur moleste le ferite;
> Ma, qual cosa é più picciola d'amore,
> Se in ogni breve spatio entra, e s' asconde
> In ogni breve spatio? hor, sotto a l'ombra
> De le palpebre, hor trà minuti rivi
> D'un biondo crine, hor dentro le pozzette
> Che forma un dolce riso in bella guancia; <220>
> E pur fa tanto grandi, e si mortali,
> E cosi immedicabili le piaghe.   *Act* 2. *sc.* 1.[41]

---

40. *Bucolics* 7.37, 41; X.37 (Dryden translations):

Fair Galatea, with silver Feet,
O, whiter than the Swan, and more than Hybla sweet

. . . deform'd like him who chaws
Sardinian Herbage to contract his Jaws

Why, Gallus, this immod'rate Grief, he cry'd:
Think'st thou that Love with Tears is satisfy'd?

41. "Small is the bee and yet with its small sting makes the most grievous and troublesome wounds; but what thing is smaller than Love who lurks in the minutest things and hides himself in every little space? Now in the shade of an eyelid, now among the fine threads of golden locks, now within the dimples which a sweet smile forms in lovely cheek, and yet he makes so great, so mortal and incurable wounds." (*Aminta,* trans. E. Grillo) Read "ricci" for "rivi."

Nor Boileau, the chastest of all writers; and that even in his art of poetry:

> Ainsi tel autrefois, qu'on vit avec Faret
> Charbonner de ses vers les murs d'un cabaret,
> S'en va mal à propos d'une voix insolente,
> Chanter du peuple Hébreu la suite triomphante,
> Et poursuivant Moise au travers des déserts,
> Court avec Pharaon se noyer dans les mers.
>
> *Chant.* 1. *l.* 21.[42]

> Mais allons voir le Vrai jusqu'en sa source même.
> Un dévot aux yeux creux, et d'abstinence blême,
> S'il n'a point le cœur juste, est affreux devant Dieu.
> L'Evangile au Chrêtien ne dit, en aucun lieu,
> Sois dévot: elle dit, Sois doux, simple, equitable;
> Car d'un dévot souvent au Chrêtien veritable
> La distance est deux fois plus longue, à mon avis,
> Que du Pôle Antarctique au Détroit de Davis.
>
> *Boileau, Satire* 11.[43]

42. Thus in times past Dubartas vainly Writ,
    Allaying sacred truth with trifling Wit,
    Impertinently, and without delight,
    Describ'd the Ismelites Triumphant Flight,
    And following Moses o'er the Sandy Plain,
    Perish'd with Pharaoh in the Arabian Main.

43. But Truth we now will to the Fountain trace,
    And see the Saint with his reserv'd Grimace,
    That look of Abstinence, that holy Leer:
    What is he? Who wou'd thus devout appear,
    To Heav'n how hideous! if he's not sincere.
    The Gospel nowhere says be Sullen, Sour,
    But bids you to be Simple, Honest, Pure.
    The Man, who is a Christian, seems to me,
    Compar'd with him who so affects to be,
    As distant from each other, as the Poles,
    From Davis Streight to where th' Antartic Rolls.
    ["A Streight under the Artic-Pole near Nova Zembla."]
        (The English editor was here mistaken: the Davis
        Strait separates Greenland from Baffin Island.)

——— But for their spirits and souls
This word *rebellion* had froze them up
As fish are in a pond.

Second part Henry IV. *act* 1. *sc.* 3.[44]

Queen. The pretty vaulting sea refus'd to drown me;
Knowing, that thou wou'dst have me drown'd on shore,
With tears as salt as sea, through thy unkindness.

Second part Henry VI. *act* 3. *sc.* 6.[45] <221>

Here there is no manner of resemblance but in the word *drown;* for there is no real resemblance between being drown'd at sea, and dying of grief at land. But perhaps this sort of tinsel wit may have a propriety in it, when used to express an affected, not a real passion, which was the Queen's case.

Pope has several similes of the same stamp. I shall transcribe one or two from the *Essay on Man,* the gravest and most instructive of all his performances:

And hence one master passion in the breast,
Like Aaron's serpent, swallows up the rest.

Epist. 2. *l.* 131.

And again, talking of this same ruling or master passion:

Nature its mother, Habit is its nurse;
Wit, spirit, faculties, but make it worse;
Reason itself but gives it edge and pow'r;
As heav'n's bless'd beam turns vinegar more sour.

Ibid. l. 145.

Lord Bolingbroke, speaking of historians:

Where their sincerity as to fact is doubtful, we strike out truth by the confrontation of different accounts; as we strike out sparks of fire by the collision of flints and steel. <222>

44. Act 1, sc. 1.
45. Act 3, sc. 2.

Let us vary the phrase a very little, and there will not remain a shadow of resemblance. Thus,

> We discover truth by the confrontation of different accounts; as we strike out sparks of fire by the collision of flints and steel.

Racine makes Pyrrhus say to Andromaque,

> Vaincu, chargé de fers, de regrets consumé,
> Brulé de plus de feux que je n'en allumai,
> Helas! fus-je jamais si cruel que vous l'êtes?[46]

And Orestes in the same strain:

> Que les Scythes sont moins cruel qu' Hermione.[47]

Similes of this kind put one in mind of a ludicrous French song:

> Je croyois Janneton
> Aussi douce que belle:
> Je croyois Janneton
> Plus douce qu'un mouton;
>   Helas! helas!
> Elle est cent fois, mille fois, plus cruelle
> Que n'est le tigre aux bois.[48]

Again:

---

46. "Defeated, bound with chains, consumed by regret, burned even more by fires that I myself lit. Alas. Was ever I as cruel as you?" (Act 1, sc. 4)

47. "The Scythians are less cruel than Hermione." (Act 2, sc. 2)

48. Molière, *Le bourgeois gentilhomme,* Act 1.2.

> I thought Jeanneton
> Fair and sweet to be;
> I thought Jeanneton
> Sweeter than sweet mutton;
> Alas! Alas!
> A hundred thousand times more cruel she
> Than the tigers of the pass.
>   (Moliere, *Don Juan and Other Plays,* trans. George Graveley and
>   Ian Maclean, Oxford: Oxford University Press, 1968)

> Helas! l'amour m'a pris,
> Comme le chat fait la souris.[49] <223>

A vulgar Irish ballad begins thus:

> I have as much love in store
> As there's apples in Portmore.

Where the subject is burlesque or ludicrous, such similes are far from being improper. Horace says pleasantly,

> Quamquam tu levior cortice.   *L. 3. ode 9.*[50]

And Shakespear,

> In breaking oaths he's stronger than Hercules.[51]

And this leads me to observe, that beside the foregoing comparisons, which are all serious, there is a species, the end and purpose of which is to excite gaiety or mirth. Take the following examples.

Falstaff, speaking to his page:

> I do here walk before thee, like a sow that hath overwhelmed all her litter
> but one.   *Second part Henry* IV. *act* 1. *sc.* 4.[52]

> I think he is not a pick-purse, nor a horse-stealer; but for his verity in love,
> I do think him as concave as a cover'd goblet, or a worm-eaten nut.
>   *As you like it, act* 3. *sc.* 10.[53] <224>

> This sword a dagger had his page,
> That was but little for his age;
> And therefore waited on him so,
> As dwarfs upon knights-errant do.   *Hudibras, canto* 1.

---

49. "Alas! Love has caught me, as the cat catches the mouse."
50. "though . . . lighter than the cork."
51. *All's Well That Ends Well.* Act 4, sc. 3. Read as: "He professes not keeping of oaths; in breaking 'em he is stronger than Hercules."
52. Act 1, sc. 2.
53. Act 3, sc. 4.

Description of Hudibras's horse:

> He was well stay'd, and in his gait
> Preserv'd a grave, majestic state.
> At spur or switch no more he skipt,
> Or mended pace, than Spaniard whipt:
> And yet so fiery, he would bound
> As if he griev'd to touch the ground:
> That Caesar's horse, who, as fame goes,
> Had corns upon his feet and toes,
> Was not by half so tender hooft,
> Nor trod upon the ground so soft.
> And as that beast would kneel and stoop,
> (Some write) to take his rider up;
> So Hubibras his ('tis well known)
> Would often do to set him down.   *Canto* 1.

> Honour is, like a widow, won
> With brisk attempt and putting on,
> With entering manfully, and urging;
> Not slow approaches, like a virgin.   *Canto* 1.

> The sun had long since in the lap
> Of Thetis taken out his nap; <225>
> And, like a lobster boil'd, the morn
> From black to red began to turn.   *Part* 2. *canto* 2.

Books, like men their authors, have but one way of coming into the world;
but there are ten thousand to go out of it, and return no more.

Tale of a Tub.

And in this the world may perceive the difference between the integrity
of a generous author, and that of a common friend. The latter is observed
to adhere close in prosperity; but on the decline of fortune, to drop suddenly off: whereas the generous author, just on the contrary, finds his hero
on the dunghill, from thence by gradual steps raises him to a throne, and

then immediately withdraws, expecting not so much as thanks for his
pains.   *Tale of a Tub.*

The most accomplish'd way of using books at present is, to serve them as
some do lords, learn their *titles,* and then brag of their acquaintance.
                                                          Tale of a Tub.

> Box'd in a chair, the beau impatient sits,
> While spouts run clatt'ring o'er the roof by fits;
> And ever and anon with frightful din
> The leather sounds; he trembles from within.
> So when Troy chairmen bore the wooden steed,
> Pregnant with Greeks, impatient to be freed,
> (Those bully Greeks, who, as the moderns do,
> Instead of paying chairmen, run them through), <226>
> Laocoon struck the outside with his spear,
> And each imprison'd hero quak'd for fear.
>   *Description of a City Shower. Swift.*

> Clubs, diamonds, hearts, in wild disorder seen,
> With throngs promiscuous strow the level green.
> Thus when dispers'd a routed army runs,
> Of Asia's troops, and Afric's sable sons,
> With like confusion, different nations fly,
> Of various habit, and of various dye,
> The pierc'd battalions disunited, fall
> In heaps on heaps; one fate o'erwhelms them all.
>   *Rape of the Lock, canto* 3.

He does not consider, that sincerity in love is as much out of fashion as
sweet snuff; nobody takes it now.   *Careless Husband.*

Lady Easy. My dear, I am afraid you have provoked her a little too far.
Sir Charles. O! Not at all. You shall see, I'll sweeten her, and she'll cool
like a dish of tea.   *Ibid.* <227>

Figures

The endless variety of expressions brought under the head of tropes and figures by ancient critics and grammarians, makes it evident, that they had no precise criterion for distinguishing tropes and figures from plain language. It was accordingly my opinion, that little could be made of them in the way of rational criticism; till discovering, by a sort of accident, that many of them depend on principles formerly explained, I gladly embrace the opportunity to show the influence of these principles where it would be the least expected. Confining myself therefore to such figures, I am luckily freed from much trash; without dropping, as far as I remember, any trope or figure that merits a proper name. And I begin with Prosopopoeia or personification, which is justly intitled to the first place. <228>

SECTION I

Personification.

The bestowing sensibility and voluntary motion upon things inanimate, is so bold a figure, as to require, one should imagine, very peculiar circumstances for operating the delusion: and yet, in the language of poetry, we find variety of expressions, which, though commonly reduced to that figure, are used without ceremony, or any sort of preparation; as, for example, *thirsty* ground, *hungry* church-yard, *furious* dart, *angry* ocean. These epithets, in their proper meaning, are attributes of sensible beings: what is their meaning, when applied to things inanimate? do they make us conceive the ground, the church-yard, the dart, the ocean, to be endued with animal functions? This is a curious inquiry; and whether so or not, it cannot be declined in handling the present subject.

The mind, agitated by certain passions, is prone to bestow sensibility upon things inanimate.* This is an additional instance of the influence of passion upon our opinions and belief.† I give examples. Antony, mourning over the body of Cae-<229>sar murdered in the senate-house, vents his passion in the following words:

> *Antony.* O pardon me, thou bleeding piece of earth,
> That I am meek and gentle with these butchers.
> Thou art the ruins of the noblest man
> That ever lived in the tide of time.
>
> *Julius Caesar, act* 3. *sc.* 4.[1]

Here Antony must have been impressed with a notion, that the body of Caesar was listening to him, without which the speech would be foolish and absurd. Nor will it appear strange, considering what is said in the chapter above cited, that passion should have such power over the mind of man. In another example of the same kind, the earth, as a common mother, is animated to give refuge against a father's unkindness:

> *Almeria.* O Earth, behold, I kneel upon thy bosom,
> And bend my flowing eyes to stream upon
> Thy face, imploring thee that thou wilt yield!
> Open thy bowels of compassion, take
> Into thy womb the last and most forlorn
> Of all thy race. Hear me, thou common parent;
> —I have no parent else.—Be thou a mother,
> And step between me and the curse of him,
> Who was—who was, but is no more a father;
> But brands my innocence with horrid crimes;
> And for the tender names of *child* and *daughter,*
> Now calls me *murderer* and *parricide.*
>
> *Mourning Bride, act* 4. *sc.* 7. <230>

---

* Page 204.
† Chap. 2. part 5.
1. Act 3, sc. 1: read "times" for "time."

Plaintive passions are extremely solicitous for vent; and a soliloquy commonly answers the purpose: but when such a passion becomes excessive, it cannot be gratified but by sympathy from others; and if denied that consolation in a natural way, it will convert even things inanimate into sympathising beings. Thus Philoctetes complains to the rocks and promontories of the isle of Lemnos;* and Alcestes dying, invokes the sun, the light of day, the clouds, the earth, her husband's palace, &c.† Moschus, lamenting the death of Bion, conceives, that the birds, the fountains, the trees, lament with him. The shepherd, who in Virgil bewails the death of Daphnis, expresseth himself thus:

> Daphni, tuum Poenos etiam ingemuisse leones
> Interitum, montesque feri sylvaeque loquuntur.
>
> *Eclogue*, v. 27.[2]

Again:

> Illum etiam lauri, illum etiam flevere myricae.
> Pinifer illum etiam sola sub rupe jacentem
> Maenalus, et gelidi fleverunt saxa Lycaei.   *Eclogue*, x. 13.[3]

Again:

> Ho visto al pianto mio
> Responder per pietate i sassi e l'onde; <231>
> E sospirar le fronde
> Ho visto al pianto mio.
> Ma non ho visto mai,

---

* Philoctetes of Sophocles, act 4. sc. 2.

† Alcestes of Euripides, act 2. sc. 1.

2. "Daphnis, the wild mountains and woods tell us that even the African lions moaned over thy death."

3. "For him, even the laurels, even the tamarisks wept. For him, as he lay beneath a lonely rock, even the pine-crowned Maenalus wept, and the crags of cold Lycacus."

Ne spero di vedere
Compassion ne la crudele, e bella.

Aminta di Tasso, act 1. *sc.* 2.[4]

That such personification is derived from nature, will not admit the least remaining doubt, after finding it in poems of the darkest ages and remotest countries. No figure is more frequent in Ossian's works; for example,

The battle is over, said the King, and I behold the blood of my friends. Sad is the heath of Lena, and mournful the oaks of Cromla.

Again:

The sword of Gaul trembles at his side, and longs to glitter in his hand.

King Richard having got intelligence of Bolingbroke's invasion, says, upon landing in England from his Irish expedition, in a mixture of joy and resentment,

———— I weep for joy
To stand upon my kingdom once again.
Dear earth, I do salute thee with my hand,
Though rebels wound thee with their horses hoofs.
As a long parted mother with her child
Plays fondly with her tears, and smiles in meeting; <232>
So weeping, smiling, greet I thee, my earth,
And do thee favour with my royal hands.
Feed not thy sovereign's foe, my gentle earth,
Nor with thy sweets comfort his rav'nous sense:
But let thy spiders that suck up thy venom,
And heavy-gaited toads, lie in their way;
Doing annoyance to the treach'rous feet,
Which with usurping steps do trample thee.
Yield stinging nettles to mine enemies;
And, when they from thy bosom pluck a flower,
Guard it, I pr'ythee, with a lurking adder;

---

4. "Rocks and waves I have seen moved to pity by my complaints—I have heard the trees accompany my tears with sighs, but I have never found, nor hope to find, compassion in this cruel fair." (*Aminta,* trans. E. Grillo)

Whose double tongue may with a mortal touch
Throw death upon thy sovereign's enemies.
Mock not my senseless conjuration, Lords:
This earth shall have a feeling; and these stones
Prove armed soldiers, ere her native king
Shall faulter under foul rebellious arms.

Richard II. *act* 3. *sc.* 2.[5]

After a long voyage, it was customary among the ancients to salute the natal soil. A long voyage being of old a greater enterprise than at present, the safe return to one's country after much fatigue and danger, was a delightful circumstance; and it was natural to give the natal soil a temporary life, in order to sympathise with the traveller. See an example, *Agamemnon* of Aeschilus, act 3. in the beginning. Regret for leaving a place one has been accustomed to, has the same effect.* <233>

Terror produceth the same effect: it is communicated in thought to every thing around, even to things inanimate:

Speaking of Polyphemus,

Clamorem immensum tollit, quo pontus et omnes
Intremuere undae, penitusque exterrita tellus
Italiae   *Aeneid.* iii. 672.[6]

———— As when old Ocean roars,
And heaves huge surges to the *trembling* shores.

Iliad ii. 249.

Go, view the settling sea. The stormy wind is laid; but the billows still tremble on the deep, and seem to fear the blast.   *Fingal.*

---

* Philoctetes of Sophocles, at the close.
5. Read "rebellion's" in the last line.
6. "He raises a mighty roar, whereat the sea and all its waves shuddered and the land of Italy was affrighted far within, and Aetna bellowed in its winding caverns." Read "Construemere" for "Intremuere."

Racine, in the tragedy of *Phedra,* describing the sea-monster that destroyed Hippolytus, conceives the sea itself to be struck with terror as well as the spectators:

> Le flot qui l' apporta recule epouvanté.[7]

A man also naturally communicates his joy to all objects around, animate or inanimate:

> ———— As when to them who sail <234>
> Beyond the Cape of Hope, and now are past
> Mozambic, off at sea north-east winds blow
> Sabean odour from the spicy shore
> Of Arabie the Blest; with such delay
> Well pleas'd, they slack their course, and many a league
> Cheer'd with the grateful smell old Ocean smiles.
>
> *Paradise Lost, b.* 4.

I have been profuse of examples, to show what power many passions have to animate their objects. In all the foregoing examples, the personification, if I mistake not, is so complete as to afford conviction, momentary indeed, of life and intelligence. But it is evident from numberless instances, that personification is not always so complete: it is a common figure in descriptive poetry, understood to be the language of the writer, and not of the persons he describes: in this case, it seldom or never comes up to conviction, even momentary, of life and intelligence. I give the following examples.

> First in *his* east the glorious lamp was seen,
> Regent of day, and all th' horizon round
> Invested with bright rays; jocund to run
> *His* longitude through heav'n's high road: the gray
> Dawn and the Pleiades before *him* danc'd,
> Shedding sweet influence. Less bright, the moon,
> But opposite, in levell'd west was set

---

7. "The wave that brought it in recoiled aghast" (act 5, sc. 5).

His mirror, with full face borrowing *her* light <235>
From *him;* for other light *she* needed none.

Paradise Lost, b. 7. l. 370.*

Night's candles are burnt out, and jocund day
Stands tiptoe on the misty mountain-tops.

Romeo and Juliet, act 3. *sc.* 7.[8]

But look, the morn, in russet mantle clad,
Walks o'er the dew of yon high eastward hill.

Hamlet, act 1. *sc.* 1.

It may, I presume, be taken for granted, that, in the foregoing instances, the personification, either with the poet or his reader, amounts not to a conviction of intelligence: that the sun, the moon, the day, the morn, are not here understood to be sensible beings. What then is the nature of this personification? I think it must be referred to the imagination: the inanimate object is imagined to be a sensible being, but without any conviction, even for a moment, that it really is so. Ideas or fictions of imagination have power to raise emotions in the mind;† and when any thing inanimate is, in imagination, supposed to be a sensible <236> being, it makes by that means a greater figure than when an idea is formed of it according to truth. This sort of personification, however, is far inferior to the other in elevation. Thus personification is of two kinds. The first, being more noble, may be termed *passionate personification:* the other, more humble, *descriptive personification;* because seldom or never is personification in a description carried to conviction.

The imagination is so lively and active, that its images are raised with very little effort; and this justifies the frequent use of descriptive personification. This figure abounds in Milton's *Allegro,* and *Penseroso.*

* The chastity of the English language, which in common usage distinguishes by genders no words but what signify beings male and female, gives thus a fine opportunity for the prosopopoeia; a beauty unknown in other languages, where every word is masculine or feminine.

† See Appendix, containing definitions and explanations of terms, § 29.

8. Act 3, sc. 5.

Abstract and general terms, as well as particular objects, are often necessary in poetry. Such terms however are not well adapted to poetry, because
they suggest not any image: I can readily form an image of Alexander or
Achilles in wrath; but I cannot form an image of wrath in the abstract, or
of wrath independent of a person. Upon that account, in works addressed
to the imagination, abstract terms are frequently personified: but such personification rests upon imagination merely, not upon conviction.

> Sed mihi vel Tellus optem prius ima dehiscat;
> Vel Pater omnipotens adigat me fulmine ad umbras,
> Pallentes umbras Erebi, noctemque profundam,
> Ante *pudor* quam te violo, aut tua jura resolvo.
>
> *Aeneid.* iv. *l.* 24.[9] <237>

Thus, to explain the effects of slander, it is imagined to be a voluntary agent:

> ———— No, 'tis Slander;
> Whose edge is sharper than the sword; whose tongue
> Out-venoms all the worms of Nile; whose breath
> Rides on the posting winds, and doth belie
> All corners of the world, kings, queens, and states,
> Maids, matrons: nay, the secrets of the grave
> This viperous Slander enters.
>
> *Shakespear, Cymbeline, act* 3. *sc.* 4.

As also human passions: take the following example:

> ———— For *Pleasure* and *Revenge*
> Have ears more deaf than adders, to the voice
> Of any true decision.   *Troilus and Cressida, act* 2. *sc.* 4.[10]

Virgil explains fame and its effects by a still greater variety of action.* And
Shakespeare personifies death and its operations in a manner singularly
fanciful:

---

* *Aeneid* iv. 173.

9. "But rather, I would pray, may earth yawn for me to its depths, or may the Almighty
Father hurl me with his bolt to the shades—the pale shades and abysmal might of Ere-
bus—before, O Shame, I violate thee or break thy laws!"

10. Act 2, sc. 2.

————— Within the hollow crown
That rounds the mortal temples of a king,
Keeps Death his court; and there the antic sits,
Scoffing his state, and grinning at his pomp;
Allowing him a breath, a little scene <238>
To monarchize, be fear'd, and kill with looks;
Infusing him with self and vain conceit,
As if his flesh, which walls about our life,
Were brass impregnable; and humour'd thus,
Comes at the last, and with a little pin
Bores through his castle-walls, and farewell king.

Richard II. *act* 3. *sc.* 4.[11]

Not less successfully is life and action given even to sleep:

King Henry. How many thousands of my poorest subjects
Are at this hour asleep! O gentle *Sleep,*
Nature's soft nurse, how have I frighted thee,
That thou no more wilt weigh my eye-lids down,
And steep my senses in forgetfulness?
Why rather, Sleep, ly'st thou in smoky cribs,
Upon uneasy pallets stretching thee,
And hush'd with buzzing night-flies to thy slumber,
Than in the perfum'd chambers of the great,
Under the canopies of costly state,
And lull'd with sounds of sweetest melody?
O thou dull god, why ly'st thou with the vile
In loathsome beds, and leav'st the kingly couch,
A watch-case to a common larum-bell?
Wilt thou, upon the high and giddy mast,
Seal up the ship-boy's eyes, and rock his brains
In cradle of the rude imperious surge,
And in the visitation of the winds,
Who take the ruffian billows by the top,
Curling their monstrous heads, and hanging them
With deaf'ning clamours in the slippery shrouds, <239>

11. Act 3, sc. 2: read "As if this flesh" for "As if his flesh."

That, with the hurly, Death itself awakes?
Can'st thou, O partial Sleep, give thy repose
To the wet sea-boy in an hour so rude;
And, in the calmest and the stillest night,
With all appliances and means to boot,
Deny it to a king? Then, happy low! lie down;
Uneasy lies the head that wears a crown.

Second part, Henry IV. *act* 3. *sc.* 1.[12]

I shall add one example more, to show that descriptive personification may be used with propriety, even where the purpose of the discourse is instruction merely:

Oh! let the steps of youth be cautious,
How they advance into a dangerous world;
Our duty only can conduct us safe.
Our passions are seducers: but of all,
The strongest *Love.* He first approaches us
In childish play, wantoning in our walks:
If heedlessly we wander after him,
As he will pick out all the dancing-way,
We're lost, and hardly to return again.
We should take warning: he is painted blind,
To show us, if we fondly follow him,
The precipices we may fall into.
Therefore let *Virtue* take him by the hand:
Directed so, he leads to certain joy.   *Southern.*[13]

Hitherto success has attended our steps: but whether we shall complete our progress with equal success, seems doubtful; for when we look back <240> to the expressions mentioned in the beginning, *thirsty* ground, *furious* dart, and such like, it seems no less difficult than at first, to say whether there be in them any sort of personification. Such expressions evidently raise not the slightest conviction of sensibility: nor do I think they amount

---

12. Second line read: "Are at this hour asleep! O Sleep! O gentle Sleep, . . ." Read "clouds" for "shrouds"; "and most stillest night" for "the stillest night."

13. Act 2, sc. 1, *The Fate of Capua—A Tragedy,* 1700.

to descriptive personification; because, in them, we do not even figure the ground or the dart to be animated. If so, they cannot at all come under the present subject. To show which, I shall endeavour to trace the effect that such expressions have in the mind. Doth not the expression *angry ocean,* for example, tacitly compare the ocean in a storm to a man in wrath? By this tacit comparison, the ocean is elevated above its rank in nature; and yet personification is excluded, because, by the very nature of comparison, the things compared are kept distinct, and the native appearance of each is preserved. It will be shown afterward, that expressions of this kind belong to another figure, which I term *a figure of speech,* and which employs the seventh section of the present chapter.

Tho' thus in general we can distinguish descriptive personification from what is merely a figure of speech, it is, however, often difficult to say, with respect to some expressions, whether they are of the one kind or of the other. Take the following instances. <241>

> The moon shines bright: in such a night as this,
> When the sweet wind did gently *kiss* the trees,
> And they did make no noise; in such a night,
> Troilus methinks mounted the Trojan wall,
> And sigh'd his soul towards the Grecian tents
> Where Cressid lay that night.
>
> *Merchant of Venice, act* 5. *sc.* I.

> ———— ———— I have seen
> Th' *ambitious* ocean swell, and rage, and foam,
> To be exalted with the threat'ning clouds.
>
> *Julius Caesar, act* I. *sc.* 6.[14]

With respect to these and numberless other examples of the same kind, it must depend upon the reader, whether they be examples of personification, or of a figure of speech merely: a sprightly imagination will advance them to the former class; with a plain reader they will remain in the latter.

14. Act I, sc. 2.

Having thus at large explained the present figure, its different kinds, and the principles upon which it is founded; what comes next in order, is, to show in what cases it may be introduced with propriety, when it is suitable, when unsuitable. I begin with observing, that passionate personification is not promoted by every passion indifferently. All dispiriting passions are averse to it; and remorse, in particular, is too serious and severe to be gratified with a phantom of the mind. I cannot <242> therefore approve the following speech of Enobarbus, who had deserted his master Antony:

> Be witness to me, O thou blessed moon,
> When men revolted shall upon record
> Bear hateful memory, poor Enobarbus did
> Before thy face repent ———
> Oh sovereign mistress of true melancholy,
> The poisonous damp of night dispunge upon me,
> That life, a very rebel to my will,
> May hang no longer on me.
>
> *Antony and Cleopatra, act* 4. *sc.* 7.[15]

If this can be justified, it must be upon the Heathen system of theology, which converted into deities the sun, moon, and stars.

Secondly, After a passionate personification is properly introduced, it ought to be confined to its proper province, that of gratifying the passion, without giving place to any sentiment or action but what answers that purpose; for personification is at any rate a bold figure, and ought to be employed with great reserve. The passion of love, for example, in a plaintive tone, may give a momentary life to woods and rocks, in order to make them sensible of the lover's distress; but no passion will support a conviction so far stretched, as that these woods and rocks should be living witnesses to report the distress to others: <243>

> Ch' i' t'ami piu de la mia vita,
> Se tu nol sai, crudele,
> Chiedilo à queste selve

15. Act 4, sc. 9.

Che te'l diranno, et te'l diran con esse
Le fere loro e i duri sterpi, e i sassi
Di questi alpestri monti,
Ch' i' ho si spesse volte
Inteneriti al suon de' miei lamenti.

Pastor Fido, act 3. *sc.* 3.[16]

No lover who is not crazed will utter such a sentiment: it is plainly the operation of the writer, indulging his inventive faculty without regard to nature. The same observation is applicable to the following passage:

In winter's tedious nights sit by the fire
With good old folks, and let them tell thee tales
Of woful ages, long ago betid:
And ere thou bid good night, to quit their grief,
Tell them the lamentable fall of me,
And send the hearers weeping to their beds.
For why! the senseless brands will sympathise
The heavy accent of thy moving tongue,
And in compassion weep the fire out.

Richard II. *act* 5. *sc.* 1.

One must read this passage very seriously to avoid laughing. The following passage is quite extravagant: the different parts of the human body are too intimately connected with self, to be personified by the power of any passion; and after con-<244>verting such a part into a sensible being, it is still worse to make it be conceived as rising in rebellion against self:

Cleopatra. Haste, bare my arm, and rouse the serpent's fury.
Coward flesh ———

---

16. That I do love thee more then I do love
    My Life (if thou doubt'st, Cruel) ask this Grove,
    And that will tell thee; and with it each beast,
    Each stupid stock there can the same attest;
    Each stone of these high mountains, which so oft
    I with the voice of my complaints made soft.

For the first line, read "Ch'i' t'ami e t'ami piu de la mia vita."

> Wouldst thou conspire with Caesar, to betray me,
> As thou wert none of mine? I'll force thee to't.
>
> *Dryden, All for Love, act* 5.

Next comes descriptive personification; upon which I must observe, in general, that it ought to be cautiously used. A personage in a tragedy, agitated by a strong passion, deals in warm sentiments; and the reader, catching fire by sympathy, relisheth the boldest personifications: but a writer, even in the most lively description, taking a lower flight, ought to content himself with such easy personifications as agree with the tone of mind inspired by the description. Nor is even such easy personification always admitted; for in plain narrative, the mind, serious and sedate, rejects personification altogether. Strada, in his history of the Belgic wars, has the following passage, which, by a strained elevation above the tone of the subject, deviates into burlesque.

> Vix descenderat a praetoria navi Caesar; cum foeda illico exorta in portu tempestas, classem impetu disjecit, <245> praetoriam hausit; quasi non vecturam amplius Caesarem, Caesarisque fortunam.
>
> *Dec.* 1. *l.* 1.[17]

Neither do I approve, in Shakespear, the speech of King John, gravely exhorting the citizens of Angiers to a surrender; though a tragic writer has much greater latitude than a historian. Take the following specimen:

> The cannons have their bowels full of wrath;
> And ready mounted are they to spit forth
> Their iron-indignation 'gainst your walls.   *Act* 2. *sc.* 3.[18]

Secondly, If extraordinary marks of respect to a person of low rank be ridiculous, no less so is the personification of a low subject. This rule chiefly regards descriptive personification; for a subject can hardly be low that is the cause of a violent passion; in that circumstance, at least, it must be of importance. But to assign any rule other than taste merely, for avoiding

---

17. "Hardly had Caesar descended from his praetorian ship, than a dreadful storm arose in the port, which by its violence scattered the fleet and sank his ship, as if it would no longer bear Caesar or the Fortune of Caesar."

18. Act 2, sc. 1.

things below even descriptive personification, will, I am afraid, be a hard task. A poet of superior genius, possessing the power of inflaming the mind, may take liberties that would be too bold in others. Homer appears not extravagant in animating his darts and arrows: nor Thomson in animating the seasons, the winds, the rains, the dews; he even <246> ventures to animate the diamond, and doth it with propriety:

> ———— That polish'd bright
> And all its native lustre let abroad,
> Dares, as it sparkles on the fair-one's breast,
> With vain ambition emulate her eyes.

But there are things familiar and base, to which personification cannot descend. In a composed state of mind, to animate a lump of matter even in the most rapid flight of fancy, degenerates into burlesque:

> How now! What noise! that spirit's possessed with haste,
> That wounds th' unresisting postern with these strokes,
> > *Shakespear, Measure for Measure, act* 4. *sc.* 6.[19]

> ———— Or from the shore
> The plovers when to scatter o'er the heath,
> And sing their wild notes to the list'ning *waste.*
> > *Thomson, Spring, l.* 23.

Speaking of a man's hand cut off in battle:

> Te decisa suum, Laride, dextera quaerit:
> Semianimesque micant digiti; ferrumque retractant.
> > *Aeneid.* x. 395.[20]

The personification here of a hand is insufferable, especially in a plain narration: not to mention that such a trivial incident is too minutely described. <247>
The same observation is applicable to abstract terms, which ought not

---

19. Act 4, sc. 2: read "unsisting" for "unresisting."
20. "while thy severed hand, Larides, seeks its master, and the dying fingers twitch and clutch again at the sword."

to be animated unless they have some natural dignity. Thomson, in this
article, is licentious; witness the following instances out of many:

> O vale of bliss! O softly swelling hills!
> On which *the power of cultivation* lies,
> And joys to see the wonders of his toil.   *Summer, l.* 1435.

> Then sated *Hunger* bids his brother *Thirst*
> Produce the mighty bowl:[21]
> Nor wanting is the brown October, drawn
> Mature and perfect, from *his* dark retreat
> Of thirty years; and now *his honest front*
> Flames in the light refulgent.   *Autumn, l.* 516.

Thirdly, It is not sufficient to avoid improper subjects: some preparation
is necessary, in order to rouse the mind; for the imagination refuses its aid,
till it be warmed at least, if not inflamed. Yet Thomson, without the least
ceremony or preparation, introduceth each season as a sensible being:

> From brightening fields of aether fair disclos'd,
> Child of the sun, refulgent *Summer* comes,
> In pride of youth, and felt through Nature's depth.
> He comes attended by the sultry hours,
> And ever fanning breezes, on his way;
> While from his ardent look, the turning Spring <248>
> Averts her blushful face, and earth and skies
> All smiling, to his hot dominion leaves.   *Summer, l.* 1.

> See *Winter* comes, to rule the vary'd year,
> Sullen and sad with all his rising train,
> *Vapours,* and *clouds,* and *storms.*   *Winter, l.* 1.

This has violently the air of writing mechanically without taste. It is not
natural that the imagination of a writer should be so much heated at the
very commencement; and, at any rate, he cannot expect such ductility in

---

21. Kames omits five lines between the second and third lines.

his readers. But if this practice can be justified by authority, Thomson has one of no mean note: Vida begins his first eclogue in the following words:

> Dicite, vos Musae, et juvenum memorate querelas;
> Dicite; nam motas ipsas ad carmina cautes
> Et requiesse suos perhibent vaga flumina cursus.[22]

Even Shakespear is not always careful to prepare the mind for this bold figure. Take the following instance

> ———— Upon these taxations,
> The clothiers all, not able to maintain
> The many to them 'longing, have put off
> The spinsters, carders, fullers, weavers; who,
> Unfit for other life, compell'd by hunger,
> And lack of other means, in desp'rate manner <249>
> Daring th' event to th' teeth, are all in uproar
> And *Danger* serves among them.
>
> *Henry* VIII. *act* I. *sc.* 4.[23]

Fourthly, Descriptive personification, still more than what is passionate, ought to be kept within the bounds of moderation. A reader warmed with a beautiful subject, can imagine, even without passion, the winds, for example, to be animated: but still the winds are the subject; and any action ascribed to them beyond or contrary to their usual operation, appearing unnatural, seldom fails to banish the illusion altogether: the reader's imagination too far strained, refuses its aid; and the description becomes obscure, instead of being more lively and striking. In this view, the following passage, describing Cleopatra on shipboard, appears to me exceptionable.

---

22. Give me, ye sacred muses, to impart
    The hidden secrets of your tuneful art;
    Give me your awful mysteries to sing,
    Unlock, and open wide, your secret spring.
    (*Vida's Art of Poetry,* trans.
    Christopher Pitt)

23. Act I, sc. 2.

> The barge she sat in, like a burnished throne,
> Burnt on the water: the poop was beaten gold,
> Purple the sails, and so perfumed, that
> The winds were love-sick with 'em.
>
> *Antony and Cleopatra, act* 2. *sc.* 3.[24]

The winds in their impetuous course have so much the appearance of fury, that it is easy to figure them wreaking their resentment against their enemies, by destroying houses, ships, *&c.;* but to figure them love-sick, has no resemblance to them in any circumstance. In another passage, where <250> Cleopatra is also the subject, the personification of the air is carried beyond all bounds:

> ───── The city cast
> Its people out upon her; and Antony
> Inthron'd i' th' market-place, did sit alone,
> Whistling to th' air, which but for vacancy,
> Had gone to gaze on Cleopatra too,
> And made a gap in nature.
>
> *Antony and Cleopatra, act* 2. *sc.* 3.[25]

The following personification of the earth or soil is not less wild:

> She shall be dignify'd with this high honour,
> To bear my Lady's train; lest the base earth
> Should from her vesture chance to steal a kiss;
> And of so great a favour growing proud,
> Disdain to root the summer-swelling flower,
> And make rough winter everlastingly.
>
> *Two Gentlemen of Verona, act* 2. *sc.* 7.[26]

Shakespear, far from approving such intemperance of imagination, puts this speech in the mouth of a ranting lover. Neither can I relish what follows:

24. Act 2, sc. 2.
25. Act 2, sc. 2.
26. Act 2, sc. 4.

Omnia quae, Phoebo quondam meditante, beatus
Audit Eurotas, jussitque ediscere lauros,
Ille canit.   *Virgil. Buc.* vi. 82.[27]

The cheerfulness singly of a pastoral song, will <251> scarce support personification in the lowest degree. But admitting, that a river gently flowing
may be imagined a sensible being listening to a song, I cannot enter into
the conceit of the river's ordering his laurels to learn the song: here all resemblance to any thing real is quite lost. This however is copied literally by
one of our greatest poets; early indeed, before maturity of taste or judgement:

Thames heard the numbers as he flow'd along,
And bade his willows learn the moving song.
                              Pope's Pastorals, past. 4. *l.* 13.

This author, in riper years, is guilty of a much greater deviation from the
rule. Dullness may be imagined a deity or idol, to be worshipped by bad
writers; but then some sort of disguise is requisite, some bastard virtue must
be bestowed, to make such worship in some degree excusible. Yet in the
Dunciad, Dullness, without the least disguise, is made the object of worship. The mind rejects such a fiction as unnatural; for dullness is a defect,
of which even the dullest mortal is ashamed:

Then he: Great tamer of all human art!
First in my care, and ever at my heart;
Dullness! whose good old cause I yet defend,
With whom my muse began, with whom shall end,
E'er since Sir Fopling's periwig was praise,
To the last honours of the Bull and Bays! <252>
O thou! of bus'ness the directing soul!

27. Sing thou on this, thy Phoebus; and the Wood
    Where once his Fane of Parian Marble stood.
    On this his ancient Oracles rehearse.
                                    (trans. Dryden)

To this our head, like bias to the bowl,
Which, as more pond'rous, made its aim more true,
Obliquely wadling to the mark in view:
O! ever gracious to perplex'd mankind,
Still spread a healing mist before the mind:
And, lest we err by Wit's wild dancing light,
Secure us kindly in our native night.
Or, if to wit a coxcomb make pretence,
Guard the sure barrier between that and sense;
Or quite unravel all the reas'ning thread,
And hang some curious cobweb in its stead!
As, forc'd from wind-guns, lead itself can fly,
And pond'rous slugs cut swiftly through the sky;
As clocks to weight their nimble motion owe,
The wheels above urg'd by the load below:
Me Emptiness and Dullness could inspire,
And were my elasticity, and fire.   *B.* i. 163.

The following instance is stretched beyond all resemblance: it is bold
to take a part or member of a living creature, and to bestow upon it
life, volition, and action: after animating two such members, it is still
bolder to make one envy the other; for this is wide of any resemblance to
reality:

───── De nostri baci
Meritamenti sia giudice quella,
Che la bocca ha più bella.
Tutte concordemente
Elesser la bellissima Amarilli;
Ed' ella i suoi begli occhi <253>
Dolcemente chinando,
Di modesto rossor tutta si tinse,
E mostrò ben, che non men bella è dentro
Di quel che sia di fuori;
O fosse, che'l bel volto
Avesse invidia all' onorata bocca,
E s'adornasse anch' egli

Della purpurea sua pomposa vesta,
Quasi volesse dir, son bello anch'io.

Pastor Fido, act 2. *sc.* 1.[28]

Fifthly, The enthusiasm of passion may have the effect to prolong passionate personification: but descriptive personification cannot be dispatched in too few words: a circumstantiate description dissolves the charm, and makes the attempt to personify appear ridiculous. Homer succeeds in animating his darts and arrows: but such personification spun out in a French translation, is mere burlesque:

Et la fléche en furie, avide de son sang,
Part, vole à lui, l'atteint, et lui perce le flanc.[29]

Horace says happily,

Post equitem sedet atra Cura.[30]

Observe how this thought degenerates by being divided, like the former, into a number of minute parts: <254>

Un sou rempli d'erreurs, que le trouble accompagne
Et malade à la ville ainsi qu' à la campagne,

28. Let her deservedly
    The Judge of all our kisses be
    Whose mouth is fairest. With one voice
    Of peerlesse Amarillis they made choice.
    She sweetly bending her fair eyes,
    Her cheeks in modest blushes dyes,
    To shew through her transparent skin
    That she is no lesse fair within
    Then shee's without; or else her countenance
    Envying the honour done her mouth perchance
    Puts on her scarlet robes, as who
    Should say, And am not I fair too?
        (*Il Pastor Fido,* trans. Richard Fanshawe)

29. "And the arrow in its fury, thirsty for blood, departs, flies towards him, reaches him, and pierces his side."

30. "Black Care even takes her seat behind the horseman" (*Odes* 3.1.40).

En vain monte à cheval pour tromper son ennui,
Le Chagrin monte en croupe, et galope avec lui.[31]

A poet, in a short and lively expression, may animate his muse, his genius,
and even his verse: but to animate his verse, and to address a whole epistle
to it, as Boileau doth,* is insupportable.

The following passage is not less faulty:

Her fate is whisper'd by the gentle breeze,
And told in sighs to all the trembling trees;
The trembling trees, in ev'ry plain and wood,
Her fate remurmer to the silver flood;
The silver flood, so lately calm, appears
Swell'd with new passion, and o'erflows with tears;
The winds, and trees, and floods, her death deplore,
Daphne, our grief! our glory! now no more.

Pope's Pastorals, iv. 61.

Let grief or love have the power to animate the winds, the trees, the floods,
provided the figure be dispatched in a single expression: even in that case,
the figure seldom has a good effect; because grief or love of the pastoral kind,
are causes rather too faint for so violent an effect as imagining the winds,
trees, or floods, to be sensible beings. But when this figure is deliberately
spread out, <255> with great regularity and accuracy, through many lines,
the reader, instead of relishing it, is struck with its ridiculous appearance.

SECTION II

Apostrophe.

This figure and the former are derived from the same principle. If, to humour a plaintive passion, we can bestow a momentary sensibility upon an

* Epistle 10.
31. "A blundering fool, whom trouble and sickness afflicts in town and country alike,
in vain mounts his steed to escape his worries, because Sorrow rides as pillion and gallops
along with him."

inanimate object, it is not more difficult to bestow a momentary presence upon a sensible being who is absent:

> Hinc Drepani me portus et illaetabilis ora
> Accipit. Hic, pelagi tot tempestatibus actus,
> Heu! genitorem, omnis curae casusque levamen,
> Amitto Anchisen: *hic me pater optime fessum*
> *Deseris,* heu! tantis nequicquam erepte periclis.
> Nec vates Helenus, cum multa horrenda moneret,
> Hos mihi praedixit luctus; non dira Celaeno.
>
> *Aeneid.* iii. 707.[32]

Strike the harp in praise of Bragela, whom I left in the isle of mist, the spouse of my love. Dost thou raise thy fair face from the rock to find the sails of Cuchullin? The sea is rolling far distant, and its white foam shall deceive thee for my sails. Retire, for it is night, my love, and the dark winds sigh in <256> thy hair. Retire to the hall of my feasts, and think of the times that are past; for I will not return till the storm of war is gone. O Connal, speak of wars and arms, and send her from my mind; for lovely with her raven-hair is the white-bosom'd daughter of Sorglan.

Fingal, b. i.

Speaking of Fingal absent,

Happy are thy people, O Fingal; thine arm shall fight their battles. Thou art the first in their dangers; the wisest in the days of their peace: thou speakest, and thy thousands obey; and armies tremble at the sound of thy steel. Happy are thy people, O Fingal.

This figure is sometimes joined with the former: things inanimate, to qualify them for listening to a passionate expostulation, are not only personified, but also conceived to be present:

32. "Next the harbour of Drepanum and its joyless shore receive me. Here I, who have been driven by so many ocean-storms, lose, alas! my father Anchises, solace of every care and chance; here, best of fathers, thou leavest me in my weariness, snatched, alas! From such mighty perils all for naught. Nor did the seer Helenus, though he warned me of many horrors, nor grim Celaeno foretell me this grief."

Et si fata Deûm, si mens non laeva fuisset,
Impulerat ferro Argolicas foedare latebras:
Trojaque nunc stares, Priamique arx alta maneres.

                              Aeneid. ii. 54.[33]

    Helena.———— Poor Lord, is't I
That chase thee from thy country, and expose
Those tender limbs of thine to the event
Of non-sparing war? And is it I
That drive thee from the sportive court, where thou
Wast shot at with fair eyes, to be the mark <257>
Of smoky muskets? *O you leaden messengers,*
That ride upon the violent speed of fire,
Fly with false aim; pierce the still moving air
That sings with piercing; do not touch my Lord.

                    All's well that ends well, act 3. *sc.* 4.[34]

And let them lift ten thousand swords, said Nathos with a smile: the sons
of car-borne Usnoth will never tremble in danger. Why dost thou roll with
all thy foam, thou roaring sea of Ullin? why do ye rustle on your dark
wings, ye whistling tempests of the sky? Do ye think, ye storms, that ye
keep Nathos on the coast? No; his soul detains him; children of the night!
Althos, bring my father's arms, *&c.*   *Fingal.*

Whither hast thou fled, O wind, said the King of Morven! Dost thou
rustle in the chambers of the south, and pursue the shower in other lands?
Why comest not thou to my sails, to the blue face of my seas? The foe is
in the land of Morven, and the King is absent.   *Fingal.*

Hast thou left thy blue course in heaven, golden-hair'd son of the sky! The
west hath open'd its gates; the bed of thy repose is there. The waves gather
to behold thy beauty: they lift their trembling heads; they see thee lovely

33. "And had the gods' decrees, had our mind not been perverse, he had driven us to
befoul with steel the Argive den, and Troy would now be standing, and thou, lofty citadel
of Priam, wouldst still abide!"
    34. Act 3, sc. 2.

in thy sleep; but they shrink away with fear. Rest in thy shadowy cave, O Sun! and let thy return be in joy.   *Fingal.*

Daughter of Heaven, fair art thou! the silence of <258> thy face is pleasant. Thou comest forth in loveliness: the stars attend thy blue steps in the east. The clouds rejoice in thy presence, O Moon! and brighten their dark-brown sides. Who is like thee in heaven, daughter of the night? The stars are ashamed in thy presence, and turn aside their sparkling eyes. Whither dost thou retire from thy course, when the darkness of thy countenance grows? Hast thou thy hall like Ossian? Dwellest thou in the shadow of grief? Have thy sisters fallen from heaven? and are they who rejoiced with thee at night no more? ——— Yes, they have fallen, fair light; and often dost thou retire to mourn. ——— But thou thyself shalt, one night, fail; and leave thy blue path in heaven. The stars will then lift their heads: they, who in thy presence were ashamed, will rejoice.   *Fingal.*

This figure, like all others, requires an agitation of mind. In plain narrative, as, for example, in giving the genealogy of a family, it has no good effect:

> ——— Fauno Picus pater; isque parentem
> Te, Saturne, refert; tu sanguinis ultimus auctor.
>
> *Aeneid.* vii. 48.[35] <259>

SECTION III

Hyperbole.

In this figure, by which an object is magnified or diminished beyond truth, we have another effect of the foregoing principle. An object of an uncommon size, either very great of its kind or very little, strikes us with surprise; and this emotion produces a momentary conviction that the object is greater or less than it is in reality:* the same effect, precisely, attends figu-

---

* See chap. 8.

35. "Faunus' sire was Picus, and he boasts thee, O Saturn, as his father; thou art first founder of the line."

rative grandeur or littleness; and hence the hyperbole, which expresses that momentary conviction. A writer, taking advantage of this natural delusion, warms his description greatly by the hyperbole: and the reader, even in his coolest moments, relishes the figure, being sensible that it is the operation of nature upon a glowing fancy.

It cannot have escaped observation, that a writer is commonly more successful in magnifying by a hyperbole than in diminishing. The reason is, that a minute object contracts the mind, and fetters its power of imagination; but that the mind, dilated and inflamed with a grand object, moulds <260> objects for its gratification with great facility. Longinus, with respect to a diminishing hyperbole, quotes the following ludicrous thought from a comic poet: "He was owner of a bit of ground no larger than a Lacedemonian letter."* But, for the reason now given, the hyperbole has by far the greater force in magnifying objects; of which take the following examples:

> For all the land which thou seest, to thee will I give it, and to thy seed for ever. And I will make thy seed as the dust of the earth: so that if a man can number the dust of the earth, then shall thy seed also be numbered.
>
> *Genesis* xiii. 15. 16.

> Illa vel intactae segetis per summa volaret
> Gramina: nec teneras cursu laesisset aristas.
>
> *Aeneid.* vii. 808.[36]

> ———— Atque imo barathri ter gurgite vastos
> Sorbet in abruptum fluctus, rursusque sub auras
> Erigit alternos, et sidera verberat undâ.   *Aeneid.* iii. 421.[37]

> ———— Horificis juxta tonat Aetna ruinis,
> Interdumque atram prorumpit ad aethera nubem,

---

* Chap. 31. of his Treatise on the Sublime.

36. "She might have flown o'er the topmost blades of unmown corn, nor in her course bruised the tender ears."

37. "And at the bottom of her seething chasm thrice she sucks the vast waves into the abyss, and again in turn casts them upwards, lashing the stars with spray."

Turbine fumantem piceo et candente favilla:
Attollitque globos flammarum, et sidera lambit.

Aeneid. iii. 571.[38] <261>

Speaking of Polyphemus,

———— Ipse arduus, altaque pulsat
Sidera.   *Aeneid.* iii. 619.[39]

———— When he speaks,
The air, a charter'd libertine, is still.   *Henry* V. *act* i. *sc.* i.

Now shield with shield, with helmet helmet clos'd,
To armour armour, lance to lance oppos'd,
Host against host with shadowy squadrons drew,
The sounding darts in iron tempests flew,
Victors and vanquish'd join promiscuous cries,
And shrilling shouts and dying groans arise;
With streaming blood the slipp'ry fields are dy'd,
And slaughter'd heroes swell the dreadful tide.

Iliad iv. 508.

The following may also pass, though far stretched.

E conjungendo à temerario ardire
Estrema forza, e infaticabil lena
Vien che si' impetuoso il ferro gire,
Che ne trema la terra, e'l ciel balena.

Gierusalem, cant. 6. *st.* 46.[40]

38. "Near at hand Aetna thunders with terrifying crashes, and now hurls forth to the sky a black cloud, smoking with pitch-black eddy and glowing ashes, and uplifts balls of flame and licks the stars."
39. "He, gigantic, strikes the stars on high."
40. Uniting force extreme, with endlesse wrath,
Supporting both with youth and strength untired,
His thundering blowes so fast about he la'th,
That skies and earth the flying sparkles fired.
(*Gerusalemme Liberata,* trans. Fairfax)

Quintilian* is sensible that this figure is natural: "For," says he, "not contented with truth, we naturally incline to augment or diminish beyond it; and for that reason the hyperbole is <262> familiar even among the vulgar and illiterate": and he adds, very justly, "That the hyperbole is then proper, when the subject of itself exceeds the common measure." From these premises, one would not expect the following inference, the only reason he can find for justifying this figure of speech, "Conceditur enim amplius dicere, quia dici quantum est, non potest: meliusque ultra quam citra stat oratio." (We are indulged to say more than enough, because we cannot say enough; and it is better to be above than under). In the name of wonder, why this childish reasoning, after observing that the hyperbole is founded on human nature? I could not resist this personal stroke of criticism; intended not against our author, for no human creature is exempt from error, but against the blind veneration that is paid to the ancient classic writers, without distinguishing their blemishes from their beauties.

Having examined the nature of this figure, and the principle on which it is erected, I proceed, as in the first section, to the rules by which it ought to be governed. And, in the first place, it is a capital fault, to introduce an hyperbole in the description of any thing ordinary or familiar; for in such a case, it is altogether unnatural, being destitute of surprise, its only foundation. Take the following instance, where the subject is extremely familiar, *viz.* swimming to gain the shore after a shipwreck. <263>

> I saw him beat the surges under him,
> And ride upon their backs; he trode the water;
> Whose enmity he flung aside, and breasted
> The surge most swoln that met him: his bold head
> 'Bove the contentious waves he kept, and oar'd
> Himself with his good arms, in lusty strokes
> To th' *shore,* that o'er his wave-borne basis bow'd,
> As stooping to relieve him.   *Tempest, act* 2. *sc.* 1.

In the next place, it may be gathered from what is said, that an hyperbole can never suit the tone of any dispiriting passion: sorrow in particular will

---

* L. 8. cap. 6. in fin.

never prompt such a figure; for which reason the following hyperboles must
be condemned as unnatural.

> *K. Rich.* Aumerle, thou weep'st, my tender-hearted cousin!
> We'll make foul weather with despised tears;
> Our sighs, and they, shall lodge the summer-corn,
> And make a dearth in this revolting land.
> > *Richard* II. *act* 3. *sc.* 6.[41]

> Draw them to Tyber's bank, and weep your tears
> Into the channel, till the lowest stream
> Do kiss the most exalted shores of all.
> > *Julius Caesar, act* 1. *sc.* 1.

Thirdly, A writer, if he wish to succeed, ought always to have the reader
in his eye: he ought in particular never to venture a bold thought or <264>
expression, till the reader be warmed and prepared. For that reason, an hyperbole in the beginning of a work can never be in its place. Example:

> Jam pauca aratro jugera regiae
> Moles relinquent.   *Horat. Carm. lib.* 2. *ode* 15.[42]

The nicest point of all, is to ascertain the natural limits of an hyperbole,
beyond which being overstrained it hath a bad effect. Longinus, in the
above-cited chapter, with great propriety of thought, enters a caveat against
an hyperbole of this kind: he compares it to a bow-string, which relaxes by
overstraining, and produceth an effect directly opposite to what is intended.
To ascertain any precise boundary, would be difficult, if not impracticable.
Mine shall be an humbler task, which is, to give a specimen of what I reckon
overstrained hyperboles; and I shall be brief upon them, because examples
are to be found every where: no fault is more common among writers of
inferior rank; and instances are found even among classical writers; witness
the following hyperbole, too bold even for an Hotspur.

41. Act 3, sc. 3.
42. "A short time and our princely piles will leave but a few acres to the plough."

Hotspur, talking of Mortimer:

> In single opposition hand to hand,
> He did confound the best part of an hour <265>
> In changing hardiment with great Glendower.
> Three times they breath'd, and three times did they drink,
> Upon agreement, of swift Severn's flood;
> Who then affrighted with their bloody looks,
> Ran fearfully among the trembling reeds,
> And hid his crisp'd head in the hollow bank,
> Blood-stained with these valiant combatants.
>
> *First part Henry* IV. *act* 1. *sc.* 4.[43]

Speaking of Henry V.

> England ne'er had a king until his time:
> Virtue he had, deserving to command:
> His brandish'd sword did blind men with its beams:
> His arms spread wider than a dragon's wings:
> His sparkling eyes, replete with awful fire,
> More dazzled, and drove back his enemies,
> Than mid-day sun fierce bent against their faces.
> What should I say? his deeds exceed all speech:
> He never lifted up his hand, but conquer'd.
>
> *First part Henry* VI. *act* 1. *sc.* 1.[44]

> Se tutti gli alberi del mondo fossero penne,
> Il cielo fosse carta, il mare inchostro,
> Non basteriano a descrivere la minima
> Parte delle vostre perfettioni.[45]

> Se tante lingue havessi, e tante voci,
> Quant' occhi il cielo, e quante arene il mare,

---

43. Act 1, sc. 3.

44. Act 1, sc. 1: read "his beams" for "its beams," "wrathful" for "awful."

45. "If all the trees were pens, the sky was paper and the sea was ink, they would not capture the smallest part of your perfections."

Perderian tutto il suono, e la favella
Nel dire a pieno le vostri lodi immensi.

Guarini.[46] <266>

It is observable, that a hyperbole, even the most extravagant, commonly produces some emotion: the present hyperbole is an exception; and the reason is, that numbers, in which the extravagance entirely consists, make no impression upon the imagination when they exceed what can easily be conceived.

Lastly, An hyperbole, after it is introduced with all advantages, ought to be comprehended within the fewest words possible: as it cannot be relished but in the hurry and swelling of the mind, a leisurely view dissolves the charm, and discovers the description to be extravagant at least, and perhaps also ridiculous. This fault is palpable in a sonnet which passeth for one of the most complete in the French language. Phillis, in a long and florid description, is made as far to outshine the sun as he outshines the stars:

Le silence regnoit sur la terre et sur l'onde,
L'air devenoit serain et l'Olimpe vermeil,
Et l'amoureux Zephir affranchi du someil,
Ressuscitoit les fleurs d'une haleine féconde.

L'Aurore déployoit l'or de sa tresse blonde,
Et semoit de rubis le chemin du soleil;
Enfin ce Dieu venoit au plus grand appareil
Qu'il soit jamais venu pour éclairer le monde.

Quand la jeune Phillis au visage riant,
Sortant de son palais plus clair que l'orient, <267>
Fit voir une lumiere et plus vive et plus belle.
Sacré flambeau du jour, n'en soiez point jaloux.

---

46. *Il Pastor Fido,* act 5, sc. 2:

O glorious Lovers! If I had tongues more
Then Heaven hath eyes, or sands are on the shore,
Their voices would be drowned in the main
Sea of your endless Praises, Glorious Dame,
Daughter of Jove (eternall as thy Father).

Vous parûtes alors aussi peu devant elle,
Que les feux de la nuit avoient fait devant vous.

Malleville.[47]

There is in Chaucer a thought expressed in a single line, which gives more lustre to a young beauty, than the whole of this much-laboured poem:

Up rose the sun, and up rose Emelie.[48]

SECTION IV

The Means or Instrument conceived to be the Agent.

When we survey a number of connected objects, that which makes the greatest figure employs chiefly our attention; and the emotion it raises, if lively, prompts us even to exceed nature in the conception we form of it. Take the following examples.

For Neleus' son Alcides' *rage* had slain.

A broken rock the *force* of Pirus threw.

In these instances, the rage of Hercules and the <268> force of Pirus, being the capital circumstances, are so far exalted as to be conceived the agents that produce the effects.

In the following instances, hunger being the chief circumstance in the description, is itself imagined to be the patient.

47. Claude de Malleville (1597–1647), cited in the first edition as from *Collection of French Epigrams,* vol. 1, p. 66. "Silence reigned over land and sea, the sky became calm and Olympus vermilion, and the amorous West Wind shaking off sleep revived the flowers with a second breath. Dawn spread out the gold of her flaxen hair, and sowed with rubies the path of the sun; at last the God appeared in his finest array, that he might ever light the world. But when young and smiling Phillis left his palace more radiant than the east, he shone forth as a light yet brighter still and more beautiful. O sacred flame of day, do not be jealous that you seemed as dim beside him as the stars of the night beside you."

48. Geoffrey Chaucer, *The Knight's Tale,* 2273.

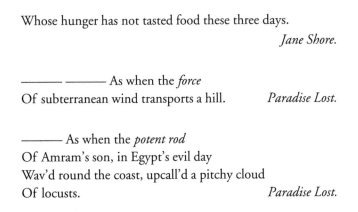

Whose hunger has not tasted food these three days.

Jane Shore.

——— ——— As when the *force*
Of subterranean wind transports a hill. *Paradise Lost.*

——— As when the *potent rod*
Of Amram's son, in Egypt's evil day
Wav'd round the coast, upcall'd a pitchy cloud
Of locusts. *Paradise Lost.*

SECTION V

*A Figure, which, among related Objects, extends the Properties
of one to another.*

This figure is not dignified with a proper name, because it has been over-looked by writers. It merits, however, a place in this work; and must be distinguished from those for-<269>merly handled, as depending on a different principle. *Giddy brink, jovial wine, daring wound,* are examples of this figure. Here are adjectives that cannot be made to signify any quality of the substantives to which they are joined: a *brink,* for example, cannot be termed *giddy* in a sense, either proper or figurative, that can signify any of its qualities or attributes. When we examine attentively the expression, we discover, that a *brink* is termed *giddy* from producing that effect in those who stand on it. In the same manner a wound is said to be *daring,* not with respect to itself, but with respect to the boldness of the person who inflicts it: and wine is said to be *jovial,* as inspiring mirth and jollity. Thus the attributes of one subject are extended to another with which it is connected; and the expression of such a thought must be considered as a figure, because the attribute is not applicable to the subject in any proper sense.

How are we to account for this figure, which we see lies in the thought, and to what principle shall we refer it? Have poets a privilege to alter the nature of things, and at pleasure to bestow attributes upon a subject to which they do not belong? We have had often occasion to inculcate, that the mind passeth easily and sweetly along a train of connected objects; and, where the objects are intimately connected, that it is disposed to carry along the good or bad properties of one to <270> another; especially when it is in any degree inflamed with these properties.* From this principle is derived the figure under consideration. Language, invented for the communication of thought, would be imperfect, if it were not expressive even of the slighter propensities and more delicate feelings: but language cannot remain so imperfect among a people who have received any polish; because language is regulated by internal feeling, and is gradually improved to express whatever passes in the mind. Thus, for example, when a sword in the hand of a coward, is termed *a coward sword,* the expression is significative of an internal operation; for the mind, in passing from the agent to its instrument, is disposed to extend to the latter the properties of the former. Governed by the same principle, we say *listening* fear, by extending the attribute *listening* of the man who listens, to the passion with which he is moved. In the expression, *bold deed,* or *audax facinus,* we extend to the effect what properly belongs to the cause. But not to waste time by making a commentary upon every expression of this kind, the best way to give a complete view of the subject, is to exhibit a table of the different relations that may give occasion to this figure. And in viewing the table, it will be observed, that the <271> figure can never have any grace but where the relations are of the most intimate kind.

1. An attribute of the cause expressed as an attribute of the effect.

Audax facinus.[49]

Of yonder fleet a *bold* discovery make.

An impious mortal gave the *daring* wound.

---

* See chap. 2. part 1. sect. 5.
49. "rash deed" (Terence, *Eunuch* 4.3.2).

——— ——— To my *advent'rous* song,
That with no middle flight intends to soar.

Paradise Lost.

2. An attribute of the effect expressed as an attribute of the cause.

Quos periisse ambos *misera* censebam in mari.

Plautus.[50]

No wonder, fallen such a *pernicious* height.

Paradise Lost.

3. An effect expressed as an attribute of the cause.

Jovial wine, Giddy brink, Drowsy night, Musing midnight, Panting height, Astonish'd thought, Mournful gloom.

Casting a dim *religious* light. *Milton, Comus.* <272>

And the *merry* bells ring round,
And the *jocund* rebecks sound. *Milton, Allegro.*

4. An attribute of a subject bestowed upon one of its parts or members.

Longing arms.

It was the nightingale, and not the lark,
That pierc'd the *fearful* hollow of thine ear.

Romeo and Juliet, act 3. sc. 7.[51]

——— ——— Oh, lay by
Those most ungentle looks and angry weapons;

50. Titus Maccius Plautus (ca. 205–184 B.C.), a comic playwright whose plays are the earliest Latin works to have survived complete: "I thought that both of them had perished in the miserable sea."
51. Act 3, sc. 5.

Unless you mean my griefs and killing fears
Should stretch me out at your *relentless* feet.

Fair Penitent, act 3.

———— ———— And ready now
To stoop with *wearied* wing, and *willing* feet,
On the bare outside of this world.   *Paradise Lost, b.* 3.[52]

5. A quality of the agent given to the instrument with which it operates.

Why peep your *coward* swords half out their shells!

6. An attribute of the agent given to the subject upon which it operates.

High-climbing hill.   *Milton.* <273>

7. A quality of one subject given to another.

Icci, *beatis* nunc Arabum invides
Gazis.   *Horat. Carm. l.* 1. *ode* 29.[53]

When sapless age, and weak unable limbs,
Should bring thy father to his *drooping* chair.

Shakespear.[54]

By art, the pilot through the boiling deep
And howling tempest, steers the *fearless* ship.

Iliad xxiii. 385.

Then, nothing loath, th' enamour'd fair he led,
And sunk transported on the *conscious* bed.

Odyssey, viii. 337.

52. *Paradise Lost,* 3.546.
53. "Iccius, art thou looking now with envious eye at the rich treasures of the Arabians."
54. *Henry VI, Part 1,* act 4, sc. 5.

A *stupid* moment motionless she stood.

Summer, l. 1336.[55]

8. A circumstance connected with a subject, expressed as a quality of the subject.

Breezy summit.

'Tis ours the chance of *fighting* fields to try.   *Iliad* i. 301.

Oh! had I dy'd before that *well-fought* wall.

Odyssey v. 395.

From this table it appears, that the adorning a cause with an attribute of the effect, is not so agreeable as the opposite expression. The progress <274> from cause to effect is natural and easy: the opposite progress resembles retrograde motion;* and therefore *panting height, astonish'd thought,* are strained and uncouth expressions, which a writer of taste will avoid.

It is not less strained, to apply to a subject in its present state, an epithet that may belong to it in some future state:

Submersasque obrue puppes.   *Aeneid.* i. 73.[56]

And mighty *ruins* fall.   *Iliad* v. 411.

Impious sons their *mangled* fathers wound.

Another rule regards this figure, That the property of one subject ought not to be bestowed upon another with which that property is incongruous:

> *K. Rich.* ——— How dare thy joints forget
> To pay their *awful* duty to our presence?

Richard II. *act* 3. *sc.* 6.[57]

---

* See chap. i.
55. Line 1346.
56. "sink and o'erwhelm the ships."
57. Act 3, sc. 3.

The connection between an awful superior and his submissive dependent is so intimate, that an attribute may readily be transferred from the one to the other: but awfulness cannot be so transferred, because it is inconsistent with submission. <275>

SECTION VI

Metaphor and Allegory.

A Metaphor differs from a simile, in form only, not in substance: in a simile, the two subjects are kept distinct in the expression, as well as in the thought; in a metaphor, the two subjects are kept distinct in the thought only, not in the expression. A hero resembles a lion, and upon that resemblance many similes have been raised by Homer and other poets. But instead of resembling a lion, let us take the aid of the imagination, and feign or figure the hero to be a lion: by that variation the simile is converted into a metaphor; which is carried on by describing all the qualities of a lion that resemble those of the hero. The fundamental pleasure here, that of resemblance, belongs to the thought. An additional pleasure arises from the expression: the poet, by figuring his hero to be a lion, goes on to describe the lion in appearance, but in reality the hero; and his description is peculiarly beautiful, by expressing the virtues and qualities of the hero in new terms, which, properly speaking, belong not to him, but to the lion. This will better be understood by examples. A family connected with a common pa-<276>rent, resembles a tree, the trunk and branches of which are connected with a common root: but let us suppose, that a family is figured, not barely to be like a tree, but to be a tree; and then the simile will be converted into a metaphor, in the following manner:

> Edward's sev'n sons, whereof thyself art one,
> Were sev'n fair branches, springing from one root:
> Some of these branches by the dest'nies cut:
> But Thomas, my dear lord, my life, my Glo'ster,
> One flourishing branch of his most royal root,

Is hack'd down, and his summer-leaves all faded,
By Envy's hand and Murder's bloody axe.

Richard II. *act* I. *sc.* 3.[58]

Figuring human life to be a voyage at sea:

There is a tide in the affairs of men,
Which, taken at the flood, leads on to fortune;
Omitted, all the voyage of their life
Is bound in shallows and in miseries.
On such a full sea are we now afloat;
And we must take the current while it serves,
Or lose our ventures.   *Julius Caesar, act* 4. *sc.* 5.[59]

Figuring glory and honour to be a garland of flowers:

Hotspur. ———— Wou'd to heav'n,
Thy name in arms were now as great as mine! <277>
Pr. Henry. I'll make it greater, ere I part from thee;
And all the budding honours on thy crest
I'll crop, to make a garland for my head.

First part Henry IV. *act* 5. *sc.* 9.[60]

Figuring a man who hath acquired great reputation and honour to be a tree
full of fruit:

58. Act I, sc. 2. Modern texts read as follows:

Edward's seven sons, wherof thyself art one,
Were as seven vials of his sacred blood,
Or seven fair branches springing from one root:
Some of those seven are dried by nature's course,
Some of those branches by the Destinies cut;
But Thomas, my dear lord, my life, my Gloucester,
One vial full of Edward's sacred blood,
One flourishing branch of his most royal root,
Is crack'd, and all the precious liquor spilt;
Is hack'd down, and his summer leaves all vaded,
By envy's hand and murder's bloody axe.

59. Act 4, sc. 3.
60. Act 5, sc. 4.

——— Oh, boys, this story
The world may read in me: my body's mark'd
With Roman swords; and my report was once
First with the best of note. Cymbeline lov'd me;
And when a soldier was the theme, my name
Was not far off: then was I as a tree,
Whose boughs did bend with fruit. But in one night,
A storm or robbery, call it what you will,
Shook down my mellow hangings, nay my leaves;
And left me bare to weather.   *Cymbeline, act* 3. *sc.* 3.

Blest be thy soul, thou king of shells, said Swaran of the dark-brown shield. In peace thou art the gale of spring; in war, the mountain-storm. Take now my hand in friendship, thou noble king of Morven.

Fingal.

Thou dwellest in the soul of Malvina, son of mighty Ossian. My sighs arise with the beam of the east: my tears descend with the drops of night. I was a lovely tree in thy presence, Oscar, with all my branches round me: but thy death came like a blast from the desert, and laid my green head low; the spring returned with its showers, but no leaf of mine arose.

Fingal. <278>

I am aware that the term *metaphor* has been used in a more extensive sense than I give it; but I thought it of consequence, in a disquisition of some intricacy, to confine the term to its proper sense, and to separate from it things that are distinguished by different names. An allegory differs from a metaphor; and what I would choose to call *a figure of speech,* differs from both. I proceed to explain these differences. A metaphor is defined above to be an act of the imagination, figuring one thing to be another. An allegory requires no such operation, nor is one thing figured to be another: it consists in choosing a subject having properties or circumstances resembling those of the principal subject; and the former is described in such a manner as to represent the latter: the subject thus represented is kept out of view; we are left to discover it by reflection; and we are pleased with the

discovery, because it is our own work. Quintilian* gives the following instance of an allegory,

> O navis, referent in mare te novi
> Fluctus. O quid agis? fortiter occupa portum.
>
> *Horat. lib.* I. *ode* 14.[61]

and explains it elegantly in the following words: "Totusque ille Horatii lo-
cus, quo navim pro re-<279>publica, fluctuum tempestates pro bellis civi-
libus, portum pro pace atque concordia, dicit."[62]

A finer or more correct allegory is not to be found than the following,
in which a vineyard is made to represent God's own people the Jews.

> Thou hast brought a vine out of Egypt: thou hast cast out the Heathen,
> and planted it. Thou didst cause it to take deep root, and it filled the land.
> The hills were covered with its shadow, and the boughs thereof were like
> the goodly cedars. Why hast thou then broken down her hedges, so that
> all which pass do pluck her? The boar out of the wood doth waste it, and
> the wild beast doth devour it. Return, we beseech thee, O God of hosts:
> look down from heaven, and behold, and visit this vine, and the vineyard
> thy right hand hath planted, and the branch thou madest strong for
> thyself.   *Psalm* 80.

In a word, an allegory is in every respect similar to an hieroglyphical
painting, excepting only that words are used instead of colours. Their effects are precisely the same: a hieroglyphic raises two images in the mind;
one seen, which represents one not seen: an allegory does the same; the
representative subject is described; and resemblance leads us to apply the
description to the subject represented. In a figure of speech, there is no
fiction of the imagination employed, as in a metaphor, nor a representative
subject introduced, as <280> in an allegory. This figure, as its name implies,

---

* L. 8. cap. 6. sect. 2. [Sect. 44]

61. "O ship, new billows threaten to bear thee out to sea again. Beware! Haste valiantly
to reach the haven!"

62. "And the rest of the ode, in which Horace represents the state under the semblance
of a ship, the civil wars as tempests, and peace and good-will as the haven."

regards the expression only, not the thought; and it may be defined, the using a word in a sense different from what is proper to it. Thus youth, or the beginning of life, is expressed figuratively by *morning of life:* morning is the beginning of the day; and in that view it is employed to signify the beginning of any other series, life especially, the progress of which is reckoned by days.

Figures of speech are reserved for a separate section; but metaphor and allegory are so much connected, that they must be handled together: the rules particularly for distinguishing the good from the bad, are common to both. We shall therefore proceed to these rules, after adding some examples to illustrate the nature of an allegory. Horace, speaking of his love to Pyrrha, which was now extinguished, expresseth himself thus:

—————— —————— Me tabulâ facer
Votivâ paries indicat uvida
Suspendisse potenti
Vestimenta maris Deo.   *Carm. l.* 1. *ode* 5.[63]

Again:

Phoebus volentem praelia me loqui,
Victas et urbes, increpuit lyrâ:
   Ne parva Tyrrhenum per aequor
    Vela darem.   *Carm. l.* 5. *ode* 15.[64] <281>

Queen. Great Lords, wise men ne'er sit and wail their loss,
But chearly seek how to redress their harms.
What though the mast be now blown overboard,
The cable broke, the holding-anchor lost,
And half our sailors swallow'd in the flood;
Yet lives our pilot still. Is't meet, that he
Should leave the helm, and, like a fearful lad,
With tearful eyes add water to the sea,

63. "As for me, the temple wall with its votive tablet shows I have hung up my dripping garments to the god who is master of the sea."
64. Book 4, ode 15: "When I wished to sing of fights and cities won, Apollo checked me, striking loud his lyre, and forbade my spreading tiny sails upon the Tuscan Sea."

And give more strength to that which hath too much;
While in his moan the ship splits on the rock,
Which industry and courage might have sav'd?
Ah, what a shame! ah, what a fault were this!

Third part Henry VI. *act* 5. *sc.* 5.[65]

Oroonoko. Ha! thou hast rous'd
The lion in his den: he stalks abroad,
And the wide forest trembles at his roar.
I find the danger now. *Oroonoko, act* 3. *sc.* 2.

My well-beloved hath a vineyard in a very fruitful hill. He fenced it, gathered out the stones thereof, planted it with the choicest vine, built a tower in the midst of it, and also made a wine-press therein: he looked that it should bring forth grapes, and it brought forth wild grapes. And now, O inhabitants of Jerusalem, and men of Judah, judge, I pray you, betwixt me and my vineyard. What could have been done more to my vineyard, that I have not done? Wherefore, when I looked that it should bring forth grapes, brought it forth wild grapes? And now go to; I will tell you what I will do to my vineyard: I will take away the hedge thereof, and it shall be eaten up; and <282> break down the wall thereof, and it shall be trodden down. And I will lay it waste: it shall not be pruned, nor digged, but there shall come up briers and thorns: I will also command the clouds that they rain no rain upon it. For the vineyard of the Lord of hosts is the house of Israel, and the men of Judah his pleasant plant.

Isaiah, v. 1.

The rules that govern metaphors and allegories, are of two kinds: the construction of these figures comes under the first kind: the propriety or impropriety of introduction comes under the other. I begin with rules of the first kind; some of which coincide with those already given for similes; some are peculiar to metaphors and allegories.

And, in the first place, it has been observed, that a simile cannot be agreeable where the resemblance is either too strong or too faint. This holds

65. Act 5, sc. 4.

equally in metaphor and allegory; and the reason is the same in all. In the following instances, the resemblance is too faint to be agreeable.

> *Malcolm.* ———— But there's no bottom, none,
> In my voluptuousness: your wives, your daughters,
> Your matrons, and your maids, could not fill up
> The cistern of my lust.   *Macbeth, act* 4. *sc.* 4.[66]

The best way to judge of this metaphor, is to convert it into a simile; which would be bad, because <283> there is scarce any resemblance between lust and a cistern, or betwixt enormous lust and a large cistern.

Again:

> He cannot buckle his distemper'd cause
> Within the belt of rule.   *Macbeth, act* 5. *sc.* 2.

There is no resemblance between a distempered cause and any body that can be confined within a belt.

Again:

> Steep me in poverty to the very lips.
>   *Othello, act* 4. *sc.* 9.[67]

Poverty here must be conceived a fluid, which it resembles not in any manner.

Speaking to Bolingbroke banished for six years:

> The sullen passage of thy weary steps
> Esteem a soil, wherein thou art to set
> The precious jewel of thy home-return.
>   *Richard* II. *act* 1. *sc.* 6.[68]

---

66. Act 4, sc. 3.
67. Act 4, sc. 2.
68. Act 1, sc. 3.

Again:

> Here is a letter, lady,
> And every word in it a gaping wound
> Issuing life-blood.
>
> *Merchant of Venice, act* 3. *sc.* 3.[69] <284>

> Tantae *molis* erat Romanam condere gentem.
>
> *Aeneid.* i. 37.[70]

The following metaphor is strained beyond all endurance: Timur-bec, known to us by the name of Tamerlane the Great, writes to Bajazet Emperor of the Ottomans in the following terms:

> Where is the monarch who dares resist us? where is the potentate who doth not glory in being numbered among our attendants? As for thee, descended from a Turcoman sailor, since the vessel of thy unbounded ambition hath been wreck'd in the gulf of thy self-love, it would be proper, that thou shouldst take in the sails of thy temerity, and cast the anchor of repentance in the port of sincerity and justice, which is the port of safety; lest the tempest of our vengeance make thee perish in the sea of the punishment thou deservest.

Such strained figures, as observed above,* are not unfrequent in the first dawn of refinement: the mind in a new enjoyment knows no bounds, and is generally carried to excess, till taste and experience discover the proper limits.

Secondly, Whatever resemblance subjects may have, it is wrong to put one for another, where they bear no mutual proportion: upon comparing a very high to a very low subject, the simile takes on an air of burlesque;

---

* Chap. 19. Comparisons.

69. Act 3, sc. 2 to read:

> Here is a letter, lady,
> The paper as the body of my friend
> And every word in it a gaping wound
> Issuing life-blood.

70. "So vast was the struggle to found the race of Rome."

and the same will be the effect, where the one is imagined to be the other, <285> as in a metaphor; or made to represent the other, as in an allegory.

Thirdly, These figures, a metaphor especially, ought not to be crowded with many minute circumstances; for in that case it is scarcely possible to avoid obscurity. A metaphor above all ought to be short: it is difficult, for any time, to support a lively image of a thing being what we know it is not; and for that reason, a metaphor drawn out to any length, instead of illustrating or enlivening the principal subject, becomes disagreeable by overstraining the mind. Here Cowley is extremely licentious: take the following instance.

> Great and wise conqu'ror, who where-e'er
> Thou com'st, doth fortify, and settle there!
> Who canst defend as well as get,
> And never hadst one quarter beat up yet;
> Now thou art in, thou ne'er wilt part
> With one inch of my vanquish'd heart;
> For since thou took'st it by assault from me,
> 'Tis garrison'd so strong with thoughts of thee,
> It fears no beauteous enemy.[71]

For the same reason, however agreeable long allegories may at first be by their novelty, they never afford any lasting pleasure: witness the *Fairy Queen,* which with great power of expression, variety of images, and melody of versification, is scarce ever read a second time. <286>

In the fourth place, the comparison carried on in a simile, being in a metaphor sunk by imagining the principal subject to be that very thing which it only resembles; an opportunity is furnished to describe it in terms taken strictly or literally with respect to its imagined nature. This suggests another rule, That in constructing a metaphor, the writer ought to make use of such words only as are applicable literally to the imagined nature of his subject: figurative words ought carefully to be avoided; for such complicated figures, instead of setting the principal subject in a strong light, involve it in a cloud; and it is well if the reader, without rejecting by the

71. "The Constant."

lump, endeavour patiently to gather the plain meaning regardless of the figures:

> A stubborn and unconquerable flame
> Creeps in his veins, and drinks the streams of life.
>
> *Lady Jane Gray, act* I. *sc.* I.

Copied from Ovid,

> Sorbent avidae praecordia flammae.
>
> *Metamorph. lib.* ix. 172.[72]

Let us analyse this expression. That a fever may be imagined a flame, I admit; though more than one step is necessary to come at the resemblance: a fever, by heating the body, resembles fire; and it is no stretch to imagine a fever to be a fire: <287> again, by a figure of speech, flame may be put for fire, because they are commonly conjoined; and therefore a fever may be termed a flame. But now admitting a fever to be a flame, its effects ought to be explained in words that agree literally to a flame. This rule is not observed here; for a flame *drinks* figuratively only, not properly.

King Henry to his son Prince Henry:

> Thou hid'st a thousand daggers in thy thoughts,
> Which thou hast whetted on thy stony heart
> To stab at half an hour of my frail life.
>
> *Second part Henry* IV. *act* 4. *sc.* II.[73]

Such faulty metaphors are pleasantly ridiculed in the *Rehearsal:*

Physician. Sir, to conclude, the place you fill has more than amply exacted the talents of a wary pilot; and all these threatening storms, which, like impregnate clouds, hover o'er our heads, will, when they once are grasp'd but by the eye of reason, melt into fruitful showers of blessings on the people.

---

72. "Greedy flames sucked in his heart."
73. Act 4, sc. 5: delete "frail."

Bayes. Pray mark that allegory. Is not that good?
Johnson. Yes, that grasping of a storm with the eye is admirable.

Act 2. *sc.* 1.

Fifthly, The jumbling different metaphors in the same sentence, beginning with one metaphor and ending with another, commonly called a mixt <288> metaphor, ought never to be indulged. Quintilian bears testimony against it in the bitterest terms; "Nam id quoque in primis est custodiendum, ut quo ex genere coeperis translationis, hoc definas. Multi enim, cum initium a tempestate sumpserunt, incendio aut ruina finiunt: quae est inconsequentia rerum foedissima." *L.* 8. *cap.* 6. § 2.[74]

K. Henry. ―――― Will you again unknit
This churlish knot of all-abhorred war,
And move in that obedient orb again,
Where you did give a fair and natural light?

First part Henry VI. *act* 5. *sc.* 1.[75]

Whether 'tis nobler in the mind, to suffer
The stings and arrows of outrag'ous fortune;
Or to take arms against a sea of troubles,
And by opposing end them.   *Hamlet, act* 3. *sc.* 2.[76]

In the sixth place, It is unpleasant to join different metaphors in the same period, even where they are preserved distinct: for when the subject is imagined to be first one thing and then another in the same period without interval, the mind is distracted by the rapid transition; and when the imagination is put on such hard duty, its images are too faint to produce any good effect: <289>

---

74. "For it is all important to follow the principle illustrated by this passage and never to mix your metaphors, But there are many who, after beginning with a tempest, will end with a fire or a falling house, with the result that they produce a hideously incongruous effect." Read "Multi autem" for "multi enim."
75. *Henry IV, Part 1,* act 5, sc. 1.
76. Act 3, sc. 1: read "slings" for "stings."

At regina gravi jamdudum saucia cura,
Vulnus alit venis, et caeco carpitur igni.   *Aeneid.* iv. 1.[77]

———— Est mollis flamma medullas
Interea, et tacitum vivit sub pectore vulnus.

                                                 Aeneid. iv. 66.[78]

Motum ex Metello consule civicum,
Bellique causas, et vitia, et modos,
    Ludumque fortunae, gravesque
        Principum amicitias, et arma
Nondum expiatis uncta cruoribus,
Periculosae plenum opus aleae,
    Tractas, et incedis per ignes
        Subpositos cineri doloso.

                                        Horat. Carm. l. 2. ode 1.[79]

In the last place, It is still worse to jumble together metaphorical and
natural expression, so as that the period must be understood in part meta-
phorically in part literally; for the imagination cannot follow with sufficient
ease changes so sudden and unprepared: a metaphor begun and not carried
on, hath no beauty; and instead of light there is nothing but obscurity and
confusion. Instances of such incorrect composition are without number. I
shall, for a specimen, select a few from different authors.

Speaking of Britain,

This precious stone set in the sea,
Which serves it in the office of a wall, <290>

---

77. "But the queen, long since smitten with a grievous love-pang, feeds the wound
with her life-blood, and is wasted with fire unseen."

78. "All the while the flame devours her tender heart-strings, and deep in her breast
lives the silent wound."

79. "Thou art treating of the civil strife that with Metellus' consulship began, the
causes of the war, its blunders, and its phases, and Fortune's game, friendships of leaders
that boded ill, and weapons stained with blood as yet unexpiated—a task full of dangerous hazard—and art walking, as it were, over fires hidden beneath treacherous ashes."

Or as a moat defensive to a house
Against the envy of less happier lands.
>   *Richard* II. *act* 2. *sc.* I.[80]

In the first line Britain is figured to be a precious stone: in the following lines, Britain, divested of her metaphorical dress, is presented to the reader in her natural appearance.

These growing feathers pluck'd from Caesar's wing,
Will make him fly an ordinary pitch,
Who else would soar above the view of men,
And keep us all in servile fearfulness.
>   *Julius Caesar, act* I. *sc.* I.

Rebus angustis animosus atque
Fortis adpare: sapienter idem
Contrahes vento nimium secundo
Turgida vela.   *Hor.*[81]

The following is a miserable jumble of expressions, arising from an unsteady view of the subject, between its figurative and natural appearance:

But now from gath'ring clouds destruction pours,
Which ruins with mad rage our halcyon hours:
Mists from black jealousies the tempest form,
Whilst late divisions reinforce the storm.
>   *Dispensary, canto* 3.

To thee, the world, its present homage pays,
The harvest early, but mature the praise.
>   *Pope's imitation of Horace, b.* 2. <291>

---

80. Read "set in the silver sea."
81. "In times of stress shew thyself bold and valiant! Yet wisely reef thy sails when they are swollen by too fair a breeze." (*Odes* II.x)

Oui, sa pudeur n'est que franche grimace,
Qu'une ombre de vertu qui garde mal la place,
Et qui s'evanouit, comme l'on peut savoir,
Aux rayons du soleil qu'une bourse fait voir.

Molière, L'Etourdi, act 3. *sc.* 2.[82]

Et son feu, depourvû de sense et de lecture,
S'eteint à chaque pas, faute de nourriture.

Boileau, L'art poetique, chant. 3. *l.* 319.[83]

Dryden, in his dedication of the translation of *Juvenal,* says,

When thus, as I may say, before the use of the loadstone, or knowledge
of the compass, I was sailing in a vast ocean, without other help than the
pole-star of the ancients, and the rules of the French stage among the
moderns, &c.

There is a time when factions, by the vehemence of their own fermen-
tation, stun and disable one another.   *Bolingbroke.*

This fault of jumbling the figure and plain expression into one confused
mass, is not less common in allegory than in metaphor. Take the following
examples.

———— ———— Heu! quoties fidem,
Mutatosque Deos flebit, et aspera
   Nigris aequora ventis
    Emirabitur insolens,
Qui nunc te fruitur credulus aureâ:

---

82. "Yes, his modesty is but a shameless grimace, that a cloak of virtue poorly dis-
guises, and which vanishes, as one comes to realise, in the light of day when a purse
appears."

83. Their Fustian Muse each accident confounds;
   Nor ever rises but by leaps and bounds,
   Till their small Stock of Learning quickly spent,
   Their poem dies for lack of nourishment.
    (Boileau, trans. N. Rowe)

Qui semper vacuam, semper amabilem
　　Sperat, nescius aurae
　　　Fallacis.　　　　　　*Horat. Carm. l. 1. ode 5.*[84] <292>

Pour moi sur cette mer, qu' ici bas nous courons,
Je songe à me pourvoir d' esquif et d'avirons,
A regler mes desirs, à prévenir l'orage,
Et sauver, s'il se peut, ma Raison du naufrage.
　　　　　　　　　　　　Boileau, epitre 5.[85]

Lord Halifax,[86] speaking of the ancient fabulists: "They (says he) wrote in signs and spoke in parables: all their fables carry a double meaning: the story is one and entire; the characters the same throughout; not broken or changed, and always conformable to the nature of the creature they introduce. They never tell you, that the dog which snapp'd at a shadow, lost his troop of horse; that would be unintelligible. This is his (Dryden's) new way of telling a story, and confounding the moral and the fable together." After instancing from the hind and panther, he goes on thus: "What relation has the hind to our Saviour? or what notion have we of a panther's Bible? If you say he means the church, how does the church feed on lawns, or range in the forest? Let it be always a church or always a cloven-footed beast, for we cannot bear his shifting the scene every line."

A few words more upon allegory. Nothing gives greater pleasure than this figure, when the representative subject bears a strong analogy, in all its

---

84. "Alas! How often shall he lament changed faith and gods, and marvel in surprise at waters rough with darkening gales, who now enjoys thee, fondly thinking thee all golden, who hopes that thou wilt ever be free of passion for another, ever lovely—ignorant of the treacherous breeze." Read "quotiens fidem" for "quoties fidem."

85. While all my Care shall be my Skiff to save,
　　From Rock and Shelf, and the devouring Wave;
　　To Govern my Desires, by Passion tost,
　　Least Reason, in the raging Storm be lost.
　　　　　　　(Boileau, trans. N. Rowe)

86. Charles Montague, Earl of Halifax (1661–1715): statesman, poet, disciple, and subsequently patron of Isaac Newton and of Addison. He was one of the commissioners who negotiated the union with Scotland in 1706.

circumstances, to that which is represented: but the choice is seldom so lucky; the analogy <293> being generally so faint and obscure, as to puzzle and not please. An allegory is still more difficult in painting than in poetry: the former can show no resemblance but what appears to the eye; the latter hath many other resources for showing the resemblance. And therefore, with respect to what the Abbé du Bos* terms mixt allegorical compositions, these may do in poetry; because, in writing, the allegory can easily be distinguished from the historical part: no person, for example, mistakes Virgil's Fame for a real being. But such a mixture in a picture is intolerable; because in a picture the objects must appear all of the same kind, wholly real or wholly emblematical. For this reason, the history of Mary de Medicis, in the palace of Luxenbourg, painted by Rubens, is unpleasant by a perpetual jumble of real and allegorical personages, which produce a discordance of parts, and an obscurity upon the whole: witness, in particular, the tablature representing the arrival of Mary de Medicis at Marseilles; where, together with the real personages, the Nereids and Tritons appear sounding their shells: such a mixture of fiction and reality in the same group, is strangely absurd. The picture of Alexander and Roxana, described by Lucian, is gay and fanciful; but it suffers by the allegorical figures. It is not in the wit of man to invent an allegorical re-<294>presentation deviating farther from any shadow of resemblance, than one exhibited by Lewis XIV. *anno* 1664; in which an enormous chariot, intended to represent that of the sun, is dragg'd along, surrounded with men and women, representing the four ages of the world, the celestial signs, the seasons, the hours, *&c.;* a monstrous composition, suggested probably by Guido's tablature of Aurora, and still more absurd.

In an allegory as well as in a metaphor, terms ought to be chosen that properly and literally are applicable to the representative subject: nor ought any circumstance to be added that is not proper to the representative subject, however justly it may be applicable properly or figuratively to the principal. The following allegory is therefore faulty:

---

* *Reflections sur la Poesie*, vol. I. sect. 24.

Ferus et Cupido,
Semper ardentes acuens sagittas
    Cote *cruentâ.*   *Horat. l. 2. ode* 8.[87]

For though blood may suggest the cruelty of love, it is an improper or immaterial circumstance in the representative subject: water, not blood, is proper for a whetstone.

We proceed to the next head, which is, to examine in what circumstance these figures are proper, in what improper. This inquiry is not alto-<295>gether superseded by what is said upon the same subject in the chapter of Comparisons; because upon trial it will be found, that a short metaphor or allegory may be proper, where a simile, drawn out to a greater length, and in its nature more solemn, would scarce be relished.

And, first, a metaphor, like a simile, is excluded from common conversation, and from the description of ordinary incidents.

Second, in expressing any severe passion that wholly occupies the mind, metaphor is improper. For which reason, the following speech of Macbeth is faulty.

> Methought I heard a voice cry, Sleep no more!
> Macbeth doth murder sleep; the innocent sleep;
> Sleep that knits up the ravell'd sleeve of Care,
> The birth of each day's life, sore Labour's bath,
> Balm of hurt minds, great Nature's second course,
> Chief nourisher in Life's feast.—   *Act* 2. *sc.* 3.[88]

The following example, of deep despair, beside the highly figurative style, hath more the air of raving than of sense:

> *Calista.* Is it the voice of thunder, or my father?
> Madness! Confusion! let the storm come on,
> Let the tumultuous roar drive all upon me,
> Dash my devoted bark; ye surges, break it;
> 'Tis for my ruin that the tempest rises. <296>

87. "cruel Cupid, ever whetting his fiery darts on blood-stained stone."
88. Act 2, sc. 2: read "death" for "birth."

When I am lost, sunk to the bottom low,
Peace shall return, and all be calm again.

Fair Penitent, act 4.

The metaphor I next introduce, is sweet and lively, but it suits not a fiery temper inflamed with passion: parables are not the language of wrath venting itself without restraint.

Chamont. You took her up a little tender flower,
Just sprouted on a bank, which the next frost
Had nip'd; and with a careful loving hand,
Transplanted her into your own fair garden,
Where the sun always shines: there long she flourish'd,
Grew sweet to sense and lovely to the eye,
Till at the last a cruel spoiler came,
Cropt this fair rose, and rifled all its sweetness,
Then cast it like a loathsome weed away.   *Orphan, act* 4.

The following speech, full of imagery, is not natural in grief and dejection of mind:

Gonsalez. O my son! from the blind dotage
Of a father's fondness these ills arose.
For thee I've been ambitious, base and bloody:
For thee I've plung'd into this sea of sin;
Stemming the tide with only one weak hand,
While t'other bore the crown, (to wreathe thy brow),
Whose weight has sunk me ere I reach'd the shore.

Mourning Bride, act 5. *sc.* 6. <297>

There is an enchanting picture of deep distress in Macbeth,* where Macduff is represented lamenting his wife and children, inhumanly murdered by the tyrant. Stung to the heart with the news, he questions the messenger over and over: not that he doubted the fact, but that his heart revolted against so cruel a misfortune. After struggling some time with his grief, he turns from his wife and children to their savage butcher; and then gives vent to his resentment, but still with manliness and dignity:

* Act 4. sc. 6. [Act 4, sc. 3: delete "then" in last line.]

> O, I could play the woman with mine eyes,
> And braggart with my tongue. But, gentle Heav'n!
> Cut short all intermission; front to front
> Bring thou this fiend of Scotland and myself;
> Within my sword's length set him.—If he 'scape,
> Then Heav'n forgive him too.

The whole scene is a delicious picture of human nature. One expression only seems doubtful: in examining the messenger, Macduff expresses himself thus:

> He hath no children—all my pretty ones!
> Did you say, all? what, all? Oh, hell-kite! all?
> What! all my pretty little chickens and their dam,
> At one fell swoop! <298>

Metaphorical expression, I am sensible, may sometimes be used with grace where a regular simile would be intolerable: but there are situations so severe and dispiriting, as not to admit even the slightest metaphor. It requires great delicacy of taste to determine with firmness, whether the present case be of that kind: I incline to think it is; and yet I would not willingly alter a single word of this admirable scene.

But metaphorical language is proper when a man struggles to bear with dignity or decency a misfortune however great: the struggle agitates and animates the mind:

> *Wolsey.* Farewell, a long farewell, to all my greatness!
> This is the state of man; to-day he puts forth
> The tender leaves of hope; to-morrow blossoms,
> And bears his blushing honours thick upon him;
> The third day comes a frost, a killing frost,
> And when he thinks, good easy man, full surely
> His greatness is a ripening, nips his root,
> And then he falls as I do.
>
> *Henry* VIII. *act* 3. *sc.* 6.[89] <299>

89. Act 3, sc. 2.

SECTION VII

Figure of Speech.

In the section immediately foregoing, a figure of speech is defined, "The using a word in a sense different from what is proper to it"; and the new or uncommon sense of the word is termed *the figurative sense*. The figurative sense must have a relation to that which is proper; and the more intimate the relation is, the figure is the more happy. How ornamental this figure is to language, will not be readily imagined by any one who hath not given peculiar attention; and therefore I shall endeavour to unfold its capital beauties and advantages. In the first place, a word used figuratively or in a new sense, suggests at the same time the sense it commonly bears: and thus it has the effect to present two objects; one signified by the figurative sense, which may be termed *the principal object;* and one signified by the proper sense, which may be termed *accessory:* the principal makes a part of the thought; the accessory is merely ornamental. In this respect, a figure of speech is precisely similar to concordant sounds in music, which, without contributing to the melody, make it harmonious. I explain myself by examples. <300> *Youth,* by a figure of speech, is termed *the morning of life.* This expression signifies *youth,* the principal object, which enters into the thought: it suggests, at the same time, the proper sense of *morning;* and this accessory object, being in itself beautiful, and connected by resemblance to the principal object, is not a little ornamental. *Imperious ocean* is an example of a different kind, where an attribute is expressed figuratively: together with *stormy,* the figurative meaning of the epithet *imperious,* there is suggested its proper meaning, *viz.* the stern authority of a despotic prince; and these two are strongly connected by resemblance. Upon this figurative power of words, Vida descants with elegance:

> Nonne vides, verbis ut veris saepe relictis
> Accersant simulata, aliundeque nomina porro
> Transportent, aptentque aliis ea rebus; ut ipsae,
> Exuviasque novas, res, insolitosque colores
> Indutae, saepe externi mirentur amictus

Unde illi, laetaeque aliena luce fruantur,
Mutatoque habitu, nec jam sua nomina mallent?
Saepe ideo, cum bella canunt, incendia credas
Cernere, diluviumque ingens surgentibus undis.
Contra etiam Martis pugnas imitabitur ignis,
Cum furit accensis acies Vulcania campis.
Nec turbato oritur quondam minor aequore pugna:
Confligunt animosi Euri certamine vasto
Inter se, pugnantque adversis molibus undae.
Usque adeo passim sua res insignia laetae <301>
Permutantque, juvantque vicissim: et mutua sese
Altera in alterius transformat protinus ora.
Tum specie capti gaudent spectare legentes:
Nam diversa simul datur è re cernere eadem
Multarum simulacra animo subeuntia rerum.

Poet. lib. 3. *l.* 44.[90]

90. See how the poet banishes with grace
    A native term to give a stranger place;
    From different images with just success,
    He cloaths his matter in the borrow'd dress,
    The borrow'd dress the things themselves admire,
    And wonder whence they drew the strange attire.
    Proud of their ravish'd spoils they now disclaim
    Their former colour, and their genuine name,
    And in another garb, more beauteous grown,
    Prefer the foreign habit to their own.
    Oft' as he paints a battle on the plain,
    The battle's imag'd by the rouring main;
    Now he the fight a fiery deluge names,
    That pours along the fields a flood of flames;
    In airy conflict, now the winds appear,
    Alarms the deeps, and wage the stormy war;
    To the fierce shock th'embattl'd tempests pour
    Waves charge on waves; th'encountering billows roar.
    Thus in a varied dress the subject shines,
    By turns the objects shift their proper signs;
    From shape to shape alternately they run,
    To borrow others charms, and lend their own;
    Pleas'd with the borrow'd charms, the readers find,

In the next place, this figure possesses a signal power of aggrandising an object, by the following means. Words, which have no original beauty but what arises from their sound, acquire an adventitious beauty from their meaning: a word signifying any thing that is agreeable, becomes by that means agreeable; for the agreeableness of the object is communicated to its name.* This acquired beauty by the force of custom, adheres to the word even when used figuratively; and the beauty received from the thing it properly signifies, is communicated to the thing which it is made to signify figuratively. Consider the foregoing expression *Imperious ocean,* how much more elevated it is than *Stormy ocean.*

Thirdly, This figure hath a happy effect by preventing the familiarity of proper names. The familiarity of a proper name, is communicated to the thing it signifies by means of their intimate connection; and the thing is thereby brought <302> down in our feeling.† This bad effect is prevented by using a figurative word instead of one that is proper; as, for example, when we express the sky by terming it *the blue vault of heaven;* for though no work of art can compare with the sky in grandeur, the expression however is relished, because it prevents the object from being brought down by the familiarity of its proper name. With respect to the degrading familiarity of proper names, Vida has the following passage:

> Hinc si dura mihi passus dicendus Ulysses,
> Non illum vero memorabo nomine, sed qui
> Et mores hominum multorum vidit, et urbes,
> Naufragus eversae post saeva incendia Trojae.
>
> *Poet. lib.* 2. *l.* 46.[91]

A crowd of different images combin'd
Rise from a single object of the mind.

* See chap. 2. part. 1. sect. 5.

† I have often regretted, that a factious spirit of opposition to the reigning family makes it necessary in public worship to distinguish the King by his proper name. One will scarce imagine who has not made the trial, how much better it sounds to pray for our Sovereign Lord the King, without any addition.

91. And hence Ulysses' toils were I to choose,
    For the main theme that should employ my muse;

Lastly, by this figure language is enriched, and rendered more copious; in which respect, were there no other, a figure of speech is a happy invention. This property is finely touched by Vida:

> Quinetiam agricolas ea fandi nota voluptas
> Exercet, dum laeta seges, dum trudere gemmas
> Incipiunt vites, sitientiaque aetheris imbrem
> Prata bibunt, ridentque satis surgentibus agri. <303>
> Hanc vulgo speciem propriae penuria vocis
> Intulit, indictisque urgens in rebus egestas.
> Quippe ubi se vera ostendebant nomina nusquam,
> Fas erat hinc atque hinc transferre simillima veris.
>
> *Poet. lib.* 3. *l.* 90.[92]

The beauties I have mentioned belong to every figure of speech. Several other beauties peculiar to one or other sort, I shall have occasion to remark afterward.

Not only subjects, but qualities, actions, effects, may be expressed figuratively. Thus, as to subjects, *the gates of breath* for the lips, *the watery kingdom* for the ocean. As to qualities, *fierce* for stormy, in the expression *Fierce winter: Altus* for *profundus; Altus puteus, Altum mare: Breathing* for *perspiring; Breathing plants.* Again, as to actions, The sea *rages,* Time will

---

By his long labours of immortal fame,
I'd paint my heroe, but conceal his name;
As one, who lost at sea, had nations seen,
And mark'd their towns, their manners and their men,
Since Troy was level'd to the dust by Greece;
['Till a few lines epitomiz'd the piece.].

92. Ev'n the rough hinds delight in such a strain,
    When the glad harvest waves the golden grain;
    And thirsty meadows drink the pearly rain;
    On the proud vine her purple gems appear;
    The smiling fields rejoice, and hail the pregnant year.
    First from necessity the figure sprung
    For things, that would not suit our scanty tongue,
    When no true names were offer'd to the view,
    Those they transferr'd that bordered on the true;
    Thence by degrees the noble license grew.

melt her frozen thoughts, Time *kills* grief. An effect is put for the cause, as *lux* for the sun; and a cause for the effect, as *boum labores* for corn. The relation of resemblance is one plentiful source of figures of speech; and nothing is more common than to apply to one object the name of another that resembles it in any respect: height, size, and worldly greatness, resemble not each other; but the emotions they produce resemble each other, and prompted by this resemblance, we naturally express worldly greatness by height or size: one feels a certain uneasiness in seeing a great depth; <304> and hence depth is made to express any thing disagreeable by excess, as *depth* of grief, *depth* of despair: again, height of place, and time long past, produce similar feelings; and hence the expression, *Ut altius repetam:* distance in past time, producing a strong feeling, is put for any strong feeling, *Nihil mihi antiquius nostra amicitia:* shortness with relation to space, for shortness with relation to time, *Brevis esse laboro, obscurus fio:*[93] suffering a punishment resembles paying a debt; hence *pendere poenas.* In the same manner, light may be put for glory, sunshine for prosperity, and weight for importance.

Many words, originally figurative, having, by long and constant use, lost their figurative power, are degraded to the inferior rank of proper terms. Thus the words that express the operations of the mind, have in all languages been originally figurative: the reason holds in all, that when these operations came first under consideration, there was no other way of describing them but by what they resembled: it was not practicable to give them proper names, as may be done to objects that can be ascertained by sight and touch. A *soft* nature, *jarring* tempers, *weight* of wo, *pompous* phrase, *beget* compassion, *assuage* grief, *break* a vow, *bend* the eye downward, *shower* down curses, *drown'd* in tears, *wrapt* in joy, *warm'd* with eloquence, *loaded* with spoils, and a thousand other expressions of the like nature, have <305> lost their figurative sense. Some terms there are, that cannot be said to be either altogether figurative or altogether proper: orig-

93. The preceding three phrases are translated as:

"I recall from the depths"
"Nothing for me is more ancient [i.e., solid] than our friendship"
"In trying to be precise, I become obscure"   [Horace]

inally figurative, they are tending to simplicity, without having lost altogether their figurative power. Virgil's *Regina saucia cura*,[94] is perhaps one of these expressions: with ordinary readers, *saucia* will be considered as expressing simply the effect of grief; but one of a lively imagination will exalt the phrase into a figure.

For epitomising this subject, and at the same time for giving a clear view of it, I cannot think of a better method, than to present to the reader a list of the several relations upon which figures of speech are commonly founded. This list I divide into two tables; one of subjects expressed figuratively, and one of attributes.

FIRST TABLE.

Subjects expressed figuratively.

1. A word proper to one subject employed figuratively to express a resembling subject.

There is no figure of speech so frequent, as what is derived from the relation of resemblance. Youth, for example, is signified figuratively by the *morning* of life. The life of a man resembles <306> a natural day in several particulars: the morning is the beginning of day, youth the beginning of life; the morning is cheerful, so is youth, &c. By another resemblance, a bold warrior is termed the *thunderbolt* of war; a multitude of troubles, a *sea* of troubles.

This figure, above all others, affords pleasure to the mind by variety of beauties. Beside the beauties above mentioned, common to all sorts, it possesses in particular the beauty of a metaphor or of a simile: a figure of speech built upon resemblance, suggests always a comparison between the principal subject and the accessory; whereby every good effect of a metaphor or simile, may in a short and lively manner, be produced by this figure of speech.

---

94. *Aeneid* 4.1: "The queen, long since smitten with a grievous love pang."

2. A word proper to the effect employed figuratively to express the cause.

Lux for the sun. *Shadow* for cloud. A helmet is signified by the expression *glittering terror.* A tree by *shadow* or *umbrage.* Hence the expression:

> Nec habet Pelion umbras. *Ovid.*[95]

> Where the dun umbrage hangs. *Spring, l.* 1023. <307>

A wound is made to signify an arrow:

> Vulnere non pedibus te consequar. *Ovid.*[96]

There is a peculiar force and beauty in this figure: the word which signifies figuratively the principal subject, denotes it to be a cause by suggesting the effect.

3. A word proper to the cause, employed figuratively to express the effect.

Boumque labores, for corn. *Sorrow* or *grief,* for tears.

> Again Ulysses veil'd his pensive head;
> Again, unmann'd, a show'r of *sorrow* shed.

> Streaming *Grief* his faded cheek bedew'd.

Blindness for darkness:

> Caecis erramus in undis. *Aeneid.* iii. 200.[97]

There is a peculiar energy in this figure, similar to that in the former: the figurative name denotes the subject to be an effect, by suggesting its cause.

95. *Metamorphoses* 12.513: "Pelion stripped of its forest shade."
96. "With my wound I will follow you, not my feet."
97. "We wander on the blind waves."

4. Two things being intimately connected, the proper name of the one employed figuratively to signify the other. <308>

Day for light. *Night* for darkness; and hence, A sudden night. *Winter* for a storm at sea:

> Interea magno misceri murmure pontum,
> Emissamque Hyemem sensit Neptunus.   *Aeneid.* i. 128.[98]

This last figure would be too bold for a British writer, as a storm at sea is not inseparably connected with winter in this climate.

5. A word proper to an attribute, employed figuratively to denote the subject.

Youth and *beauty* for those who are young and beautiful:

> Youth and beauty shall be laid in dust.

Majesty for the King:

> What are thou, that usurp'st this time of night,
> Together with that fair and warlike form,
> In which the *Majesty* of buried Denmark
> Did sometime march?   *Hamlet, act* i. sc. i.

> ——— Or have ye chosen this place
> After the toils of battle, to repose
> Your weary'd *virtue.*   *Paradise Lost.*

> *Verdure* for a green field.   *Summer, l.* 301. <309>

Speaking of cranes,

> The pigmy nations wounds and death they bring,
> And all the *war* descends upon the wing.   *Iliad* iii. 10.

---

98. "Meanwhile Neptune saw the sea in a turmoil of wild uproar."

Cool *age* advances venerably wise. *Iliad* iii. 149.

The peculiar beauty of this figure arises from suggesting an attribute that embellishes the subject, or puts it in a stronger light.

6. A complex term employed figuratively to denote one of the component parts.

Funus for a dead body. *Burial* for a grave.

7. The name of one of the component parts instead of the complex term.

Taeda for a marriage. The *East* for a country situated east from us. *Jovis vestigia servat,* for imitating Jupiter in general.

8. A word signifying time or place, employed figuratively to denote what is connected with it.

Clime for a nation, or for a constitution of government: hence the expression, *Merciful clime, Fleecy winter* for snow, *Seculum felix.* <310>

9. A part for the whole.

The *Pole* for the earth. The *head* for the person:

Triginta minas pro capite tuo dedi. *Plautus.*[99]

Tergum for the man:

Fugiens tergum. *Ovid.*[100]

Vultus for the man:

---

99. *Circilio* 2.3.65: "I gave thirty minae for your head."
100. "Fleeing, with back turned."

Jam fulgor armorum fugaces
Terret equos, equitumque vultus.   *Horat.*[101]

Quis desiderio sit pudor aut modus
Tam chari *capitis?*   *Horat.*[102]

Dumque virent *genua?*   *Horat.*[103]

Thy growing virtues justify'd my cares,
And promis'd comfort to my *silver hairs.*   *Iliad* ix. 616.

———— Forthwith from the pool he rears
His mighty *stature.*   *Paradise Lost.*

The silent *heart* with grief assails.   *Parnell.*[104]

The peculiar beauty of this figure consists in marking that part which makes the greatest figure.

10. The name of the container, employed figuratively to signify what is contained. <311>

Grove for the birds in it, Vocal *grove. Ships* for the seamen, Agonizing *ships. Mountains* for the sheep pasturing upon them, Bleating *mountains. Zacynthus, Ithaca,* &c. for the inhabitants. *Ex moestis domibus,* Livy.

11. The name of the sustainer, employed figuratively to signify what is sustained.

Altar for the sacrifice. *Field* for the battle fought upon it, Well-fought *field.*

101. *Odes* 2.1: "Even now the gleam of weapons strikes terror into timid horses and into the horsemen's faces."
    102. *Odes* 1.24: "What restraint should there be to grief for one so dear?"
    103. *Epodes* 13.4: "While our limbs are strong [literally 'knees']"
    104. Thomas Parnell (1679–1718), friend of Swift, and of Pope who published his works posthumously.

12. The name of the materials, employed figuratively to signify the things made of them.

Ferrum for *gladius.*

13. The names of the Heathen deities, employed figuratively to signify what they patronise.

Jove for the air, *Mars* for war, *Venus* for beauty, *Cupid* for love, *Ceres* for corn, *Neptune* for the sea, *Vulcan* for fire.

This figure bestows great elevation upon the subject; and therefore ought to be confined to the higher strains of poetry. <312>

SECOND TABLE.
Attributes expressed figuratively.

1. When two attributes are connected, the name of the one may be employed figuratively to express the other.

Purity and virginity are attributes of the same person: hence the expression, *Virgin* snow, for pure snow.

2. A word signifying properly an attribute of one subject, employed figuratively to express a resembling attribute of another subject.

Tottering state. *Imperious* ocean. *Angry* flood. *Raging* tempest. *Shallow* fears.

> My sure divinity shall bear the shield,
> And edge thy sword to *reap* the glorious field.
> *Odyssey* xx. 61.

Black omen, for an omen that portends bad fortune.

Ater odor.   *Virgil.*[105]

The peculiar beauty of this figure arises from suggesting a comparison.
<313>

3. A word proper to the subject, employed to express one of its attributes.

Mens for *intellectus. Mens* for a resolution:

Istam, oro, exue mentem.[106]

4. When two subjects have a resemblance by a common quality, the name of the one subject may be employed figuratively to denote that quality in the other.

Summer life for agreeable life.

5. The name of the instrument made to signify the power of employing it.

———— Melpomene, cui liquidam pater
Vocem cum *cithara* dedit.[107]

The ample field of figurative expression displayed in these tables, affords great scope for reasoning. Several of the observations relating to metaphor, are applicable to figures of speech: these I shall slightly retouch, with some additions peculiarly adapted to the present subject.

In the first place, as the figure under consideration is built upon relation, we find from experience, and it must be obvious from reason, that the beauty of the figure depends on the intimacy <314> of the relation between the figurative and proper sense of the word. A slight resemblance, in par-

105. "Black odour" (bad smell).
106. "I beg you, make clear your resolution."
107. Horace *Odes* 3.13: "O Melpomene, thou to whom the Father gave a liquid voice and music of the lyre."

ticular, will never make this figure agreeable: the expression, for example, *Drink down a secret,* for listening to a secret with attention, is harsh and uncouth, because there is scarce any resemblance between *listening* and *drinking.* The expression *weighty crack,* used by Ben Johnson for *loud crack,* is worse if possible: a loud sound has not the slightest resemblance to a piece of matter that is weighty. The following expression of Lucretius is not less faulty, "Et lepido quae sunt *fucata* sonore." i. 645.[108]

> —————— —————— Sed magis
> Pugnas et exactos tyrannos
> Densum humeris *bibit* aure vulgus.
> > *Horat. Carm. l.* 2. *ode* 13.[109]

> Phemius! let acts of gods, and heroes old,
> What ancient bards in hall and bow'r have told,
> Attemper'd to the lyre, your voice employ,
> Such the pleas'd *ear will drink* with silent joy.
> > *Odyssey,* i. 433.

> Strepitumque exterritus *hausit.*　　　　*Aeneid.* vi. 559.[110]

> —————— —————— Write, my Queen,
> And with mine eyes I'll *drink* the words you send.
> > *Cymbeline, act* i. *sc.* 2.

> As thus th' effulgence tremulous I *drink.*
> > *Summer, l.* 1684. <315>

> Neque *audit* currus habenas.　　　　*Georg.* i. 514.[111]

---

108. "And are varnished over with finely sounding phrase."
　　　(trans. H. A. J. Munro, London, 1864)
109. "But the dense throng, shoulder to shoulder packed, drinks in more eagerly with listening ear stories of battles and of tyrants banished."
110. "Rooted to the spot in terror of the din."
111. "The chariot heeds not the rein."

O Prince! (Lycaon's valiant son reply'd),
As thine the steeds, be thine the talk to guide.
The horses practis'd to their lord's command,
Shall *hear* the rein, and answer to thy hand.

Iliad, v. 288.

The following figures of speech seem altogether wild and extravagant, the figurative and proper meaning having no connection whatever. *Moving* softness, Freshness *breathes, Breathing* prospect, *Flowing* spring, *Dewy* light, *Lucid* coolness, and many others of this false coin, may be found in Thomson's *Seasons.*

Secondly, The proper sense of the word ought to bear some proportion to the figurative sense, and not soar much above it, nor sink much below it. This rule, as well as the foregoing, is finely illustrated by Vida:

Haec adeo cum sint, cum fas audere poetis
Multa modis multis; tamen observare memento
Si quando haud propriis rem mavis dicere verbis,
Translatisque aliunde notis, longeque petitis,
Ne nimiam ostendas, quaerendo talia, curam.
Namque aliqui exercent vim duram, et rebus inique
Nativam eripiunt formam, indignantibus ipsis,
Invitasque jubent alienos sumere vultus
Haud magis imprudens mihi erit, et luminis expers,
Qui puero ingentes habitus det ferre gigantis, <316>
Quam siquis stabula alta lares appellet equinos,
Aut crines magnae genitricis gramina dicat.

Poet. iii. 148.[112]

112. But tho' our fond indulgence grants the muse,
A thousand liberties in different view;
When e'er you chuse an image to express
In foreign terms, and scorn the native dress,
Yet be discreete; nor strain the point too far,
Let the transition still unforc'd appear,
Nor e'er discover an excess of care;
For some we know with awkward silence

Thirdly, In a figure of speech, every circumstance ought to be avoided that agrees with the proper sense only, not the figurative sense; for it is the latter that expresses the thought, and the former serves for no other purpose but to make harmony:

> Zacynthus green with ever-shady groves,
> And Ithaca, presumptuous boast their loves;
> Obtruding on my choice a second lord,
> They press the Hymenean rite abhorr'd.
>
> *Odyssey,* xix. 152.

Zacynthus here standing figuratively for the inhabitants, the description of the island is quite out of place: it puzzles the reader, by making him doubt whether the word ought to be taken in its proper or figurative sense.

> ———— ———— Write, my Queen,
> And with mine eyes I'll drink the words you send,
> Though ink be made of gall.   *Cymbeline, act* 1. *sc.* 2.

The disgust one has to drink ink in reality, is not to the purpose where the subject is drinking ink figuratively.

In the fourth place, To draw consequences from <317> a figure of speech, as if the word were to be understood literally, is a gross absurdity, for it is confounding truth with fiction:

> Be Moubray's sins so heavy in his bosom,
> That they may break his foaming courser's back,

> Distort the subject, and disguise the sense;
> Quite change the genuine figure, and deface
> The native shape with ev'ry living grace;
> And force unwilling objects to put on
> An alien face, and features not their own.
> A low conceit in disproportion'd terms,
> Is like a boy dress'd up in giants arms;
> Blind to the truth, all reason they exceed,
> Who name a stall, the palace of a steed,
> Or grass the tresses of great Rhea's head.

> And throw the rider headlong in the lists,
> A caitiff recreant to my cousin Hereford.
>
> Richard II. act I. sc. 3.[113]

Sin may be imagined heavy in a figurative sense: but weight in a proper sense belongs to the accessory only; and therefore to describe the effects of weight, is to desert the principal subject, and to convert the accessory into a principal:

> *Cromwell.* How does your Grace?
> *Wolsey.* Why, well;
> Never so truly happy, my good Cromwell.
> I know myself now, and I feel within me
> A peace above all earthly dignities,
> A still and quiet conscience. The King has cur'd me,
> I humbly thank his Grace; and from these shoulders,
> These ruin'd pillars, out of pity, taken
> A load would sink a navy, too much honour.
>
> Henry VIII. act 3. sc. 6.[114]

Ulysses speaking of Hector:

> I wonder now how yonder city stands,
> When we have here the base and pillar by us.
>
> Troilus and Cressida, act 4. sc. 9.[115] <318>

> *Othello.* No; my heart is turn'd to stone: I strike it, and it hurts my hand.   *Othello, act* 4. *sc.* 5.[116]

> Not less, even in this despicable now,
> Than when my name fill'd Afric with affrights,
> And froze your hearts beneath your torrid zone.
>
> Don Sebastian King of Portugal, act 1.[117]

113. Act 1, sc. 2.
114. Act 3, sc. 2.
115. Act 4, sc. 5.
116. Act 4, sc. 1.
117. John Dryden.

How long a space, since first I lov'd, it is!
   To look into a glass I fear,
And am surpris'd with wonder, when I miss
   Grey hairs and wrinkles there.   *Cowley, vol.* i. *p.* 86.[118]

I chose the flourishing'st tree in all the park,
   With freshest boughs, and fairest head;
I cut my love into his gentle bark,
   And in three days behold 'tis dead;
My very written flames so violent be,
   They've burnt and wither'd up the tree.
                    Cowley, vol. i. *p.* 136.[119]

Ah, mighty Love, that it were inward heat
Which made this precious limbeck sweat!
   But what, alas! ah what does it avail,
That she weeps tears so wond'rous cold,
As scarce the ass's hoof can hold,
   So cold, that I admire they fall not hail.
                    Cowley, vol. i. *p.* 132.[120]

Such a play of words is pleasant in a ludicrous poem.

Almeria. O Alphonso, Alphonso!
Devouring seas have wash'd thee from my sight, <319>
No time shall rase thee from my memory;
No, I will live to be thy monument:
The cruel ocean is no more thy tomb;
But in my heart thou art interr'd.   *Mourning Bride, act* i. *sc.* i.

This would be very right, if there were any inconsistence, in being interred in one place really, and in another place figuratively.

Je crains que cette saison
Ne nous amene la peste;

118. From "The Long Life."
119. From "The Tree."
120. From "Weeping."

La gueule du chien celeste
Vomit feu sur l'horison.
Afin que je m'en delivre,
Je veux lire ton gros livre
Jusques an dernier feüillet:
Tout ce que ta plume trace,
Robinet, a de la glace
A faire trembler Juillet.   *Maynard.*[121]

In me tota ruens Venus
    Cyprum deseruit.   *Horat. Carm. l.* 1. *ode* 19.[122]

From considering that a word used in a figurative sense suggests at the same time its proper meaning, we discover a fifth rule, That we ought not to employ a word in a figurative sense, the proper sense of which is inconsistent or incongruous with the subject: for every inconsistency, and even incongruity, though in the expression only and not real, is unpleasant: <320>

Interea genitor Tyberini ad fluminis undam
Vulnera *siccabat* lymphis ———   *Aeneid.* x. 833.[123]

Tres adeo incertos caeca caligine *soles*
Erramus pelago, totidem sine sidere noctes.
                                    Aeneid. iii. 203.[124]

---

121. François de Maynard (1583–1646) *Oeuvres poétiques:* untitled epigram.

I fear that the season will bring in the plague; the mouth of the Celestial Dog is vomiting fire on the horizon. Before I am released from it I want to read your great book to the very last page: everything that your pen inscribes, Robinet, has a coolness that makes July shiver.

122. "Upon me Venus, leaving her Cyprus, has fallen with all her power."
123. "Meanwhile by the wave of the Tiber river, the father staunched his wounds with water, and rested his reclining frame against a tree's trunk."
124. "For full three days, shrouded in misty gloom, we wander in the deep, for as many starless nights."

The foregoing rule may be extended to form a sixth, That no epithet ought to be given to the figurative sense of a word that agrees not also with its proper sense:

> ———— Dicat Opuntiae
> Frater Megillae, quo *beatus*
> Vulnere.   *Horat. Carm. lib.* i. *ode.* 27.[125]

> Parcus deorum cultor, et infrequens,
> *Insanientis* dum sapientiae
>   Consultus erro.   *Horat. Carm. lib.* i. *ode* 34.[126]

Seventhly, The crowding into one period or thought different figures of speech, is not less faulty than crowding metaphors in that manner: the mind is distracted in the quick transition from one image to another, and is puzzled instead of being pleased:

> I am of ladies most deject and wretched,
> That suck'd the honey of his music-vows.   *Hamlet.*[127]

> My bleeding bosom sickens at the sound.
>   *Odyssey,* i. 439. <321>

> ———— ———— Ah miser,
>   Quantâ laboras in *Charybdi!*
>   Digne puer meliore *flammâ.*
>   Quae saga, quis te solvere Thessalis
>   Magus *venenis,* quis poterit deus?
>   Vix illigatum te triformi
>   Pegasus expediet *Chimerâ.*
>   *Horat. Carm. lib.* i. *ode* 27.[128]

125. "Then let Opuntian Megylla's brother tell with what wound, what shaft, he languishes in bliss."

126. "I, a chary and infrequent worshipper of the gods, what time I wandered, the votary of a foolish wisdom."

127. Act 3, sc. 1: read "And I of ladies" for "I am of ladies."

128. "Ah! Wretched youth! In what fatal whirlpool art thou caught, lad worthy of a better flame! What witch, what wizard with Thessalian charms, nay, what god, can rescue

Eighthly, If crowding figures be bad, it is still worse to graft one figure upon another: For instance,

> While his keen falchion drinks the warriors' lives.
>
> *Iliad* xi. 211.

A falchion[129] drinking the warriors' blood is a figure built upon resemblance, which is passable. But then in the expression, *lives* is again put for *blood;* and by thus grafting one figure upon another, the expression is rendered obscure and unpleasant.

Ninthly, Intricate and involved figures that can scarce be analysed, or reduced to plain language, are least of all tolerable:

> Votis incendimus aras.   *Aeneid.* iii. 279.[130]

> ———— Onerantque canistris
> Dona laboratae Cereris.   *Aeneid.* viii. 180.[131] <322>

Vulcan to the Cyclopes:

> Arma acri facienda viro: nunc viribus usus,
> Nunc manibus rapidis, omni nunc arte magistra:
> *Praecipitate* moras.   *Aeneid.* viii. 441.[132]

> ———— Huic gladio, perque aerea suta
> Per tunicam squalentem auro, latus *haurit* apertum.
>
> *Aeneid.* x. 313.[133]

---

thee! Entangled, as thou art, in the triple-formed Chimaera's toils, scarce Pegasus shall set thee free."

129. Broad, curved convex-edged sword.

130. "And kindle the altars with offerings."

131. "And pile on baskets the gifts of Ceres."

132. "Arms for a brave warrior must ye make. Now is need of strength, now of swift hands, now of all your masterful skill. Fling off delay!"

133. "Driven through the brazen joints and through tunic rough with gold, the sword drank from his pierced side."

Semotique prius tarda necessitas
Lethi, corripuit gradum.   *Horat. Carm. lib.* i. *ode* 3.[134]

Scribêris Vario fortis, et hostium
Victor, Maeonii carminis *alite.*

Horat. Carm. lib. i. *ode* 6.[135]

Else shall our fates be number'd with the dead.

Iliad v. 294.

Commutual death the fate of war confounds.

Iliad viii. 85. *and* xi. 117.

Speaking of Proteus,

Instant he wears, elusive of the rape,
The mimic force of every savage shape.   *Odyssey* iv. 563.

Rolling convulsive on the floor, is seen
The piteous object of a prostrate Queen.   *Ibid.* iv. 952.

The mingling tempest weaves its gloom.

Autumn, 337.[136] <323>

A various sweetness swells the gentle race.   *Ibid.* 640.[137]

A sober calm fleeces unbounded ether.   *Ibid.* 967.[138]

The distant water-fall swells in the breeze.

Winter, 738.[139]

134. "And the doom of death, that before had been slow and distant, quickened its pace."
135. "Thou shalt be heralded by Varius, a poet of Homeric flight, as valiant and victorious o'er the foe."
136. Line 333.
137. Line 633.
138. Line 957.
139. Line 735.

In the tenth place, When a subject is introduced by its proper name, it is absurd to attribute to it the properties of a different subject to which the word is sometimes apply'd in a figurative sense:

> Hear me, oh Neptune! thou whose arms are hurl'd
> From shore to shore, and gird the solid world.
>
> Odyssey. ix. 617.

Neptune is here introduced personally, and not figuratively for the ocean: the description therefore, which is only applicable to the latter, is altogether improper.

It is not sufficient, that a figure of speech be regularly constructed, and be free from blemish: it requires taste to discern when it is proper when improper; and taste, I suspect, is our only guide. One however may gather from reflection and experience, that ornaments and graces suit not any of the dispiriting passions, nor are proper for expressing any thing grave and important. In familiar conversation, they are in some measure ridicu-<324>lous: Prospero, in the *Tempest,* speaking to his daughter Miranda, says,

> The fringed curtains of thine eyes advance,
> And say what thou seest yond.[140]

No exception can be taken to the justness of the figure; and circumstances may be imagined to make it proper; but it is certainly not proper in familiar conversation.

In the last place, Though figures of speech have a charming effect when accurately constructed and properly introduced, they ought however to be scattered with a sparing hand: nothing is more luscious, and nothing consequently more satiating, than redundant ornaments of any kind. <325>

---

140. Act I, sc. 2.

Narration and Description

Horace, and many critics after him, exhort writers to choose a subject adapted to their genius. Such observations would multiply rules of criticism without end; and at any rate belong not to the present work, the object of which is human nature in general, and what is common to the species. But though the choice of a subject comes not under such a plan, the manner of execution comes under it; because the manner of execution is subjected to general rules, derived from principles common to the species. These rules, as they concern the things expressed as well as the language or expression, require a division of this chapter into two parts; first of thoughts, and next of words. I pretend not to justify this division as entirely accurate: for in discoursing of thoughts, it is difficult to abstract altogether from the words; and still more difficult, in discoursing of words, to abstract altogether from the thought.

The first rule is, That in history, the reflections ought to be chaste and solid; for while the mind <326> is intent upon truth, it is little disposed to the operations of the imagination. Strada's Belgic history is full of poetical images, which, discording with the subject, are unpleasant; and they have a still worse effect, by giving an air of fiction to a genuine history. Such flowers ought to be scattered with a sparing hand, even in epic poetry; and at no rate are they proper, till the reader be warmed, and by an enlivened imagination be prepared to relish them: in that state of mind, they are agreeable; but while we are sedate and attentive to an historical chain of facts, we reject with disdain every fiction. This Belgic history is indeed wofully vicious both in matter and in form: it is stuffed with frigid and unmeaning reflections; and its poetical flashes, even laying aside their impropriety, are mere tinsel.

Second, Vida,* following Horace, recommends a modest commencement of an epic poem; giving for a reason, That the writer ought to husband his fire. This reason has weight; but what is said above suggests a reason still more weighty: bold thoughts and figures are never relished till the mind be heated and thoroughly engaged, which is not the reader's case at the commencement. Homer introduces not a single simile in <327> the first book of the Iliad, nor in the first book of the Odyssey. On the other hand, Shakespear begins one of his plays with a sentiment too bold for the most heated imagination:

> *Bedford.* Hung be the heav'ns with black, yield day to night!
> Comets, importing change of times and states,
> Brandish your crystal tresses in the sky,
> And with them scourge the bad revolting stars,
> That have consented unto Henry's death!
> Henry the Fifth, too famous to live long!
> England ne'er lost a king of so much worth.
>
> *First part Henry* VI.[1]

The passage with which Strada begins his history, is too poetical for a subject of that kind; and at any rate too high for the beginning of a grave performance. A third reason ought to have no less influence than either of the former, That a man who, upon his first appearance, strains to make a figure, is too ostentatious to be relished. Hence the first sentences of a work ought to be short, natural, and simple. Cicero, in his oration *pro Archia poeta,* errs against this rule: his reader is out of breath at the very first period; which seems never to end. Burnet begins the History of his Own Times with a period long and intricate.

A third rule or observation is, That where the subject is intended for entertainment solely, not <328> for instruction, a thing ought to be de-

---

* Poet. lib. 2. l. 30.
1. Act 1, sc. 1.

scribed as it appears, not as it is in reality. In running, for example, the impulse upon the ground is proportioned in some degree to the celerity of motion: though in appearance it is otherwise; for a person in swift motion seems to skim the ground, and scarcely to touch it. Virgil, with great taste, describes quick running according to appearance; and raises an image far more lively than by adhering scrupulously to truth:

> Hos super advenit Volsca de gente Camilla,
> Agmen agens equitum et florentes aere catervas,
> Bellatrix: non illa colo calathisve Minervae
> Foemineas assueta manus; sed praelia virgo
> Dura pati, cursuque pedum praevertere ventos.
> Illa vel intactae segetis per summa volaret
> Gramina: nec teneras cursu laesisset aristas:
> Vel mare per medium, fluctu suspensa tumenti,
> Ferret iter; celeres nec tingeret aequore plantas.
>
> *Aeneid.* vii. 803.[2]

This example is copied by the author of *Telemachus:*

> Les Brutiens sont legeres à la course comme les cerfs, et comme les daims. On croiroit que l'herbe même la plus tendre n'est point foulée sous leurs pieds; à peine laissent-ils dans le sable quelques traces de leurs pas.
>
> *Liv.* 10. <329>

Again:

> Déjà il avoit abattu Eusilas si léger à la course, qu'à peine il imprimoit la trace de ses pas dans le sable, et qui devançoit dans son pays les plus rapides flots de l'Eurotas et dé l'Alphée.   *Liv.* 20.[3]

---

2. "To crown the array comes Camilla, of Volscian race, leading her troop of horse, and squadrons gay with brass, a warrior-maid, never having trained her woman's hand to Minerva's distaff or basket of wool, but hardy to bear the battle-brunt and in speed of foot to outstrip the winds. She might have flown o'er the topmost blades of unmown corn, nor in her course bruised the tender ears; or sped her way o'er mid sea, poised above the swelling wave, nor dipped her swift feet in the flood."

3. Fénelon: *Les aventures de Télémaque,* 1699: Bks. 10, 20 (trans. Tobias Smollett:

Fourth, In narration as well as in description, objects ought to be painted so accurately as to form in the mind of the reader distinct and lively images. Every useless circumstance ought indeed to be suppressed, because every such circumstance loads the narration; but if a circumstance be necessary, however slight, it cannot be described too minutely. The force of language consists in raising complete images;* which have the effect to transport the reader as by magic into the very place of the important action, and to convert him as it were into a spectator, beholding every thing that passes. The narrative in an epic poem ought to rival a picture in the liveliness and accuracy of its representations: no circumstance must be omitted that tends to make a complete image; because an imperfect image, as well as any other imperfect conception, is cold and uninteresting. I shall illustrate this rule by several examples, giving the first place to a beautiful passage from Virgil: <330>

> Qualis *populeâ* moerens Philomela sub umbrâ
> Amissos queritur foetus, quos durus *arator*
> Observans nido *implumes* detraxit.   *Georg. lib. 4. l.* 511.[4]

The poplar, ploughman, and unfledged young, though not essential in the description, tend to make a complete image, and upon that account are an embellishment.

The Adventures of Telemachus, Son of Ulysses, London, 1776). Fénelon's popular work received at least 150 French editions by 1830 and 18 English translations by 1800:

> The Brutians are swift of foot, and in running equal the stag or deer. They seem hardly to touch the grass they run over, and the print of their feet is scarce visible in the sand.

> Already he had overthrown Eusilas, so swift in running, that he scarce left the prints of his feet on the sand, and in his own country outstripped the most rapid billows of Eurotas and Alpheus.

* Chap. 2. part 1. sect. 7.

4. "Even as the nightingale, mourning beneath the poplar's shade, bewails the loss of her brood, that a churlish ploughman hath espied and torn unfledged from the nest."

Again:

> Hic viridem Aeneas *frondenti ex ilice* metam
> Constituit, signum nautis.   *Aeneid.* v. 129.[5]

Horace, addressing to Fortune:

> Te pauper ambit sollicita prece
> Ruris colonus: te dominam aequoris,
>   Quicumque Bithynâ lacessit
>   Carpathium pelagus carinâ.   *Carm. lib.* 1. *ode* 35.[6]

> —— Illum ex moenibus hosticis
>   Matrona bellantis tyranni
>   Prospiciens, et adulta virgo,
> Suspiret: Eheu, ne rudis agminum
> Sponsus lacessat regius asperum
>   Tactu leonem, quem cruenta
>   Per medias rapit ira caedes.
>   *Carm. lib.* 3. *ode* 2.[7] <331>

Shakespear says,* "You may as well go about to turn the sun to ice by fanning in his face with a *peacock's* feather." The peacock's feather, not to mention the beauty of the object, completes the image: an accurate image cannot be formed of that fanciful operation, without conceiving a particular feather; and one is at a loss when this is neglected in the description. Again, "The rogues slighted me into the river with as little remorse, as they would have drown'd a bitch's blind puppies, fifteen i' th' litter."†

> *Old Lady.* You would not be a queen?
> *Anne.* No, not for all the riches under heav'n.

---

* Henry V. act 4. sc. 4.
† *Merry Wives of Windsor,* act 3. sc. 15.
5. "Here as a signal for sailors Aeneas set up a green cone of leafy ilex."
6. "Thee the poor peasant entreats with anxious prayer; thee, as sovereign of the deep, whoever braves the Carpathian Sea in Bythnian bark."
7. "At sight of him from foeman's battlements may the consort of the warring tyrant and the ripe maiden sigh: 'Ah, let not our royal lover, unpractised in the fray, rouse the lion fierce to touch, whom rage for blood hurries through the midst of carnage.'"

> *Old Lady.* 'Tis strange: a threepence bow'd would hire me
> Old as I am, to queen it.   *Henry* VIII. *act* 2. *sc.* 5.[8]

In the following passage, the action, with all its material circumstances, is represented so much to the life, that it would scarce appear more distinct to a real spectator; and it is the manner of description that contributes greatly to the sublimity of the passage.

> He spake; and to confirm his words, out-flew
> Millions of flaming swords, drawn from the thighs
> Of mighty cherubim; the sudden blaze
> Far round illumin'd hell: highly they rag'd <332>
> Against the Highest, and fierce with grasped arms
> Clash'd on their sounding shields the din of war,
> Hurling defiance toward the vault of heav'n.
>
> *Milton, b.* 1.

A passage I am to cite from Shakespear, falls not much short of that now mentioned in particularity of description:

> O you hard hearts! you cruel men of Rome!
> Knew you not Pompey? Many a time and oft
> Have you climb'd up to walls and battlements,
> To towers and windows, yea, to chimney-tops,
> Your infants in your arms; and there have sat
> The live-long day with patient expectation
> To see great Pompey pass the streets of Rome;
> And when you saw his chariot but appear,
> Have you not made an universal shout,
> That Tyber trembled underneath his banks,
> To hear the replication of your sounds,
> Made in his concave shores?   *Julius Caesar, act.* 1. *sc.* 1.[9]

The following passage is scarce inferior to either of those mentioned:

Far before the rest, the son of Ossian comes; bright in the smiles of youth, fair as the first beams of the sun. His long hair waves on his back: his dark

---

8. Act 2, sc. 3.
9. Read "her banks" for "his banks" and "her concave shores" for "his concave shores."

brow is half beneath his helmet. The sword hangs loose on the hero's side; and his spear glitters as he moves. I fled from his terrible eye, King of high Temora. *Fingal.* <333>

The *Henriade* of Voltaire errs greatly against the foregoing rule: every incident is touched in a summary way, without ever descending to circumstances. This manner is good in a general history, the purpose of which is to record important transactions: but in a fable it is cold and uninteresting; because it is impracticable to form distinct images of persons or things represented in a manner so superficial.

It is observed above, that every useless circumstance ought to be suppressed. The crowding such circumstances, is, on the one hand, no less to be avoided, than the conciseness for which Voltaire is blamed, on the other. In the *Aeneid,** Barce, the nurse of Sichaeus, whom we never hear of before nor after, is introduced for a purpose not more important than to call Anna to her sister Dido: and that it might not be thought unjust in Dido, even in this trivial circumstance, to prefer her husband's nurse before her own, the poet takes care to inform his reader, that Dido's nurse was dead. To this I must oppose a beautiful passage in the same book, where, after Dido's last speech, the poet, without detaining his readers by describing the manner of her death, hastens to the lamentation of her attendants:

> Dixerat: atque illam media inter talia ferro
> Collapsam aspiciunt comites, ensemque cruore <334>
> Spumantem, sparsasque manus. It clamor ad alta
> Atria, concussam bacchatur fama per urbem;
> Lamentis gemituque et foemineo ululatu
> Tecta fremunt, resonat magnis plangoribus aether.
> *Lib.* 4. *l.* 663.[10]

As an appendix to the foregoing rule, I add the following observation, That to make a sudden and strong impression, some single circumstance

---

* Lib. 4. l. 632.

10. "And even as she spoke her handmaids see her fallen on the sword, the blade reeking with blood and her hands bespattered. A scream rises to the lofty roof; Rumour riots through the startled city. The palace rings with lamentation, with sobbing and women's shrieks, and heaven echoes with loud wails." Read "conlapsam" for "collapsam."

happily selected, has more power than the most laboured description. Macbeth, mentioning to his lady some voices he heard while he was murdering the King, says,

> There's one did laugh in sleep, and one cry'd Murder!
> They wak'd each other; and I stood and heard them;
> But they did say their prayers, and address them
> Again to sleep.
>   *Lady.* There are two lodg'd together.
>   *Macbeth.* One cry'd, God bless us! and, Amen the other;
> As they had seen me with these hangman's hands.
> Listening their fear, I could not say Amen,
> When they did say, God bless us.
>   *Lady.* Consider it not so deeply.
>   *Macbeth.* But wherefore could not I pronounce Amen?
> I had most need of blessing, and Amen
> Stuck in my throat.
>   *Lady.* These deeds must not be thought
> After these ways; so, it will make us mad.
>   *Macbeth.* Methought, I heard a voice cry,
> Sleep no more!
> Macbeth doth murder sleep, *&c.*   *Act.* 2. *sc.* 3.[11] <335>

Alphonso, in the *Mourning Bride,* shut up in the same prison where his father had been confined:

> In a dark corner of my cell I found
> This paper, what it is this light will show.
> "If my Alphonso"—Ha!   [*Reading.*
> "If my Alphonso live, restore him, Heav'n;
> Give me more weight, crush my declining years

---

11. Act 2, sc. 2: read opening lines as:

> There's one did laugh in's sleep, and one cry'd Murder!
> They did wake each other; I stood and heard them
> But they did say their prayers, and address'd them
> Again to sleep.

With bolts, with chains, imprisonment, and want;
But bless my son, visit not him for me."
It is his hand; this was his pray'r.—Yet more:
"Let ev'ry hair, which sorrow by the roots   [*Reading.*
Tears from my hoary and devoted head,
Be doubled in thy mercies to my son:
Not for myself, but him, hear me, all-gracious"—
'Tis wanting what should follow—Heav'n should follow,
But 'tis torn off—Why should that word alone
Be torn from his petition? 'Twas to Heav'n,
But Heav'n was deaf, Heav'n heard him not; but thus,
Thus as the name of Heav'n from this is torn,
So did it tear the ears of mercy from
His voice, shutting the gates of pray'r against him.
If piety be thus debarr'd access
On high, and of good men the very best
Is singled out to bleed, and bear the scourge,
What is reward? or what is punishment?
But who shall dare to tax eternal justice?

Mourning Bride, act 3. *sc.* 1.

This incident is a happy invention, and a mark of uncommon genius.
<336>
Describing Prince Henry:

I saw young Harry, with his beaver on,
His cuisses on his thighs, gallantly arm'd,
Rise from the ground like feather'd Mercury;
And vaulted with such ease into his seat,
As if an angel dropt down from the clouds,
To turn and wind a fiery Pegasus,
And witch the world with noble horsemanship.

First part Henry IV. *act* 4. *sc.* 2.[12]

12. Act 4, sc. 1: read "cushes" for "cuisses."

King Henry. Lord Cardinal, if thou think'st on Heaven's bliss,
Hold up thy hand, make signal of thy hope.
He dies, and makes no sign!
                    Second part Henry VI. *act* 3. *sc.* 10.[13]

The same author speaking ludicrously of an army debilitated with diseases, says,

Half of them dare not shake the snow from off their cassocks, lest they shake themselves to pieces.[14]

I have seen the walls of Balclutha, but they were desolate. The flames had resounded in the halls: and the voice of the people is heard no more. The stream of Clutha was removed from its place by the fall of the walls. The thistle shook there its lonely head: the moss whistled to the wind. The fox looked out from the windows: and the rank grass of the wall waved round his head. Desolate is the dwelling of Morna: silence is in the house of her fathers.   *Fingal.* <337>

To draw a character is the master-stroke of description. In this Tacitus excels: his portraits are natural and lively, not a feature wanting nor misplaced. Shakespear, however, exceeds Tacitus in liveliness, some characteristical circumstance being generally invented or laid hold of, which paints more to the life than many words. The following instances will explain my meaning, and at the same time prove my observation to be just.

Why should a man, whose blood is warm within,
Sit like his grandsire cut in alabaster?
Sleep when he wakes, and creep into the jaundice,
By beeing peevish? I tell thee what, Anthonio,
(I love thee, and it is my love that speaks),
There are a sort of men, whose visages

13. Act 3, sc. 3.
14. *All's Well,* act 4, sc. 3.

Do cream and mantle like a standing pond;
And do a wilful stillness entertain,
With purpose to be dress'd in an opinion
Of wisdom, gravity, profound conceit;
As who should say, I am Sir Oracle,
And when I ope my lips, let no dog bark!
O my Anthonio, I do know of those,
That therefore only are reputed wise,
For saying nothing. *Merchant of Venice, act* I. *sc.* 2.

Again:

Gratiano speaks an infinite deal of nothing, more than any man in all
Venice: his reasons are two grains of wheat hid in two bushels of chaff;
you shall seek all day ere you find them, and when you have them they
are not worth the search. *Ibid.*[15] <338>

In the following passage a character is completed by a single stroke.

Shallow. O the mad days that I have spent; and to see how many of
mine old acquaintance are dead.
Silence. We shall all follow, Cousin.
Shallow. Certain, 'tis certain, very sure, very sure; Death (as the Psalmist
saith) is certain to all: all shall die. How a good yoke of bullocks at Stam-
ford fair?
Slender. Truly, Cousin, I was not there.
Shallow. Death is certain. Is old *Double* of your town living yet?
Silence. Dead, Sir.
Shadow. Dead! see, see; he drew a good bow: and dead. He shot a fine
shoot. How a score of ewes now?
Silence. Thereafter as they be. A score of good ewes may be worth ten
pounds.
Shallow. And is old *Double* dead?
Second part Henry IV. *act* 3. *sc.* 3.[16]

15. Act I, sc. I; act I, sc. I.
16. Act 3, sc. 2: Kames omits five lines from Shadow's penultimate speech.

Describing a jealous husband:

> Neither press, coffer, chest, trunk, well, vault, but he hath an abstract for
> the remembrance of such places, and goes to them by his note. There is
> no hiding you in the house.
>
> *Merry Wives of Windsor, act* 4. *sc.* 3.

Congreve has an inimitable stroke of this kind in his comedy of *Love for
Love:*

> *Ben Legend.* Well, father, and how do all at home? how does brother
> Dick, and brother Val?
> *Sir Sampson.* Dick! body o' me, Dick has been dead <339> these two
> years. I writ you word when you were at Leghorn.
> *Ben.* Mess, that's true; marry, I had forgot. Dick's dead, as you say.
>
> *Act* 3. *sc.* 6.

Falstaff speaking of ancient Pistol:

> He's no swaggerer, hostess; a tame cheater i'faith; you may stroak him as
> gently as a puppy-greyhound; he will not swagger with a Barbary hen, if
> her feathers turn back in any shew of resistance.
>
> *Second Part Henry* IV. *act* 2. *sc.* 9.

Ossian, among his other excellencies, is eminently successful in drawing
characters; and he never fails to delight his reader with the beautiful attitudes of his heroes. Take the following instances.

> O Oscar! bend the strong in arm; but spare the feeble hand. Be thou a
> stream of many tides against the foes of thy people; but like the gale that
> moves the grass to those who ask thine aid.—So Tremor lived; such Trathal
> was; and such has Fingal been. My arm was the support of the injured;
> and the weak rested behind the lightning of my steel.

> We heard the voice of joy on the coast, and we thought that the mighty
> Cathmore came. Cathmore the friend of strangers! the brother of red-
> haired Cairbar. But their souls were not the same; for the light of heaven
> was in the bosom of Cathmor. His towers rose on the banks of Atha: seven
> paths led to his halls: seven <340> chiefs stood on these paths, and called

the stranger to the feast. But Cathmor dwelt in the wood to avoid the voice of praise.

Dermid and Oscar were one: they reaped the battle together. Their friendship was strong as their steel; and death walked between them to the field. They rush on the foe like two rocks falling from the brow of Ardven. Their swords are stained with the blood of the valiant: warriors faint at their name. Who is equal to Oscar but Dermid? who to Dermid but Oscar?

Son of Comhal, replied the chief, the strength of Morni's arm has failed; I attempt to draw the sword of my youth, but it remains in its place: I throw the spear, but it falls short of the mark: and I feel the weight of my shield. We decay like the grass of the mountain, and our strength returns no more. I have a son, O Fingal, his soul has delighted in the actions of Morni's youth; but his sword has not been fitted against the foe, neither has his fame begun. I come with him to battle, to direct his arm. His renown will be a sun to my soul, in the dark hour of my departure. O that the name of Morni were forgot among the people! that the heroes would only say, "Behold the father of Gaul."

Some writers, through heat of imagination, fall into contradiction; some are guilty of downright absurdities; and some even rave like madmen. Against such capital errors one cannot be more effectually warned than by collecting instances; and the first shall be of a contradiction, the most venial of all. Virgil speaking of Neptune, <341>

> Interea magno misceri murmure pontum,
> Emissamque hyemem sensit Neptunus, et imis
> Stagna refusa vadis: *graviter commotus,* et alto
> Prospiciens, summâ *placidum* caput extulit undâ.
>
> *Aeneid.* i. 128.[17]

17. "Meanwhile Neptune saw the sea in a turmoil of wild uproar, the storm let loose and the still waters upheaved from their lowest depths. Greatly troubled was he, and gazing out over the deep he raised his serene face above the water's surface."

Again:

> When first young Maro, in his boundless mind,
> A work t' outlast *immortal* Rome design'd.
>
> > *Essay on Criticism, l.* 130.

The following examples are of absurdities.

Alii pulsis e tormento catenis discerpti sectique, dimidiato corpore pug-nabant sibi superstites, ac peremptae partis ultores.

> > *Strada, Dec.* 2. *l.* 2.[18]

> Il povér huomo, che non sen' era accorto,
> Andava combattendo, ed era morto.   *Berni.*[19]

> He fled; but flying, left his life behind.   *Iliad* xi. 433.

> Full through his neck the weighty falchion sped:
> Along the pavement roll'd the mutt'ring head.
>
> > *Odyssey* xxii. 365.

The last article is of raving like one mad. Cleopatra speaking to the aspic,

> ——— Welcome, thou kind deceiver,
> Thou best of thieves; who, with an easy key, <342>
> Dost open life, and unperceiv'd by us,
> Ev'n steal us from ourselves; discharging so
> Death's dreadful office, better than himself;
> Touching our limbs so gently into slumber,
> That Death stands by, deceiv'd by his own image,
> And thinks himself but Sleep.
>
> > *Dryden, All for Love, act* 5.

---

18. "Others, mangled and ripped by the chains that were pulled from the catapult, fought with their halved bodies, surviving for themselves and avengers that half that was taken from them."

19. F. Berni, *Il primo libro dell'Opere Burlesche,* 1497–1535: "The poor man who did not realize, when he was fighting, that he was already dead."

Reasons that are common and known to every one, ought to be taken for granted: to express them is childish, and interrupts the narration. Quintus Curtius, relating the battle of Issus,

> Jam in conspectu, sed extra teli jactum, utraque acies erat; quum priores Persae inconditum et trucem sustulere clamorem. Redditur et a Macedonibus major, exercitus impar numero, sed jugis montium vastisque saltibus repercussus: *quippe semper circumjecta nemora petraeque, quantumcumque accepere vocem, multiplicato sono referunt.*[20]

Having discussed what observations occurred upon the thoughts or things expressed, I proceed to what more peculiarly concern the language or verbal dress. The language proper for expressing passion being handled in a former chapter, several observations there made are applicable to the present subject; particularly, That as words are intimately connected with the ideas they represent, the emotions raised by the sound and by the sense ought to be concordant. An elevated subject requires an elevated style; what is familiar, ought <343> to be familiarly expressed: a subject that is serious and important, ought to be clothed in plain nervous language: a description, on the other hand, addressed to the imagination, is susceptible of the highest ornaments that sounding words and figurative expression can bestow upon it.

I shall give a few examples of the foregoing rules. A poet of any genius is not apt to dress a high subject in low words; and yet blemishes of that kind are found even in classical works. Horace, observing that men are satisfied with themselves, but seldom with their condition, introduces Jupiter indulging to each his own choice:

> Jam faciam quod vultis: eris tu, qui modo miles,
> Mercator: tu, consultus modo, rusticus: hinc vos,
> Vos hinc mutatis discedite partibus: eia,
> Quid statis? nolint: atqui licet esse beatis.

---

20. "When the two armies were already in sight of each other but still out of reach of javelin-range, the Persian front raised a wild, fierce shout. The Macedonians returned it, the echoes from the mountain tops and vast forests making them sound more numerous than they were; surrounding woods and rocks always return any sound they receive with increased volume" [bk 3.10]. (*The History of Alexander,* trans. John Yardley)

Quid causae est, merito quin illis *Jupiter ambas*
Iratas buccas inflet? neque se fore posthac
Tam facilem dicat, votis ut praebeat aurem?

Sat. lib. 1. *sat.* 1. *l.* 16.[21]

Jupiter in wrath puffing up both cheeks, is a low and even ludicrous expression, far from suitable to the gravity and importance of the subject: every one must feel the discordance. The following couplet, sinking far below the subject, is no less ludicrous. <344>

Not one looks backward, onward still he goes,
Yet ne'er looks forward farther than his nose.

Essay on Man, ep. iv. 223.

Le Rhin tremble et fremit à ces tristes nouvelles;
Le feu sort à travers ses humides prunelles.
C'est donc trop peu, dit-il, que l'Escaut en deux mois
Ait appris à couler sous de nouvelles loix;
Et de mille remparts mon onde environnee
De ces fleuves sans nom suivrà la destinèe?
Ah! perissent mes eaux, ou par d'illustres coups
Montrons qui doit cédar des mortels ou de nous.
A ces mots *essuiant sa barbe limonneuse,*
Il prend d'un vieux guerrier la figure poudreuse.
Son front cicatricé rend son air furieux,
Et l'ardeur du combat étincelle en ses yeux.

Boileau, epitre 4. *l.* 61.[22]

---

21. "Here I am! I will grant your prayers forthwith. You, who were but now a soldier, shall be a trader; you, but now a lawyer, shall be a farmer. Change parts; away with you— and with you! Well! Why standing still? They would refuse. And yet 'tis in their power to be happy. What reason is there why Jove should not, quite properly, puff out both cheeks at them in anger, and say that never again will be so easy-going as to lend ear to their prayers?"

22. The monarch Rhine, the dreadful tidings heard,
    And for himself and subject Waters fear'd,
    The fires that sparked his humid Eyes,
    Confess'd at once his Fury and Surprize.
    "Was't not enough, that in two months, the Schelde,

A god wiping his dirty beard is proper for burlesque poetry only; and altogether unsuitable to the strained elevation of this poem.

On the other hand, to raise the expression above the tone of the subject, is a fault than which none is more common. Take the following instances.

> Orcan le plus fidéle à server ses desseins,
> Né sous le ciel brûlant des plus noirs Affricains.
>
> *Bajazet, act* 3. *sc.* 8.[23]

> Les ombres par trois fois ont obscurci les cieux
> Depuis que le sommeil n'est entré dans vos yeux; <345>
> Et le jour a trois fois chasse la nuit obscure
> Depuis que votre corps languit sans nourriture.
>
> *Phedra, act* 1. *sc.* 3.[24]

> Shou'd to new Laws with vile Submission yield?
> Must I, encompass'd with a hundred Walls,
> Fall as a mean, a nameless River falls?
> First Perish all my Streams! He cry'd; no more
> My rapid current wash the German shore!
> Or I'll by some distinguish'd Effort try,
> Who's Master, or a Mortal here, or I."
> He Spoke; and starting from his Oozy Bed,
> He shook the slimy Honours of his Head,
> He wip'd his filthy Beard, and fierce he rose,
> To meet in Arms, and to repel his Foes.
> [His Front, which gap'd with many a dreadful Scar,
> In vengeful Furows Rolls, and bids the War.
> Rage glows in ev'ry Glance, he burns to Fight,
> Assert his Empire, and defend his Right.]
> (Boileau, trans. N. Rowe)

23. "Orcan the most faithful to fulfil his designs, born under the burning sun of the blackest Africans."

24. And thrice the day has driven forth dim night
> Since last your fainting lips took nourishment.
> (Racine, trans. John Cairncross)

Assuerus. Ce mortel, qui montra tant de zéle pour moi, Vit-il encore?
Asaph. ———— Il voit l'astre qui vous éclaire.

Esther, act 2. *sc.* 3.[25]

Oui, c'est Agamemnon, c'est ton roi qui t'eveille;
Viens, reconnois la voix qui frappe ton oreille.

Iphigenie.[26]

No jocund health that Denmark drinks to-day,
But the great cannon to the clouds shall tell;
And the King's rowse the heav'ns shall bruit again,
Respeaking earthly thunder.   *Hamlet, act* 1. *sc.* 2.

———— In the inner room
I spy a winking lamp, that weakly strikes
The ambient air, scarce kindling into light.

Southern, Fate of Capua, act 3.

In the funeral orations of the Bishop of Meaux, the following passages are raised far above the tone of the subject:

L'Ocean etonné de se voir traversé tant de fois, en des appareils si divers, et pour des causes si differentes, *&c.*   *p.* 6.[27]

Grande Reine, je satisfais à vos plus tendres desires, quand je célébre ce monarque; et son cœur qui n'a jamais vêcu que pour lui, se eveille, tout poudre qu'il est, <346> et devient sensible, même sous ce drap mortuaire, au nom d'un epoux si cher.   *p.* 32.[28]

25. This mortal, who showed such zeal for me. Does he still?
    He sees the star that shines upon you.
26. "Yes, it is Agamemnon your king who wakes you; Come, hear the voice that strikes your ear."
27. "The ocean, astonished to see itself crossed so many times, in such differing ways, and for such diverse causes."
28. "Great Queen, I honour your most tender wishes when I celebrate the monarch; his heart which was never conquered except by her, awakes, in dust though it is, and becomes aware, even in the shrouds of death, of the name of a wife so dear."

Montesquieu, in a didactic work, *L'esprit des Loix,* gives too great indulgence to imagination: the tone of his language swells frequently above his subject. I give an example:

> Mr. le Comte de Boulainvilliers et Mr. l'Abbé Dubos ont fait chacun un systeme, dont l'un semble être une conjuration contre le tiers-etat, et l'autre une conjuration contre la noblesse. Lorsque le Soleil donna à Phaéton son char à conduire, il lui dit, Si vous montez trop haut, vous brulerez la demeure céleste; si vous descendez trop bas, vous réduirez en cendres la terre n'allez point trop à droite, vous tomberiez dans la constellation du serpent; n'allez point trop à gauche, vous iriez dans celle de l'autel: tenez-vous centre les deux. *L.* 30. *ch.* 10.[29]

The following passage, intended, one would imagine, as a receipt to boil water, is altogether burlesque by the laboured elevation of the diction:

> A massy caldron of stupendous frame
> They brought, and plac'd it o'er the rising flame:
> Then heap the lighted wood; the flame divides
> Beneath the vase, and climbs around the sides:
> In its wide womb they pour the rushing stream:
> The boiling water bubbles to the brim.
> *Iliad,* xviii. 405. <347>

In a passage at the beginning of the 4th book of Telemachus, one feels a sudden bound upward without preparation, which accords not with the subject:

> Calypso, qui avoit été jusqu' à ce moment immobile et transportee de plaisir en écoutant les avantures de Télémaque, l'interrompit pour lui faire prendre quelque repôs. Il est tems, lui dit-elle, qui vous alliez goûter la

---

29. "The Count de Boulainvilliers and the Abbé du Bos have formed two different systems, one of which seems to be a conspiracy against the commons, and the other against the nobility. When the sun gave leave to Phaeton to drive his chariot, he said to him ' If you ascend too high, you will burn the heavenly mansions; if you descend too low, you will reduce the earth to ashes; do not drive to the right, you will meet there with the constellation of the Serpent; avoid going too much to the left, or you will fall in with that of the Altar: keep in the middle.'" (Montesquieu, *The Spirit of the Laws,* trans. Thomas Nugent, 1750; quotation from Ovid, *Metamorphoses,* bk. 2)

douceur du sommeil aprés tant de travaux. Vous n'avez rien à craindre ici; tout vous est favorable. Abandonnez vous donc à la joye. Goutez la paix, et tous les autres dons des dieux dont vous allez être comble. Demain, *quand l'Aurore avec ses doigts de rôses entr'ouvira les portes dorées de l'Orient, et que le Chevaux du Soleil sortans de l'onde amére répandront les flames du jour, pour chasser devant eux toutes les etoiles du ciel,* nous reprendrons, mon cher Télémaque, l'histoire de vos malheurs.[30]

This obviously is copied from a similar passage in the *Aeneid,* which ought not to have been copied, because it lies open to the same censure; but the force of authority is great:

> At regina gravi jamdudum saucia cura
> Vulnus alit venis, et caeco carpitur igni.
> Multa viri virtus animo, multusque recursat
> Gentis honos: haerent infixi pectore vultus,
> Verbaque: nec placidam membris dat cura quietem.
> *Postera Phoebea lustrabat lampade terras,*
> *Humentemque Aurora polo dimoverat umbram;*
> Cum sic unanimem alloquitur malesana sororem.
>
> *Lib.* iv. 1.[31] <348>

Take another example where the words rise above the subject.

> Ainsi les peuples y accoururent bientôt en foule de toutes parts; le commerce de cette ville étoit semblable au flux et au reflux de la mer. Les trésors

---

30. "Calypso, who had thus far heard Telemachus recount his adventures, with the utmost attention and transport, now interrupted him, that he might take a little repose. 'It is time,' said she, 'that you refresh yourself with a little rest after such immense fatigue. Here you have nothing to make you uneasy; all if friendly and favourable. Let your heart then give way to joy; let it relish the quiet, and all the other gifts which the gods are going to pour down upon you. Tomorrow, when Aurora with her rosy fingers shall begin to unlock the gilded gates of the east, and the horses of the sun issuing from the briny waves, shall spread abroad the light of day, driving before them all the stars of heaven, you shall resume the recital of your misfortunes.'" (Fénelon, trans. Tobias Smollett)

31. "But the queen, long since smitten with a grievous love-pang, feeds the wound with her life-blood, and is wasted with fire unseen. Oft to her heart rushes back the chief's valour, oft his glorious stock; his looks and words cling fast within her bosom, and the pang withholds calm rest from her limbs. The morrow's dawn was lighting the earth with the lamp of Phoebus, and had scattered from the sky the dewy shades, when, much distraught, she thus speaks to her sister, sharer of her heart." (Virgil, trans. H. R. Fairclough)

y entroient comme les flots viennent l'un sur l'autre. Tout y étoit apporté et en sortoit librement; tout ce qui y entroit, étoit utile; tout ce qui en sortoit, laissoit en sortant d'autres richesses en sa place. La justice sevére presidoit dans le port au milieu de tant de nations. La franchise, la bonne foi, la candeur, sembloient du haut de ces superbs tours appeller les marchands des terres le plus éloignées: chacun de ces marchands, *soit qu'il vint des rives orientales où le soleil sort chaque jour du sein des ondes, soit qu'il fût parti de cette grande mer où le soleil lassé de son cours va eteindre ses feux,* vivoit paisible et en sureté dans Salente comme dans sa patrie!

Telemaque, l. 12.[32]

The language of Homer is suited to his subject, no less accurately than the actions and sentiments of his heroes are to their characters. Virgil, in that particular, falls short of perfection: his language is stately throughout; and though he descends at times to the simplest branches of cookery, roasting and boiling for example, yet he never relaxes a moment from the high tone.* In adjusting his language to his subject, no writer equals Swift. I can recollect but one exception, which at the same <349> time is far from being gross: *The journal of a modern lady* is composed in a style blending sprightliness with familiarity, perfectly suited to the subject: in one passage, however, the poet deviating from that style, takes a tone above his subject. The passage I have in view begins, *l.* 116. *But let me now a while survey, &c.* and ends at *l.* 135.

It is proper to be observed upon this head, that writers of inferior rank are continually upon the stretch to enliven and enforce their subject by

---

* See *Aeneid.* lib. i. 188.–219.

32. "In consequence of these regulations, great numbers of people came from all parts to settle at Salentum. The trade of that city might be compared to the ebbing and flowing of the sea, ships with merchandise and treasure coming in and going out in a constant succession, like the waves of the ocean. Every thing useful was imported and exported without restraint. What was carried out was more than balanced, by what was brought in return. Justice was dispensed with the utmost exactness and impartiality to the several nations that used the port. Freedom, probity, and fair dealing seemed from the top of the lofty towers to invite merchants from the most distant nations; and all these merchants, whether they came from the extremity of the East, where the sun every day rises from the bosom of the deep, or from that vast ocean, where, after a tedious course, he quenches his fires at eve, lived in as much peace and security at Salentum, as in his own country" (Fénelon, trans. Tobias Smollett).

exaggeration and superlatives. This unluckily has an effect contrary to what is intended; the reader, disgusted with language that swells above the subject, is led by contrast to think more meanly of the subject than it may possibly deserve. A man of prudence, beside, will be no less careful to husband his strength in writing than in walking: a writer too liberal of superlatives, exhausts his whole stock upon ordinary incidents, and reserves no share to express, with greater energy, matters of importance.* <350>

Many writers of that kind abound so in epithets, as if poetry consisted entirely in high-sounding words. Take the following instance.

> When black-brow'd Night her dusky mantle spread,
>   And wrapt in solemn gloom the sable sky;
> When soothing Sleep her opiate dews had shed,
>   And seal'd in silken slumbers ev'ry eye:
> My wakeful thoughts admit no balmy rest,
>   Nor the sweet bliss of soft oblivion share:
> But watchful wo distracts my aching breast,
>   My heart the subject of corroding care:
> From haunts of men with wand'ring steps and slow
> I solitary steal, and sooth my pensive wo.

Here every substantive is faithfully attended by some tumid epithet; like young master, who cannot walk abroad without having a lac'd livery-man at his heels. Thus in reading without taste, an emphasis is laid on every word; and in singing without taste, every note is grac'd. Such redundancy of epithets, instead of pleasing, produce satiety and disgust!

The power of language to imitate thought, is not confined to the capital circumstances above mentioned: it reacheth even the slighter modifications. Slow action, for example, is imitated by words pronounced slow;

---

* Montaigne, reflecting upon the then present modes, observes, that there never was at any other time so abject and servile prostitution of words in the addresses made by people of fashion to one another; the humblest tenders of life and soul, no professions under that of devotion and adoration; the writer constantly declaring himself a vassal, nay a slave: so that when any more serious occasion of friendship or gratitude requires more genuine professions, words are wanting to express them.

labour or toil, by words harsh or rough in their sound. But this subject has been already handled.* <351>

In dialogue-writing, the condition of the speaker is chiefly to be regarded in framing the expression. The sentinel in *Hamlet,* interrogated with relation to the ghost whether his watch had been quiet, answers with great propriety for a man in his station, "Not a mouse stirring."†

I proceed to a second remark, no less important than the former. No person of reflection but must be sensible, that an incident makes a stronger impression on an eye-witness, than when heard at second hand. Writers of genius, sensible that the eye is the best avenue to the heart, represent every thing as passing in our sight; and, from readers or hearers, transform us as it were into spectators: a skilful writer conceals himself, and presents his personages: in a word, every thing becomes dramatic as much as possible. Plutarch, *de gloria Atheniensium,* observes, that Thucydides makes his reader a spectator, and inspires him with the same passions as if he were an eye-witness; and the same observation is applicable to our countryman Swift. From this happy talent arises that energy of style which is peculiar to him: he can-<352>not always avoid narration; but the pencil is his choice, by which he bestows life and colouring upon his objects. Pope is richer in ornament, but possesseth not in the same degree the talent of drawing from the life. A translation of the sixth satire of Horace, begun by the former and finished by the latter, affords the fairest opportunity for a comparison. Pope obviously imitates the picturesque manner of his friend: yet every one of taste must be sensible, that the imitation, though fine, falls short of the original. In other instances, where Pope writes in his own style, the difference of manner is still more conspicuous.

Abstract or general terms have no good effect in any composition for amusement; because it is only of particular objects that images can be

---

* Ch. 18. sect. 3.

† One can scarce avoid smiling at the blindness of a certain critic, who, with an air of self-sufficiency, condemns this expression as low and vulgar. A French poet, says he, would express the same thought in a more sublime manner: "Mais tout dort, et l'armée, et les vents, et Neptune." ["But everything went wrong: the army, the winds, even Neptune."] And he adds, "The English poet may please at London, but the French every where else."

formed.* Shakespear's style in that respect is excellent: every article in his descriptions is particular, as in nature; and if accidentally a vague expression slip in, the blemish is discernible by the bluntness of its impression. Take the following example: Falstaff, excusing himself for running away at a robbery, says,

> By the Lord, I knew ye, as well as he that made ye. Why, hear ye, my masters; was it for me to kill the heir-apparent? should I turn upon the true prince? Why, thou knowest, I am as valiant as Hercules; but <353> beware instinct, the lion will not touch the true prince: *instinct is a great matter.* I was a coward on instinct: I shall think the better of myself, and thee, during my life; I for a valiant lion, and thou for a true prince. But, by the Lord, lads, I am glad you have the money. Hostess, clap to the doors, watch tonight, pray to-morrow. Gallants, lads, boys, hearts of gold, all the titles of good fellowship come to you! What, shall we be merry? shall we have a play *extempore?*   *First part Henry* IV. *act* 2. *sc.* 9.[33]

The sentence I object to is, *instinct is a great matter,* which makes but a poor figure, compared with the liveliness of the rest of the speech. It was one of Homer's advantages, that he wrote before general terms were multiplied: the superior genius of Shakespear displays itself in avoiding them after they were multiplied. Addison describes the family of Sir Roger de Coverley in the following words:

> You would take his valet de chambre for his brother, his butler is gray-headed, his groom is one of the gravest men that I have ever seen, and his coachman has the looks of a privy counsellor.
>
> *Spectator,* No. 106.

The description of the groom is less lively than of the others; plainly because the expression, being vague and general, tends not to form any image. <354> "Dives opum variarum,"† is an expression still more vague; and so are the following:

---

* See chap. 4.
† *Georg.* ii. 468. ["rich in treasures manifold"]
33. Act 2, sc. 4.

———— Maecenas, *mearum*
Grande decus, columenque *rerum.*

Horat. Carm. lib. 2. *ode* 17.[34]

———— et fide Teia
Dices *laborantes in uno*
Penelopen, vitreamque Circen.   *Ibid. lib.* 1. *ode* 17.[35]

———— Ridiculum acri
Fortius et melius magnas plerumque *secat res.*

Horat. Satir. lib. 1. *sat.* 10.[36]

In the fine arts it is a rule, to put the capital objects in the strongest point of view; and even to present them oftener than once, where it can be done. In history-painting, the principal figure is placed in the front, and in the best light: an equestrian statue is placed in a centre of streets, that it may be seen from many places at once. In no composition is there greater opportunity for this rule than in writing:

———— Sequitur pulcherrimus Astur,
Astur equo fidens et versicoloribus armis.

Aeneid x. 180.[37]

———— Full many a lady
I've ey'd with best regard, and many a time <355>
Th' harmony of their tongues hath into bondage
Brought my too diligent ear; for several virtues
Have I lik'd several women, never any
With so full soul, but some defect in her
Did quarrel with the noblest grace she ow'd,
And put it to the soil. But you, O you,

34. "Maecenas, the great glory and prop of my own existence."
35. "And sing on Teian lyre Penelope and Circe of the glassy sea, enamoured of the self-same hero."
36. "Jesting oft cuts hard knots more forcefully and effectively than gravity."
37. "Then follows Astyr, of wondrous beauty—Astyr, relying on his steed and many coloured arms."

So perfect, and so peerless, are created
Of every creature's best.   *The Tempest, act* 3. *sc.* 1.

    Orlando. ——— Whate'er you are
That in this desert inaccessible,
Under the shade of melancholy boughs,
Lose and neglect the creeping hours of time;
If ever you have look'd on better days;
If ever been where bells have knoll'd to church;
If ever sat at any good man's feast;
If ever from your eye-lids wip'd a tear,
And know what 'tis to pity and be pity'd;
Let gentleness my strong enforcement be,
In the which hope I blush and hide my sword.
    Duke sen. True is it that we have seen better days;
And have with holy bell been knoll'd to church;
And sat at good mens feasts; and wip'd our eyes
Of drops that sacred pity had engender'd:
And therefore sit you down in gentleness,
And take upon command what help we have,
That to your wanting may be ministred.   *As you like it.*[38]

With thee conversing I forget all time;
All seasons and their change, all please alike.
Sweet is the breath of morn, her rising sweet,
With charm of earliest birds; pleasant the sun <356>
When first on this delightful land he spreads
His orient beams, on herbs, tree, fruit, and flow'r,
Glist'ring with dew; fragrant the fertile earth
After soft showers; and sweet the coming on
Of grateful evening mild, the silent night
With this her solemn bird, and this fair moon,
And these the gems of heav'n, her starry train.
But neither breath of morn, when she ascends
With charm of earliest birds, nor rising sun

38. Act 2, sc. 7.

On this delightful land, nor herb, fruit, flow'r,
Glistering with dew, nor fragrance after showers,
Nor grateful evening mild, nor silent night,
With this her solemn bird, nor walk by moon
Or glittering star-light, without thee is sweet.

Paradise Lost, b. 4. l. 634.

What mean ye, that ye use this proverb, The fathers have eaten four grapes, and the children's teeth are set on edge? As I live, saith the Lord God, ye shall not have occasion to use this proverb in Israel. If a man keep my judgements to deal truly, he is just, he shall surely live. But if he be a robber, a shedder of blood; if he have eaten upon the mountains, and defiled his neighbour's wife; if he have oppressed the poor and needy, have spoiled by violence, have not restored the pledge, have lift up his eyes to idols, have given forth upon usury, and have taken increase: shall he live? he shall not live: he shall surely die; and his blood shall be upon him. Now, lo, if he beget a son, that seeth all his father's sins, and considereth, and doeth not such like; that hath not eaten upon the mountains, hath not lift up his eyes to idols, nor defiled his neighbour's wife, hath not oppressed any, nor with-held the pledge, neither hath spoiled by violence, but hath given <357> his bread to the hungry, and covered the naked with a garment; that hath not received usury nor increase, that hath executed my judgements, and walked in my statutes; he shall not die for the iniquity of his father; he shall surely live. The soul that sinneth, it shall die; the son shall not bear the iniquity of the father, neither shall the father bear the iniquity of the son; the righteousness of the righteous shall be upon him, and the wickedness of the wicked shall be upon him. Have I any pleasure that the wicked should die, saith the Lord God; and not that he should return from his ways and live? *Ezekiel.* xviii.

The repetitions in Homer, which are frequent, have been the occasion of much criticism. Suppose we were at a loss about the reason, might not taste be sufficient to justify them? At the same time, we are at no loss about the reason: they evidently make the narration dramatic, and have an air of truth, by making things appear as passing in our sight. But such repetitions are unpardonable in a didactic poem. In one of Hesiod's poems of that kind, a long passage occurs twice in the same chapter.

A concise comprehensive style is a great ornament in narration; and a superfluity of unnecessary words, no less than of circumstances, a great nuisance. A judicious selection of the striking circumstances clothed in a nervous style, is delightful. In this style, Tacitus excels all writers, ancient and modern. Instances are numberless: take the following specimen. <358>

> Crebra hinc praelia, et saepius in modum latrocinii: per saltus, per paludes; ut cuique fors aut virtus: temere, proviso, ob iram, ob praedam, jussu, et aliquando ignaris ducibus.   *Annal. lib.* 12. § 39.[39]

After Tacitus, Ossian in that respect justly merits the place of distinction. One cannot go wrong for examples in any part of the book; and at the first opening the following instance meets the eye:

> Nathos cloathed his limbs in shining steel. The stride of the chief is lovely: the joy of his eye terrible. The wind rustles in his hair. Darthula is silent at his side: her look is fixed on the chief. Striving to hide the rising sigh, two tears swell in her eyes.

I add one other instance, which, beside the property under consideration, raises delicately our most tender sympathy.

> Son of Fingal! dost thou not behold the darkness of Crothar's hall of shells? My soul was not dark at the feast, when my people lived. I rejoiced in the presence of strangers, when my son shone in the hall. But, Ossian, he is a beam that is departed, and left no streak of light behind. He is fallen, son of Fingal, in the battles of his father.—Rothmar, the chief of grassy Tromlo, heard that my eyes had failed; he heard that my arms were fixed in the hall, and the pride of his soul arose. He came towards Croma: my people fell before him. I took my arms in the hall, but what could sightless Crothar do? My steps were <359> unequal; my grief was great. I wished for the days that were past; days! wherein I fought, and won in the field of blood. My son returned from the chace; the fair-haired Fovargormo. He had not lifted his sword in battle, for his arm was young. But the soul of the youth was great; the fire of valour burnt in his eye. He saw

---

39. "They met in sudden encounters, as chance directed, or valour prompted; in the fens, in the woods, in the narrow defiles; the men, on some occasions, led on by their chiefs, and frequently without their knowledge, as resentment, or the love of booty, happened to incite their fury" (Tacitus, *De Moribus Germanorum,* trans. Arthur Murphy, 1793).

the disordered steps of his father, and his sigh arose. King of Croma, he said, is it because thou hast no son? is it for the weakness of Fovar-gormo's arm that thy sighs arise: I begin, my father, to feel the strength of my arm; I have drawn the sword of my youth, and I have bent the bow. Let me meet this Rothmar, with the youths of Croma: let me meet him, O my father, for I feel my burning soul.

And thou shalt meet him, I said, son of the sightless Crothar! But let others advance before thee, that I may hear the tread of thy feet at thy return; for my eyes behold thee not, fair-haired Fovar-gormo!—He went; he met the foe; he fell. The foe advances towards Croma. He who slew my son is near, with all his pointed spears.

If a concise or nervous style be a beauty, tautology must be a blemish; and yet writers, fettered by verse, are not sufficiently careful to avoid this slovenly practice: they may be pitied, but they cannot be justified. Take for a specimen the following instances, from the best poet, for versification at least, that England has to boast of.

> High on his helm celestial lightnings play,
> His beamy shield emits a living ray, <360>
> Th' unweary'd blaze incessant streams supplies,
> Like the red star that fires th' autumnal skies.   *Iliad* v. 5.

> Strength and omnipotence invest thy throne.
>   *Iliad* viii. 576.

> So silent fountains, from a rock's tall head,
> In sable streams soft trickling waters shed.   *Iliad* ix. 19.

> His clanging armour rung.   *Iliad* xii. 94.

> Fear on their cheek, and horror in their eye.   *Iliad* xv. 4.

> The blaze of armour flash'd against the day.
>   *Iliad* xvii. 736.

> As when the piercing blasts of Boreas blow.
>   *Iliad* xix. 380.

And like the moon, the broad refulgent shield
Blaz'd with long rays, and gleam'd athwart the field.

Iliad xix. 402.

No—could our swiftness o'er the winds prevail,
Or beat the pinions of the western gale,
All were in vain—   *Iliad* xix. 460.

The humid sweat from ev'ry pore descends.

Iliad xxiii. 829. <361>

Redundant epithets, such as *humid* in the last citation, are by Quintilian disallowed to orators; but indulged to poets,* because his favourite poets, in a few instances, are reduced to such epithets for the sake of versification; for instance, *Prata canis albicant pruinis* of Horace,[40] and *liquidos fontes* of Virgil.

As an apology for such careless expressions, it may well suffice, that Pope, in submitting to be a translator, acts below his genius. In a translation, it is hard to require the same spirit or accuracy, that is cheerfully bestowed on an original work. And to support the reputation of that author, I shall give some instances from Virgil and Horace, more faulty by redundancy than any of those above mentioned:

Saepe etiam immensum coelo venit agmen aquarum,
Et foedam glomerant tempestatem imbribus atris
Collectae ex alto nubes: ruit arduus ether,
Et pluviâ ingenti fata laeta, boumque labores
Diluit.   *Georg. lib.* i. 322.[41]

Postquam altum tenuere rates, nec jam amplius ullae
Apparent terrae; coelum undique et undique pontus:

---

* L. 8. cap. 6. sect. 2.

40. "Nor are the meadows any longer white with hoary frost." (Horace *Odes* I.4.4)

41. "Often, too, there appears in the sky a mighty column of waters, and clouds mustered from on high roll up a murky tempest of black showers: down falls the lofty heaven, and with its deluge of rain washes away the gladsome crops and the labours of oxen."

Tum mihi caeruleus supra caput astitit imber,
Noctem hyememque ferens: et inhorruit unda tenebris.

Aeneid. lib. iii. 192.[42]

———— Hinc tibi copia
Manabit ad plenum benigno <362>
Ruris honorum opulenta cornu.

Horat. Carm. lib. i. *ode* 17.[43]

Videre fessos vomerem inversum boves
Collo trahentes languido. *Horat. epod.* ii. 63.[44]

Here I can luckily apply Horace's rule against himself:

Est brevitate opus, ut currat sententia, neu se
Impediat verbis lassas onerantibus aures.

Satir. lib. i. *sat.* x. 9.[45]

I close this chapter with a curious inquiry. An object, however ugly to the sight, is far from being so when represented by colours or by words. What is the cause of this difference? With respect to painting, the cause is obvious: a good picture, whatever the subject be, is agreeable by the pleasure we take in imitation; and this pleasure overbalancing the disagreeableness of the subject, makes the picture upon the whole agreeable. With respect to the description of an ugly object, the cause follows. To connect individuals in the social state, no particular contributes more than language, by the power it possesses of an expeditious communication of thought, and a lively representation of transactions. But nature hath not been satisfied to recommend language by its utility merely: independent of utility, it is

42. "After our ships gained the deep, and now no longer any land is seen, but sky on all sides and on all sides sea, then a murky rain-cloud loomed over-head, bringing night and tempest, while the wave shuddered darkling."

43. "In this spot shall rich abundance of the glories of the field flow to the full for thee from bounteous horn."

44. "To see the wearied oxen dragging along the upturned ploughshares on their tired necks."

45. "You need terseness, so that the thought may run on, and not become entangled in verbiage that weighs upon wearied ears."

made suceptible of many <363> beauties, which are directly felt, without any intervening reflection.* And this unfolds the mystery; for the pleasure of language is so great, as in a lively description to overbalance the disagreeableness of the image raised by it.† This, however, is no encouragement to choose a disagreeable subject; for the pleasure is incomparably greater where the subject and the description are both of them agreeable.

The following description is upon the whole agreeable, though the subject described is in itself dismal:

> Nine times the space that measures day and night
> To mortal men, he with his horrid crew
> Lay vanquish'd, rowling in the fiery gulf,
> Confounded though immortal! but his doom
> Reserv'd him to more wrath; for now the thought
> Both of lost happiness and lasting pain
> Torments him; round he throws his baleful eyes
> That witness'd huge affliction and dismay,
> Mix'd with obdurate pride and stedfast hate:
> At once as far as angels ken he views
> The dismal situation waste and wild:
> A dungeon horrible, on all sides round
> As one great furnace flam'd; yet from those flames
> No light, but rather darkness visible
> Serv'd only to discover sights of wo,
> Regions of sorrow, doleful shades, where peace <364>
> And rest can never dwell, hope never comes
> That comes to all; but torture without end
> Still urges, and a fiery deluge, fed
> With ever-burning sulphur unconsum'd!
> Such place eternal justice had prepar'd
> For those rebellious.   *Paradise Lost, book* 1. *l.* 50.

An unmanly depression of spirits in time of danger is not an agreeable sight; and yet a fine description or representation of it will be relished:

---

* See chap. 18.
† See chap. 2. part 4.

K. Richard. What must the King do now? must he submit?
The King shall do it: must he be depos'd?
The King shall be contented: must he lose
The name of King? o' God's name, let it go;
I'll give my jewels for a set of beads;
My gorgeous palace, for a hermitage;
My gay apparel, for an almsman's gown;
My figur'd goblets, for a dish of wood;
My sceptre, for a palmer's walking-staff;
My subjects, for a pair of carved saints;
And my large kingdom, for a little grave;
A little, little grave;—an obscure grave.
Or I'll be bury'd in the King's highway;
Some way of common tread, where subjects feet
May hourly trample on their sovereign's head;
For on my heart they tread now, whilst I live;
And, bury'd once, why not upon my head?

Richard II. *act* 3. *sc.* 6.[46]

Objects that strike terror in a spectator, have in <365> poetry and painting a fine effect. The picture, by raising a slight emotion of terror, agitates the mind; and in that condition every beauty makes a deep impression. May not contrast heighten the pleasure, by opposing our present security to the danger of encountering the object represented?

———— The other shape,
If shape it might be call'd, that shape had none
Distinguishable in member, joint, or limb;
Or substance might be call'd that shadow seem'd,
For each seem'd either; black it stood as night,
Fierce as ten furies, terrible as hell,
And shook a dreadful dart.   *Paradise Lost, book* 2. *l. 666.*

---

46. Act 3, sc. 3: read "Some way of common trade" for "Some way of common tread."

———— Now storming fury rose,
And clamour such as heard in heaven till now
Was never: arms on armour clashing bray'd
Horrible discord, and the madding wheels
Of brazen chariots rag'd; dire was the noise
Of conflict: overhead the dismal hiss
Of fiery darts in flaming vollies flew,
And flying vaulted either host with fire.
So under fiery cope together rush'd
Both battles main, with ruinous assault
And inextinguishable rage: all heaven
Resounded; and had earth been then, all earth
Had to her centre shook.   *Paradise Lost, book* 6. *l.* 207.

Ghost. ———— But that I am forbid
To tell the secrets of my prison-house,
I could a tale unfold, whose lightest word
Would harrow up thy soul, freeze thy young blood, <366>
Make thy two eyes, like stars, start from their spheres,
Thy knotty and combined locks to part,
And each particular hair to stand on end,
Like quills upon the fretful porcupine:
But this eternal blazon must not be
To ears of flesh and blood.   *Hamlet, act* 1. *sc.* 8.[47]

Gratiano. Poor Desdemona! I'm glad thy father's dead:
Thy match was mortal to him; and pure grief
Shore his old thread in twain. Did he live now,
This sight would make him do a desp'rate turn:
Yea, curse his better angel from his side,
And fall to reprobation.   *Othello, act* 5. *sc.* 8.[48]

47. Act 1, sc. 5.
48. Act 5, sc. 2.

Objects of horror must be excepted from the foregoing theory; for no description, however lively, is sufficient to overbalance the disgust raised even by the idea of such objects. Every thing horrible ought therefore to be avoided in a description. Nor is this a severe law: the poet will avoid such scenes for his own sake, as well as for that of his reader; and to vary his descriptions, nature affords plenty of objects that disgust us in some degree without raising horror. I am obliged therefore to condemn the picture of Sin in the second book of *Paradise Lost,* though a masterly performance: the original would be a horrid spectacle; and the horror is not much softened in the copy: <367>

> ———— Pensive here I sat
> Alone; but long I sat not, till my womb,
> Pregnant by thee, and now excessive grown,
> Prodigious motion felt and rueful throes.
> At last this odious offspring whom thou seest,
> Thine own begotten, breaking violent way,
> Tore through my intrails, that with fear and pain
> Distorted, all my nether shape thus grew
> Transform'd; but he my inbred enemy
> Forth issu'd, brandishing his fatal dart,
> Made to destroy: I fled, and cry'd out Death;
> Hell trembl'd at the hideous name, and sigh'd
> From all her caves, and back resounded Death.
> I fled; but he pursu'd, (though more, it seems,
> Inflam'd with lust than rage), and swifter far,
> Me overtook, his mother all dismay'd,
> And in embraces forcible and foul
> Ingendring with me, of that rape begot
> These yelling monsters that with ceaseless cry
> Sorround me, as thou saw'st, hourly conceiv'd
> And hourly born, with sorrow infinite
> To me; for when they list, into the womb
> That bred them they return, and howl and gnaw
> My bowels, their repast; then bursting forth,

Afresh with conscious terrors vex me round,
That rest or intermission none I find.
Before mine eyes in opposition sits
Grim Death, my son and foe, who sets them on,
And me his parent would full soon devour
For want of other prey, but that he knows
His end with mine involv'd; and knows that I
Should prove a bitter morsel, and his bane,
Whenever that shall be.   *Book* 2. *l. 777.* <368>

Iago's character in the tragedy of *Othello,* is insufferably monstrous and
Satanical: not even Shakespear's masterly hand can make the picture
agreeable.

Though the objects introduced in the following scenes are not altogether
so horrible as Sin is in Milton's description; yet with every person of delicacy, disgust will be the prevailing emotion:

————— Strophades Graio stant nomine dictae
Insulae Ionio in magno: quas dira Celaeno,
Harpyiaeque colunt aliae: Phineia postquam
Clausa domus, mensasque metu liquere priores.
Tristius haud illis monstrum, nec saevior ulla
Pestis et ira Deûm Stygiis sese extulit undis.
Virginei volucrum vultus, foedissima ventris
Proluvies, uncaeque manus, et pallida semper
Ora fame.
Huc ubi delati portus intravimus: ecce
Laeta boum passim campis armenta videmus,
Caprigenumque pecus, nullo custode, per herbas.
Irruimus ferro, et Divos ipsumque vocamus
In praedam partemque Jovem: tunc littore curvo
Extruimusque toros, dapibusque epulamur opimis.
At subitae horrifico lapsu de montibus adsunt
Harpyiae: et magnis quatiunt clangoribus alas:

Diripiuntque dapes, contactuque omnia foedant
Immundo: tum vox tetrum dira inter odorem.

Aeneid. lib. iii. 210.[49]

Sum patria ex Ithaca, comes infelicis Ulyssei,
Nomen Achemenides: Trojam, genitore Adamasto <369>
Paupere (mansissetque utinam fortuna!) profectus.
Hic me, dum trepidi crudelia limina linquunt,
Immemores socii vasto Cyclopis in antro
Deseruere. Domus sanie dapibusque cruentis,
Intus opaca, ingens: ipse arduus, altaque pulsat
Sidera: (Dii, talem terris avertite pestem)
Nec visu facilis, nec dictu affabilis ulli.
Visceribus miserorum, et sanguine vescitur atro.
Vidi egomet, duo de numero cum corpora nostro,
Prensa manu magna, medio resupinus in antro,
Frangeret ad saxum, sanieque aspersa natarent
Limina: vidi, atro cum membra fluentia tabo
Manderet, et tepidi tremerent sub dentibus artus.
Haud impune quidem: nec talia passus Ulysses,
Oblitusve sui est Ithacus discrimine tanto.
Nam simul expletus dapibus, vinoque sepultus
Cervicem inflexam posuit, jacuitque per antrum
Immensus, saniem eructans, ac frusta cruento
Per somnum commixta mero; nos, magna precati

---

49. "Strophades the Greek name they bear—islands set in the great Ionian sea, where dwell dread Celaeno and the other Harpies, since Phineus' house was closed on them, and in fear they left their former tables. No monster more baneful than these, no fiercer plague or wrath of the gods ever rose from the Stygian waves. Maiden faces have these birds, foulest filth they drop, clawed hands are theirs, and faces ever gaunt with hunger.

"When hither borne we entered the harbour, lo! We see goodly herds of cattle scattered over the plains and flocks of goats untended on the grass. We rush upon them with the sword, calling the gods and Jove himself to share our spoil; then on the winding shore we build couches and banquet on the rich dainties. But suddenly, with fearful swoop from the mountains the Harpies are upon us, and with loud clanging shake their wings, plunder the feast, and with unclean touch mire every dish; then amid the foul stench comes a hideous scream."

Numina, sortitique vices, unà undique circum
Fundimur, et telo lumen terebramus acuto
Ingens, quod torva solum sub fronte latebat.

Aeneid. lib. iii. 613.[50] <370>

50. "I come from the land of Ithaca, a companion of luckless Ulysses, Achaemenides by name, and, since my father Adamastus was poor—and would to heaven that fortune had so stayed!—I set out for Troy. Here my comrades, when hastily quitting the grim gateway, thoughtlessly left me in the Cyclops' vast cave. It is a house of gore and blood-stained feasts, dark and huge within. The master, gigantic, strikes the stars on high—ye gods, take such a pest away from earth!—in aspect forbidding, in speech to be accosted by none. He feeds on the flesh of wretched men and their dark blood. I myself saw when he seized in his huge hand two of our company and, lying back in the midst of the cave, crushed them on the rock, and the splashed courts swam with gore; I saw when he munched their limbs, all dripping with black blood-clots, and the warm joints quivered beneath his teeth. Yet not unpunished! Ulysses brooked not this, nor in such a strait was he forgetful of himself. For when, gorged with the feast and drowned in wine, the monster rested his drooping neck, and lay in endless length throughout the cave, in his sleep vomiting gore and morsels mixed with blood and wine, we prayed to the great gods, then, with our parts allotted, poured round him on every side, and with pointed weapon pierced the one huge eye, that lay deep-set beneath his savage brow."

Epic and Dramatic Composition

Tragedy differs not from the epic in substance: in both the same ends are pursued, namely, instruction and amusement; and in both the same mean is employed, namely, imitation of human actions. They differ only in the manner of imitating: epic poetry employs narration; tragedy represents its facts as passing in our sight: in the former, the poet introduces himself as an historian; in the latter, he presents his actors, and never himself.* <371>

This difference, regarding form only, may be thought slight: but the effects it occasions, are by no means so; for what we see makes a deeper impression than what we learn from others. A narrative poem is a story told by another: facts and incidents passing upon the stage, come under our own

---

* The dialogue in a dramatic composition distinguishes it so clearly from other compositions, that no writer has thought it necessary to search for any other distinguishing mark. But much useless labour has been bestowed, to distinguish an epic poem by some peculiar mark. Bossu defines it to be, "A composition in verse, intended to form the manners by instructions disguised under the allegories of an important action"; which excludes every epic poem founded upon real facts, and perhaps includes several of Aesop's fables. Voltaire reckons verse so essential, as for that single reason to exclude the adventures of Telemachus. See his *Essay upon Epic Poetry.* Others, affected with substance more than with form, hesitate not to pronounce that poem to be epic. It is not a little diverting to see so many profound critics hunting for what is not: they take for granted, without the least foundation, that there must be some precise criterion to distinguish epic poetry from every other species of writing. Literary compositions run into each other, precisely like colours: in their strong tints they are easily distinguished; but are susceptible of so much variety and of so many different forms, that we never can say where one species ends and another begins. As to the general taste, there is little reason to doubt, that a work where heroic actions are related in an elevated style, will, without further requisite, be deemed an epic poem.

observation; and are beside much enlivened by action and gesture, expressive of many sentiments beyond the reach of words.

A dramatic composition has another property, independent altogether of action; which is, that it makes a deeper impression than narration: in the former, persons express their own sentiments; in the latter, sentiments are related at second hand. For that reason, Aristotle, the father of critics, lays it down as a rule, That in an epic poem the author ought to take every opportunity of introducing his actors, and of confining the nar-<372> rative part within the narrowest bounds.* Homer understood perfectly the advantage of this method; and his two poems abound in dialogue. Lucan runs to the opposite extreme, even so far as to stuff his *Pharsalia* with cold and languid reflections; the merit of which he assumes to himself, and deigns not to share with his actors. Nothing can be more injudiciously timed, than a chain of such reflections, which suspend the battle of Pharsalia after the leaders had made their speeches, and the two armies are ready to engage.†

Aristotle, regarding the fable only, divides tragedy into simple and complex: but it is of greater moment, with respect to dramatic as well as epic poetry, to found a distinction upon the different ends attained by such compositions. A poem, whether dramatic or epic, that has nothing in view but to move the passions and to exhibit pictures of virtue and vice, may be distinguished by the name of *pathetic:* but where a story is purposely contrived to illustrate some moral truth, by showing that disorderly passions naturally lead to external misfortunes; such composition may be denominated *moral.*‡ Beside making a deeper <373> impression than can be done by cool reasoning, a moral poem does not fall short of reasoning in affording conviction: the natural connection of vice with misery, and of virtue

---

* *Poet.* chap. 25. sect. 6.

† Lib. 7. from line 385. to line 460.

‡ The same distinction is applicable to that sort of fable which is said to be the invention of Aesop. A moral, it is true, is by all critics considered as essential to such a fable. But nothing is more common than to be led blindly by authority; for of the numerous collections I have seen, the fables that clearly inculcate a moral, make a very small part. In many fables, indeed, proper pictures of virtue and vice are exhibited: but the bulk of these collections convey no instruction, nor afford any amusement beyond what a child receives in reading an ordinary story.

with happiness, may be illustrated by stating a fact as well as by urging an argument. Let us assume, for example, the following moral truths; that discord among the chiefs renders ineffectual all common measures; and that the consequences of a slightly-founded quarrel, fostered by pride and arrogance, are no less fatal than those of the grossest injury: these truths may be inculcated, by the quarrel between Agamemnon and Achilles at the siege of Troy. If facts or circumstances be wanting, such as tend to rouse the turbulent passions, they must be invented; but no accidental nor unaccountable event ought to be admitted; for the necessary or probable connection between vice and misery is not learned from any events but what are naturally occasioned by the characters and passions of the persons represented, acting in such and such circumstances. A real event of which we see not the <374> cause, may afford a lesson, upon the presumption that what hath happened may again happen: but this cannot be inserted from a story that is known to be a fiction.

Many are the good effects of such compositions. A pathetic composition, whether epic or dramatic, tends to a habit of virtue, by exciting us to do what is right, and restraining us from what is wrong.* Its frequent pictures of human woes, produce, beside, two effects extremely salutary: they improve our sympathy, and fortify us to bear our own misfortunes. A moral composition obviously produces the same good effects, because by being moral it ceaseth not to be pathetic: it enjoys beside an excellence peculiar to itself; for it not only improves the heart, as above mentioned, but instructs the head by the moral it contains. I cannot imagine any entertainment more suited to a rational being, than a work thus happily illustrating some moral truth: where a number of persons of different characters are engaged in an important action, some retarding, others promoting, the great catastrophe: and where there is dignity of style as well as of matter. A work of that kind has our sympathy at command; and can put in motion the whole train of the social affections: our curiosity in some scenes is excited, in others gratified; and our delight is consummated <375> at the close, upon finding, from the characters and situations exhibited at the commencement, that every incident down to the final catastrophe is nat-

---

* See chap. 2. part I. sect. 4.

ural, and that the whole in conjunction make a regular chain of causes and effects.

Considering that an epic and a dramatic poem are the same in substance, and have the same aim or end, one will readily imagine, that subjects proper for the one must be equally proper for the other. But considering their difference as to form, there will be found reason to correct that conjecture, at least in some degree. Many subjects may indeed be treated with equal advantage in either form; but the subjects are still more numerous for which they are not equally qualified; and there are subjects proper for the one, and not for the other. To give some slight notion of the difference, as there is no room here for enlarging upon every article, I observe, that dialogue is better qualified for expressing sentiments, and narrative for displaying facts. Heroism, magnanimity, undaunted courage, and other elevated virtues, figure best in action: tender passions, and the whole tribe of sympathetic affections, figure best in sentiment. It clearly follows, that tender passions are more peculiarly the province of tragedy, grand and heroic actions of epic poetry.* <376>

I have no occasion to say more upon the epic, considered as peculiarly adapted to certain subjects. But as dramatic subjects are more complex, I must take a narrower view of them; which I do the more willingly, in order to clear a point involved in great obscurity by critics.

In the chapter of Emotions and Passions,† it is occasionally shown, that the subject best fitted for tragedy is where a man has himself been the cause of his misfortune; not so as to be deeply guilty, nor altogether innocent: the misfortune must be occasioned by a fault incident to human nature, and therefore in some degree venial. Such misfortunes call forth the social affections, and warmly interest the spectator. An accidental misfortune, if not extremely singular, doth not greatly move our pity: the person who suffers, being innocent, is freed from the greatest of all torments, that anguish of mind which is occasioned by remorse:

---

* In Racine tender sentiments prevail; in Corneille, grand and heroic manners. Hence clearly the preference of the former before the latter, as dramatic poets. Corneille would have figured better in an heroic poem.

† Part 4.

Poco é funesta
L'altrui fortuna
Quando non resta
Ragione alcuna
Ne di pentirsi, né darrosir.   *Metastasio.*[1] <377>

An atrocious criminal, on the other hand, who brings misfortunes upon himself, excites little pity, for a different reason: his remorse, it is true, aggravates his distress, and swells the first emotions of pity; but these are immediately blunted by our hatred of him as a criminal. Misfortunes that are not innocent, nor highly criminal, partake the advantages of each extreme: they are attended with remorse to embitter the distress, which raises our pity to a height; and the slight indignation we have at a venial fault, detracts not sensibly from our pity. The happiest of all subjects accordingly for raising pity, is where a man of integrity falls into a great misfortune by doing an action that is innocent, but which, by some singular means, is conceived by him to be criminal: his remorse aggravates his distress; and our compassion, unrestrained by indignation, knows no bounds. Pity comes thus to be the ruling passion of a pathetic tragedy; and, by proper representation, may be raised to a height scarce exceeded by any thing felt in real life. A moral tragedy takes in a larger field; as it not only exercises our pity, but raises another passion, which, though selfish, deserves to be cherished equally with the social affection. The passion I have in view is fear or terror; for when a misfortune is the natural consequence of some wrong bias in the temper, every spectator who is conscious of such a bias in himself, takes the alarm, and dreads his falling in-<378>to the same misfortune: and by the emotion of fear or terror, frequently reiterated in a variety of moral tragedies, the spectators are put upon their guard against the disorders of passion.

The commentators upon Aristotle, and other critics, have been much gravelled about the account given of tragedy by that author: "That by means of pity and terror, it refines or purifies in us all sorts of passion." But no one who has a clear conception of the end and effects of a good

---

1. Metastasio: "when there is no reason for repentance or blushing, another man's fortune is not fatal."

tragedy, can have any difficulty about Aristotle's meaning: our pity is engaged for the persons represented; and our terror is upon our own account. Pity indeed is here made to stand for all the sympathetic emotions, because of these it is the capital. There can be no doubt, that our sympathetic emotions are refined or improved by daily exercise; and in what manner our other passions are refined by terror, I have just now said. One thing is certain, that no other meaning can justly be given to the foregoing doctrine than that now mentioned; and that it was really Aristotle's meaning, appears from his 13th chapter, where he delivers several propositions conformable to the doctrine as here explained. These, at the same time, I take liberty to mention; because, as far as authority can go, they confirm the foregoing reasoning about subjects proper for tragedy. The first proposition is, That it being the province of tragedy to excite pity and terror, an <379> innocent person falling into adversity ought never to be the subject. This proposition is a necessary consequence of his doctrine as explained: a subject of that nature may indeed excite pity and terror; but the former in an inferior degree, and the latter in no degree for moral instruction. The second proposition is, That the history of a wicked person in a change from misery to happiness, ought not to be represented. It excites neither terror nor compassion, nor is agreeable in any respect. The third is, That the misfortunes of a wicked person ought not to be represented. Such representation may be agreeable in some measure upon a principle of justice: but it will not move our pity; nor any degree of terror, except in those of the same vicious disposition with the person represented. The last proposition is, That the only character fit for representation lies in the middle, neither eminently good nor eminently bad; where the misfortune is not the effect of deliberate vice, but of some involuntary fault, as our author expresses it.* The only objection I find to Aristotle's account of tragedy, is, that he confines it within too narrow bounds, by refusing admittance to the pathetic kind: for if terror be es-<380>sential to tragedy, no representation deserves that name but the moral kind, where the misfortunes exhibited

---

* If any one can be amused with a grave discourse which promiseth much and performs nothing, I refer to Brumoy in his *Theatre Grec,* Preliminary discourse on the origin of tragedy. [Pierre Brumoy, *Le théâtre des Grecs,* 1730, trans. English 1759.]

are caused by a wrong balance of mind, or some disorder in the internal constitution: such misfortunes always suggest moral instruction; and by such misfortunes only, can terror be excited for our improvement.

Thus Aristotle's four propositions above mentioned, relate solely to tragedies of the moral kind. Those of the pathetic kind, are not confined within so narrow limits: subjects fitted for the theatre, are not in such plenty as to make us reject innocent misfortunes which rouse our sympathy, tho' they inculcate no moral. With respect indeed to subjects of that kind, it may be doubted, whether the conclusion ought not always to be fortunate. Where a person of integrity is represented as suffering to the end under misfortunes purely accidental, we depart discontented, and with some obscure sense of injustice: for seldom is man so submissive to Providence, as not to revolt against the tyranny and vexations of blind chance; he will be tempted to say, This ought not to be. Chance, giving an impression of anarchy and misrule, produces always a damp upon the mind. I give for an example the *Romeo and Juliet* of Shakespear, where the fatal catastrophe is occasioned by Friar Laurence's coming to the monument a minute too late: we are vexed at the unlucky chance, and go away dissatisfied. Such impres-<381>sions, which ought not to be cherished, are a sufficient reason for excluding stories of that kind from the theatre. The misfortunes of a virtuous person, arising from necessary causes or from a chain of unavoidable circumstances, are considered in a different light. A regular chain of causes and effects directed by the general laws of nature, never fails to suggest the hand of Providence; to which we submit without resentment, being conscious that submission is our duty.* For that reason, we are not disgusted with the distresses of Voltaire's *Mariamne,* though redoubled on her till her death, without the least fault or failing on her part: her misfortunes are owing to a cause extremely natural, and not unfrequent, the jealousy of a barbarous husband. The fate of Desdemona, in the *Moor of Venice,* affects us in the same manner. We are not so easily reconciled to the fate of Cordelia in *King Lear:* the causes of her misfortune are by no means so evident, as to exclude the gloomy notion of chance. In short, a perfect character suffering under misfortunes, is qualified for being the subject of a pathetic

* See *Essays on the Principles of Morality,* edit. 2. p. 291.

tragedy, provided chance be excluded. Nor is a perfect character altogether inconsistent with a moral tragedy: it may successfully be introduced in an under-part, if the chief <382> place be occupied by an imperfect character, from which a moral can be drawn. This is the case of Desdemona and Mariamne just mentioned; and it is the case of Monimia and Belvidera, in Otway's two tragedies, *The Orphan,* and *Venice Preserv'd.*

I had an early opportunity to unfold a curious doctrine, That fable operates on our passions, by representing its events as passing in our sight, and by deluding us into a conviction of reality.* Hence, in epic and dramatic compositions, every circumstance ought to be employ'd that may promote the delusion; such as the borrowing from history some noted event, with the addition of circumstances that may answer the author's purpose: the principal facts are known to be true; and we are disposed to extend our belief to every circumstance. But in choosing a subject that makes a figure in history, greater precaution is necessary than where the whole is a fiction. In the latter case there is full scope for invention: the author is under no restraint other than that the characters and incidents be just copies of nature. But where the story is founded on truth, no circumstances must be added, but such as connect naturally with what are known to be true; history may be supplied, but must not be contradicted: further, the subject chosen must be distant in time, or at <383> least in place; for the familiarity of recent persons and events ought to be avoided. Familiarity ought more especially to be avoided in an epic poem, the peculiar character of which is dignity and elevation: modern manners make no figure in such a poem.†

After Voltaire, no writer, it is probable, will think of rearing an epic poem upon a recent event in the history of his own country. But an event of that

---

* Chap. 2. part 1. sect. 7.

† I would not from this observation be thought to under-value modern manners. The roughness and impetuosity of ancient manners, may be better fitted for an epic poem, without being better fitted for society. But without regard to that circumstance, it is the familiarity of modern manners that unqualifies them for a lofty subject. The dignity of our present manners, will be better understood in future ages, when they are no longer familiar.

kind is perhaps not altogether unqualified for tragedy: it was admitted in
Greece; and Shakespear has employ'd it successfully in several of his pieces.
One advantage it possesses above fiction, that of more readily engaging our
belief, which tends above any other circumstance to raise our sympathy.
The scene of comedy is generally laid at home: familiarity is no objection;
and we are peculiarly sensible of the ridicule of our own manners.

After a proper subject is chosen, the dividing it into parts requires some
art. The conclusion of a book in an epic poem, or of an act in a play, can-
<384>not be altogether arbitrary; nor be intended for so slight a purpose
as to make the parts of equal length. The supposed pause at the end of
every book, and the real pause at the end of every act, ought always to
coincide with some pause in the action. In this respect, a dramatic or epic
poem ought to resemble a sentence or period in language, divided into
members that are distinguished from each other by proper pauses; or it
ought to resemble a piece of music, having a full close at the end, preceded
by imperfect closes that contribute to the melody. Every act in a dramatic
poem ought therefore to close with some incident that makes a pause in
the action; for otherwise there can be no pretext for interrupting the representation: it would be absurd to break off in the very heat of action;
against which every one would exclaim: the absurdity still remains where
the action relents, if it be not actually suspended for some time. This rule
is also applicable to an epic poem: though in it a deviation from the rule is
less remarkable; because it is in the reader's power to hide the absurdity, by
proceeding instantly to another book. The first book of *Paradise Lost* ends
without any close, perfect or imperfect: it breaks off abruptly, where Satan,
seated on his throne, is prepared to harangue the convocated host of the
fallen angels; and the second book begins with the speech. Milton seems
to have copied the *Aeneid,* of which the two first <385> books are divided
much in the same manner. Neither is there any proper pause at the end of
the fifth book of the *Aeneid.* There is no proper pause at the end of the
seventh book of *Paradise Lost,* nor at the end of the eleventh. In the *Iliad*
little attention is given to this rule.

This branch of the subject shall be closed with a general rule, That action
being the fundamental part of every composition whether epic or dramatic,
the sentiments and tone of language ought to be subservient to the action,

so as to appear natural, and proper for the occasion. The application of this rule to our modern plays, would reduce the bulk of them to a skeleton.*

<386>

---

* En général il y a beaucoup de discours et peu d'action sur la scene Françoise. Quelqu'un disoit en sortant d'une piece de Denis le Tiran, Je n'ai rien vu, mais j'ai entendu force paroles. Voila ce qu'on peut dire en sortant des pieces Françoises. Racine et Corneille avec tout leur génie ne sont eux-mémes que des parleurs; et leur successeur est le premier qui, à l'imitation des Anglois, ait osé mettre quelquefois la scene en représentation. Communément tout se passe en beaux dialogues bien agencés, bien ronflans, où l'on voit d'abord que le premier soin de chaque interlocuteur est tonjours celui de briller. Presque tout s'enonce en maximes générales. Quelque agités qu'ils puissent être, ils songent toujours plus au public qu'à eux mêmes; une sentence leur coute moins qu'un sentiment; les pieces de Racine et de Moliere exceptées, le *je* est presque aussi scrupuleusement banni de la scene Françoise que des écrits de Port-Royal; et les passions humaines, aussi modestes que l'humilité Chrétienne, n'y parlent jamais que par *on*. Il y a encore une certaine dignité manierée dans le geste et dans le propos, qui ne permet jamais à la passion de parler exactement son language, ni à l'auteur de revetir son personage, et de se transporter au lieu de la scene; mais le tient toujours enchainé sur le théatre, et sous les yeux des spectateurs. Aussi les situations les plus vives ne lui font-elles jamais oublier un bel arrangement de phrases, ni des attitudes élégantes; et si le desespoir lui plonge un poignard dans le cœur, non content d'observer la décence en tombant comme Polixene, il ne tombe point; la décence le maintient debout après sa mort, et tous ceux qui viennent d'expirer s'en retournent l'instant d'après sur leurs jambes.   *Rousseau.*

[*La Nouvelle Héloïse* II, Lettre XVII. "In general there is more talk and less action on the French stage.{ . . .} Someone said this about a play of Denis the Tyrant—I haven't seen it—but I understand the force of the remark. One can say this is distinctive of French plays. Racine and Corneille, for all their genius, are themselves only talkers; and their successor is the first who, following the English, has dared to put some action into the play. Usually everyone spends their time in beautifully constructed and high sounding speeches, where the first priority of every speaker is to be brilliant. Almost everyone expounds general maxims. However worked up they may be, they are always thinking more of the public than of themselves; a sentence cuts them less than a sentiment. Racine and Molière apart, the pronoun 'I' is scrupulously banned by writers of the Port-Royal from the French stage; and human passions, even Christian humility, are almost always prefaced by 'one.' There is, of course, a certain mannered dignity in their gesture and propriety, which forbids an author from burdening his characters with the explicit expression of a passion, and placing himself in the context; but it ensures he is chained to the theatre, under the eyes of the spectator. Even the most lively situations are not allowed to forget the finest arrangement of words, or elegant attitudes; and so if despair plunges a dagger in the heart, not content with observing the decency of falling, Polixene does not fall at all; decency requires him to remain upright after his death, and all those who have just died scramble up again onto their feet." Kames omits a brief passage at the beginning.]

After carrying on together epic and dramatic compositions, I shall mention circumstances peculiar to each; beginning with the epic kind. In a theatrical entertainment, which employs both the eye and the ear, it would be a gross absurdity, to introduce upon the stage superior beings in a visible shape. There is no place for such objection in an epic poem; and Boileau,* with many other critics, declares strongly for that sort of machinery in an epic poem. But waving authority, which is apt to impose upon the judgement, let us draw what light we can from reason. I begin with a preliminary remark, That this matter is but indistinctly handled by critics: the poetical privilege of animating insensible objects for enlivening a de-<387>scription, is very different from what is termed *machinery,* where deities, angels, devils, or other supernatural powers, are introduced as real personages, mixing in the action, and contributing to the catastrophe; and yet these are constantly jumbled together in the reasoning. The former is founded on a natural principle;† but can the latter claim the same authority? far from it; nothing is more unnatural. Its effects, at the same time, are deplorable. First, it gives an air of fiction to the whole; and prevents that impression of reality, which is requisite to interest our affections, and to move our passions.‡ This of itself is sufficient to explode machinery, whatever entertainment it may afford to readers of a fantastic taste or irregular imagination. And, next, were it possible, by disguising the fiction, to delude us into a notion of reality, which I think can hardly be; an insuperable objection would still remain, that the aim or end of an epic poem can never be attained in any perfection, where machinery is introduced; for an evident reason, that virtuous emotions cannot be raised successfully, but by the actions of those who are endued with passions and affections like our own, that is, by human actions: and as for moral instruction, it is clear, that none can be drawn from <388> beings who act not upon the same principles with us. A fable in Aesop's manner is no objection to this reasoning: his lions, bulls, and goats, are truly men in disguise: they act and feel in every respect as human beings; and the moral we draw is founded on that supposition. Homer, it

* Third part of his art of poetry.
† Chap. 20. sect. 1.
‡ See chap. 2. part 1. sect. 7.

is true, introduces the gods into his fable: but the religion of his country authorised that liberty; it being an article in the Grecian creed, that the gods often interpose visibly and bodily in human affairs. I must however observe, that Homer's deities do no honour to his poems: fictions that transgress the bounds of nature, seldom have a good effect; they may inflame the imagination for a moment, but will not be relished by any person of a correct taste. They may be of some use to the lower rank of writers; but an author of genius has much finer materials of Nature's production, for elevating his subject, and making it interesting.

One would be apt to think, that Boileau, declaring for the Heathen deities as above, intended them only for embellishing the diction: but unluckily he banishes angels and devils, who undoubtedly make a figure in poetic language, equal to the Heathen deities. Boileau, therefore, by pleading for the latter in opposition to the former, certainly meant, if he had any distinct meaning, that the Heathen deities may be introduced as actors. And, in fact, he himself is guilty of that <389> glaring absurdity, where it is not so pardonable as in an epic poem. In his ode upon the taking of Namur he demands with a most serious countenance, whether the walls were built by Apollo or Neptune? and in relating the passage of the Rhine, *anno* 1672, he describes the god of that river as fighting with all his might to oppose the French monarch; which is confounding fiction with reality at a strange rate. The French writers in general run into this error: wonderful the effect of custom, to hide from them how ridiculous such fictions are!

That this is a capital error in the *Gierusalemme liberata,* Tasso's greatest admirers must acknowledge: a situation can never be intricate, nor the reader ever in pain about the catastrophe, as long as there is an angel, devil, or magician, to lend a helping hand. Voltaire, in his essay upon epic poetry, talking of the *Pharsalia,* observes judiciously, "That the proximity of time, the notoriety of events, the character of the age, enlightened and political, joined with the solidity of Lucan's subject, deprived him of poetical fiction." Is it not amazing, that a critic who reasons so justly with respect to others, can be so blind with respect to himself? Voltaire, not satisfied to enrich his language with images drawn from invisible and superior beings, introduces them into the action: in the sixth canto of the *Henriade,* St. Louis appears in person, and terri-<390>fies the soldiers; in the seventh canto, St. Louis sends the god of Sleep to Henry; and, in the tenth, the demons of Discord, Fanaticism, War, &c. assist Aumale in a single combat with Turenne, and are driven away by a good angel brandishing the sword of God. To blend such fictitious personages in the same action with mortals, makes a bad figure at any rate; and is intolerable in a history so recent as that of Henry IV. But perfection is not the lot of man.*

I have tried serious reasonings upon this subject; but ridicule, I suppose, will be found a more successful weapon, which Addison has applied in an elegant manner:

> Whereas the time of a gene-<391>ral peace is, in all appearance, drawing near; being informed that there are several ingenious persons who intend to show their talents on so happy an occasion, and being willing, as much as in me lies, to prevent that effusion of nonsense, which we have good cause to apprehend; I do hereby strictly require every person who shall write on this subject, to remember that he is a Christian, and not to sacrifice his catechism to his poetry. In order to it, I do expect of him, in the first place, to make his own poem, without depending upon Phoebus for any part of it, or calling out for aid upon any of the muses by name. I do likewise positively forbid the sending of Mercury with any particular message or dispatch relating to the peace; and shall by no means suffer Minerva to take upon her the shape of any plenipotentiary concerned in this great work. I do farther declare, that I shall not allow the destinies to have had an hand in the deaths of the several thousands who have been slain in the late war; being of opinion that all such deaths may be well accounted for by the Christian system of powder and ball. I do therefore strictly forbid

---

* When I commenced author, my aim was to amuse, and perhaps to instruct, but never to give pain. I accordingly avoided every living author, till the Henriade occurred to me as the best instance I could find for illustrating the doctrine in the text; and I yielded to the temptation, judging that my slight criticisms would never reach M. de Voltaire. They have however reached him; and have, as I am informed, stirred up some resentment. I am afflicted at this information; for what title have I to wound the mind more than the body? It would beside show ingratitude to a celebrated writer, who is highly entertaining, and who has bestow'd on me many a delicious morsel. My only excuse for giving offence is, that it was undesigned; for to plead that the censure is just, is no excuse. As the offence was public, I take this opportunity to make the apology equally so. I hope it will be satisfactory: perhaps not.—I owe it however to my own character.

the fates to cut the thread of man's life upon any pretence whatsoever, unless it be for the sake of the rhyme. And whereas I have good reason to fear, that Neptune will have a great deal of business on his hands in several poems which we <392> may now suppose are upon the anvil, I do also prohibit his appearance, unless it be done in metaphor, simile, or any very short allusion; and that even here he may not be permitted to enter, but with great caution and circumspection. I desire that the same rule may be extended to his whole fraternity of Heathen gods; it being my design, to condemn every poem to the flames in which Jupiter thunders, or exercises any other act of authority which does not belong to him. In short, I expect that no Pagan agent shall be introduced, or any fact related which a man cannot give credit to with a good conscience. Provided always, that nothing herein contained shall extend, or be construed to extend, to several of the female poets in this nation, who shall still be left in full possession of their gods and goddesses, in the same manner as if this paper had never been written.*

The marvellous is indeed so much promoted by machinery, that it is not wonderful to find it embraced by the plurality of writers, and perhaps of readers. If indulged at all, it is generally indulged to excess. Homer introduceth his deities with no greater ceremony than his mortals; and Virgil has still less moderation: a pilot spent with watching cannot fall asleep, and drop into the sea by na-<393>tural means: one bed cannot receive the two lovers, Aeneas and Dido, without the immediate interposition of superior powers. The ridiculous in such fictions, must appear even through the thickest vail of gravity and solemnity.

Angels and devils serve equally with Heathen deities as materials for figurative language; perhaps better among Christians, because we believe in them, and not in Heathen deities. But every one is sensible, as well as Boileau, that the invisible powers in our creed make a much worse figure as actors in a modern poem, than the invisible powers in the Heathen creed did in ancient poems; the cause of which is not far to seek. The Heathen deities, in the opinion of their votaries, were beings elevated one step only above mankind, subject to the same passions, and directed by the same

* *Spectator,* No. 523.

motives; therefore not altogether improper to mix with men in an important action. In our creed, superior beings are placed at such a mighty distance from us, and are of a nature so different, that with no propriety can
we appear with them upon the same stage: man, a creature much inferior,
loses all dignity in the comparison.

There can be no doubt, that an historical poem admits the embellishment of allegory, as well as of metaphor, simile, or other figure. Moral truth,
in particular, is finely illustrated in the allegorical manner: it amuses the
fancy to find abstract terms, by a sort of magic, metamorphos'd into active
be-<394>ings; and it is highly pleasing to discover a general proposition in
a pictured event. But allegorical beings should be confined within their own
sphere, and never be admitted to mix in the principal action, nor to co-
operate in retarding or advancing the catastrophe. This would have a still
worse effect than invisible powers; and I am ready to assign the reason. The
impression of real existence, essential to an epic poem, is inconsistent with
that figurative existence which is essential to an allegory;* and therefore no
means can more effectually prevent the impression of reality, than to introduce allegorical beings co-operating with those whom we conceive to be
really existing. The love-episode, in the *Henriade*,† insufferable by the discordant mixture of allegory with real life, is copied from that of Rinaldo
and Armida, in the *Gierusalemme liberata,* which hath no merit to intitle
it to be copied. An allegorical object, such as Fame in the *Aeneid,* and the
Temple of Love in the *Henriade,* may find place in a description: but to
introduce Discord as a real personage, imploring the assistance of Love, as
another real personage, to enervate the courage of the hero, is making these
figurative beings act beyond their sphere, and creating a strange jumble of
truth and fiction. The allegory of Sin and Death in the *Paradise Lost,* is, I
presume, not generally relish-<395>ed, though it is not entirely of the same
nature with what I have been condemning: in a work comprehending the
achievements of superior beings, there is more room for fancy than where
it is confined to human actions.

What is the true notion of an episode? or how is it to be distinguished

* See chap. 20. sect. 6.
† Canto 9.

from the principal action? Every incident that promotes or retards the catastrophe, must be part of the principal action. This clears the nature of
an episode; which may be defined, "An incident connected with the principal action, but contributing neither to advance nor to retard it." The descent of Aeneas into hell doth not advance nor retard the catastrophe, and
therefore is an episode. The story of Nisus and Euryalus, producing an
alteration in the affairs of the contending parties, is a part of the principal
action. The family-scene in the sixth book of the *Iliad* is of the same nature;
for by Hector's retiring from the field of battle to visit his wife, the Grecians
had opportunity to breathe, and even to turn upon the Trojans. The unavoidable effect of an episode, according to this definition, must be, to
break the unity of action; and therefore it ought never to be indulged, unless
to unbend the mind after the fatigue of a long narration. An episode, when
such is its purpose, requires the following conditions: It ought to be well
connected with the principal action: it ought to be lively and interesting:
it ought to be short: <396> and a time ought to be chosen when the principal action relents.*

   In the following beautiful episode, which closes the second book of Fingal, all these conditions are united.

   Comal was a son of Albion; the chief of an hundred hills. His deer drunk
   of a thousand streams; and a thousand rocks replied to the voice of his
   dogs. His face was the mildness of youth; but his hand the death of heroes.
   One was his love, and fair was she; the daughter of mighty Conloch. She
   appeared like a sun-beam among women, and her hair was like the wing
   of the raven. Her soul was fixed on Comal, and she was his companion
   in the chace. Often met their eyes of love, and happy were their words in
   secret. But Gormal loved the maid, the chief of gloomy Ardven. He
   watched her lone steps on the heath, the foe of unhappy Comal.
      One day tired of the chace, when the mist had concealed their friends,
   Comal and the daughter of Conloch met in the cave of Ronan. It was the
   wonted haunt of Comal. Its sides were hung with his arms; a hundred

   * Homer's description of the shield of Achilles is properly introduced at a time when
the action relents, and the reader can bear an interruption. But the author of Telemachus
describes the shield of that young hero in the heat of battle: a very improper time for
an interruption.

shields of thongs were there, a hundred helms of sounding steel. Rest here, said he, my love Galvina, thou light of the cave of Ronan: a deer appears on Mora's brow; I go, but soon will return. I <397> fear, said she, dark Gormal my foe: I will rest here; but soon return, my love.

He went to the deer of Mora. The daughter of Conloch, to try his love, cloathed her white side with his armour, and strode from the cave of Ronan. Thinking her his foe, his heart beat high, and his colour changed. He drew the bow: the arrow flew: Galvina fell in blood. He ran to the cave with hasty steps, and called the daughter of Conloch. Where art thou, my love? but no answer.—He marked, at length, her heaving heart beating against the mortal arrow. O Conlach's daughter, is it thou! he sunk upon her breast.

The hunters found the hapless pair. Many and silent were his steps round the dark dwelling of his love. The fleet of the ocean came: he fought, and the strangers fell: he searched for death over the field; but who could kill the mighty Comal? Throwing away his shield, an arrow found his manly breast. He sleeps with his Galvina: their green tombs are seen by the mariner, when he bounds on the waves of the north.

Next, upon the peculiarities of a dramatic poem. And the first I shall mention is a double plot; one of which must resemble an episode in an epic poem; for it would distract the spectator, instead of entertaining him, if he were forc'd to attend, at the same time, to two capital plots equally interesting. And even supposing it an under-plot like an episode, it seldom hath a good effect in tragedy, of which simplicity is a chief property; for an <398> interesting subject that engages our affections, occupies our whole attention, and leaves no room for any separate concern.* Variety is more

---

* Racine, in his preface to the tragedy of *Berenice,* is sensible that simplicity is a great beauty in tragedy, but mistakes the cause. "Nothing (says he) but verisimilitude pleases in tragedy: but where is the verisimilitude, that within the compass of a day, events should be crowded which commonly are extended through months?" This is mistaking the accuracy of imitation for the probability or improbability of future events. I explain myself. The verisimilitude required in tragedy is, that the actions correspond to the manners, and the manners to nature. When this resemblance is preserved, the imitation is just, because it is a true copy of nature. But I deny that the verisimilitude of future events, meaning the probability of future events, is any rule in tragedy. A number of extraordinary events, are, it is true, seldom crowded within the compass of a day: but what seldom happens may happen; and when such events fall out, they appear no less natural

tolerable in comedy, which pretends only to amuse, without totally occupying the mind. But even <399> there, to make a double plot agreeable, is no slight effort of art: the under-plot ought not to vary greatly in its tone from the principal; for discordant emotions are unpleasant when jumbled together; which, by the way, is an insuperable objection to tragi-comedy. Upon that account, the *Provok'd Husband* deserves censure: all the scenes that bring the family of the Wrongheads into action, being ludicrous and farcical, are in a very different tone from the principal scenes, displaying severe and bitter expostulations between Lord Townley and his lady. The same objection touches not the double plot of the *Careless Husband;* the different subjects being sweetly connected, and having only so much variety as to resemble shades of colours harmoniously mixed. But this is not all. The under-plot ought to be connected with that which is principal, so much at least as to employ the same persons: the under-plot ought to occupy the intervals or pauses of the principal action; and both ought to be concluded together. This is the case of the *Merry Wives of Windsor.*

Violent action ought never to be represented on the stage. While the dialogue goes on, a thousand particulars concur to delude us into an impression of reality; genuine sentiments, passionate language, and persuasive gesture: the spectator once engaged, is willing to be deceived, loses sight of himself, and without scruple enjoys the <400> spectacle as a reality. From this absent state, he is roused by violent action: he wakes as from a pleasing dream, and gathering his senses about him, finds all to be a fiction. Horace delivers the same rule, and founds it upon the same reason:

> Ne pueros coram populo Medea trucidet;
> Aut humana palam coquat exta nefarius Atreus;

---

than the most ordinary accidents. To make verisimilitude in the sense of probability a governing rule in tragedy, would annihilate that sort of writing altogether; for it would exclude all extraordinary events, in which the life of tragedy consists. It is very improbable or unlikely, pitching upon any man at random, that he will sacrifice his life and fortune for his mistress or for his country: yet when that event happens, supposing it comformable to the character, we recognise the verisimilitude as to nature, whatever want of verisimilitude or of probability there was *a priori* that such would be the event.

Aut in avem Procne vertatur, Cadmus in anguem:
Quodcumque ostendis mihi sic, incredulus odi.[2]

The French critics join with Horace in excluding blood from the stage; but overlooking the most substantial objection, they urge only, that it is barbarous, and shocking to a polite audience. The Greeks had no notion of such delicacy, or rather effeminacy; witness the murder of Clytemnestra by her son Orestes, passing behind the scene as represented by Sophocles: her voice is heard calling out for mercy, bitter expostulations on his part, loud shrieks upon her being stabb'd, and then a deep silence. I appeal to every person of feeling, whether this scene be not more horrible than if the deed had been committed in sight of the spectators upon a sudden gust of passion. If Corneille, in representing the affair between Horatius and his sister, upon which murder ensues behind the scene, had no other view but to remove from the spectators a shocking action, he was guilty of a capital mistake: for murder in cold <401> blood, which in some measure was the case as represented, is more shocking to a polite audience, even where the conclusive stab is not seen, than the same act performed in their presence by violent and unpremeditated passion, as suddenly repented of as committed. I heartily agree with Addison,* that no part of this incident ought to have been represented, but reserved for a narrative, with every alleviating circumstance in favour of the hero.

A few words upon the dialogue; which ought to be so conducted as to be a true representation of nature. I talk not here of the sentiments, nor of the language; for these come under different heads: I talk of what properly belongs to dialogue-writing; where every single speech, short or long, ought to arise from what is said by the former speaker, and furnish matter for what comes after, till the end of the scene. In this view, all the speeches, from first to last, represent so many links of one continued chain. No author, ancient or modern, possesses the art of dialogue equal to Shakespear.

* *Spectator,* No. 44.
2. "So that Medea is not to butcher her boys before the people, nor impious Atreus cook human flesh upon the stage, nor Procne be turned into a bird, Cadmus into a snake" (*Ars poetica* 185).

Dryden, in that particular, may justly be placed as his opposite: he frequently introduces three or four persons speaking upon the same subject, each throwing out his own notions separately, without regarding what is said by the <402> rest: take for an example the first scene of *Aurenzebe*. Sometimes he makes a number club in relating an event, not to a stranger, supposed ignorant of it; but to one another, for the sake merely of speaking: of which notable sort of dialogue, we have a specimen in the first scene of the first part of the *Conquest of Granada*. In the second part of the same tragedy, scene second, the King, Abenamar, and Zulema, make their separate observations, like so many soliloquies, upon the fluctuating temper of the mob. A dialogue so uncouth, puts one in mind of two shepherds in a pastoral, excited by a prize to pronounce verses alternately, each in praise of his own mistress.

This manner of dialogue-writing, beside an unnatural air, has another bad effect: it stays the course of the action, because it is not productive of any consequence. In Congreve's comedies, the action is often suspended to make way for a play of wit. But of this more particularly in the chapter immediately following.

No fault is more common among writers, than to prolong a speech after the impatience of the person to whom it is addressed ought to prompt him or her to break in. Consider only how the impatient actor is to behave in the mean time. To express his impatience in violent action without interrupting, would be unnatural; and yet to dissemble his impatience, by appearing cool where <403> he ought to be highly inflamed, would be no less so.

Rhyme being unnatural and disgustful in dialogue, is happily banished from our theatre: the only wonder is that it ever found admittance, especially among a people accustomed to the more manly freedom of Shakespear's dialogue. By banishing rhyme, we have gained so much, as never once to dream of any further improvement. And yet, however suitable blank verse may be to elevated characters and warm passions, it must appear improper and affected in the mouths of the lower sort. Why then should it be a rule, That every scene in tragedy must be in blank verse? Shakespear, with great judgement, has followed a different rule; which is, to intermix prose with verse, and only to employ the latter where it is required by the importance or dignity of the subject. Familiar thoughts and ordinary facts ought to be expressed in plain language: to hear, for example, a footman deliver a simple message in blank verse, must appear ridiculous to every one who is not biassed by custom. In short, that variety of characters and of situations, which is the life of a play, requires not only a suitable variety in the sentiments, but also in the diction. <404>

The Three Unities

In the first chapter is explained the pleasure we have in a chain of connected facts. In histories of the world, of a country, of a people, this pleasure is faint; because the connections are slight or obscure. We find more entertainment in biography; because the incidents are connected by their relation to a person who makes a figure, and commands our attention. But the greatest entertainment is in the history of a single event, supposing it interesting; and the reason is, that the facts and circumstances are connected by the strongest of all relations, that of cause and effect: a number of facts that give birth to each other form a delightful train; and we have great mental enjoyment in our progress from the beginning to the end.

But this subject merits a more particular discussion. When we consider the chain of causes and effects in the material world, independent of purpose, design, or thought, we find a number of incidents in succession, without beginning, middle, or end: every thing that happens is both a cause and an effect; being the effect of what goes be-<405>fore, and the cause of what follows: one incident may affect us more, another less; but all of them are links in the universal chain: the mind, in viewing these incidents, cannot rest or settle ultimately upon any one; but is carried along in the train without any close.

But when the intellectual world is taken under view, in conjunction with the material, the scene is varied. Man acts with deliberation, will, and choice: he aims at some end, glory, for example, or riches, or conquest, the procuring happiness to individuals, or to his country in general: he proposes means, and lays plans to attain the end purposed. Here are a number of facts or incidents leading to the end in view, the whole composing one chain by the relation of cause and effect. In running over a series of such facts or incidents, we cannot rest upon any one; because they are presented to us as means only, leading to some end: but we rest with satisfaction upon the end or ultimate event; because there the purpose or aim of the chief person or persons is accomplished. This indicates the beginning, the middle, and the end, of what Aristotle calls *an entire action.** The story naturally begins with describing those circumstances which move the principal person to form a plan, in order to compass some desired event: the prosecution of that plan and the <406> obstructions, carry the reader into the heat of action: the middle is properly where the action is the most involved; and the end is where the event is brought about, and the plan accomplished.

A plan thus happily accomplished after many obstructions, affords wonderful delight to the reader; to produce which, a principle mentioned above† mainly contributes, the same that disposes the mind to complete every work commenced, and in general to carry every thing to a conclusion.

I have given the foregoing example of a plan crowned with success, because it affords the clearest conception of a beginning, a middle, and an end, in which consists *unity* of action; and indeed stricter unity cannot be imagined than in that case. But an action may have unity, or a beginning, middle, and end, without so intimate a relation of parts; as where the catastrophe is different from what is intended or desired, which frequently happens in our best tragedies. In the *Aeneid,* the hero, after many obstructions, makes his plan effectual. The *Iliad* is formed upon a different model: it begins with the quarrel between Achilles and Agamemnon; goes on to describe the several effects produced by that cause; and ends in a reconciliation. Here is unity of ac-<407>tion, no doubt, a beginning, a middle, and an end; but inferior to that of the *Aeneid,* which will thus appear. The mind hath a propensity to go forward in the chain of history: it keeps always in view the expected event; and when the incidents or under-parts are connected by their relation to the event, the mind runs sweetly and easily along them. This pleasure we have in the *Aeneid.* It is not altogether so pleasant, as in the *Iliad,* to connect effects by their common cause; for such con-

* *Poet.* cap. 6. See also cap. 7.
† Chap. 8.

nection forces the mind to a continual retrospect: looking back is like walk-ing backward.

Homer's plan is still more defective, upon another account, That the events described are but imperfectly connected with the wrath of Achilles, their cause: his wrath did not exert itself in action; and the misfortunes of his countrymen were but negatively the effects of his wrath, by depriving them of his assistance.

If unity of action be a capital beauty in a fable imitative of human affairs, a plurality of unconnected fables must be a capital deformity. For the sake of variety, we indulge an under-plot that is connected with the principal: but two unconnected events are extremely unpleasant, even where the same actors are engaged in both. Ariosto is quite licentious in that particular: he carries on at the same time a plurality of unconnected stories. His only excuse is, that his plan is perfectly well <408> adjusted to his subject; for every thing in the *Orlando Furioso* is wild and extravagant.

Tho' to state facts in the order of time is natural, yet that order may be varied for the sake of conspicuous beauties.* If, for example, a noted story, cold and simple in its first movements, be made the subject of an epic poem, the reader may be hurried into the heat of action; reserving the prelimi-naries for a conversation-piece, if thought necessary; and that method, at the same time, hath a peculiar beauty from being dramatic.† But a privilege that deviates from nature ought to be sparingly indulged; and yet romance-writers make no difficulty of presenting to the reader, without the least preparation, unknown persons engaged in some arduous adventure equally unknown. In *Cassandra*,[1] two personages, who afterward are discovered to be the heroes of the fable, start up completely armed upon the banks of the Euphrates, and engage in a single combat.‡

---

* See chap. 1.

† See chap. 21.

‡ I am sensible that a commencement of this sort is much relished by readers disposed to the marvellous. Their curiosity is raised, and they are much tickled in its gratification. But curiosity is at an end with the first reading, because the personages are no longer unknown; and therefore at the second reading, a commencement so artificial loses its power even over the vulgar. A writer of genius prefers lasting beauties.

1. Gauthier de Costes (1614–63), *Cassandra*, 1644–50 (translated into English 1667).

A play analysed, is a chain of connected facts, < 409 > of which each scene makes a link. Each scene, accordingly, ought to produce some incident relative to the catastrophe or ultimate event, by advancing or retarding it. A scene that produceth no incident, and for that reason may be termed *barren,* ought not to be indulged, because it breaks the unity of action: a barren scene can never be intitled to a place, because the chain is complete without it. In the *Old Bachelor,* the 3d scene of act 2. and all that follow to the end of that act, are mere conversation-pieces, productive of no consequence. The 10th and 11th scenes, act 3. *Double Dealer,* the 10th, 11th, 12th, 13th, and 14th scenes, act 1. *Love for Love,* are of the same kind. Neither is *The Way of the World* entirely guiltless of such scenes. It will be no justification, that they help to display characters: it were better, like Dryden in his *dramatis personae,* to describe characters beforehand, which would not break the chain of action. But a writer of genius has no occasion for such artifice: he can display the characters of his personages much more to the life in sentiment and action. How successfully is this done by Shakespear! in whose works there is not to be found a single barren scene.

Upon the whole, it appears, that all the facts in an historical fable, ought to have a mutual connection, by their common relation to the grand event or catastrophe. And this relation, in which the *unity* of action consists, is equally essential to epic and dramatic compositions. < 410 >

In handling unity of action, it ought not to escape observation, that the mind is satisfied with slighter unity in a picture than in a poem; because the perceptions of the former are more lively than the ideas of the latter. In *Hogarth's Enraged Musician,*[2] we have a collection of every grating sound in nature, without any mutual connection except that of place. But the horror they give to the delicate ear of an Italian fidler, who is represented almost in convulsions, bestows unity upon the piece, with which the mind is satisfied.

How far the unities of time and of place are essential, is a question of greater intricacy. These unities were strictly observed in the Greek and Roman theatres; and they are inculcated by the French and English critics, as essential to every dramatic composition. They are also acknowledged by

2. Engraving published in 1741.

our best poets, though in practice they make frequent deviation, which they pretend not to justify, against the practice of the Greeks and Romans, and against the solemn decision of their own countrymen. But in the course of this inquiry it will be made evident, that in this article we are under no necessity to copy the ancients; and that our critics are guilty of a mistake, in admitting no greater latitude of place and time than was admitted in Greece and Rome.

Suffer me only to premise, that the unities of place and time, are not, by the most rigid critics, <411> required in a narrative poem. In such a composition, if it pretend to copy nature, these unities would be absurd; because real events are seldom confined within narrow limits either of place or of time. And yet we can follow history, or an historical fable, through all its changes, with the greatest facility: we never once think of measuring the real time by what is taken in reading; nor of forming any connection between the place of action and that which we occupy.

I am sensible, that the drama differs so far from the epic, as to admit different rules. It will be observed, "That an historical fable, intended for reading solely, is under no limitation of time nor of place, more than a genuine history; but that a dramatic composition cannot be accurately represented, unless it be limited, as its representation is, to one place and to a few hours; and therefore that it can admit no fable but what has these properties; because it would be absurd to compose a piece for representation that cannot be justly represented." This argument, I acknowledge, has at least a plausible appearance; and yet one is apt to suspect some fallacy, considering that no critic, however strict, has ventured to confine the unities of place and of time within so narrow bounds.* <412>

A view of the Grecian drama, compared with our own, may perhaps relieve us from this dilemma: if they be differently constructed, as shall be made evident, it is possible that the foregoing reasoning may not be equally

---

* Bossu, after observing, with wondrous critical sagacity, that winter is an improper season for an epic poem, and night no less improper for tragedy; admits however, that an epic poem may be spred through the whole summer months, and a tragedy through the whole sunshine hours of the longest summer-day. *Du poeme epique, l. 3. chap.* 12. At that rate an English tragedy may be longer than a French tragedy; and in Nova Zembla the time of a tragedy and of an epic poem may be the same.

applicable to both. This is an article that, with relation to the present subject, has not been examined by any writer.

All authors agree, that tragedy in Greece was derived from the hymns in
praise of Bacchus, which were sung in parts by a chorus. Thespis, to relieve
the singers and for the sake of variety, introduced one actor; whose province
it was to explain historically the subject of the song, and who occasionally
represented one or other personage. Eschylus, introducing a second actor,
formed the dialogue, by which the performance became dramatic; and the
actors were multiplied when the subject represented made it necessary. But
still, the chorus, which gave a beginning to tragedy, was considered as an
essential part. The first scene, generally, unfolds the preliminary circumstances that lead to the grand event: and this <413> scene is by Aristotle
termed the *prologue.* In the second scene, where the action properly begins,
the chorus is introduced, which, as originally, continues upon the stage
during the whole performance: the chorus frequently makes one in the dialogue; and when the dialogue happens to be suspended, the chorus, during
the interval, is employ'd in singing. Sophocles adheres to this plan reli-
giously. Euripides is not altogether so correct. In some of his pieces, it
becomes necessary to remove the chorus for a little time. But when that
unusual step is risked, matters are so ordered as not to interrupt the
representation: the chorus never leave the stage of their own accord, but
at the command of some principal personage, who constantly waits their
return.

Thus the Grecian drama is a continued representation without interruption; a circumstance that merits attention. A continued representation
without a pause, affords not opportunity to vary the place of action, nor
to prolong the time of the action beyond that of the representation. To a
representation so confined in place and time, the foregoing reasoning is
strictly applicable: a real or feigned action that is brought to a conclusion
after considerable intervals of time and frequent changes of place, cannot
accurately be copied in a representation that admits no latitude in either.
Hence it is, that the unities of place and of time, were, or ought to have
been, strictly observed in the Greek <414> tragedies; which is made necessary by the very constitution of their drama, for it is absurd to compose
a tragedy that cannot be justly represented.

Modern critics, who for our drama pretend to establish rules founded
on the practice of the Greeks, are guilty of an egregious blunder. The unities
of place and of time were in Greece, as we see, a matter of necessity, not
of choice; and I am now ready to show, that if we submit to such fetters,
it must be from choice, not necessity. This will be evident upon taking a
view of the constitution of our drama, which differs widely from that of
Greece; whether more or less perfect, is a different point, to be handled
afterward. By dropping the chorus, opportunity is afforded to divide the
representation by intervals of time, during which the stage is evacuated and
the spectacle suspended. This qualifies our drama for subjects spread
through a wide space both of time and of place: the time supposed to pass
during the suspension of the representation, is not measured by the time
of the suspension; and any place may be supposed when the representation
is renewed, with as much facility as when it commenced: by which means,
many subjects can be justly represented in our theatres, that were excluded
from those of ancient Greece. This doctrine may be illustrated, by comparing a modern play to a set of historical pictures; let us suppose them five
in number, and the resemblance will be complete. Each of the pictures
<415> resembles an act in one of our plays: there must necessarily be the
strictest unity of place and of time in each picture; and the same necessity
requires these two unities during each act of a play, because during an act
there is no interruption in the spectacle. Now, when we view in succession
a number of such historical pictures, let it be, for example, the history of
Alexander by Le Brun,[3] we have no difficulty to conceive, that months or
years have passed between the events exhibited in two different pictures,
though the interruption is imperceptible in passing our eye from the one
to the other; and we have as little difficulty to conceive a change of place,
however great. In which view, there is truly no difference between five acts
of a modern play, and five such pictures. Where the representation is suspended, we can with the greatest facility suppose any length of time or any
change of place: the spectator, it is true, may be conscious, that the real
time and place are not the same with what are employed in the representation: but this is a work of reflection; and by the same reflection he may

3. See above vol. 1, pp. 101, 322.

also be conscious, that Garrick is not King Lear, that the playhouse is not Dover cliffs, nor the noise he hears thunder and lightning. In a word, after an interruption of the representation, it is no more difficult for a spectator to imagine a new place, or a different time, than at the commencement of the play, to imagine himself at Rome, or in a period of time two thou- <416>sand years back. And indeed, it is abundantly ridiculous, that a critic, who is willing to hold candle-light for sun-shine, and some painted canvasses for a palace or a prison, should be so scrupulous about admitting any latitude of place or of time in the fable, beyond what is necessary in the representation.

There are, I acknowledge, some effects of great latitude in time that ought never to be indulged in a composition for the theatre: nothing can be more absurd, than at the close to exhibit a full-grown person who appears a child at the beginning: the mind rejects, as contrary to all probability, such latitude of time as is requisite for a change so remarkable. The greatest change from place to place hath not altogether the same bad effect. In the bulk of human affairs place is not material; and the mind, when occupied with an interesting event, is little regardful of minute circumstances: these may be varied at will, because they scarce make any impression.

But though I have taken arms to rescue modern poets from the despotism of modern critics, I would not be understood to justify liberty without any reserve. An unbounded licence with relation to place and time, is faulty for a reason that seems to have been overlooked, which is, that it seldom fails to break the unity of action. In the ordinary course of human affairs, single events, such as are fit to be represented on the stage, are confined to a <417> narrow spot, and commonly employ no great extent of time: we accordingly seldom find strict unity of action in a dramatic composition, where any remarkable latitude is indulged in these particulars. I say further, that a composition which employs but one place, and requires not a greater length of time than is necessary for the representation, is so much the more perfect: because the confining an event within so narrow bounds, contributes to the unity of action; and also prevents that labour, however slight, which the mind must undergo in imagining frequent changes of place and many intervals of time. But still I must insist, that such limitation of place and time as was necessary in the Grecian drama, is no rule to us; and therefore, that though such limitation adds one beauty more to the composition, it is at best but a refinement, which may justly give place to a thousand beauties more substantial. And I may add, that it is extremely difficult, I was about to say impracticable, to contract within the Grecian limits, any fable so fruitful of incidents in number and variety, as to give full scope to the fluctuation of passion.

It may now appear, that critics who put the unities of place and of time upon the same footing with the unity of action, making them all equally essential, have not attended to the nature and constitution of the modern drama. If they admit an interrupted representation, with which no writer <418> finds fault, it is absurd to reject its greatest advantage, that of representing many interesting subjects excluded from the Grecian stage. If there needs must be a reformation, why not restore the ancient chorus and the ancient continuity of action? There is certainly no medium: for to admit an interruption without relaxing from the strict unities of place and of time, is in effect to load us with all the inconveniences of the ancient drama, and at the same time to with-hold from us its advantages.

The only proper question, therefore, is, Whether our model be or be not a real improvement? This indeed may fairly be called in question; and in order to a comparative trial, some particulars must be premised. When a play begins, we have no difficulty to adjust our imagination to the scene of action, however distant it be in time or in place; because we know that the play is a representation only. The case is very different after we are engaged: it is the perfection of representation to hide itself, to impose on the spectator, and to produce in him an impression of reality, as if he were a spectator of a real event;* but any interruption annihilates that impression, by rousing him out of his waking dream, and unhappily restoring him to his senses. So difficult it is to support the impression of reality, that much slighter <419> interruptions than the interval between two acts, are sufficient to dissolve the charm: in the 5th act of the *Mourning Bride,* the three first scenes are in a room of state, the fourth in a prison; and the change is operated by shifting the scene, which is done in a trice: but however quick the transition may be, it is impracticable to impose upon the spectators, so

---

* Chap. 2. part 1. sect. 7.

as to make them conceive that they are actually carried from the palace to the prison; they immediately reflect, that the palace and prison are imaginary, and that the whole is a fiction.

From these premises, one will naturally be led, at first view, to pronounce the frequent interruptions in the modern drama to be an imperfection. It will occur, "That every interruption must have the effect to banish the dream of reality, and with it to banish our concern, which cannot subsist while we are conscious that all is a fiction; and therefore, that in the modern drama sufficient time is not afforded for fluctuation and swelling of passion, like what is afforded in that of Greece, where there is no interruption." This reasoning, it must be owned, has a specious appearance: but we must not become faint-hearted upon the first repulse; let us rally our troops for a second engagement.

Considering attentively the ancient drama, we find, that though the representation is never interrupted, the principal action is suspended not less <420> frequently than in the modern drama: there are five acts in each; and the only difference is, that in the former, when the action is suspended as it is at the end of every act, opportunity is taken of the interval to employ the chorus in singing. Hence it appears, that the Grecian continuity of representation cannot have the effect to prolong the impression of reality: to banish that impression, a pause in the action while the chorus is employ'd in singing, is no less effectual than a total suspension of the representation.

But to open a larger view, I am ready to show, that a representation with proper pauses, is better qualified for making a deep impression, than a continued representation without a pause. This will be evident from the following considerations. Representation cannot very long support an impression of reality; for when the spirits are exhausted by close attention and by the agitation of passion, an uneasiness ensues, which never fails to banish the waking dream. Now supposing the time that a man can employ with strict attention without wandering, to be no greater than is requisite for a single act, a supposition that cannot be far from truth; it follows, that a continued representation of longer endurance than an act, instead of giving scope to fluctuation and swelling of passion, would overstrain the attention, and produce a total absence of mind. In that respect, the four pauses have a fine effect; for by affording to the audience <421> a seasonable respite when the impression of reality is gone, and while nothing material is in agitation, they relieve the mind from its fatigue; and consequently prevent a wandering of thought at the very time possibly of the most interesting scenes.

In one article, indeed, the Grecian model has greatly the advantage: its chorus, during an interval, not only preserves alive the impressions made upon the audience, but also prepares their hearts finely for new impressions. In our theatres, on the contrary, the audience, at the end of every act, being left to trifle time away, lose every warm impression; and they begin the next act cool and unconcerned, as at the commencement of the representation. This is a gross malady in our theatrical representations; but a malady that luckily is not incurable. To revive the Grecian chorus, would be to revive the Grecian slavery of place and time; but I can figure a detached chorus coinciding with a pause in the representation, as the ancient chorus did with a pause in the principal action. What objection, for example, can there lie against music between the acts, vocal and instrumental, adapted to the subject? Such detached chorus, without putting us under any limitation of time or place, would recruit the spirits, and would preserve entire the tone, if not the tide, of passion: the music, after an act, should commence in the tone of the preceding passion, and be gradually varied till it accord with the tone of the <422> passion that is to succeed in the next act. The music and the representation would both of them be gainers by their conjunction; which will thus appear. Music that accords with the present tone of mind, is, on that account, doubly agreeable; and accordingly, though music singly hath not power to raise a passion, it tends greatly to support a passion already raised. Further, music prepares us for the passion that follows, by making cheerful, tender, melancholy, or animated impressions, as the subject requires. Take for an example the first scene of the *Mourning Bride,* where soft music,[4] in a melancholy strain, prepares us for Almeria's deep distress. In this manner, music and representation support each other delightfully: the impression made upon the audience by the representation, is a fine preparation for the music that succeeds; and the impression made by the music, is a fine preparation for the representation that succeeds. It

4. The music was by Gottfried Finger.

appears to me evident, that, by some such contrivance, the modern drama
may be improved, so as to enjoy the advantage of the ancient chorus without its slavish limitation of place and time. And as to music in particular,
I cannot figure any means that would tend more to its improvement: composers, those for the stage at least, would be reduced to the happy necessity
of studying and imitating nature; instead of deviating, according to the
present mode, into wild, fantastic, and unnatural conceits. But we must
return to our sub-<423>ject, and finish the comparison between the ancient
and the modern drama.

The numberless improprieties forced upon the Greek dramatic poets by
the constitution of their drama, may be sufficient, one should think, to
make us prefer the modern drama, even abstracting from the improvement
proposed. To prepare the reader for this article, it must be premised, that
as in the ancient drama the place of action never varies, a place necessarily
must be chosen, to which every person may have access without any improbability. This confines the scene to some open place, generally the court
or area before a palace; which excludes from the Grecian theatre transactions within doors, though these commonly are the most important. Such
cruel restraint is of itself sufficient to cramp the most pregnant invention;
and accordingly Greek writers, in order to preserve unity of place, are reduced to woful improprieties. In the *Hippolytus* of Euripides,* Phedra, dis-
tressed in mind and body, is carried without any pretext from her palace to
the place of action: is there laid upon a couch, unable to support herself
upon her limbs, and made to utter many things improper to be heard by
a number of women who form the chorus: and what is still more improper,
her female attendant uses the strongest intreaties to make her reveal the
secret <424> cause of her anguish; which at last Phedra, contrary to decency
and probability, is prevailed upon to do in presence of that very chorus.†
Alcestes, in Euripides, at the point of death, is brought from the palace to
the place of action, groaning, and lamenting her untimely fate.‡ In the
Trachiniens of Sophocles,§ a secret is imparted to Dejanira, the wife of

* Act 1. sc. 6.
† Act 2. sc. 2.
‡ Act 2. sc. 1.
§ Act 2.

Hercules, in presence of the chorus. In the tragedy of *Iphigenia*, the messenger employ'd to inform Clitemnestra that Iphigenia was sacrificed, stops short at the place of action, and with a loud voice calls the Queen from her palace to hear the news. Again, in the *Iphigenia in Tauris*, the necessary presence of the chorus forces Euripides into a gross absurdity, which is to form a secret in their hearing;* and to disguise the absurdity, much court is paid to the chorus, not one woman but a number, to engage them to secrecy. In the *Medea* of Euripides, that princess makes no difficulty, in presence of the chorus, to plot the death of her husband, of his mistress, and of her father the King of Corinth, all by poison. It was necessary to bring Medea upon the stage, and there is but one place of action, which is always occupied by the chorus. This scene closes the second act: and in the end of the third, she frankly makes the chorus her <425> confidents in plotting the murder of her own children. Terence, by identity of place, is often forc'd to make a conversation within doors be heard on the open street: the cries of a woman in labour are there heard distinctly.

The Greek poets are not less hampered by unity of time than by that of place. In the *Hippolytus* of Euripides, that prince is banished at the end of the fourth act; and in the first scene of the following act, a messenger relates to Theseus the whole particulars of the death of Hippolytus by the sea-monster: that remarkable event must have occupied many hours; and yet in the representation, it is confined to the time employed by the chorus upon the song at the end of the 4th act. The inconsistency is still greater in the *Iphigenia in Tauris:*† the song could not exhaust half an hour; and yet the incidents supposed to have happened during that time, could not naturally have been transacted in less than half a day.

The Greek artists are forc'd, no less frequently, to transgress another rule, derived also from a continued representation. The rule is, that as a vacuity, however momentary, interrupts the representation, it is necessary that the place of action be constantly occupied. Sophocles, with regard to that rule as well as to others, is generally correct. But Euripides cannot bear such restraint: <426> he often evacuates the stage, and leaves it empty for others.

* Act 4. at the close.
† Act 5. sc. 4.

Iphigenia in Tauris, after pronouncing a soliloquy in the first scene, leaves the place of action, and is succeeded by Orestes and Pylades: they, after some conversation, walk off; and Iphigenia re-enters, accompanied with the chorus. In the *Alcestes,* which is of the same author, the place of action is void at the end of the third act. It is true, that to cover the irregularity, and to preserve the representation in motion, Euripides is careful to fill the stage without loss of time: but this still is an interruption, and a link of the chain broken; for during the change of the actors, there must be a space of time, during which the stage is occupied by neither set. It makes indeed a more remarkable interruption, to change the place of action as well as the actors; but that was not practicable upon the Grecian stage.

It is hard to say upon what model Terence has formed his plays. Having no chorus, there is a pause in the representation at the end of every act. But advantage is not taken of the cessation, even to vary the place of action: for the street is always chosen, where every thing passing may be seen by every person; and by that choice, the most sprightly and interesting parts of the action, which commonly pass within doors, are excluded; witness the last act of the *Eunuch.* He hath submitted to the like slavery with respect to time. In a word, a <427> play with a regular chorus, is not more confined in place and time than his plays are. Thus a zealous sectary follows implicitly ancient forms and ceremonies, without once considering whether their introductive cause be still subsisting. Plautus, of a bolder genius than Terence, makes good use of the liberty afforded by an interrupted representation: he varies the place of action upon all occasions, when the variation suits his purpose.

The intelligent reader will by this time understand, that I plead for no change of place in our plays but after an interval, nor for any latitude in point of time but what falls in with an interval. The unities of place and time ought to be strictly observed during each act; for during the representation, there is no opportunity for the smallest deviation from either. Hence it is an essential requisite, that during an act the stage be always occupied; for even a momentary vacuity makes an interval or interruption. Another rule is no less essential: it would be a gross breach of the unity of action, to exhibit upon the stage two separate actions at the same time; and therefore, to preserve that unity, it is necessary that each personage introduced during an act, be linked to those in possession of the stage, so as to join all in one action. These things follow from the very conception of an act, which admits not the slightest interruption: the moment the representation is intermitted, there is an end of that act; and we <428> have no notion of a new act, but where, after a pause or interval, the representation is again put in motion. French writers, generally speaking, are correct in this particular. The English, on the contrary, are so irregular, as scarce to deserve a criticism. Actors, during the same act, not only succeed each other in the same place without connection, but what is still less excusable, they frequently succeed each other in different places. This change of place in the same act, ought never to be indulged; for, beside breaking the unity of the act, it has a disagreeable effect. After an interval, the imagination readily adapts itself to any place that is necessary, as readily as at the commencement of the play; but during the representation, we reject change of place. From the foregoing censure must be excepted the *Mourning Bride* of Congreve, where regularity concurs with the beauty of sentiment and of language, to make it one of the most complete pieces England has to boast of. I must acknowledge, however, that in point of regularity, this elegant performance is not altogether unexceptionable. In the four first acts, the unities of place and time are strictly observed: but in the last act, there is a capital error with respect to unity of place; for in the three first scenes of that act, the place of action is a room of state, which is changed to a prison in the fourth scene: the chain also of the actors is broken; as the persons introduced in the prison, are different from <429> those who made their appearance in the room of state. This remarkable interruption of the representation, makes in effect two acts instead of one: and therefore, if it be a rule that a play ought not to consist of more acts than five, this performance is so far defective in point of regularity. I may add, that even admitting six acts, the irregularity would not be altogether removed, without a longer pause in the representation than is allowed in the acting; for more than a momentary interruption is requisite for enabling the imagination readily to fall in with a new place, or with a wide space of time. In *The Way of the World,* of the same author, unity of place is preserved during every act, and a stricter unity of time during the whole play, than is necessary. <430>

Gardening and Architecture

The books we have upon architecture and upon embellishing ground, abound in practical instruction, necessary for a mechanic: but in vain should we rummage them for rational principles to improve our taste. In a general system, it might be thought sufficient to have unfolded the principles that govern these and other fine arts, leaving the application to the reader: but as I would neglect no opportunity of showing the extensive influence of these principles, the purpose of the present chapter is to apply them to gardening and architecture; but without intending any regular plan of these favourite arts, which would be unsuitable not only to the nature of this work, but to the inexperience of its author.

Gardening was at first an useful art: in the garden of Alcinous, described by Homer, we find nothing done for pleasure merely. But gardening is now improved into a fine art; and when we talk of a garden without any epithet, a pleasure-garden, by way of eminence, is understood: the garden of Alcinous, in modern language, was but a kitchen-garden. Architecture has run the <431> same course: it continued many ages an useful art merely, without aspiring to be classed with the fine arts. Architecture, therefore, and gardening, being useful arts as well as fine arts, afford two different views. The reader, however, will not here expect rules for improving any work of art in point of utility; it being no part of my plan to treat of any useful art as such: but there is a beauty in utility; and in discoursing of beauty, that of utility must not be neglected. This leads us to consider gardens and buildings in different views: they may be destined for use solely, for beauty solely, or for both. Such variety of destination, bestows upon these arts a great command of beauties, complex no less than various.

Hence the difficulty of forming an accurate taste in gardening and architecture: and hence that difference and wavering of taste in these arts, greater
than in any art that has but a single destination.

Architecture and gardening cannot otherwise entertain the mind, but
by raising certain agreeable emotions or feelings; with which we must begin,
as the true foundation of all the rules of criticism that govern these arts.
Poetry, as to its power of raising emotions, possesses justly the first place
among the fine arts; for scarce any one emotion of human nature is beyond
its reach. Painting and sculpture are more circumscribed, having the command of no emotions but of what are raised by sight: they are peculiarly
successful in ex-<432>pressing painful passions, which are displayed by external signs extremely legible.* Gardening, beside the emotions of beauty
from regularity, order, proportion, colour, and utility, can raise emotions
of grandeur, of sweetness, of gaiety, of melancholy, of wildness, and even
of surprise or wonder. In architecture, the beauties of regularity, order, and
proportion, are still more conspicuous than in gardening: but as to the
beauty of colour, architecture is far inferior. Grandeur can be expressed in
a building, perhaps more successfully than in a garden; but as to the other
emotions above mentioned, architecture hitherto has not been brought to
the perfection of expressing them distinctly. To balance that defect, architecture can display the beauty of utility in the highest perfection.

Gardening indeed possesses one advantage, never to be equalled in the
other art: in various scenes, it can raise successively all the different emotions
above mentioned. But to produce that delicious effect, the garden must be
extensive, so as to admit a slow succession: for a small garden, comprehended at one view, ought to be confined to one expression;† it may be gay,
it may be sweet, it may be gloomy; but an attempt to mix these, would
create a jumble of emotions not a <433> little unpleasant.‡ For the same
reason, a building, even the most magnificent, is necessarily confined to
one expression.

---

* See chap. 15.
† See chap. 8.
‡ "The citizen, who in his villa has but an acre for a garden, must have it diversified
with every object that is suited to an extensive garden. There must be woods, streams,
lawns, statues, and temples to every goddess as well as to Cloacina."

Architecture, considered as a fine art, instead of being a rival to gardening in its progress, seems not far advanced beyond its infant state. To bring it to maturity, two things mainly are wanted. First, a greater variety of parts and ornaments than at present it seems provided with. Gardening here has greatly the advantage: it is provided with plenty of materials for raising scenes without end, affecting the spectator with variety of emotions. In architecture, on the contrary, materials are so scanty, that artists hitherto have not been successful in raising any emotions but of beauty and grandeur: with respect to the former, there are indeed plenty of means, regularity, order, symmetry, simplicity, utility; and with respect to the latter, the addition of size is sufficient. But though it is evident, that every building ought to have a certain character or expression suited to its destination; yet this refinement has scarce been attempted by any artist. A death's head and bones employ'd in monumental buildings, will indeed <434> produce an emotion of gloom and melancholy; but such ornaments, if these can be termed so, ought to be rejected, because they are in themselves disagreeable. The other thing wanted to bring the art to perfection, is, to ascertain the precise impression made by every single part and ornament, cupolas, spires, columns, carvings, statues, vases, &c.: for in vain will an artist attempt rules for employing these, either singly or in combination, until the different emotions they produce be distinctly explained. Gardening in that particular also, hath the advantage: the several emotions raised by trees, rivers, cascades, plains, eminencies, and its other materials, are understood; and each emotion can be described with some degree of precision, which is attempted occasionally in the foregoing parts of this work.

In gardening as well as in architecture, simplicity ought to be a ruling principle. Profuse ornament hath no better effect than to confound the eye, and to prevent the object from making an impression as one entire whole. An artist destitute of genius for capital beauties, is naturally prompted to supply the defect by crowding his plan with slight embellishments: hence in a garden, triumphal arches, Chinese houses, temples, obelisks, cascades, fountains, without end; and in a building, pillars, vases, statues, and a profusion of carved work. Thus some women defective in taste, are apt to overcharge every part of their <435> dress with ornament. Superfluity of decoration hath another bad effect: it gives the object a diminutive look:

an island in a wide extended lake makes it appear larger; but an artificial lake, which is always little, appears still less by making an island in it.*

In forming plans for embellishing a field, an artist without taste employs straight lines, circles, squares; because these look best upon paper. He perceives not, that to humour and adorn nature, is the perfection of his art; and that nature, neglecting regularity, distributes her objects in great variety with a bold hand. A large field laid out with strict regularity, is stiff and artificial.† Nature indeed, in organized bodies comprehended under one view, studies regularity; which, for the same reason, ought to be studied in architecture: but in large objects, which cannot otherwise be surveyed but in parts and by succession, regularity and uniformity would be useless properties, because they cannot be discovered by the eye.‡ Nature therefore, in her large works, ne-<436>glects these properties; and in copying nature, the artist ought to neglect them.

Having thus far carried on a comparison between gardening and architecture; rules peculiar to each come next in order, beginning with gardening. The simplest plan of a garden, is that of a spot embellished with a number of natural objects, trees, walks, polish'd parterres, flowers, streams, &c. One more complex comprehends statues and buildings, that nature and art may be mutually ornamental. A third, approaching nearer perfection, is of objects assembled together in order to produce, not only an emotion of beauty, but also some other particular emotion, grandeur, for example, gaiety, or any other above mentioned. The completest plan of a garden is an improvement upon the third, requiring the several parts to be so arranged, as to inspire all the different emotions that can be raised by gardening. In this plan, the arrangement is an important circumstance; for it has been shown, that some emotions figure best in conjunction, and that others ought always to appear in succession, and never in conjunction. It

---

* See appendix to part 5. chap. 2.

† In France and Italy a garden is disposed like the human body, alleys, like legs and arms, answering each other; the great walk in the middle representing the trunk of the body. Thus an artist void of taste carries self along into every operation.

‡ A square field appears not such to the eye when viewed from any part of it; and the centre is the only place where a circular field preserves in appearance its regular figure.

is mentioned above,* <437> that when the most opposite emotions, such as gloominess and gaiety, stillness and activity, follow each other in succession, the pleasure on the whole will be the greatest; but that such emotions ought not to be united, because they produce an unpleasant mixture.† For this reason, a ruin affording a sort of melancholy pleasure, ought not to be seen from a flower-parterre which is gay and cheerful. But to pass from an exhilarating object to a ruin, has a fine effect; for each of the emotions is the more sensibly felt by being contrasted with the other. Similar emotions, on the other hand, such as gaiety and sweetness, stillness and gloominess, motion and grandeur, ought to be raised together; for their effects upon the mind are greatly heightened by their conjunction.‡

Kent's method of embellishing a field,[1] is admirable; which is, to replenish it with beautiful objects, natural and artificial, disposed as they ought to be upon a canvas in painting. It requires indeed more genius to paint in the gardening way: in forming a landscape upon a canvas, no more is required but to adjust the figures to each other: an artist who would form a garden in Kent's manner, has an additional task; which is, to adjust his figures to the several varieties of the field.

A single garden must be distinguished from a <438> plurality; and yet it is not obvious in what the unity of a garden consists. We have indeed some notion of unity in a garden surrounding a palace, with views from each window, and walks leading to every corner: but there may be a garden without a house; in which case, it is the unity of design that makes it one garden; as where a spot of ground is so artfully dressed as to make the several portions appear to be parts of one whole. The gardens of Versailles, properly expressed in the plural number, being no fewer than sixteen, are indeed all of them connected with the palace, but have scarce any mutual connection: they appear not like parts of one whole, but rather like small gardens in contiguity. A greater distance between these gardens would produce

---

* Chap. 8.
† Chap. 2. part 4.
‡ See the place immediately above cited.
1. William Kent (1685–1748), architect, designer, landscape gardener, studied painting in Rome, and worked with Lord Burlington from 1719 to 1748. Best known for Holkham Hall (begun 1734) and the Horse Guards, London.

a better effect: their junction breeds confusion of ideas, and upon the whole gives less pleasure than would be felt in a slower succession.

Regularity is required in that part of a garden which is adjacent to the dwelling-house; because an immediate accessory ought to partake the regularity of the principal object:* but in proportion <439> to the distance from the house considered as the centre, regularity ought less and less to be studied; for in an extensive plan, it hath a fine effect to lead the mind insensibly from regularity to a bold variety. Such arrangement tends to make an impression of grandeur: and grandeur ought to be studied as much as possible, even in a more confined plan, by avoiding a multiplicity of small parts.† A small garden, on the other hand, which admits not grandeur, ought to be strictly regular.

Milton, describing the garden of Eden, prefers justly grandeur before regularity:

> Flowers worthy of paradise, which not nice art
> In beds and curious knots, but Nature boon <440>
> Pour'd forth profuse on hill, and dale, and plain;
> Both where the morning-sun first warmly smote
> The open field, and where the unpierc'd shade
> Imbrown'd the noontide bow'rs.   *Paradise Lost, b.* 4.

A hill covered with trees, appears more beautiful as well as more lofty than when naked. To distribute trees in a plain requires more art: near the

---

* The influence of this connection surpassing all bounds, is still visible in many gardens, formed of horizontal plains forc'd with great labour and expence, perpendicular faces of earth supported by massy stone walls, terrace-walks in stages one above another, regular ponds and canals without the least motion, and the whole surounded, like a prison, with high walls excluding every external object. At first view it may puzzle one to account for a taste so opposite to nature in every particular. But nothing happens without a cause. Perfect regularity and uniformity are required in a house; and this idea is extended to its accessory the garden, especially if it be a small spot incapable of grandeur or of much variety: the house is regular, so must the garden be; the floors of the house are horizontal, and the garden must have the same position; in the house we are protected from every intruding eye, so must we be in the garden. This, it must be confessed, is carrying the notion of resemblance very far: but where reason and taste are laid asleep, nothing is more common than to carry resemblance beyond proper bounds.

† See chap. 4.

dwelling-house they ought to be scattered so distant from each other, as not to break the unity of the field; and even at the greatest distance of distinct vision, they ought never to be so crowded as to hide any beautiful object.

In the manner of planting a wood or thicket, much art may be display'd. A common centre of walks, termed *a star,* from whence are seen remarkable objects, appears too artificial, and consequently too stiff and formal, to be agreeable: the crowding withal so many objects together, lessens the pleasure that would be felt in a slower succession. Abandoning therefore the star, let us try to substitute some form more natural, that will display all the remarkable objects in the neighbourhood. This may be done by various apertures in the wood, purposely contrived to lay open successively every such object; sometimes a single object, sometimes a plurality in a line, and sometimes a rapid succession of them: the mind at intervals is roused and cheered by agreeable objects; <441> and by surprise, upon viewing objects of which it had no expectation.

Attending to the influence of contrast, explained in the eighth chapter, we discover why the lowness of the ceiling increases in appearance the size of a large room, and why a long room appears still longer by being very narrow, as is remarkable in a gallery: by the same means, an object terminating a narrow opening in a wood, appears at a double distance. This suggests another rule for distributing trees in some quarter near the dwelling-house; which is, to place a number of thickets in a line, with an opening in each, directing the eye from one to another; which will make them appear more distant from each other than they are in reality, and in appearance enlarge the size of the whole field. To give this plan its utmost effect, the space between the thickets ought to be considerable: and in order that each may be seen distinctly, the opening nearest the eye ought to be wider than the second, the second wider than the third, and so on to the end.* <442>

By a judicious distribution of trees, other beauties may be produced. A landscape so rich as to ingross the whole attention, and so limited as sweetly

---

* An object will appear more distant than it really is, if different coloured evergreens be planted between it and the eye. Suppose holly and laurel, and the holly, which is of the deeper colour, nearer the eye: the degradation of colour in the laurel, makes it appear at a great distance from the holly, and consequently removes the object, in appearance, to a greater distance than it really is.

to be comprehended under a single view, has a much finer effect than the most extensive landscape that requires a wandering of the eye through successive scenes. This observation suggests a capital rule in laying out a field; which is, never at any one station to admit a larger prospect than can easily be taken in at once. A field so happily situated as to command a great extent of prospect, is a delightful subject for applying this rule: let the prospect be split into proper parts by means of trees; studying at the same time to introduce all the variety possible. A plan of this kind executed with taste will produce charming effects: the beautiful prospects are multiplied: each of them is much more agreeable than the entire prospect was originally: and, to crown the whole, the scenery is greatly diversified.

As gardening is not an inventive art, but an imitation of nature, or rather nature itself ornamented; it follows necessarily, that every thing unnatural ought to be rejected with disdain. Statues of wild beasts vomiting water, a common ornament in gardens, prevail in those of Versailles. Is that ornament in a good taste? A *jet d'eau,* being purely artificial, may, without disgust, be tortured into a thousand shapes: but a representation of what really exists in nature, admits not any un-<443>natural circumstance. In the statues of Versailles the artist has displayed his vicious taste without the least colour or disguise. A lifeless statue of an animal pouring out water, may be endured without much disgust: but here the lions and wolves are put in violent action, each has seized its prey, a deer or a lamb, in act to devour; and yet, as by hocus-pocus, the whole is converted into a different scene: the lion, forgetting his prey, pours out water plentifully; and the deer, forgetting its danger, performs the same work: a representation no less absurd than that in the opera, where Alexander the Great,[2] after mounting the wall of a town besieged, turns his back to the enemy, and entertains his army with a song.*

---

* Ulloa, a Spanish writer, describing the city of Lima, says, that the great square is finely ornamented. "In the centre is a fountain, equally remarkable for its grandeur and capacity. Raised above the fountain is a bronze statue of Fame, and four small basons on the angles. The water issues from the trumpet of the statue, and from the mouths of eight lions surrounding it, which (in his opinion) greatly heighten the beauty of the whole." [Antonio de Ulloa, *Relacion historica del viaga a la America meridional . . . ,*1748. Translated as *A Voyage to South America . . . ,* 1758.]

2. Handel, *Alessandro.*

In gardening, every lively exhibition of what is beautiful in nature has a fine effect: on the other hand, distant and faint imitations are displeasing to every one of taste. The cutting evergreens in the shape of animals, is very ancient; as appears from the epistles of Pliny, who seems to be a <444> great admirer of the conceit. The propensity to imitation gave birth to that practice; and has supported it wonderfully long, considering how faint and insipid the imitation is. But the vulgar, great and small, are entertained with the oddness and singularity of a resemblance, however distant, between a tree and an animal. An attempt in the gardens of Versailles to imitate a grove of trees by a group of *jets d'eau,* appears, for the same reason, no less childish.

In designing a garden, every thing trivial or whimsical ought to be avoided. Is a labyrinth then to be justified? It is a mere conceit, like that of composing verses in the shape of an axe or an egg: the walks and hedges may be agreeable; but in the form of a labyrinth, they serve to no end but to puzzle: a riddle is a conceit not so mean; because the solution is proof of sagacity, which affords no aid in tracing a labyrinth.

The gardens of Versailles, executed with boundless expence by the best artists of that age, are a lasting monument of a taste the most depraved: the faults above mentioned, instead of being avoided, are chosen as beauties, and multiplied without end. Nature, it would seem, was deemed too vulgar to be imitated in the works of a magnificent monarch; and for that reason preference was given to things unnatural, which probably were mistaken for supernatural. I have often amused myself with a fanciful resemblance between these <445> gardens and the Arabian tales: each of them is a performance intended for the amusement of a great king: in the sixteen gardens of Versailles there is no unity of design, more than in the thousand and one Arabian tales: and, lastly, they are equally unatural; groves of *jets d'eau,* statues of animals conversing in the manner of Aesop, water issuing out of the mouths of wild beasts, give an impression of fairy-land and witchcraft, no less than diamond-palaces, invisible rings, spells and incantations.

A straight road is the most agreeable, because it shortens the journey. But in an embellished field, a straight walk has an air of formality and confinement: and at any rate is less agreeable than a winding or waving walk; for in surveying the beauties of an ornamented field, we love to roam from place to place at freedom. Winding walks have another advantage: at every step they open new views. In short, the walks in pleasure-ground[3] ought not to have any appearance of a road: my intention is not to make a journey, but to feast my eye on the beauties of art and nature. This rule excludes not openings directing the eye to distant objects. Such openings, beside variety, are agreeable in various respects: first, as observed above, they extend in appearance the size of the field: next, an object, at whatever distance, continues the opening, and deludes the spectator into a conviction, that the trees which confine the view < 446 > are continued till they join the object. Straight walks in recesses do well: they vary the scenery, and are favourable to meditation.

Avoid a straight avenue directed upon a dwelling-house: better far an oblique approach in a waving line, with single trees and other scattered objects interposed. In a direct approach, the first appearance is continued to the end: we see a house at a distance, and we see it all along in the same spot without any variety. In an oblique approach, the interposed objects put the house seemingly in motion: it moves with the passenger, and appears to direct its course so as hospitably to intercept him. An oblique approach contributes also to variety: the house, seen successively in different directions, assumes at each step a new figure.

A garden on a flat ought to be highly and variously ornamented, in order to occupy the mind, and prevent our regretting the insipidity of an uniform plain. Artificial mounts in that view are common: but no person has thought of an artificial walk elevated high above the plain. Such a walk is airy, and tends to elevate the mind: it extends and varies the prospect; and it makes the plain, seen from a height, appear more agreeable.

Whether should a ruin be in the Gothic or Grecian form? In the former, I think; because it exhibits the triumph of time over strength; a melancholy, but not unpleasant thought: a Gre-< 447 >cian ruin suggests rather the triumph of barbarity over taste; a gloomy and discouraging thought.

There are not many fountains in a good taste. Statues of animals vomiting water, which prevail every where, stand condemned as unnatural. A

3. First edition: "the walks in a field intended for entertainment."

statue of a whale spouting water upward from its head, is in one sense natural, as certain whales have that power; but it is a sufficient objection, that
its singularity would make it appear unnatural; there is another reason
against it, that the figure of a whale is in itself not agreeable. In many Roman fountains, statues of fishes are employed to support a large bason of
water. This unnatural conceit is not accountable, unless from the connection that water hath with the fish that swim in it; which by the way shows
the influence of even the slighter relations. The best design for a fountain
I have met with, is what follows. In an artificial rock, rugged and abrupt,
there is a cavity out of sight at the top: the water, conveyed to it by a pipe,
pours or trickles down the broken parts of the rock, and is collected into
a bason at the foot: it is so contrived, as to make the water fall in sheets or
in rills at pleasure.

Hitherto a garden has been treated as a work intended solely for pleasure,
or, in other words, for giving impressions of intrinsic beauty. What comes
next in order, is the beauty of a garden destined for use, termed *relative
beauty;** and <448> this branch shall be dispatched in a few words. In gardening, luckily, relative beauty need never stand in opposition to intrinsic
beauty: all the ground that can be requisite for use, makes but a small proportion of an ornamented field; and may be put in any corner without
obstructing the disposition of the capital parts. At the same time, a kitchen-
garden or an orchard is susceptible of intrinsic beauty; and may be so artfully disposed among the other parts, as by variety and contrast to contribute to the beauty of the whole. In this respect, architecture requires a greater
stretch of art, as will be seen immediately; for as intrinsic and relative beauty
must often be blended in the same building, it becomes a difficult task to
attain both in any perfection.

In a hot country, it is a capital object to have what may be termed a
summer-garden; that is, a spot of ground disposed by art and by nature to
exclude the sun, but to give free access to the air. In a cold country, the
capital object should be a *winter-garden,* open to the sun, sheltered from
wind, dry under foot, and taking on the appearance of summer by variety
of evergreens. The relish of a country-life, totally extinct in France, is de-

---

* See these terms defined, chap. 3.

caying fast in Britain. But as still many people of fashion, and some of taste, pass the winter, or part of it, in the country, it is amazing that winter-gardens should be overlooked. During summer, every field is a garden; but during <449> half of the year, the weather is seldom so good in Britain as to afford comfort in the open air without shelter; and yet seldom so bad as not to afford comfort with shelter. I say more, that beside providing for exercise and health, a winter-garden may be made subservient to education, by introducing a habit of thinking. In youth, lively spirits give too great a propensity to pleasure and amusement, making us averse to serious occupation. That untoward bias may be corrected in some degree by a winter-garden, which produces in the mind a calm satisfaction, free from agitation of passion, whether gay or gloomy; a fine tone of mind for meditation and reasoning.* <450>

Gardening being in China brought to greater perfection than in any other known country, we shall close our present subject with a slight view of Chinese gardens,[4] which are found entirely obsequious to the principles that govern every one of the fine arts. In general, it is an indispensable law

---

* A correspondent, whose name I hitherto have concealed that I might not be thought vain, and which I can no longer conceal (a), writes to me as follows: "In life we generally lay our account with prosperity, and seldom, very seldom, prepare for adversity. We carry that propensity even into the structure of our gardens: we cultivate the gay ornaments of summer, relishing no plants but what flourish by mild dews and gracious sunshine: we banish from our thoughts ghastly winter, when the benign influences of the sun cheering us no more, are doubly regretted by yielding to the piercing north wind and nipping frost. Sage is the gardener, in the metaphorical as well as literal sense, who procures a friendly shelter to protect us from December storms, and cultivates the plants that adorn and enliven that dreary season. He is no philosopher who cannot retire into the Stoic's walk, when the gardens of Epicurus are out of bloom: he is too much a philosopher who will rigidly proscribe the flowers and aromatics of summer, to sit constantly under the cypress-shade."(a) Mrs. Montagu. [Elizabeth Montague (1720–1800): London bluestocking, who visited Kames in 1766. In 1769 she published a book on the relative virtues of Shakespeare and French literature, which was dismissed by Dr. Johnson.]

4. The references are to William Chambers (1723–96), *Designs of Chinese Buildings, Furniture, Dresses, Machines and Utensils*, 1757; *Plans, Elevations, Sections, and Perspective Views of the Gardens and Buildings at Kew*, 1763. Edmund Burke had republished Chambers's essay on Chinese gardens in *Annual Register*, 1758.

there, never to deviate from nature: but in order to produce that degree of variety which is pleasing, every method consistent with nature is put in practice. Nature is strictly imitated in the banks of their artificial lakes and rivers; which sometimes are bare and gravelly, sometimes covered with wood quite to the brink of the water. To flat spots adorned with flowers and shrubs, are opposed others steep and rocky. We see meadows covered with cattle; rice-grounds that run into lakes; groves into which enter navigable creeks and rivulets: these generally conduct to some interesting object, a magnificent building, terraces cut in a mountain, a cascade, a grotto, an artificial rock. Their artificial rivers are generally serpentine; sometimes narrow, noisy, and rapid; sometimes deep, broad, and slow: and to make the scene still more active, mills and other <451> moving machines are often erected. In the lakes are interspersed islands; some barren, surrounded with rocks and shoals; others enriched with every thing that art and nature can furnish. Even in their cascades they avoid regularity, as forcing nature out of its course: the waters are seen bursting from the caverns and windings of the artificial rocks, here a roaring cataract, there many gentle falls; and the stream often impeded by trees and stones, that seem brought down by the violence of the current. Straight lines are sometimes indulged, in order to keep in view some interesting object at a distance.

Sensible of the influence of contrast, the Chinese artists deal in sudden transitions, and in opposing to each other, forms, colours, and shades. The eye is conducted, from limited to extensive views, and from lakes and rivers to plains, hills, and woods: to dark and gloomy colours, are opposed the more brilliant: the different masses of light and shade are disposed in such a manner, as to render the composition distinct in its parts, and striking on the whole. In plantations, the trees are artfully mixed according to their shape and colour; those of spreading branches with the pyramidal, and the light green with the deep green. They even introduce decayed trees, some erect, and some half out of the ground.* In order to <452> heighten con-

---

* Taste has suggested to Kent the same artifice. A decayed tree placed properly, contributes to contrast; and also in a pensive or sedate state of mind produces a sort of pity, grounded on an imaginary personification.

trast, much bolder strokes are risked: they sometimes introduce rough rocks, dark caverns, trees ill formed, and seemingly rent by tempests, or blasted by lightening; a building in ruins, or half consumed by fire. But to relieve the mind from the harshness of such objects, the sweetest and most beautiful scenes always succeed.

The Chinese study to give play to the imagination: they hide the termination of their lakes; and commonly interrupt the view of a cascade by trees, through which are seen obscurely the waters as they fall. The imagination once roused, is disposed to magnify every object.

Nothing is more studied in Chinese gardens than to raise wonder or surprise. In scenes calculated for that end, every thing appears like fairyland: a torrent, for example, conveyed under ground, puzzles a stranger by its uncommon sound to guess what it may be; and, to multiply such uncommon sounds, the rocks and buildings are contrived with cavities and interstices. Sometimes one is led insensibly into a dark cavern, terminating unexpectedly in a landscape enriched with all that nature affords the most delicious. At other times, beautiful walks insensibly conduct to a rough uncultivated field, where bushes, briers, and <453> stones interrupt the passage: looking about for an outlet, some rich prospect unexpectedly opens to view. Another artifice is, to obscure some capital part by trees or other interposed objects: our curiosity is raised to know what lies beyond; and after a few steps, we are greatly surprised with some scene totally different from what was expected.

These cursory observations upon gardening, shall be closed with some reflections that must touch every reader. Rough uncultivated ground, dismal to the eye, inspires peevishness and discontent: may not this be one cause of the harsh manners of savages? A field richly ornamented, containing beautiful objects of various kinds, displays in full lustre the goodness of the Deity, and the ample provision he has made for our happiness. Ought not the spectator to be filled with gratitude to his Maker, and with benevolence to his fellow-creatures? Other fine arts may be perverted to excite irregular, and even vicious, emotions: but gardening, which inspires the purest and most refined pleasures, cannot fail to promote every good affection. The gaiety and harmony of mind it produceth, inclining the spectator to communicate his satisfaction to others, and to make them happy as he is himself, tend naturally to establish in him a habit of humanity and benevolence.* <454>

It is not easy to suppress a degree of enthusiasm, when we reflect on the advantages of gardening with respect to virtuous education. In the beginning of life the deepest impressions are made; and it is a sad truth, that the young student, familiarized to the dirtiness and disorder of many colleges pent within narrow bounds in populous cities, is rendered in a measure insensible to the elegant beauties of art and nature. Is there no man of fortune sufficiently patriotic to think of reforming this evil? It seems to me far from an exaggeration, that good professors are not more essential to a college, than a spacious garden sweetly ornamented, but without any thing glaring or fantastic, so as upon the whole to inspire our youth with a taste no less for simplicity than for elegance. In that respect, the university of Oxford may justly be deemed a model.

Having finished what occurred on gardening, I proceed to rules and observations that more peculiarly concern architecture. Architecture, being an useful as well as a fine art, leads us to distinguish buildings and parts of buildings into three kinds, namely, what are intended for utility solely, what for ornament solely, and what for both. <455> Buildings intended for utility solely, such as detached offices, ought in every part to correspond precisely to that intention: the slightest deviation from the end in view, will by every person of taste be thought a blemish. In general, it is the perfection of every work of art, that it fulfils the purpose for which it is intended; and every other beauty, in opposition, is improper. But in things intended for ornament, such as pillars, obelisks, triumphal arches, beauty ought alone to be regarded. A Heathen temple must be considered as merely ornamental; for being dedicated to some deity, and not intended for habitation, it is susceptible of any figure and any embellishment that fancy can suggest and beauty admit. The great difficulty of contrivance, respects buildings that are intended to be useful as well as ornamental. These ends, employing

---

* The manufactures of silk, flax, and cotton, in their present advance toward perfection, may be held as inferior branches of the fine arts; because their productions in dress and in furniture inspire, like them, gay and kindly emotions favourable to morality.

different and often opposite means, are seldom united in perfection; and the only practicable method in such buildings is, to favour ornament less or more according to the character of the building: in palaces, and other edifices sufficiently extensive to admit a variety of useful contrivance, regularity justly takes the lead; but in dwelling-houses that are too small for variety of contrivance, utility ought to prevail, neglecting regularity as far as it stands in opposition to convenience.* <456>

Intrinsic and relative beauty being founded on different principles, must be handled separately. I begin with relative beauty, as of the greater importance.

The proportions of a door are determined by the use to which it is destined. The door of a dwelling-house, which ought to correspond to the human size, is confined to seven or eight feet in height, and three or four in breadth. The proportions proper for the door of a barn or coach-house, are widely different. Another consideration enters. To study intrinsic beauty in a coach-house or barn, intended merely for use, is obviously improper. But a dwelling-house may admit ornaments; and the principal door of a palace demands all the grandeur that is consistent with the foregoing proportions dictated by utility: it ought to be elevated, and approached by steps; and it may be adorned with pillars supporting an architrave, or in any other beautiful manner. The door of a church ought to be wide, in order to afford an easy passage for a multitude: the width, at the same time, regulates the height, as will appear by and by. The size of windows ought to be proportioned to that of the room they illuminate; for if the apertures be not sufficiently large <457> to convey light to every corner, the room is unequally lighted, which is a great deformity. The steps of a stair ought to be accommodated to the human figure, without regarding any other proportion: they are accordingly the same in large and in small buildings, because both are inhabited by men of the same size.

I proceed to consider intrinsic beauty blended with that which is relative. Though a cube in itself is more agreeable than a parallelopipedon, yet a

---

* A building must be large to produce any sensible emotion of regularity, proportion, or beauty; which is an additional reason for minding convenience only in a dwelling-house of small size.

large parallelopipedon set on its smaller base, is by its elevation more agree-able; and hence the beauty of a Gothic tower. But supposing this figure to be destined for a dwelling-house, to make way for relative beauty, we im-mediately perceive that utility ought chiefly to be regarded, and that the figure, inconvenient by its height, ought to be set upon its larger base: the loftiness is gone; but that loss is more than compensated by additional con-venience; for which reason, a figure spread more upon the ground than raised in height, is always preferred for a dwelling-house, without excepting even the most superb palace.

As to the divisions within, utility requires that the rooms be rectangular; for otherwise void spaces will be left, which are of no use. A hexagonal figure leaves no void spaces; but it determines the rooms to be all of one size, which is inconvenient. A room of a moderate size may be a square; but in very large rooms this figure must, <458> for the most part, give place to a parallelogram, which can more easily be adjusted, than a square, to the smaller rooms contrived entirely for convenience. A parallelogram, at the same time, is the best calculated for receiving light; because, to avoid cross lights, all the windows ought to be in one wall; and the opposite wall must be so near as to be fully lighted, otherwise the room will be obscure. The height of a room exceeding nine or ten feet, has little or no relation to utility; and therefore proportion is the only rule for determining a greater height.

As all artists who love what is beautiful, are prone to entertain the eye, they have opportunity to exert their taste upon palaces and sumptuous buildings, where, as above observed, intrinsic beauty ought to have the as-cendant over that which is relative. But such propensity is unhappy with respect to dwelling-houses of moderate size; because in these, intrinsic beauty cannot be displayed in any perfection, without wounding relative beauty: a small house admits not much variety of form; and in such houses there is no instance of internal convenience being accurately adjusted to external regularity: I am apt to believe that it is beyond the reach of art. And yet architects never give over attempting to reconcile these two incom-patibles: how otherwise should it happen, that of the endless variety of private dwelling-houses, there is scarce an instance of any one being chosen <459> for a pattern? The unwearied propensity to make a house regular as

well as convenient, forces the architect, in some articles, to sacrifice convenience to regularity, and in others, regularity to convenience; and the
house, which turns out neither regular nor convenient, never fails to displease: the faults are obvious; and the difficulty of doing better is known
to the artist only.*

Nothing can be more evident, than that the form of a dwelling-house
ought to be suited to the climate: and yet no error is more common, than
to copy in Britain the form of Italian houses; not forgetting even those parts
that are purposely contrived for air, and for excluding the sun. I shall give
one or two instances. A colonnade along the front of a building, hath a fine
effect in Greece and Italy, by producing coolness and obscurity, agreeable
properties in warm and luminous climates: but the cold climate of Britain
is altogether averse to that ornament; and therefore, a colonnade can never
be proper in this country, unless for a portico, or to communicate with a
detached building. Again, a logio laying the house open to the north, contrived in Italy for gathering cool air, is, if possible, still more improper for
<460> this climate: scarce endurable in summer, it, in winter, exposes the
house to the bitter blasts of the north, and to every shower of snow and
rain.

Having said what appeared necessary upon relative beauty, the next step
is, to view architecture as one of the fine arts; which will lead us to the
examination of such buildings, and parts of buildings, as are calculated
solely to please the eye. In the works of Nature, rich and magnificent, variety prevails; and in works of Art that are contrived to imitate Nature, the
great art is to hide every appearance of art; which is done by avoiding regularity, and indulging variety. But in works of art that are original, and not
imitative, the timid hand is guided by rule and compass; and accordingly
in architecture strict regularity and uniformity are studied, as far as consistent with utility.

Proportion is no less agreeable than regularity and uniformity; and therefore in buildings intended to please the eye, they are all equally essential.
By many writers it is taken for granted, that in buildings there are certain

---

* "Houses are built to live in, and not to look on; therefore let use be preferred before
uniformity, except where both may be had." *Lord Verulam, essay* 45. ["Of Building."]

proportions that please the eye, as in sounds there are certain proportions that please the ear; and that in both equally the slightest deviation from the precise proportion is disagreeable. Others seem to relish more a comparison between proportion in numbers and proportion in quantity; and hold that the same pro-<461>portions are agreeable in both. The proportions, for example, of the numbers 16, 24, and 36, are agreeable; and so, say they, are the proportions of a room, the height of which is 16 feet, the breadth 24, and the length 36. May I hope from the reader, that he will patiently accompany me in examining this point, which is useful as well as curious. To refute the notion of a resemblance between musical proportions and those of architecture, it might be sufficient to observe in general, that the one is addressed to the ear, the other to the eye; and that objects of different senses have no resemblance, nor indeed any relation to each other. But more particularly, what pleases the ear in harmony, is not proportion among the strings of the instrument, but among the sounds that these strings produce. In architecture, on the contrary, it is the proportion of different quantities that pleases the eye, without the least relation to sound. Were quantity to be the ground of comparison, we have no reason to presume, that there is any natural analogy between the proportions that please in a building, and the proportions of strings that produce concordant sounds. Let us take for example an octave, produced by two similar strings, the one double of the other in length: this is the most perfect of all concords; and yet I know not that the proportion of one to two is agreeable in any two parts of a building. I add, that concordant notes are pro-<462>duced by wind-instruments, which, as to proportion, appear not to have even the slightest resemblance to a building.

With respect to the other notion, namely a comparison between proportion in numbers and proportion in quantity; I urge, that number and quantity are so different, as to afford no probability of any natural relation between them. Quantity is a real quality of every body; number is not a real quality, but merely an idea that arises upon viewing a plurality of things, whether conjunctly or in succession. An arithmetical proportion is agreeable in numbers; but have we any reason to infer that it must also be agreeable in quantity? At that rate, a geometrical proportion, and many others which are agreeable in numbers, ought also to be agreeable in quantity. In an endless variety of proportions, it would be wonderful, if there never should happen a coincidence of any one agreeable proportion in both. One example is given in the numbers 16, 24, and 36; but to be convinced that this agreeable coincidence is merely accidental, we need only reflect, that the same proportions are not applicable to the external figure of a house, and far less to a column.

That we are framed by nature to relish proportion as well as regularity, is indisputable; but that agreeable proportion should, like concord in sounds, be confined to certain precise measures, is not warranted by experience: on the contrary, we <463> learn from experience, that proportion admits more and less; that several proportions are each of them agreeable; and that we are not sensible of disproportion, till the difference between the quantities compared become the most striking circumstance. Columns evidently admit different proportions, equally agreeable; and so do houses, rooms, and other parts of a building. This leads to an interesting reflection: the foregoing difference between concord and proportion, is an additional instance of that admirable harmony which subsists among the several branches of the human frame. The ear is an accurate judge of sounds, and of their smallest differences; and that concord in sounds should be regulated by accurate measures, is perfectly well suited to this accuracy of perception: the eye is more uncertain about the size of a large object, than of one that is small; and at a distance an object appears less than at hand. Delicacy of perception, therefore, with respect to proportion in quantities, would be an useless quality; and it is much better ordered, that there should be such a latitude with respect to agreeable proportions, as to correspond to the uncertainty of the eye with respect to quantity.

But all the beauties of this subject are not yet displayed; and it is too interesting to be passed over in a cursory view. I proceed to observe, that to make the eye as delicate with respect to proportion as the ear is with respect to concord, would <464> not only be an useless quality, but be the source of continual pain and uneasiness. I need go no farther for a proof than the very room I occupy at present; for every step I take varies to me, in appearance, the proportion of length to breadth: at that rate, I should not be happy but in one precise spot, where the proportion appears agreeable. Let me further observe, that it would be singular indeed to find, in the nature of man, any two principles in perpetual opposition to each other: and yet this would be the case, if proportion were circumscribed like concord; for it would exclude all but one of those proportions that utility requires in different buildings, and in different parts of the same building.

It provokes a smile to find writers acknowledging the necessity of accurate proportions, and yet differing widely about them. Laying aside reasoning and philosophy, one fact universally allowed ought to have undeceived them, that the same proportions which are agreeable in a model, are not agreeable in a large building: a room 40 feet in length and 24 in breadth and height, is well proportioned; but a room 12 feet wide and high and 24 long, approaches to a gallery.

Perrault, in his comparison of the ancients and moderns,* is the only author who runs to the opposite extreme; maintaining, that the different <465> proportions assigned to each order of columns are arbitrary, and that the beauty of these proportions is entirely the effect of custom. This betrays ignorance of human nature, which evidently delights in proportion, as well as in regularity, order, and propriety. But without any acquaintance with human nature, a single reflection might have convinced him of his error, That if these proportions had not originally been agreeable, they could not have been established by custom.

To illustrate the present point, I shall add a few examples of the agreeableness of different proportions. In a sumptuous edifice, the capital rooms ought to be large, for otherwise they will not be proportioned to the size of the building: and for the same reason, a very large room is improper in a small house. But in things thus related, the mind requires not a precise or single proportion, rejecting all others; on the contrary, many different proportions are made equally welcome. In all buildings accordingly, we find rooms of different proportions equally agreeable, even where the proportion is not influenced by utility. With respect to the height of a room, the proportion it ought to bear to the length and breadth, is arbitrary; and it cannot be otherwise, considering the uncertainty of the eye as to the height of a room, when it exceeds 17 or 18 feet. In columns again, even architects must confess, that the proportion <466> of height and thickness varies

---

* Pag. 94. [Charles Perrault (1628–1703), *Parallèle des Anciens et Modernes,* 1688.]

betwixt 8 diameters and 10, and that every proportion between these extremes is agreeable. But this is not all. There must certainly be a farther
variation of proportion, depending on the size of the column: a row of
columns 10 feet high, and a row twice that height, require different proportions: the intercolumniations must also differ according to the height
of the row.

Proportion of parts is not only itself a beauty, but is inseparably connected with a beauty of the highest relish, that of concord or harmony;
which will be plain from what follows. A room of which the parts are all
finely adjusted to each other, strikes us with the beauty of proportion. It
strikes us at the same time with a pleasure far superior: the length, the
breadth, the height, the windows, raise each of them separately an emotion:
these emotions are similar; and though faint when felt separately, they produce in conjunction the emotion of concord or harmony, which is extremely pleasant.* On the other hand, where the length of a room far exceeds the breadth, the mind, comparing together parts so intimately
connected, immediately perceives a disagreement or disproportion which
disgusts. But this is not all: viewing them separately, different emotions are
produced, < 467 > that of grandeur from the great length, and that of meanness or littleness from the small breadth, which in union are disagreeable
by their discordance. Hence it is, that a long gallery, however convenient
for exercise, is not an agreeable figure of a room: we consider it, like a stable,
as destined for use, and expect not that in any other respect it should be
agreeable.†

Regularity and proportion are essential in buildings destined chiefly or
solely to please the eye, because they produce intrinsic beauty. But a skilful
artist will not confine his view to regularity and proportion: he will also
study congruity, which is perceived when the form and ornaments of a
structure are suited to the purpose for which it is intended. The sense of
congruity dictates the following rule, That every building have an expres-

* Chap. 2. part 4.
† A covered passage connecting a winter-garden with the dwelling-house, would answer the purpose of walking in bad weather much better than a gallery. A slight roof
supported by slender pillars, whether of wood or stone, would be sufficient; filling up
the spaces between the pillars with evergreens, so as to give verdure and exclude wind.

sion corresponding to its destination: A palace ought to be sumptuous and grand; a private dwelling, neat and modest; a play-house, gay and splendid; and a monument, gloomy and melancholy.* A Heathen temple has a dou-ble destina-<468>tion: It is considered chiefly as a house dedicated to some divinity; and in that respect it ought to be grand, elevated, and magnificent: it is considered also as a place of worship; and in that respect it ought to be somewhat dark or gloomy, because dimness produces that tone of mind which is suited to humility and devotion. A Christian church is not con-sidered to be a house for the Deity, but merely a place of worship: it ought therefore to be decent and plain, without much ornament: a situation ought to be chosen low and retired; because the congregation, during worship, ought to be humble, and disengaged from the world. Columns, beside their chief service of being supports, may contribute to that peculiar ex-pression which the destination of a building requires: columns of different proportions, serve to express loftiness, lightness, &c. as well as strength. Situation also may contribute to expression: conveniency regulates the sit-uation of a private dwelling-house; but, as I have had occasion to ob-<469>serve,† the situation of a palace ought to be lofty.

And this leads to a question, Whether the situation, where there happens to be no choice, ought, in any measure, to regulate the form of the edifice? The connection between a large house and the neighbouring fields, though not intimate, demands however some congruity. It would, for example, displease us to find an elegant building thrown away upon a wild uncul-tivated country: congruity requires a polished field for such a building; and beside the pleasure of congruity, the spectator is sensible of the pleasure of concordance from the similarity of the emotions produced by the two ob-jects. The old Gothic form of building, seems well suited to the rough

---

* A house for the poor ought to have an appearance suited to its destination. The new hospital in Paris for foundlings, errs against this rule; for it has more the air of a palace than of an hospital. [Hospice des Enfants Assistes, founded in 1638 near Notre Dame: the new buildings were opposite the Observatoire, near the present Rue Denfert-Rochereau.] Propriety and convenience ought to be studied in lodging the indigent; but in such houses splendor and magnificence are out of all rule. For the same reason, a naked statue or picture, scarce decent any where, is in a church intolerable. A sumptuous charity-school, beside its impropriety, gives the children an unhappy taste for high living.

† Chap. 10.

uncultivated regions where it was invented: the only mistake was, the trans-
ferring this form to the fine plains of France and Italy, better fitted for
buildings in the Grecian taste; but by refining upon the Gothic form, every
thing possible has been done to reconcile it to its new situation. The profuse
variety of wild and grand objects about Inverary,[5] demanded a house in the
Gothic form; and every one must approve the taste of the proprietor, in
adjusting so finely the appearance of his house to that of the country where
it is placed.

The external structure of a great house, leads <470> naturally to its internal structure. A spacious room, which is the first that commonly receives
us, seems a bad contrivance in several respects. In the first place, when immediately from the open air we step into such a room, its size in appearance
is diminished by contrast: it looks little compared with that great canopy
the sky. In the next place, when it recovers its grandeur, as it soon doth, it
gives a diminutive appearance to the rest of the house: passing from it, every
apartment looks little. This room therefore may be aptly compared to the
swoln commencement of an epic poem,

> Bella per Emathios plusquam civilia campos.[6]

In the third place, by its situation it serves only for a waiting-room, and a
passage to the principal apartments; instead of being reserved, as it ought
to be, for entertaining company: a great room, which enlarges the mind
and gives a certain elevation to the spirits, is destined by nature for conversation. Rejecting therefore this form, I take a hint from the climax in
writing for another form that appears more suitable: a handsome portico,
proportioned to the size and fashion of the front, leads into a waiting-room
of a larger size, and that to the great room; all by a progression from small
to great. If the house be very large, there may be space for the following
suit of rooms: first, a portico; second, a passage within the house, <471>
bounded by a double row of columns connected by arcades; third, an oc-

---

5. The Gothic designs for the Duke of Argyll, and completed 1753–60, were by Roger
Morris (1695–1749) and William Adam (1689–1748).
6. Lucan, *Pharsalia,* line 1: "I sing of wars worse than civil wars waged throughout
the Emathian plain."

tagon room, or of any other figure, about the centre of the building; and, lastly, the great room.

A double row of windows must be disagreeable by distributing the light unequally: the space in particular between the rows is always gloomy. For that reason, a room of greater height than can be conveniently served by a single row, ought regularly to be lighted from the roof. Artists have generally an inclination to form the great room into a double cube,[7] even with the inconvenience of a double row of windows: they are pleased with the regularity, overlooking that it is mental only, and not visible to the eye, which seldom can distinguish between the height of 24 feet and that of 30.*

Of all the emotions that can be raised by architecture, grandeur is that which has the greatest influence on the mind; and it ought therefore to be the chief study of the artist, to raise this emotion in great buildings destined to please the eye. But as grandeur depends partly on size, it seems <472> so far unlucky for architecture, that it is governed by regularity and proportion, which never deceive the eye by making objects appear larger than they are in reality: such deception, as above observed, is never found but with some remarkable disproportion of parts. But though regularity and proportion contribute nothing to grandeur as far as that emotion depends on size, they in a different respect contribute greatly to it, as has been explained above.†

Next of ornaments, which contribute to give buildings a peculiar expression. It has been doubted whether a building can regularly admit any ornament but what is useful, or at least has that appearance. But considering the different purposes of architecture, a fine as well as an useful art, there is no good reason why ornaments may not be added to please the eye without any relation to use. This liberty is allowed in poetry, painting, and gar-

---

* One who has not given peculiar attention will scarce imagine how imperfect our judgement is about distances, without experience. Our looks being generally directed to objects upon the ground around us, we judge tolerably of horizontal distances: but seldom having occasion to look upward in a perpendicular line, we scarce can form any judgement of distances in that direction.

† Chap. 4.

7. Double Cube: the famous room at Wilton House renovated by John Webb (1611–72) in 1649, after the fire.

dening, and why not in architecture considered as a fine art? A private dwelling-house, it is true, and other edifices where use is the chief aim, admit not regularly any ornament but what has the appearance, at least, of use: but temples, triumphal arches, and other buildings intended chiefly or solely for show, admit every sort of ornament.

A thing intended merely as an ornament,[8] may <473> be of any figure and of any kind that fancy can suggest: if it please the spectator, the artist gains his end. Statues, vases, sculpture upon stone, whether basso or alto relievo, are beautiful ornaments, relished in all civilized countries. The placing such ornaments so as to produce the best effect, is the only nicety. A statue in perfection is an enchanting work; and we naturally require that it should be seen in every direction and at different distances; for which reason, statues employed as ornaments are proper to adorn the great stair-case that leads to the principal door of a palace, or to occupy the void between pillars. But a niche in the external front is not a proper place for a statue: and statues upon the roof, or upon the top of a wall, would give pain by seeming to be in danger of tumbling. To adorn the top of a wall with a row of vases is an unhappy conceit, by placing things apparently of use where they cannot be of any use. As to basso and alto relievo, I observe, that in architecture as well as in gardening, contradictory expressions ought to be avoided: for which reason, the lightness and delicacy of carved work suits ill with the firmness and solidity of a pedestal: upon the pedestal, whether of a statue or a column, the ancients never ventured any bolder ornament than the basso relievo.

One at first view will naturally take it for granted, that in the ornaments under consideration beauty is indispensable. It goes a great way un-<474>doubtedly; but, upon trial, we find many things esteemed as highly ornamental that have little or no beauty. There are various circumstances, beside beauty, that tend to make an agreeable impression. For instance, the reverence we have for the ancients is a fruitful source of ornaments. Amalthea's horn has always been a favourite ornament, because of its connection with a lady who was honoured with the care of Jupiter in his infancy. A fat old fellow and a goat are surely not graceful forms; and yet Selinus and his

---

8. The remainder of the chapter is a considerably expanded version of the first edition.

companions are every where fashionable ornaments. What else but our fondness for antiquity can make the horrid form of a Sphinx so much as endurable? Original destination is another circumstance that has influence to add dignity to things in themselves abundantly trivial. In the sculpture of a marble chimney-piece, instruments of a Grecian or Roman sacrifice are beheld with pleasure; original destination rendering them venerable as well as their antiquity. Let some modern cutlery ware be substituted, though not less beautiful; the artist will be thought whimsical, if not absurd. Triumphal arches, pyramids, obelisks, are beautiful forms; but the nobleness of their original destination has greatly enhanced the pleasure we take in them. A statue, supposed to be an Apollo, will with an antiquary lose much of its grace when discovered to have been done for a barber's apprentice. Long robes appear noble, not singly for their flowing <475> lines, but for their being the habit of magistrates; and a scarf acquires an air of dignity by being the badge of a superior order of churchmen. These examples may be thought sufficient for a specimen: a diligent inquiry into human nature will discover other influencing principles; and hence it is, that of all subjects ornaments admit the greatest variety in point of taste.

Things merely ornamental appear more gay and showy than things that take on the appearance of use. A knot of diamonds in the hair is splendid; but diamonds have a more modest appearance when used as clasps or buttons. The former are more proper for a young beauty, the latter after marriage.

And this leads to ornaments having relation to use. Ornaments of that kind are governed by a different principle, which is, That they ought to be of a form suited to their real or apparent destination. This rule is applicable as well to ornaments that make a component part of the subject, as to ornaments that are only accessory. With relation to the former, it never can proceed from a good taste to make a tea-spoon resemble the leaf of a tree; for such a form is inconsistent with the destination of a tea-spoon. An eagle's paw[9] is an ornament no less improper for the foot of a chair or table; because it gives it the appearance of weakness, inconsistent with its desti-

---

9. Eagle's paw: a design popularized in Britain by Thomas Chippendale (1718–79) but familiar from the Italian Renaissance.

nation of bearing weight. Blind windows are sometimes intro-<476>duced to preserve the appearance of regularity: in which case the deceit ought carefully to be concealed: if visible, it marks the irregularity in the clearest manner, signifying, that real windows ought to have been there, could they have been made consistent with the internal structure. A pilaster is another example of the same sort of ornament; and the greatest error against its seeming destination of a support, is to sink it so far into the wall as to make it lose that seeming. A composition representing leaves and branches, with birds perching upon them, has been long in fashion for a candlestick; but none of these particulars is in any degree suited to that destination.

A large marble bason supported by fishes, is a conceit much relished in fountains. This is an example of accessory ornaments in a bad taste; for fishes here are unsuitable to their apparent destination. No less so are the supports of a coach, carved in the figure of Dolphins or Tritons: for what have these marine beings to do on dry land? and what support can they be to a coach?

In a column we have an example of both kinds of ornament. Where columns are employed in the front of a building to support an entablature, they belong to the first kind: where employed to connect with detached offices, they are rather of the other kind. As a column is a capital orna-<477>ment in Grecian architecture, it well deserves to be handled at large.

With respect to the form of this ornament, I observe, that a circle is a more agreeable figure than a square, a globe than a cube, and a cylinder than a parallelopipedon. This last, in the language of architecture, is saying that a column is a more agreeable figure than a pilaster; and for that reason, it ought to be preferred, all other circumstances being equal. Another reason concurs, that a column connected with a wall, which is a plain surface, makes a greater variety than a pilaster. There is an additional reason for rejecting pilasters in the external front of a building, arising from a principle unfolded above,* namely, a tendency in man, to advance every thing to its perfection, and to its conclusion. If, for example, I see a thing obscurely in a dim light and by disjointed parts, that tendency prompts me to connect the disjointed parts into a whole: I supposed it to be, for example, a horse;

* Chap. 4.

and my eye-sight being obedient to the conjecture, I immediately perceive a horse, almost as distinctly as in day-light. This principle is applicable to the case in hand. The most superb front, at a great distance, appears a plain surface: approaching gradually, we begin first to perceive inequalities, and then pillars; but whether round or square, <478> we are uncertain: our curiosity anticipating our progress, cannot rest in suspense: being prompted, by the tendency mentioned, to suppose the most complete pillar, or that which is the most agreeable to the eye, we immediately perceive, or seem to perceive, a number of columns: if upon a near approach we find pilasters only, the disappointment makes these pilasters appear disagreeable; when abstracted from that circumstance, they would only have appeared some-what less agreeable. But as this deception cannot happen in the inner front inclosing a court, I see no reason for excluding pilasters from such a front, when there is any cause for preferring them before columns.

With respect now to the parts of a column, a bare uniform cylinder without a capital, appears naked; and without a base, appears too ticklishly placed to stand firm:* it ought therefore to have some finishing at the top and at the bottom. Hence the three chief parts of a column, the shaft, the base, and the capital. Nature undoubtedly requires proportion among these parts, but it admits variety of proportion. I suspect that the proportions in use have been influenced in some degree by the human figure; the capital being con-<479>ceived as the head, the base as the feet. With respect to the base, indeed, the principle of utility interposes to vary it from the hu-man figure: the base must be so proportioned to the whole, as to give the column the appearance of stability.

We find three orders of columns among the Greeks, the Dorick, the Ionic, and the Corinthian, distinguished from each other by their desti-nation as well as by their ornaments. It has been warmly disputed, whether any new order can be added to these: some hold the affirmative, and give for instances the Tuscan and Composite: others deny, and maintain that these properly are not distinct orders, but only the original orders with some

---

* A column without a base is disagreeable, because it seems in a tottering condition; yet a tree without a base is agreeable; and the reason is, that we know it to be firmly rooted. This observation shows how much taste is influenced by reflection.

slight variations. Among writers who do not agree upon any standard for distinguishing the different orders from each other, the dispute can never have an end. What occurs to me on this subject is what follows.

The only circumstances that can serve to distinguish one order from another, are the form of the column, and its destination. To make the first a distinguishing mark, without regard to the other, would multiply these orders without end; for a colour is not more susceptible of different shades, than a column is of different forms. Destination is more limited, as it leads to distinguish columns into three kinds or orders; one plain and strong, for the purpose of supporting <480> plain and massy buildings; one delicate and graceful, for supporting buildings of that character; and between these, one for supporting buildings of a middle character. This distinction, which regards the different purposes of a column, is not naturally liable to any objection, considering that it tends also to regulate the form, and in some measure the ornaments, of a column. To enlarge the division by taking in a greater variety of purposes, would be of little use, and, if admitted, would have no end; for from the very nature of the foregoing division, there can be no good reason for adding a fourth order, more than a fifth, a sixth, &c. without any possible circumscription.

To illustrate this doctrine, I make the following observation. If we regard destination only, the Tuscan is of the same order with the Doric, and the Composite with the Corinthian; but if we regard form merely, they are of different orders.

The ornaments of these three orders ought to be so contrived as to make them look like what they are intended for. Plain and rustic ornaments would be not a little discordant with the elegance of the Corinthian order; and ornaments sweet and delicate no less so, with the strength of the Doric. For that reason, I am not altogether satisfied with the ornaments of the last-mentioned order: if they be not too delicate, they are at least too numerous for a pillar in which the character of utility prevails over that of beauty. The crowding of <481> ornaments would be more sufferable in a column of an opposite character. But this is a slight objection, and I wish I could think the same of what follows. The Corinthian order has been the favourite of two thousand years, and yet I cannot force myself to relish its capital. The invention of this florid capital is ascribed to the sculptor Callimachus, who took a hint from the plant *Acanthus,* growing round a basket placed accidentally upon it; and in fact the capital under consideration represents pretty accurately a basket so ornamented. This object, or its imitation in stone, placed upon a pillar, may look well; but to make it the capital of a pillar intended to support a building, must give the pillar an appearance inconsistent with its destination: an Acanthus, or any tender plant, may require support, but is altogether insufficient to support any thing heavier than a bee or a butterfly. This capital must also bear the weight of another objection: to represent a vine wreathing round a column with its root seemingly in the ground, is natural; but to represent an Acanthus, or any plant, as growing on the top of a column, is unnatural. The elegance of this capital did probably at first draw a vail over its impropriety; and now by long use it has gained an establishment, respected by every artist. Such is the force of custom, even in contradiction to nature! <482>

It will not be gaining much ground to urge, that the basket, or vase, is understood to be the capital, and that the stems and leaves of the plant are to be considered as ornaments merely; for, excepting a plant, nothing can be a more improper support for a great building than a basket or vase even of the firmest texture.

With respect to buildings of every sort, one rule, dictated by utility, is, that they be firm and stable. Another rule, dictated by beauty, is, that they also appear so: for what appears tottering and in hazard of tumbling, produceth in the spectator the painful emotion of fear, instead of the pleasant emotion of beauty; and, accordingly, it is the great care of the artist, that every part of his edifice appear to be well supported. Procopius,[10] describing the church of St. Sophia in Constantinople, one of the wonders of the world, mentions with applause a part of the fabric placed above the east front in form of a half-moon, so contrived as to inspire both fear and admiration: for though, says he, it is perfectly well supported, yet it is suspended in such a manner as if it were to tumble down the next moment.

---

10. Procopius (ca. A.D. 490–560): Byzantine historian, trained as a lawyer in Constantinople. Kames refers to *De aedificiis,* an account of public works carried out during the reign of Justinian (A.D. 527–565), especially the building of St. Sophia; his *History of the Wars* and *Anecdota* were available in English translations of 1653 and 1674, respectively.

This conceit is a sort of false wit in architecture, which men were fond of in the infancy of the fine arts. A turret jutting out from an angle in the uppermost story of a Gothic tower, is a witticism of the same kind.

To succeed in allegorical or emblematic orna-<483>ments, is no slight effort of genius; for it is extremely difficult to dispose them so in a building as to produce any good effect. The mixing them with realities, makes a miserable jumble of truth and fiction.* In a basso-relievo on Antonine's pillar, rain obtained by the prayers of a Christian legion, is expressed by joining to the group of soldiers a rainy Jupiter, with water in abundance falling from his head and beard. De Piles, fond of the conceit, carefully informs his reader,[11] that he must not take this for a real Jupiter, but for a symbol which among the Pagans signified rain: he never once considers, that a symbol or emblem ought not to make part of a group representing real objects or real events; but be so detached, as even at first view to appear an emblem. But this is not all, nor the chief point: every emblem ought to be rejected that is not clearly expressive of its meaning; for if it be in any degree obscure, it puzzles, and doth not please. The temples of Ancient and Modern Virtue in the gardens of Stow,[12] appear not at first view emblematical; and when we are informed that they are so, it is not easy to gather their meaning: the spectator sees one temple entire, another in ruins; but without an explanatory inscription, he may guess, but cannot be certain, that the former being dedicated to Ancient Virtue, the latter to Modern Virtue, are intended <484> a satire upon the present times. On the other hand, a trite emblem, like a trite simile, is disgustful.† Nor ought an emblem more than a simile to be founded on low or familiar objects; for if these be not agreeable as well as their meaning, the emblem upon the whole will not be relished. A room in a dwelling-house containing a monument to a deceased friend, is dedicated to Melancholy: it has a clock that strikes

---

* See chap. 20. sect. 5.
† See chap. 8.
11. *The Art of Painting*, ch. 23.
12. Stowe: the temples of Ancient and Modern Virtue, designed by John Vanbrugh, James Gibbs, and William Kent for Lord Cobham. Statues were carved by John Michael Rysbrack (1694–1770) and Peter Scheemakers (1691–1781). Lancelot (Capability) Brown (1716–83) took over gardening supervision after the death of Kent in 1748.

every minute, to signify how swiftly time passes—upon the monument, weeping figures and other hackney'd ornaments commonly found upon tomb-stones, with a stuffed raven in a corner—verses on death, and other serious subjects, inscribed all around. The objects are too familiar, and the artifice too apparent, to produce the intended effect.*

The statue of Moses striking a rock from which water actually issues, is also in a false taste; for it is mixing reality with representation. Moses himself may bring water out of the rock, but this miracle is too much for his statue. The same objec-<485>tion lies against a cascade where the statue of a water-god pours out of his urn real water.

I am more doubtful whether the same objection lies against the employing statues of animals as supports, that of a Negro, for example, supporting a dial, statues of fish supporting a bason of water, *Termes* supporting a chimney-piece; for when a stone is used as a support, where is the incongruity, it will be said, to cut it into the form of an animal? But leaving this doubtful, another objection occurs, That such designs must in some measure be disagreeable, by the appearance of giving pain to a sensitive being.

It is observed above of gardening, that it contributes to rectitude of manners, by inspiring gaiety and benevolence. I add another observation, That both gardening and architecture contribute to the same end, by inspiring a taste for neatness and elegance. In Scotland, the regularity and polish even of a turnpike-road has some influence of this kind upon the low people in the neighbourhood. They become fond of regularity and neatness; which is displayed, first upon their yards and little inclosures, and next within doors. A taste for regularity and neatness thus acquired, is extended by degrees to dress, and even to behaviour and manners. The author of a history of Switzerland,[13] describing the fierce manners of the plebeians of Bern three or four centuries ago, continually inured to success in war, which made them <486> insolently aim at a change of government in order to

---

* In the city of Mexico, there was a palace termed *the house of affliction,* where Montezuma retired upon losing any of his friends, or upon any public calamity. This house was better adjusted to its destination: it inspired a sort of horror: all was black and dismal: small windows shut up with grates, scarce allowing passage to the light.

13. Possibly Abraham Stanyan, *An Account of Switzerland,* 1714.

establish a pure democracy, observes, that no circumstance tended more to sweeten their manners, and to make them fond of peace, than the public buildings carried on by the senate for ornamenting their capital; particularly a fine town-house, and a magnificent church, which to this day, says our author, stands its ground as one of the finest in Europe. <487>

CHAPTER XXV

Standard of Taste

"That there is no disputing about taste," meaning taste in its figurative as well as proper sense, is a saying so generally received as to have become a proverb. One thing even at first view is evident, that if the proverb hold true with respect to taste in its proper meaning, it must hold equally true with respect to our other external senses: if the pleasures of the palate disdain a comparative trial, and reject all criticism, the pleasures of touch, of smell, of sound, and even of sight, must be equally privileged. At that rate, a man is not within the reach of censure, even where he prefers the Saracen's head upon a signpost before the best tablature of Raphael, or a rude Gothic tower before the finest Grecian building; or where he prefers the smell of a rotten carcass before that of the most odoriferous flower, or discords before the most exquisite harmony.

But we cannot stop here. If the pleasures of external sense be exempted from criticism, why not every one of our pleasures, from whatever source derived? if taste in its proper sense cannot <488> be disputed, there is little room for disputing it in its figurative sense. The proverb accordingly comprehends both; and in that large sense may be resolved into the following general proposition, That with respect to the perceptions of sense, by which some objects appear agreeable some disagreeable, there is not such a thing as a *good* or a *bad,* a *right* or a *wrong;* that every man's taste is to himself an ultimate standard without appeal, and consequently that there is no ground of censure against any one, if such a one there be, who prefers Blackmore before Homer,[1] selfishness before benevolence, or cowardice before magnanimity.

1. In "Of the Standard of Taste" (1757), Hume had contrasted John Ogilby

The proverb in the foregoing examples is indeed carried very far: it seems difficult, however, to sap its foundation, or with success to attack it from any quarter: for is not every man equally a judge of what ought to be agreeable or disagreeable to himself? doth it not seem whimsical, and perhaps absurd, to assert, that a man *ought not* to be pleased when he is, or that he *ought* to be pleased when he is not?

This reasoning may perplex, but will never afford conviction: every one of taste will reject it as false, however unqualified to detect the fallacy. At the same time, though no man of taste will assent to the proverb as holding true in every case, no man will affirm that it holds true in no case: objects there are, undoubtedly, that we may like or <489> dislike indifferently, without any imputation upon our taste. Were a philosopher to make a scale for human pleasures, he would not think of making divisions without end; but would rank together many pleasures arising perhaps from different objects, either as equally conducing to happiness, or differing so imperceptibly as to make a separation unnecessary. Nature hath taken this course, at least it appears so to the generality of mankind. There may be subdivisions without end; but we are only sensible of the grosser divisions, comprehending each of them various pleasures equally affecting: to these the proverb is aplicable in the strictest sense; for with respect to pleasures of the same rank, what ground can there be for preferring one before another? if a preference in fact be given by any individual, it cannot proceed from taste, but from custom, imitation, or some peculiarity of mind.

Nature, in her scale of pleasures, has been sparing of divisions: she hath wisely and benevolently filled every division with many pleasures; in order that individuals may be contented with their own lot, without envying that of others. Many hands must be employed to procure us the conveniences of life; and it is necessary that the different branches of business, whether more or less agreeable, be filled with hands: a taste too refined would obstruct that plan; for it would crowd some employments, leaving others, no less useful, to-<490>tally neglected. In our present condition, lucky it is

---

(1600–1676) with Milton, alluding to Dryden's list of dunces in his poem "Mac-Flecknoe" (1682). Swift and Pope had added the name of Blackmore, and Kames follows Pope.

that the plurality are not delicate in their choice, but fall in readily with the occupations, pleasures, food, and company, that fortune throws in their way; and if at first there be any displeasing circumstance, custom soon makes it easy.

The proverb will hold true as to the particulars now explained; but when applied in general to every subject of taste, the difficulties to be encountered are insuperable. We need only to mention the difficulty that arises from human nature itself; do we not talk of a good and a bad taste? of a right and a wrong taste? and upon that supposition, do we not, with great confidence, censure writers, painters, architects, and every one who deals in the fine arts? Are such criticisms absurd, and void of common sense? have the foregoing expressions, familiar in all languages and among all people, no sort of meaning? This can hardly be; for what is universal, must have a foundation in nature. If we can reach that foundation, the standard of taste will no longer be a secret.

We have a sense or conviction of a common nature, not only in our own species, but in every species of animals: and our conviction is verified by experience; for there appears a remarkable uniformity among creatures of the same kind, and a deformity no less remarkable among creatures of different kinds. This common nature is con-<491>ceived to be a model or standard for each individual that belongs to the kind. Hence it is a wonder to find an individual deviating from the common nature of the species, whether in its internal or external construction: a child born with aversion to its mother's milk, is a wonder, no less than if born without a mouth, or with more than one.* This conviction of a common nature in every species, paves the way finely for distributing things into *genera* and *species;* to which we are extremely prone, not only with regard to animals and vegetables, where nature has led the way; but also with regard to many other things, where there is no ground for such distribution, but fancy merely.

With respect to the common nature of man in particular, we have a conviction that it is invariable not less than universal; that it will be the same hereafter as at present, and as it was in time past; the same among all nations and in all corners of the earth. Nor are we deceived; because, giving

---

* See *Essays on Morality and Natural Religion,* part 1. essay 2. ch. 1.

allowance for the difference of culture and gradual refinement of manners, the fact corresponds to our conviction.

We are so constituted, as to conceive this common nature, to be not only invariable, but also *perfect* or *right;* and consequently that indi-<492> viduals *ought* to be made conformable to it. Every remarkable deviation from the standard, makes accordingly an impression upon us of imperfection, irregularity, or disorder: it is disagreeable, and raises in us a painful emotion: monstrous births, exciting the curiosity of a philosopher, fail not at the same time to excite a sort of horror.

This conviction of a common nature or standard and of its perfection, accounts clearly for that remarkable conception we have, of a right and a wrong sense or taste in morals. It accounts not less clearly for the conception we have of a right and a wrong sense or taste in the fine arts. A man who, avoiding objects generally agreeable, delights in objects generally disagreeable, is condemned as a monster: we disapprove his taste as bad or wrong, because we have a clear conception that he deviates from the common standard. If man were so framed as not to have any notion of a common standard, the proverb mentioned in the beginning would hold universally, not only in the fine arts, but in morals: upon that supposition, the taste of every man, with respect to both, would to himself be an ultimate standard. But as the conviction of a common standard is universal and a branch of our nature, we intuitively conceive a taste to be right or good if conformable to the common standard, and wrong or bad if disconformable.

No particular in human nature is more univer-<493>sal, than the uneasiness a man feels when in matters of importance his opinions are rejected by others: why should difference in opinion create uneasiness, more than difference in stature, in countenance, or in dress? The conviction of a common standard explains the mystery: every man, generally speaking, taking it for granted that his opinions agree with the common sense of mankind, is therefore disgusted with those who think differently, not as differing from him, but as differing from the common standard: hence in all disputes, we find the parties, each of them equally, appealing constantly to the common sense of mankind as the ultimate rule or standard. With respect to points arbitrary or indifferent, which are not supposed to be regulated by any standard, individuals are permitted to think for themselves with impunity: the same liberty is not indulged with respect to points that are reckoned of moment; for what reason, other than that the standard by which these are regulated, ought, as we judge, to produce an uniformity of opinion in all men? In a word, to this conviction of a common standard must be wholly attributed, the pleasure we take in those who espouse the same principles and opinions with ourselves, as well as the aversion we have at those who differ from us. In matters left indifferent by the standard, we find nothing of the same pleasure or pain: a bookish man, unless swayed by convenience, relisheth not the contem-<494>plative man more than the active; his friends and companions are chosen indifferently out of either class: a painter consorts with a poet or musician, as readily as with those of his own art; and one is not the more agreeable to me for loving beef, as I do, nor the less agreeable for preferring mutton.

I have ventured to say, that my disgust is raised, not by differing from me, but by differing from what I judge to be the common standard. This point, being of importance, ought to be firmly established. Men, it is true, are prone to flatter themselves, by taking it for granted that their opinions and their taste are in all respects conformable to the common standard; but there may be exceptions, and experience shows there are some: there are instances without number, of persons who are addicted to the grosser amusements of gaming, eating, drinking, without having any relish for more elegant pleasures, such, for example, as are afforded by the fine arts; yet these very persons, talking the same language with the rest of mankind, pronounce in favour of the more elegant pleasures, and they invariably approve those who have a more refined taste, being ashamed of their own as low and sensual. It is in vain to think of giving a reason for this singular impartiality, other than the authority of the common standard with respect to the dignity of human nature:* <495> and from the instances now given we discover, that the authority of that standard, even upon the most groveling souls, is so vigorous, as to prevail over self-partiality, and to make them despise their own taste compared with the more elevated taste of others.

Uniformity of taste and sentiment resulting from our conviction of a common standard, leads to two important final causes; the one respecting

* See chap. II.

our duty, the other our pastime. Barely to mention the first shall be sufficient, because it does not properly belong to the present undertaking. Unhappy it would be for us did not uniformity prevail in morals: that our
actions should uniformly be directed to what is good and against what is
ill, is the greatest blessing in society; and in order to uniformity of action,
uniformity of opinion and sentiment is indispensable.

With respect to pastime in general, and the fine arts in particular, the final
cause of uniformity is illustrious. Uniformity of taste gives opportunity for
sumptuous and elegant buildings, for fine gardens, and extensive embellishments, which please universally: and the reason is, that without uniformity
of taste, there could not be any suitable reward, either of profit or honour,
to encourage men of genius to labour in such works, and to advance them
toward perfection. The same uniformity of taste is equally necessary to perfect the art of music, sculpture, and painting, and to sup-<496>port the
expence they require after they are brought to perfection. Nature is in every
particular consistent with herself: we are framed by Nature to have a high
relish for the fine arts, which are a great source of happiness, and friendly in
a high degree to virtue: we are, at the same time, framed with uniformity of
taste, to furnish proper objects for that high relish; and if uniformity did not
prevail, the fine arts could never have made any figure.

And this suggests another final cause no less illustrious. The separation
of men into different classes, by birth, office, or occupation, however necessary, tends to relax the connection that ought to be among members of
the same state; which bad effect is in some measure prevented by the access
all ranks of people have to public spectacles, and to amusements that are
best enjoyed in company. Such meetings, where every one partakes of the
same pleasures in common, are no slight support to the social affections.

Thus, upon a conviction common to the species, is erected a standard
of taste, which without hesitation is applied to the taste of every individual.
That standard, ascertaining what actions are right what wrong, what proper
what improper, hath enabled moralists to establish rules for our conduct,
from which no person is permitted to swerve. We have the same standard
for ascertaining in all the fine arts, what is beautiful or ugly, high or low,
<497> proper or improper, proportioned or disproportioned: and here, as
in morals, we justly condemn every taste that deviates from what is thus
ascertained by the common standard.

That there exists a rule or standard in nature for trying the taste of individuals, in the fine arts as well as in morals, is a discovery; but is not sufficient to complete the task undertaken. A branch still more important remains upon hand; which is, to ascertain what is truly the standard of nature, that we may not lie open to have a false standard imposed on us. But what means shall be employed for bringing to light this natural standard? This is not obvious: for when we have recourse to general opinion and general practice, we are betrayed into endless perplexities. History informs us, that nothing is more variable than taste in the fine arts: judging by numbers, the Gothic taste of architecture must be preferred before that of Greece, and the Chinese taste probably before either. It would be endless to recount the various tastes that have prevailed in different ages with respect to gardening, and still prevail in different countries. Despising the modest colouring of nature, women of fashion in France daub their cheeks with a red powder; nay, an unnatural swelling in the neck, peculiar to the inhabitants of the Alps, is relished by that people. But we ought not to be discouraged by such untoward instances, when we find as great variety in moral <498> opinions: was it not among some nations held lawful for a man to sell his children for slaves, to expose them in their infancy to wild beasts, and to punish them for the crime of their parents? was any thing more common than to murder an enemy in cold blood? nay more, did not law once authorise the abominable practice of human sacrifices, no less impious than immoral? Such aberrations from the rules of morality prove only, that men, originally savage and brutal, acquire not rationality nor delicacy of taste till they be long disciplined in society. To ascertain the rules of morality, we appeal not to the common sense of savages, but of men in their more perfect state: and we make the same appeal in forming the rules that ought to govern the fine arts: in neither can we safely rely on a local or transitory taste; but on what is the most general and the most lasting among polite nations.

In this very manner, a standard for morals has been ascertained with a good deal of accuracy, and is daily applied by able judges with general satisfaction. The standard of taste in the fine arts, is not yet brought to such perfection; and we can account for its slower progress: the sense of right and wrong in actions is vivid and distinct, because its objects are clearly distinguishable from each other; whereas the sense of right and wrong in the fine arts is faint and wavering, because its objects are commonly not so clearly distinguishable from <499> each other. And there appears to me a striking final cause in thus distinguishing the moral sense from the sense of right and wrong in the fine arts. The former, as a rule of conduct, and as a law we ought to obey, must be clear and authoritative. The latter is not intitled to the same privilege, because it contributes to our pleasure and amusement only: were it strong and lively, it would usurp upon our duty, and call off the attention from matters of greater moment: were it clear and authoritative, it would banish all difference of taste, leaving no distinction between a refined taste and one that is not so; which would put an end to rivalship, and consequently to all improvement.

But to return to our subject. However languid and cloudy the common sense of mankind may be as to the fine arts, it is notwithstanding the only standard in these as well as in morals. True it is indeed, that in gathering the common sense of mankind, more circumspection is requisite with respect to the fine arts than with respect to morals: upon the latter, any person may be consulted; but in the former, a wary choice is necessary, for to collect votes indifferently would certainly mislead us. Those who depend for food on bodily labour, are totally void of taste; of such a taste at least as can be of use in the fine arts. This consideration bars the greater part of mankind; and of the remaining part, many by a corrupted taste are unqualified for voting. The common sense of <500> mankind must then be confined to the few that fall not under these exceptions. But as such selection seems to throw matters again into uncertainty, we must be more explicit upon this branch of our subject.

Nothing tends more than voluptuousness to corrupt the whole internal frame, and to vitiate our taste, not only in the fine arts, but even in morals: Voluptuousness never fails, in course of time, to extinguish all the sympathetic affections, and to bring on a beastly selfishness, which leaves nothing of man but the shape: about excluding such persons there will be no dispute. Let us next bring under trial, the opulent who delight in expence: the appetite for superiority and respect, inflamed by riches, is vented upon costly furniture, numerous attendants, a princely dwelling, sumptuous feasts, every thing superb and gorgeous, to amaze and humble all beholders: simplicity, elegance, propriety, and things natural, sweet, or amiable, are despised or neglected; for these are not appropriated to the rich, nor make a figure in the public eye: in a word, nothing is relished, but what serves to gratify pride, by an imaginary exaltation of the possessor above those who surround him. Such sentiments contract the heart, and make every principle give way to self-love: benevolence and public spirit, with all their refined emotions, are little felt, and less regarded; and if these be <501> excluded, there can be no place for the faint and delicate emotions of the fine arts.

The exclusion of classes so many and numerous, reduces within a narrow compass those who are qualified to be judges in the fine arts. Many circumstances are necessary to form such a judge: there must be a good natural taste; that is, a taste approaching, at least in some degree, to the delicacy of taste above described:* that taste must be improved by education, reflection, and experience:† it must be preserved in vigour by living regularly, by using the goods of fortune with mo-<502>deration, and by following the dictates of improved nature, which give welcome to every rational pleasure without indulging any excess. This is the tenor of life which of all contributes the most to refinement of taste; and the same tenor of life contributes the most to happiness in general.

* Chap. 2. part 2.
† That these particulars are useful, it may be said necessary, for acquiring a discerning taste in the fine arts, will appear from the following facts, which show the influence of experience singly. Those who live in the world and in good company, are quick-sighted with respect to every defect or irregularity in behaviour: the every slightest singularity in motion, in speech, or in dress, which to a peasant would be invisible, escapes not their observation. The most minute differences in the human countenance, so minute as to be far beyond the reach of words, are distinctly perceived by the plainest person; while, at the same time, the generality have very little discernment in the faces of other animals to which they are less accustomed: Sheep, for example, appear to have all the same face, except to the shepherd, who knows every individual in his flock as he does his relations and neighbours. The very populace in Athens were critics in language, in pronunciation, and even in eloquence, harangues being their daily entertainment. In Rome, at present, the most illiterate shopkeeper is a better judge of statues and of pictures, than persons of refined education in London. [A reference to the influential report in Charles Burney, *The Present State of Music in France and Italy,* London, 1771.] These facts afford convincing evidence, that a discerning taste depends still more on experience than on nature. But these facts merit peculiar regard for another reason, that they open to us a sure method of improving our taste in the fine arts; which, with those who have leisure for improvements, ought to be a powerful incitement to cultivate a taste in these arts: an occupation that cannot fail to embellish their manners, and to sweeten society.

If there appear much uncertainty in a standard that requires so painful and intricate a selection, we may possibly be reconciled to it by the following consideration, That, with respect to the fine arts, there is less difference of taste than is commonly imagined. Nature hath marked all her works with indelible characters of high or low, plain or elegant, strong or weak: these, if at all perceived, are seldom misapprehended; and the same marks are equally perceptible in works of art. A defective taste is incurable; and it hurts none but the possessor, because it carries no authority to impose upon others. I know not if <503> there be such a thing as a taste naturally bad or wrong; a taste, for example, that prefers a groveling pleasure before one that is high and elegant: groveling pleasures are never preferred; they are only made welcome by those who know no better. Differences about objects of taste, it is true, are endless; but they generally concern trifles, or possibly matters of equal rank, where preference may be given either way with impunity: if, on any occasion, persons differ where they ought not, a depraved taste will readily be discovered on one or other side, occasioned by imitation, custom, or corrupted manners, such as are described above. And considering that every individual partakes of a common nature, what is there that should occasion any wide difference in taste or sentiment? By the principles that constitute the sensative part of our nature, a wonderful uniformity is preserved in the emotions and feelings of the different races of men; the same object making upon every person the same impression, the same in kind, if not in degree. There have been, as above observed, aberrations from these principles; but soon or late they prevail, and restore the wanderer to the right tract.

I know but of one other means for ascertaining the common sense of mankind; which I mention, not in despair, but in great confidence of success. As the taste of every individual ought to be governed by the principles above mentioned, an ap-<504>peal to these principles must necessarily be decisive of every controversy that can arise upon matters of taste. In general, every doubt with relation to the common sense of man, or standard of taste, may be cleared by the same appeal; and to unfold these principles is the declared purpose of the present undertaking. <505>

APPENDIX

Terms defined or explained

1. Every thing we perceive or are conscious of, whether a being or a quality, a passion or an action, is with respect to the percipient termed an *object*. Some objects appear to be internal, or within the mind; passion, for example, thinking, volition; Some external; such as every object of sight, of hearing, of smell, of touch, of taste.

2. That act of the mind which makes known to me an external object, is termed *perception*. That act of the mind which makes known to me an internal object, is termed *consciousness*. The power or faculty from which consciousness proceeds, is termed an *internal sense*. The power or faculty from which perception proceeds, is termed an *external sense*. This distinction refers to the objects of our knowledge; for the senses, whether external or internal, are all of them powers or faculties of the mind.* <506>

---

* I have complied with all who have gone before me in describing the senses internal and external to be powers or faculties; and yet, after much attention, I have not discovered any thing active in their operations to entitle them to that character. The following chain of thought has led me to hesitate. One being operates on another: the first is active, the other passive. If the first act, it must have a power to act: if an effect be produced on the other, it must have a *capacity* to have that effect produced upon it. Fire melts wax: *ergo* fire has a power to produce that effect; and wax must be capable to have that effect produced in it. Now as to the senses. A tree in flourish makes an impression on me, and by that means I see the tree. But in this operation I do not find that the mind is active: seeing the tree is only an effect produced on it by intervention of the rays of light. What seems to have led us into an error is the word *seeing*, which, under the form of an active verb, has a passive signification. *I feel* is a similar example; for to feel is certainly not to act, but the effect of being acted upon: the feeling pleasure is the effect produced in my mind when a beautiful object is presented. Perception accordingly is not an action, but an effect produced in the mind. Sensation is another effect: it is the pleasure I feel upon perceiving what is agreeable.

3. But as self is an object that cannot be termed either external or internal, the faculty by which I have knowledge of myself, is a sense that cannot properly be termed either internal or external.

4. By the eye we perceive figure, colour, motion, &c.: by the ear we perceive the different qualities of sound, high, low, loud, soft: by touch we perceive rough, smooth, hot, cold, &c.: by taste we perceive sweet, sour, bitter, &c.: by smell we perceive fragrant, fetid, &c. These qualities partake the common nature of all qualities, that they are not capable of an independent existence, but must belong to some being of which they <507> are properties or attributes. A being with respect to its properties or attributes is termed a *subject,* or *substratum.* Every substratum of visible qualities, is termed *substance;* and of tangible qualities, *body.*

5. Substance and sound are perceived as existing at a distance from the organ; often at a considerable distance. But smell, touch, and taste, are perceived as existing at the organ of sense.

6. The objects of external sense are various. Substances are perceived by the eye; bodies by the touch. Sounds, tastes, and smells, passing commonly under the name of secondary qualities, require more explanation than there is room for here. All the objects of internal sense are attributes: witness deliberation, reasoning, resolution, willing, consenting, which are internal actions. Passions and emotions, which are internal agitations, are also attributes. With regard to the former, I am conscious of being active; with regard to the latter, I am conscious of being passive.

7. Again, we are conscious of internal action as in the head; of passions and emotions as in the heart.

8. Many actions may be exerted internally, and many effects produced, of which we are unconscious: when we investigate the ultimate cause of the motion of the blood, and of other internal motions upon which life depends, it is the most probable opinion that some internal power is the cause; and if so, we are unconscious of the operations of <508> that power. But consciousness being implied in the very meaning of deliberating, reasoning, resolving, willing, consenting, such operations cannot escape our knowledge. The same is the case of passions and emotions; for no internal agitation is denominated a passion or emotion, but what we are conscious of.

9. The mind is not always the same: by turns it is cheerful, melancholy, calm, peevish, &c. These differences may not improperly be denominated *tones*.

10. Perception and sensation are commonly reckoned synonymous terms, signifying that internal act by which external objects are made known to us. But they ought to be distinguished. *Perceiving* is a general term for hearing, seeing, tasting, touching, smelling; and therefore *perception* signifies every internal act by which we are made acquainted with external objects: thus we are said to perceive a certain animal, a certain colour, sound, taste, smell, &c. *Sensation* properly signifies that internal act by which we are made conscious of pleasure or pain felt at the organ of sense: thus we have a sensation of the pleasure arising from warmth, from a fragrant smell, from a sweet taste; and of the pain arising from a wound, from a fetid smell, from a disagreeable taste. In perception, my attention is directed to the external object: in sensation, it is directed to the pleasure or pain I feel. <509>

The terms *perception* and *sensation* are sometimes employed to signify the objects of perception and sensation. Perception in that sense is a general term for every external thing we perceive; and sensation a general term for every pleasure and pain felt at the organ of sense.

11. Conception is different from perception. The latter includes a conviction of the reality of its object: the former does not; for I can conceive the most extravagant stories told in a romance, without having any conviction of their reality. Conception differs also from imagination. By the power of fancy I can imagine a golden mountain, or an ebony ship with sails and ropes of silk. When I describe a picture of that kind to another, the idea he forms of it is termed a *conception*. Imagination is active, conception is passive.

12. Feeling, beside denoting one of the external senses, is a general term, signifying that internal act by which we are made conscious of our pleasures and our pains; for it is not limited, as sensation is, to any one sort. Thus, feeling being the genus of which sensation is a species, their meaning is the same when applied to pleasure and pain felt at the organ of sense: and accordingly we say indifferently, "I feel pleasure from heat, and pain from cold"; or, "I have a sensation of pleasure from heat, and of pain from cold."

But the meaning of feeling, as is said, is much <510> more extensive: It is proper to say, I feel pleasure in a sumptuous building, in love, in friendship; and pain in losing a child, in revenge, in envy: sensation is not properly applied to any of these.

The term *feeling* is frequently used in a less proper sense, to signify what we feel or are conscious of; and in that sense it is a general term for all our passions and emotions, and for all our other pleasures and pains.

13. That we cannot perceive an external object till an impression is made upon our body, is probable from reason, and is ascertained by experience. But it is not necessary that we be made sensible of the impression: in touching, in tasting, and in smelling, we are sensible of the impression; but not in seeing and hearing. We know indeed from experiments, that before we perceive a visible object, its image is spread upon the *retina tunica;* and that before we perceive a sound, an impression is made upon the drum of the ear: but we are not conscious either of the organic image or of the organic impression; nor are we conscious of any other operation preparatory to the act of perception: all we can say, is, that we see that river, or hear that trumpet.* <511>

14. Objects once perceived may be recalled to the mind by the power of memory. When I recall an object of sight in that manner, it appears to me precisely the same as in the original survey, only less distinct. For example, having seen yesterday a spreading oak growing on the brink of a river, I endeavour to recall these objects to my mind. How is this operation performed? Do I endeavour to form in my mind a picture of them or representative image? Not so. I transport myself ideally to the place where I saw

---

* Yet a singular opinion that impressions are the only objects of perception, has been espoused by some philosophers of no mean rank; not attending to the foregoing peculiarity in the senses of seeing and hearing, that we perceive objects without being conscious of an organic impression, or of any impression. See the Treatise upon Human Nature: where we find the following passage, book 1. p. 4. sect. 2. "Properly speaking, it is not our body we perceive when we regard our limbs and members; so that the ascribing a real and corporeal existence to these impressions, or to their objects, is an act of the mind as difficult to explain," &c. [Kames earlier stated (2.390n) he would cite only dead writers but had quoted Voltaire's *Henriade* (1.103, 2.233, 389; cf. also 2.381) and Hume's *History* (2.23, 31, 36). Hume died in 1776, fourteen years after the first edition of 1762, in which Kames cited his works.]

the tree and river yesterday; upon which I have a perception of these objects, similar in all respects to the perception I had when I viewed them with my eyes, only less distinct. And in this recollection, I am not conscious of a picture or representative image, more than in the original survey: the perception is of the tree and river themselves, as at first. I confirm this by another experiment. After attentively surveying a fine statue, I close my eyes. What follows? The same object continues, with-<512>out any difference but that it is less distinct than formerly.* This indistinct secondary perception of an object, is termed an *idea*. And therefore <513> the precise and accurate definition of an idea in contradistinction to an original per-

---

* This experiment, which every one may reiterate till entire satisfaction be obtained, is of greater importance than at first view may appear; for it strikes at the root of a celebrated doctrine, which for more than two thousand years has misled many philosophers. This doctrine as delivered by Aristotle is in substance, [This note did not appear in the first edition: the passages are not quotations but, as Kames says, they represent Aristotle's doctrine "in substance."] "That of every object of thought there must be in the mind some form, phantasm, or species; that things sensible are perceived and remembered by means of sensible phantasms, and things intelligible by intelligible phantasms; and that these phantasms have the form of the object without the matter, as the impression of a seal upon wax has the form of the seal without its matter." The followers of Aristotle add, "That the sensible and intelligible forms of things, are sent forth from the things themselves, and make impressions upon the passive intellect, which impressions are perceived by the active intellect." This notion differs very little from that of Epicurus, which is, "That all things send forth constantly and in every direction, slender ghosts or films of themselves, (*tenuia simulacra,* as expressed by his commentator Lucretius); which striking upon the mind, are the means of perception, dreaming," &c. Des Cartes, bent to oppose Aristotle, rejects the doctrine of sensible and intelligible phantasms; maintaining however the same doctrine in effect, namely, That we perceive nothing external but by means of some image either in the brain or in the mind: and these images he terms *ideas*. According to these philosophers, we perceive nothing immediately but phantasms or ideas: and from these we infer, by reasoning, the existence of external objects. Locke, adopting this doctrine, employs almost the whole of his book about ideas. He holds, that we cannot perceive, remember, nor imagine, any thing, but by having an idea or image of it in the mind. He agrees with Des Cartes, that we can have no knowledge of things external, but what we acquire by reasoning upon their ideas or images in the mind; taking it for granted, that we are conscious of these ideas or images, and of nothing else. Those who talk the most intelligibly explain the doctrine thus: When I see in a mirror a man standing behind me, the immediate object of my sight is his image, without which I could not see him: in like manner, when I see a tree or a house, there must be an image of these objects in my brain or in my mind; which

ception, is, "That perception of a real object which is raised <514> in the mind by the power of memory." Every thing we have any knowledge of, whether inter-<515>nal or external, passions, emotions, thinking, resolving,

---

image is the immediate object of my perception; and by means of that image I perceive the external object.

One would not readily suspect any harm in this ideal system, other than the leading us into a labyrinth of metaphysical errors, in order to account for our knowledge of external objects, which is more truly and more simply accounted for by direct perception. And yet some late writers have been able to extract from it death and destruction to the whole world, levelling all down to a mere chaos of ideas. Dr. Berkeley, upon authority of the philosophers named, taking for granted that we cannot perceive any object but what is in the mind, discovered, that the reasoning employed by Des Cartes and Locke to infer the existence of external objects, is inconclusive; and upon that discovery ventured, against common sense, to annihilate totally the material world. And a later writer, discovering that Berkeley's arguments might with equal success be applied against immaterial beings, ventures still more boldly to reject by the lump the immaterial world as well as the material; leaving nothing in nature but images or ideas floating *in vacuo,* without affording them a single mind for shelter or support.

When such wild and extravagant consequences can be drawn from the ideal system, it might have been expected, that no man who is not crazy would have ventured to erect such a superstructure, till he should first be certain beyond all doubt of a solid foundation. And yet upon inquiry, we find the foundation of this terrible doctrine to be no better than a shallow metaphysical argument, *namely,* "That no being can act but where it is; and, consequently, that it cannot act upon any subject at a distance." This argument possesses indeed one eminent advantage, that its obscurity, like that of an oracle, is apt to impose upon the reader, who is willing to consider it as a demonstration, because he does not clearly see the fallacy. The best way to give it a fair trial, is to draw it out of its obscurity, and to state it in a clear light, as follows. "No subject can be perceived unless it act upon the mind; but no distant subject can act upon the mind, because no being can act but where it is: and, therefore, the immediate object of perception must be something united to the mind, so as to be able to act upon it." Here the argument is completed in all its parts; and from it is derived the supposed necessity of phantasms or ideas united to the mind, as the only objects of perception. It is singularly unlucky, that this argument concludes directly against the very system of which it is the only foundation; for how can phantasms or ideas be raised in the mind by things at a distance, if things at a distance cannot act upon the mind? I say more, that it assumes a proposition as true, without evidence, *namely,* That no distant subject can act upon the mind. This proposition undoubtedly requires evidence, for it is not intuitively certain. And, therefore, till the proposition be demonstrated, every man without scruple may rely upon the conviction of his senses, that he hears and sees things at a distance.

But I venture a bolder step, which is, to show that the proposition is false. Admitting that no being can act but where it is, is there any thing more simple or more common, than the acting upon subjects at a distance by intermediate means? This holds in fact

willing, heat, cold, &c. as well as ex-<516>ternal objects, may be recalled as above, by the power of memory.*

15. External objects are distinguishable into <517> simple and complex. Certain sounds are so simple as not to be resolvable into parts; and so are certain tastes and smells. Objects of touch are for the most part complex: they are not only hard or soft, but also smooth or rough, hot or cold. Of all external objects, visible objects are commonly the most complex: a tree is composed of a trunk, branches, leaves: it has colour, figure, size. But as an action is not resolvable into parts, a perception, being an act of sense, is always simple. The colour, figure, umbrage of a spreading oak, raise not different perceptions: the perception is one, that of a tree, coloured, figured, &c. A quality is never perceived separately from the subject; nor a part from

---

with respect both to seeing and hearing. When I see a tree, for example, rays of light are reflected from the tree to my eye, forming a picture upon the *retina tunica:* but the object perceived is the tree itself, not the rays of light, nor the picture. In this manner distant objects are perceived, without any action of the object upon the mind, or of the mind upon the object. Hearing is in a similar case: the air, put in motion by thunder, makes an impression upon the drum of the ear; but this impression is not what I hear, it is the thunder itself by means of that impression.

With respect to vision in particular, we are profoundly ignorant by what means and in what manner the picture on the *retina tunica* contributes to produce a sight of the object. One thing only is clear, that as we have no knowledge of that picture, it is as natural to conceive that it should be made the instrument of discovering the external object, and not itself, as of discovering itself only, and not the external object.

Upon the chimerical consequences drawn from the ideal system, I shall make but a single reflection. Nature determines us necessarily to rely on the veracity of our senses; and upon their evidence the existence of external objects is to us a matter of intuitive knowledge and absolute certainty. Vain therefore is the attempt of Dr. Berkeley and of his followers, to deceive us, by a metaphysical subtilty, into a disbelief of what we cannot entertain even the slightest doubt.

* From this definition of an idea, the following proposition must be evident, That there can be no such thing as an innate idea. If the original perception of an object be not innate, which is obvious; it is not less obvious, that the idea or secondary perception of that object cannot be innate. And yet, to prove this self-evident proposition, Locke has bestowed a whole book of his Treatise upon Human Understanding. So necessary it is to give accurate definitions, and so preventive of dispute are definitions when accurate. Dr. Berkeley has taken great pains to prove another proposition equally evident, That there can be no such thing as a general idea: all our original perceptions are of particular objects, and our secondary perceptions or ideas must be equally so.

the whole. There is a mental power of abstraction, of which afterward; but the eye never abstracts, nor any other external sense.

16. Many particulars beside those mentioned enter into the perception of visible objects, motion, rest, place, space, time, number, &c. These, all of them, denote simple ideas, and for that reason admit not of a definition. All that can be done, is to point out how they are acquired. The ideas of motion and of rest, are familiar even to a child, from seeing its nurse sometimes walking, sometimes sitting: the former it is taught to call *motion;* the latter, *rest.* Place enters into every perception of a visible object: the object is perceived to exist, <518> and to exist somewhere, on the right hand or on the left, and where it exists is termed *place.* Ask a child where its mother is, or in what place: it will answer readily, she is in the garden. Space is connected with size or bulk: every piece of matter occupies *room* or *space* in proportion to its bulk. A child perceives that when its little box is filled with playthings, there is no room or space for more. Space is also applied to signify the distance of visible objects from each other; and such space accordingly can be measured. Dinner comes after breakfast, and supper after dinner: a child perceives an interval, and that interval it learns to call *time.* A child sometimes is alone with its nurse: its mother is sometimes in the room; and sometimes also its brothers and sisters. It perceives a difference between many and few; and that difference it is taught to call *number.*

17. The primary perception of a visible object, is more complete, lively, and distinct, than that of any other object. And for that reason, an idea or secondary perception of a visible object, is also more complete, lively, and distinct, than that of any other object. A fine passage in music, may, for a moment, be recalled to the mind with tolerable accuracy; but, after the shortest interval, it becomes no less obscure than the ideas of the other objects mentioned.

18. As the range of an individual is commonly <519> within a narrow space, it rarely happens, that every thing necessary to be known comes under our own perceptions. Language is an admirable contrivance for supplying that deficiency; for by language every man's perceptions may be communicated to all: and the same may be done by painting and other imitative arts. The facility of communication depends on the liveliness of the ideas; especially in language, which hitherto has not arrived at greater

perfection than to express clear ideas: hence it is, that poets and orators, who are extremely successful in describing objects of sight, find objects of the other senses too faint and obscure for language. An idea thus acquired of an object at second hand, ought to be distinguished from an idea of memory, though their resemblance has occasioned the same term *idea* to be applied to both; which is to be regreted, because ambiguity in the signification of words is a great obstruction to accuracy of conception. Thus Nature hath furnished the means of multiplying ideas without end, and of providing every individual with a sufficient stock to answer, not only the necessities, but even the elegancies of life.

19. Further, man is endued with a sort of creative power: he can fabricate images of things that have no existence. The materials employed in this operation, are ideas of sight, which he can take to pieces and combine into new forms at <520> pleasure: their complexity and vivacity make them fit materials. But a man hath no such power over any of his other ideas, whether of the external or internal senses: he cannot, after the utmost effort, combine these into new forms, being too obscure for that operation. An image thus fabricated cannot be called a secondary perception, not being derived from an original perception: the poverty of language, however, as in the case immediately above mentioned, has occasioned the same term *idea* to be applied to all. This singular power of fabricating images without any foundation in reality, is distinguished by the name *imagination*.

20. As ideas are the chief materials employed in reasoning and reflecting, it is of consequence that their nature and differences be understood. It appears now, that ideas may be distinguished into three kinds: first, Ideas derived from original perceptions, properly termed *ideas of memory;* second, Ideas communicated by language or other signs; and, third, Ideas of imagination. These ideas differ from each other in many respects; but chiefly in respect of their proceeding from different causes: The first kind is derived from real existences that have been objects of our senses: language is the cause of the second, or any other sign that has the same power with language: and a man's imagination is to himself the cause of the third. It is scarce necessary to add, that an idea, originally of <521> imagination, being conveyed to others by language or any other vehicle, becomes in their mind an idea of the second kind; and again, that an idea of this kind, being

afterward recalled to the mind, becomes in that circumstance an idea of memory.

21. We are not so constituted as to perceive objects with indifference: these, with very few exceptions, appear agreeable or disagreeable; and at the same time raise in us pleasant or painful emotions. With respect to external objects in particular, we distinguish those which produce organic impressions, from those which affect us from a distance. When we touch a soft and smooth body, we have a pleasant feeling as at the place of contact; which feeling we distinguish not, at least not accurately, from the agreeableness of the body itself; and the same holds in general with regard to all organic impressions. It is otherwise in hearing and seeing: a sound is perceived as in itself agreeable, and raises in the hearer a pleasant emotion: an object of sight appears in itself agreeable, and raises in the spectator a pleasant emotion. These are accurately distinguished: the pleasant emotion is felt as within the mind; the agreeableness of the object is placed upon the object, and is perceived as one of its qualities or properties. The agreeable appearance of an object of sight is termed *beauty;* and the disagreeable appearance of such an object is termed *ugliness.* <522>

22. But though beauty and ugliness, in their proper and genuine signification, are confined to objects of sight; yet in a more lax and figurative signification, they are applied to objects of the other senses: they are sometimes applied even to abstract terms: for it is not unusual to say, *a beautiful theorem, a beautiful constitution of government.*

23. A line composed by a single rule, is perceived and said to be regular: a straight line, a parabola, a hyperbola, the circumference of a circle, and of an ellipse, are all of them regular lines. A figure composed by a single rule, is perceived and said to be regular: a circle, a square, a hexagon, an equilateral triangle, are regular figures, being composed by a single rule that determines the form of each. When the form of a line or of a figure is ascertained by a single rule that leaves nothing arbitrary, the line and the figure are said to be perfectly regular; which is the case of the figures now mentioned, and the case of a straight line and of the circumference of a circle. A figure and a line that require more than one rule for their construction, or that have any of their parts left arbitrary, are not perfectly regular: a parallelogram and a rhomb are less regular than a square; the

parallelogram being subjected to no rule as to the length of sides, other than that the opposite sides be equal; the rhomb being subjected to no rule as to its angles, other than that the opposite angles be equal: for the same reason, the <523> circumference of an ellipse, the form of which is susceptible of much variety, is less regular than that of a circle.

24. Regularity, properly speaking, belongs, like beauty, to objects of sight; and, like beauty, it is also applied figuratively to other objects: thus we say, *a regular government, a regular composition of music,* and, *regular discipline.*

25. When two figures are composed of similar parts, they are said to be uniform. Perfect uniformity is where the constituent parts of two figures are equal: thus two cubes of the same dimensions are perfectly uniform in all their parts. Uniformity less perfect is, where the parts mutually correspond, but without being equal: the uniformity is imperfect between two squares or cubes of unequal dimensions; and still more so between a square and a parallelogram.

26. Uniformity is also applicable to the constituent parts of the same figure. The constituent parts of a square are perfectly uniform; its sides are equal and its angles are equal. Wherein then differs regularity from uniformity? for a figure composed of uniform parts must undoubtedly be regular. Regularity is predicated of a figure considered as a whole composed of uniform parts: uniformity is predicated of these parts as related to each other by resemblance: we say, a square is a regular, not an uniform, figure; but with respect to the constituent parts of a square, we say <524> not, that they are regular, but that they are uniform.

27. In things destined for the same use, as legs, arms, eyes, windows, spoons, we expect uniformity. Proportion ought to govern parts intended for different uses: we require a certain proportion between a leg and an arm; in the base, the shaft, the capital of a pillar; and in the length, the breadth, the height of a room: some proportion is also required in different things intimately connected, as between a dwelling-house, the garden, and the stables; but we require no proportion among things slightly connected, as between the table a man writes on and the dog that follows him. Proportion and uniformity never coincide: things equal are uniform; but proportion is never applied to them: the four sides and angles of a square are equal and

perfectly uniform; but we say not that they are proportional. Thus, proportion always implies inequality or difference; but then it implies it to a certain degree only: the most agreeable proportion resembles a *maximum* in mathematics; a greater or less inequality or difference is less agreeable.

28. Order regards various particulars. First, in tracing or surveying objects, we are directed by a sense of order: we perceive it to be more orderly, that we should pass from a principal to its accessories, and from a whole to its parts, than in the contrary direction. Next, with respect to the <525> position of things, a sense of order directs us to place together things intimately connected. Thirdly, in placing things that have no natural connection, that order appears the most perfect, where the particulars are made to bear the strongest relation to each other that position can give them. Thus parallelism is the strongest relation that position can bestow upon straight lines: if they be so placed as by production to intersect, the relation is less perfect. A large body in the middle, and two equal bodies of less size, one on each side, is an order that produces the strongest relation the bodies are susceptible of by position: the relation between the two equal bodies would be stronger by juxtaposition; but they would not both have the same relation to the third.

29. The beauty or agreeableness of a visible object, is perceived as one of its qualities; which holds, not only in the primary perception, but also in the secondary perception or idea: and hence the pleasure that arises from the idea of a beautiful object. An idea of imagination is also pleasant, though in a lower degree than an idea of memory, where the objects are of the same kind; for an evident reason, that the former is more distinct and lively than the latter. But this inferiority in ideas of imagination, is more than compensated by their greatness and variety, which are boundless; for by the imagination, exerted without controul, we can fabricate ideas of finer visible ob-<526>jects, of more noble and heroic actions, of greater wickedness, of more surprising events, than ever in fact existed: and in communicating such ideas by words, painting, sculpture, &c. the influence of the imagination is no less extensive than great.

30. In the nature of every man, there is somewhat original, which distinguishes him from others, which tends to form his character, and to make him meek or fiery, candid or deceitful, resolute or timorous, cheerful or

morose. This original bent, termed *disposition,* must be distinguished from a *principle:* the latter, signifying a law of human nature, makes part of the common nature of man; the former makes part of the nature of this or that man. *Propensity* is a name common to both; for it signifies a principle as well as a disposition.

31. *Affection,* signifying a settled bent of mind toward a particular being or thing, occupies a middle place between disposition on the one hand, and passion on the other. It is clearly distinguishable from disposition, which, being a branch of one's nature originally, must exist before there can be an opportunity to exert it upon any particular object; whereas affection can never be original, because, having a special relation to a particular object, it cannot exist till the object have once at least been presented. It is no less clearly distinguishable from passion, which, depending on the real or ideal presence of its object, vanishes with its object: whereas affection is a lasting con-<527>nection; and, like other connections, subsists even when we do not think of the person. A familiar example will clear the whole. I have from nature a disposition to gratitude, which, through want of an object, happens never to be exerted; and which therefore is unknown even to myself. Another who has the same disposition, meets with a kindly office which makes him grateful to his benefactor: an intimate connection is formed between them, termed *affection;* which, like other connections, has a permanent existence, though not always in view. The affection, for the most part, lies dormant, till an opportunity offer for exerting it: in that circumstance, it is converted into the passion of gratitude; and the opportunity is greedily seized of testifying gratitude in the warmest manner.

32. *Aversion,* I think, is opposed to affection; not to desire, as it commonly is. We have an affection to one person; we have an aversion to another: the former disposes us to do good to its object, the latter to do ill.

33. What is a sentiment? It is not a perception; for a perception signifies the act by which we become conscious of external objects. It is not consciousness of an internal action, such as thinking, suspending thought, inclining, resolving, willing, *&c.* Neither is it the conception of a relation among objects; a conception of that kind being termed *opinion.* The term *sentiment* is ap-<528>propriated to such thoughts as are prompted by passion.

34. *Attention* is that state of mind which prepares one to receive impressions. According to the degree of attention, objects make a strong or weak impression.* Attention is requisite even to the simple act of seeing: the eye can take in a considerable field at one look; but no object in the field is seen distinctly, but that singly which fixes the attention: in a profound reverie that totally occupies the attention, we scarce see what is directly before us. In a train of perceptions, the attention being divided among various objects, no particular object makes such a figure as it would do single and apart. Hence, the stillness of night contributes to terror, there being nothing to divert the attention:

> Horror ubique animos, simul ipsa silentia terrent.
>
> Aeneid. ii.[1]

> *Zara.* Silence and solitude are ev'ry where!
> Through all the gloomy ways and iron doors <529>
> That hither lead, nor human face nor voice
> is seen or heard. A dreadful din was wont
> To grate the sense, when enter'd here, from groans
> And howls of slaves condemn'd, from clink of chains,
> And crash of rusty bars and creaking hinges:
> And ever and anon the sight was dash'd
> With frightful faces and the meagre looks
> Of grim and ghastly executioners.
> Yet more this stillness terrifies my soul
> Than did that scene of complicated horrors.
>
> Mourning Bride, act 5. sc. 8.

And hence it is, that an object seen at the termination of a confined view, is more agreeable than when seen in a group with the surrounding objects:

---

* Bacon, in his Natural History, makes the following observations. Sounds are meliorated by the intension of the sense, where the common sense is collected most to the particular sense of hearing, and the sight suspended. Therefore sounds are sweeter, as well as greater, in the night than in the day; and I suppose they are sweeter to blind men than to others: and it is manifest, that between sleeping and waking, when all the senses are bound and suspended, music is far sweeter than when one is fully waking.

1. *Aeneid* 2.755: "Everywhere dread fills my heart, the very silence, too, dismays."

The crow doth sing as sweetly as the lark
When neither is attended; and, I think,
The nightingale, if she should sing by day,
When ev'ry goose is cackling, would be thought
No better a musician than the wren.

Merchant of Venice.[2]

35. In matters of slight importance, attention is mostly directed by will; and for that reason, it is our own fault if trifling objects make any deep impression. Had we power equally to with-hold our attention from matters of importance, we might be proof against any deep impression. But our power fails us here: an interesting object seizes and fixes the attention beyond the possibility of controul; <530> and while our attention is thus forcibly attached to one object, others may solicit for admittance; but in vain, for they will not be regarded. Thus a small misfortune is scarce felt in presence of a greater:

Lear. Thou think'st 'tis much, that this contentious storm
Invades us to the skin; so 'tis to thee;
But where the greater malady is fix'd,
The lesser is scarce felt. Thou'dst shun a bear;
But if thy flight lay tow'rd the roaring sea,
Thou'dst meet the bear i' th' mouth. When the mind's free,
The body's delicate: the tempest in my mind
Doth from my senses take all feeling else,
Save what beats there. *King Lear, act* 3. *sc.* 5.[3]

36. *Genus, species, modification,* are terms invented to distinguish beings from each other. Individuals are distinguished by their qualities: a number of individuals considered with respect to qualities that distinguish them from others, is termed a *species:* a plurality of *species* considered with respect to their distinguishing qualities, is termed a *genus.* That quality which distinguisheth one genus, one species, or even one individual, from another, is termed a *modification:* thus the same particular that is termed a *property* or *quality* when considered as belonging to an individual, or a class of in-

2. Act 5, sc. 1.
3. Act 3, sc. 4.

dividuals, is termed a *modification* when consi-<531>dered as distinguishing the individual or the class from another: a black skin and soft curled hair, are properties of a negro: the same circumstances considered as marks that distinguish a negro from a man of a different species, are denominated *modifications*.

37. Objects of sight, being complex, are distinguishable into the several particulars that enter into the composition: these objects are all of them coloured; and they all have length, breadth, and thickness. When I behold a spreading oak, I distinguish in that object, size, figure, colour, and sometimes motion: in a flowing river, I distinguish colour, figure, and constant motion; a dye has colour, black spots, six plain surfaces, all equal and uniform. Objects of touch have all of them extension: some of them are felt rough, some smooth: some of them are hard, some soft. With respect to the other senses, some of their objects are simple, some complex: a sound, a taste, a smell, may be so simple as not to be distinguishable into parts: others are perceived to be compounded of different sounds, different tastes, and different smells.

38. The eye at one look can grasp a number of objects, as of trees in a field, or men in a crowd: these objects having each a separate and independent existence, are distinguishable in the mind as well as in reality; and there is nothing more easy than to abstract from some and to confine our contemplation to others. A large oak with its spreading <532> branches fixes our attention upon itself, and abstracts us from the shrubs that surround it. In the same manner, with respect to compound sounds, tastes, or smells, we can fix our thoughts upon any one of the component parts, abstracting our attention from the rest. The power of abstraction is not confined to objects that are separable in reality as well as mentally; but also takes place where there can be no real separation: the size, the figure, the colour, of a tree, are inseparably connected, and have no independent existence; the same of length, breadth, and thickness: and yet we can mentally confine our observations to one of these, abstracting from the rest. Here abstraction takes place where there cannot be a real separation.

39. Space and time have occasioned much metaphysical jargon; but after the power of abstraction is explained as above, there remains no difficulty about them. It is mentioned above, that space as well as place enter into

the perception of every visible object: a tree is perceived as existing in a certain place, and as occupying a certain space. Now, by the power of abstraction, space may be considered abstractedly from the body that occupies it; and hence the abstract term space. In the same manner, existence may be considered abstractedly from any particular thing that exists; and place may be considered abstractedly from any particular thing that may be in it. Every series or succession of things, suggests the idea of time; and <533> time may be considered abstractedly from any series of succession. In the same manner, we acquire the abstract term motion, rest, number, and a thousand other abstract terms; an excellent contrivance for improving speech, as without it speech would be wofully imperfect. Brute animals may have some obscure notion of these circumstances, as connected with particular objects: an ox probably perceives that he takes longer time to go round a long ridge in the plough, than a short one; and he probably perceives when he is one of four in the yoke, or only one of two. But the power of abstraction is not bestowed on brute animals; because to them it would be altogether useless, as they are incapable of speech.

40. This power of abstraction is of great utility. A carpenter considers a log of wood with regard to hardness, firmness, colour, and texture: a philosopher, neglecting these properties, makes the log undergo a chymical analysis; and examines its taste, its smell, and its component principles: the geometrician confines his reasoning to the figure, the length, breadth, and thickness. In general, every artist, abstracting from all other properties, confines his observations to those which have a more immediate connection with his profession.

41. It is observed above, p. 516. that there can be no such thing as a general idea; that all our perceptions are of particular objects, and that our secondary perceptions or ideas must be equally so. <534> Precisely, for the same reason, there can be no such thing as an abstract idea. We cannot form an idea of a part without taking in the whole; nor of motion, colour, figure, independent of a body. No man will say that he can form any idea of beauty, till he think of a person endued with that quality; nor that he can form an idea of weight, till he takes under consideration a body that is weighty. And when he takes under consideration a body endued with one or other of the properties mentioned, the idea he forms is not an abstract or general idea,

but the idea of a particular body with its properties. But though a part and the whole, a subject and its attributes, an effect and its cause, are so intimately connected, as that an idea cannot be formed of the one independent of the other; yet we can reason upon the one abstracting from the other.

This is done by words signifying the thing to which the reasoning is confined; and such words are denominated *abstract terms.* The meaning and use of an abstract term is well understood, though of itself, unless other particulars be taken in, it raises no image nor idea in the mind. In language it serves excellent purpose; by it different figures, different colours, can be compared, without the trouble of conceiving them as belonging to any particular subject; and they contribute with words significant to raise images or ideas in the mind. <535>

42. The power of abstraction is bestowed on man, for the purpose solely of reasoning. It tends greatly to the facility as well as clearness of any process of reasoning, that, laying aside every other circumstance, we can confine our attention to the single property we desire to investigate.

43. Abstract terms may be separated into three different kinds, all equally subservient to the reasoning faculty. Individuals appear to have no end; and did we not possess the faculty of distributing them into classes, the mind would be lost in an endless maze, and no progress be made in knowledge. It is by the faculty of abstraction that we distribute beings into *genera* and *species:* finding a number of individuals connected by certain qualities common to all, we give a name to these individuals considered as thus connected, which name, by gathering them together into one class, serves to express the whole of these individuals as distinct from others. Thus the word *animal* serves to denote every being that can move voluntarily; and the words *man, horse, lion, &c.* answer similar purposes. This is the first and most common sort of abstraction; and it is of the most extensive use, by enabling us to comprehend in our reasoning whole kinds and sorts, instead of individuals without end. The next sort of abstract terms comprehends a number of individual objects, considered as connected by some occasional relation. A great number of persons collected in one place, without <536> any other relation but merely that of contiguity, are denominated *a crowd:* in forming this term, we abstract from sex, from age, from condition, from dress, *&c.* A number of persons connected by the same

laws and by the same government, are termed *a nation:* and a number of men under the same military command, are termed *an army.* A third sort of abstraction is, where a single property or part, which may be common to many individuals, is selected to be the subject of our contemplation; for example, whiteness, heat, beauty, length, roundness, head, arm.

44. Abstract terms are a happy invention: it is by their means chiefly, that the particulars which make the subject of our reasoning, are brought into close union, and separated from all others however naturally connected. Without the aid of such terms, the mind could never be kept steady to its proper subject, but be perpetually in hazard of assuming foreign circumstances, or neglecting what are essential. We can, without the aid of language, compare real objects by intuition, when these objects are present; and, when absent, we can compare them in idea. But when we advance farther, and attempt to make inferences and draw conclusions, we always employ abstract terms, even in thinking: it would be as difficult to reason without them, as to perform operations in algebra without signs; for there is scarce any reasoning without some degree of ab-<537>straction, and we cannot easily abstract without using abstract terms. Hence it follows, that without language man would scarce be a rational being.

45. The same thing, in different respects, has different names. With respect to certain qualities, it is termed a *substance;* with respect to other qualities, a *body;* and with respect to qualities of all sorts, a *subject.* It is termed a *passive subject* with respect to an action exerted upon it; an *object* with respect to a percipient; a *cause* with respect to the effect it produces; and an *effect* with respect to its cause. <538> <539>

INDEX

Aristaeus) the episode of Aristaeus in
the Georgics censured ii. 176.
Aristotle) censured ii. 512. *note.*
Army) defined ii. 536.
Arrangement) the best arrangement of
words is to place them if possible in
an increasing series ii. 16. Arrange-
ment of members in a period ii. 16.
Of periods in a discourse ii. 17.
Ambiguity from wrong arrangement
ii. 54. Arrangement natural and
inverted ii. 81. 82.
Articulate sounds) how far agreeable
ii. 6. 7. 8. 9. 10.
Artificial mount ii. 446.
Arts). *See* Fine arts.
Ascent) pleasant, but descent not pain-
ful i. 220.
Athalie) of Racine censured i. 486.
Attention) defined ii. 528. Impression
made by objects depends on the
degree of attention ii. 528. Attention
not always voluntary ii. 529. 530.
Attractive passions i. 440.
Attractive object i. 184.
Attractive signs of passion i. 439.
Attributes) transferred by a figure of
speech from one subject to another
ii. 269, *&c.*
Avarice) defined i. 40.
Avenue) to a house ii. 446.
Aversion) defined i. 119. 120. 405.
ii. 527. <542>

Bacchius ii. 179.
Bajazet) of Racine censured i. 505.
Barren scene) defined ii. 409.
Base) of a column ii. 478.
Basso-relievo ii. 473.
Batrachomuomachia) censured i. 368.
Beauty) ch. 3. Intrinsic and relative
i. 197. ii. 447. Beauty of simplicity

i. 200. of figure i. 201. of the circle
i. 203. of the square i. 203. of a
regular polygon i. 203. of a parallelogram i. 203. of an equilateral
triangle i. 204. Whether beauty be a
primary or secondary quality of
objects i. 207. Beauty distinguished
from grandeur i. 213. Beauty of
natural colours i. 327. Beauty distinguished from congruity i. 337.
Consummate beauty seldom produces a constant lover i. 414.
Wherein consists the beauty of the
human visage i. 426. Beauty proper
and figurative ii. 522. 523.
Behaviour) gross and refined i. 113.
Belief) of the reality of external
objects i. 88. Enforced by a lively
narrative, or a good historical painting i. 100, 101. Influenced by passion
i. 162, 163. ii. 228. 259. Influenced by
propensity i. 163. Influenced by
affection i. 163.
Benevolence operates in conjunction
with self-love to make us happy
i. 185. Benevolence inspired by gardening ii. 453.
Berkeley) censured ii. 513. *note.*
Blank verse ii. 119. 160. Its aptitude
for inversion ii. 163. Its melody
ii. 163. How far proper in tragedy
ii. 403.
Body) defined ii. 507.
Boileau) censured ii. 254. 388.
Bombast i. 243. Bombast in action
i. 247.
Bossu) censured ii. 411. *note.*
Burlesque) machinery does well in a
burlesque poem i. 103. Burlesque
distinguished into two kinds i. 366.
Business) men of middle age best qualified for it i. 307.

Cadence ii. 94. 104.

Capital) of a column ii. 478.

Careless Husband) its double plot well contrived ii. 399.

Cascade i. 252.

Cause) resembling causes may produce effects that have no resemblance; and causes that have no resemblance may produce resembling effects ii. 86. Cause defined ii. 537.

Chance) the mind revolts against misfortunes that happen by chance ii. 380. <543>

Character) to draw a character is the master-stroke of description ii. 337, 338.

Characteristics) of Shaftsbury criticised i. 339. *note.*

Children) love to them accounted for i. 71. A child can discover a passion from its external signs i. 441. Hides none of its emotions i. 450.

Chinese gardens ii. 450. Wonder and surprise studied in them ii. 452.

Choreus ii. 178.

Choriambus ii. 180.

Chorus) an essential part of the Grecian tragedy ii. 412.

Church) what ought to be its form and situation ii. 468.

Cicero censured ii. 80. 96. 99.

Cid) of Corneille censured i. 464. 490.

Cinna) of Corneille censured i. 341. 459. 487.

Circle) its beauty i. 201.

Circumstances) in a period, where they should be placed ii. 61. 68.

Class) all living creatures distributed into classes ii. 491. 492.

Climax) in sense i. 226. 462. ii. 74. In sound ii. 17. When these are joined, the sentence is delightful ii. 92.

Coephores) of Eschylus censured i. 424.

Coexistent) emotions and passions i. 124, &c.

Colonnade) where proper ii. 459.

Colour) gold and silver esteemed for their beautiful colours i. 199. A secondary quality i. 107. Natural colours i. 327. Colouring of the human face, exquisite i. 327.

Columns) every column ought to have a base i. 179. The base ought to be square i. 179. Columns admit different proportions ii. 465. 468. What emotions they raise ii. 468. Column more beautiful than a pilaster ii. 477. Its form ii. 478. Five orders of columns ii. 479. Capital of the Corinthian order censured ii. 481.

Comedy) double plot in a comedy ii. 397. 399. Modern manners do best in comedy ii. 383. Immorality of English comedy i. 55.

Comet) motion of the comets and planets compared with respect to beauty i. 251.

Commencement) of a work ought to be modest and simple ii. 326.

Common nature) in every species of animals i. 108. ii. 490. We have a conviction that this common nature is invariable ii. 491. Also that it is perfect or right i. 108. ii. 491.

Common sense ii. 493. 503.

Communication of passion to related objects. *See* Passion. <544> Communication of qualities to related objects. *See* Propensity.

Comparison i. 279, &c. ch. 19. In the early composition of all nations, comparisons are carried beyond proper bounds ii. 184. Comparisons

that resolve into a play of words
ii. 218.

Complex emotion i. 125, &c.

Complex object) its power to generate
passion i. 75. 76. 239.

Complex perception ii. 517.

Complexion) what colour of dress is
the most suitable to different com-
plexions i. 297.

Conception) defined ii. 509.

Concord) or harmony in objects of
sight i. 129.

Concordant sounds) defined i. 125.

Congreve) censured i. 57. 368. 432.
note. ii. 402. 409.

Congruity and propriety ch. 10. A secondary relation i. 336. note.
Congruity distinguished from
beauty i. 337. Distinguished from
propriety i. 337. As to quantity, congruity coincides with proportion
i. 346.

Connection) essential in all compositions i. 27.

Conquest of Granada) of Dryden censured i. 492.

Consonants ii. 7.

Constancy) consummate beauty the
cause of inconstancy i. 414.

Construction) of language explained
ii. 44, &c.

Contemplation) when painful i. 315.

Contempt) raised by improper action
i. 274.

Contrast ch. 8. Its effect in language
ii. 12. In a series of objects ii. 15.
Contrast in the thought requires
contrast in the members of the
expression ii. 37, 38. The effect of
contrast in gardening ii. 451.

Conviction) intuitive. See Intuitive
conviction.

Copulative) to drop the copulative
enlivens the expression ii. 41, &c.

Coriolanus) of Shakespeare censured
i. 491.

Corneille) censured i. 459. 480. 503.
509.

Corporeal pleasure i. 1, 2. Low and
sometimes mean i. 356.

Couplet ii. 120. Rules for its composition ii. 160. 161.

Courage) of greater dignity than justice i. 355.

Creticus ii. 179.

Criminal) the hour of execution seems
to him to approach with a swift pace
i. 167.

Criticism) its advantages i. 7, &c. Its
terms not accurately defined i. 443.
<545>

Crowd) defined ii. 533.

Curiosity i. 258. 278, &c.

Custom and habit ch. 14. Renders
objects familiar i. 259. Custom distinguished from habit i. 400, 401.
Custom puts the rich and poor
upon a level i. 419. Taste in the fine
arts improved by custom ii. 501.
note.

Dactyle ii. 179.

Davila) censured i. 323.

Declensions) explained ii. 46. 47.

Dedications. See Epistles Dedicatory.

Delicacy) of taste i. 111. ii. 501.

Derision i. 344. 366.

Des Cartes) censured ii. 512. note.

Descent) not painful i. 220.

Description) it animates a description
to represent things past as present
i. 98. The rules that ought to govern
it ii. 325. A lively description is
agreeable, though the subject

Epithets) redundant ii. 359.

Epitritus ii. 181.

Essays on man) criticised ii. 176.

Esteem) love of i. 192. 231.

Esther) of Racine censured i. 485. 490.
<548>

Eunuch) of Terence censured i. 509.

Euripides) censured i. 508. ii. 424.

Evergreens) cut in the shape of animals
ii. 443.

Effect of experience with respect to
taste in the fine arts ii. 501. *note.*

Expression) elevated, low i. 223.
Expression that has no distinct
meaning i. 517. Members of a sentence expressing a resemblance
betwixt two objects, ought to resemble each other ii. 34. *&c.* Force of
expression by suspending the
thought till the close ii. 76.

External objects) their reality i. 88.

External senses) distinguished into
two kinds i. 1. External sense ii. 505.

External signs) of emotions and passions ch. 15. External signs of
passion, what emotions they raise in
a spectator i. 106. *&c.*

Eye-sight) influenced by passion i. 176,
177. 288. 291.

Face) though uniformity prevail in
the human face, yet every face is
distinguishable from another
i. 331.

Faculty) by which we know passion
from its external signs i. 441.

Fairy Queen) criticised ii. 285.

False quantity) painful to the ear
ii. 123.

Fame) love of i. 192.

Familiarity) its effect i. 118. 259. ii. 301.
it wears off by absence i. 266.

Fashion) its influence accounted for
i. 69. Fashion is in a continual flux
i. 206.

Fear) explained i. 81. *&c.* Rises often to
its utmost pitch in an instant i. 119.
Fear arising from affection or aversion i. 120. Fear is infectious i. 180.

Feeling) its different significations
ii. 509.

Fiction) emotions raised by fiction
i. 88. *&c.*

Figure) beauty of i. 201. Definition of
a regular figure ii. 521.

Figures) some passions favourable
to figurative expression i. 497.
ii. 204.

Figures ch. 20. Figure of speech
ii. 240. 278. 299, *&c.* Figures were
of old much strained ii. 184. 284.

Final cause) defined i. 358. Final cause
of our sense of order and connection i. 32. of the sympathetic
emotion of virtue i. 64, 65. of the
instinctive passion of fear i. 81. 82,
of the instinctive passion of anger
i. 86. of ideal presence i. 100. *&c.*
of the power that fiction has over
the mind i. 103. of emotions and
passions i. 181. *&c.* of the communication of passion to related objects
i. 192. of regularity, uniformity, or-
<549>der, and simplicity, i. 201. of
proportion i. 202. of beauty i. 208.
Why certain objects are neither
pleasant nor painful i. 219. 220. 250.
of the pleasure we have in motion
and force i. 257. of curiosity i. 258.
of wonder i. 269. of surprise i. 270.
of the principle that prompts us to
perfect every work i. 295. of the
pleasure or pain that results from
the different circumstances of a

Hatred) how produced i. 119. Signifies more commonly affection than passion i. 119. Its endurance i. 123.

Hearing) in hearing we feel no impression ii. 510.

Henriade) censured ii. 333. 383. 389. 394.

Hexameter) Virgil's hexameters extremely melodious, those of Horace seldom so ii. 101. And the reason why they are not ii. 118. Structure of an hexameter line ii. 105. Rules for its structure ii. 107, 108. Musical pauses in an Hexameter line ii. 107. *note.* Wherein its melody consists ii. 118.

Hiatus) defined ii. 9.

Hippolytus) of Euripides censured i. 489. ii. 423. 424.

History) why the history of heroes and conquerors is singularly agreeable i. 63. 228. By what means does history raise our passions i. 95, 96, 97. It rejects poetical images ii. 326, 327.

History-painting. *See* Painting. <552>

Homer) defective in order and connection i. 27. His language finely suited to his subject ii. 348. His repetitions defended ii. 357. His poems in a great measure dramatic ii. 372. Censured ii. 392.

Hope i. 120.

Horace) defective in connection i. 27. His hexameters not melodious ii. 101. Their defects pointed out ii. 118.

Horror) objects of horror should be banished from poetry and painting ii. 366.

House) a fine house gives lustre to the owner i. 70. *note.*

Human nature) a complicated machine i. 34.

Humanity) the finest temper of mind i. 112.

Humour) defined i. 369. Humour in writing distinguished from humour in character i. 360.

Hyperbole i. 243. ii. 259, *&c.*

Hippobachius ii. 179.

Iambic verse) its modulation faint ii. 101.

Iambus ii. 178.

Jane Shore) censured i. 466. 478. 479.

Idea) not so easily remembered as a perception is i. 170, 171. Succession of ideas i. 305. Pleasure and pain of ideas in a train i. 313, *&c.* Idea of memory defined ii. 511. Cannot be innate ii. 516. *note.* There are no general ideas ii. 516. *note.* Idea of an object of sight more distinct than of any other object ii. 518. Ideas distinguished into three kinds ii. 520. Ideas of imagination not so pleasant as ideas of memory ii. 525.

Ideal presence i. 90, *&c.* raised by theatrical representation i. 96. raised by painting i. 96.

Ideal system ii. 512. *note.*

Identity of a passion or of an emotion i. 116.

Jet d'eau i. 253. ii. 442. 444, 445.

Jingle of words ii. 160. 169.

Iliad) criticised ii. 406. 407.

Images) the life of poetry and rhetoric i. 93. 100. 238.

Imagination) the great instrument of recreation i. 272. To give play to it has a good effect in gardening ii. 452. Its power in fabricating images ii. 519. 525. Agreeableness of ideas of imagination ii. 525.

Object (*continued*)
ii. 440. Object defined ii. 505.
Objects of external sense in what
place perceived ii. 505. 506. Objects
of internal sense ii. 507. All objects
of sight are complex ii. 517. 530. Objects simple and complex ii. 530. 531.
Obstacles) to gratification inflame a
passion i. 121.
Old Bachelor) censured ii. 409.
Opera) censured i. 338.
Opinion) influenced by passion i. 152,
&c. ii. 228. influenced by propensity
i. 164. influenced by affection i. 165.
Why differing from me in opinion
is disagreeable ii. 493. Opinion
defined ii. 526.
Oration) of Cicero *pro Archia poeta*
censured ii. 80.
Orchard ii. 448.
Order i. 22, &c. 204. ii. 524. Pleasure
we have in order i. 25. necessary in
all compositions i. 27. Sense of
order has an influence upon our passions i. 76. Order and proportion
contribute to grandeur i. 212. When
a list of many particulars is brought
into a period, in what order should
they be placed? ii. 73, &c. Order in
stating facts ii. 407.
Organ of sense i. 1.
Organic pleasure i. 1. 2, &c.
Orlando Furioso) censured ii. 408.
Ornament) ought to be suited to the
subject i. 338, &c. Redundant ornaments ought to be avoided ii. 324.
Ornaments distinguished into what
are merely such, and what have relation to use ii. 472. Allegorical or
emblematic ornaments ii. 482. 483.
Ossian) excels in drawing characters
ii. 339.

Othello) censured ii. 366.
Ovid) censured i. 323.

Paeon ii. 180.
Pain) cessation of pain extremely
pleasant i. 60. Pain, voluntary and
involuntary i. 112. 113. Different
effects of <559> pain upon the temper i. 113. Social pain less severe than
selfish i. 113. Pain of a train of perceptions in certain circumstances
i. 314. Pain lessens by custom i. 416.
ii. 489. Pain of want i. 417.
Painful emotions and passions i. 105,
&c.
Painting) power of painting to move
our passions i. 96. Its power to
engage our belief i. 101. What
degree of variety is requisite i. 321.
322. A picture ought to be so simple
as to be seen at one view i. 322. In
grotesque painting the figures ought
to be small, in historical painting as
great as the life i. 225. Grandeur of
manner in painting i. 238. A landscape admits not variety of
expression i. 302. Painting is an imitation of nature ii. 3. In
history-painting the principal figure
ought to be in the best light ii. 354.
A good picture agreeable though the
subject be disagreeable ii. 362.
Objects that strike terror have a fine
effect in painting ii. 364. Objects of
horror ought not to be represented
ii. 366. Unity of action in a picture
ii. 410. What emotions can be raised
by painting ii. 431.
Panic) cause of it. i. 180.
Paradise Lost) the richness of its melody ii. 163. censured ii. 384. 385.
Parallelogram) its beauty i. 203.

Pedestal) ought to be sparingly ornamented ii. 473.

Perceptions) more easily remembered than ideas i. 171. Succession of perceptions i. 17. 305. Unconnected perceptions find not easy admittance to the mind i. 308. 314. Pleasure and pain of perceptions in a train i. 313, &c. Perception defined ii. 508. described ii. 534. Original and secondary ii. 511, &c. Simple and complex ii. 510.

Period) has a fine effect when its members proceed in the form <561> of an increasing series ii. 16. In the periods of a discourse variety ought to be studied ii. 17. Different thoughts ought not to be crowded into one period ii. 32. The scene ought not to be changed in a period ii. 39. A period so arranged as to express the sense clearly, seems more musical than where the sense is left doubtful ii. 62. In what part of the period doth a word make the greatest figure ii. 71. A period ought to be closed with that word which makes the greatest figure ii. 73. When there is occasion to mention many particulars, in what order ought they to be placed? ii. 73, &c. A short period is lively and familiar, a long period grave and solemn ii. 79. A discourse ought not to commence with a long period ii. 80.

Personification ii. 228, &c. Passionate and descriptive ii. 236.

Perspicuity) a capital requisite in writing ii. 19. Perspicuity in arrangement ii. 54.

Phantasm ii. 512. note.

Pharsalia) censured ii. 372.

Phedra) of Racine censured i. 423. 504.

Picture) See Painting.

Pilaster) less beautiful than a column ii. 477.

Pindar) defective in order and connection i. 27.

Pity) defined i. 42. apt to produce love i. 79. always painful, yet always agreeable i. 110. resembles its cause i. 181. What are the proper subjects for raising pity ii. 376, &c.

Place) explained ii. 532.

Plain) a large plain, a beautiful object i. 176.

Planetary system) its beauty i. 248. 256.

Plautus) the liberty he takes as to place and time ii. 427.

Play) is a chain of connected facts, each scene making a link ii. 408. 409.

Play of words) i. 391. 514, &c. gone into disrepute i. 392. Comparisons that resolve into a play of words ii. 218, &c.

Pleasant emotions and passions i. 105, &c. Social passions more pleasant than the selfish i. 112. Pleasant pain explained i. 127. 128.

Pleasure) pleasures of seeing and hearing distinguished from those of the other senses i. 1, &c. pleasure of order i. 25. of connection i. 25. Pleasures of taste, touch, and smell, not termed *emotions* or *passions* i. 33. Pleasure of a reverie i. 93. 315. Pleasures refined and gross i. 112. Pleasure of a train of perceptions in certain circumstances i. 313, &c. <562> Corporeal pleasure low, and sometimes mean i. 356. Pleasures of the eye and ear never low or mean i. 356. Pleasures of the understand-

Propensity (*continued*)
every work that is begun, and to
carry things to perfection i. 293.
ii. 477. Propensity to communicate
to others every thing that affects us
i. 494. Propensity to place together
things mutually connected ii. 62.
Propensity defined ii. 526. 527. *See*
Principle.

Properties) transferred from one subject to another i. 66. 176. 177. 198.
ii. 4. 62. 66. 85. 112. 144. 145. 269. 301.

Property) the affection man bears to
his property i. 72. A secondary relation i. 336. *note.*

Prophecy) those who believe in proph-
ecies wish the accomplishment
i. 193.

Propriety) ch. 10. a secondary relation
i. 336. *note.* distinguished from congruity i. 337. distinguished from
proportion i. 346. Propriety in
buildings ii. 467. 468.

Proportion) contributes to grandeur
i. 212. distinguished from propriety
i. 346. As to quantity coincides with
congruity i. 346. examined as
applied to architecture ii. 460. Proportion defined ii. 523.

Prose) distinguished from verse ii. 98,
&c.

Prospect) an unbounded prospect disagreeable i. 294. *note.* By what
means a prospect may be improved
ii. 441. 442.

Provoked Husband) censured ii. 399.

Pun) defined i. 396.

Punishment) in the place where the
crime was committed i. 298. Punishment of impropriety i. 343, *&c.* 349.

Public games) of the Greeks i. 254.

Phyrrhichius ii. 178. <564>

Qualities) primary and secondary
i. 206. 207. A quality cannot be conceived independent of the subject to
which it belongs ii. 50. Different
qualities perceived by different
senses ii. 505. 506. Communicated
to related objects. *See* Propensity.

Quantity) with respect to melody
ii. 105. Quantity with respect to
English verse ii. 120. False quantity
ii. 122.

Quintilian) censured ii. 261. 262.

Quintus Curtius) censured i. 465.

Racine) criticised i. 504. Censured
i. 509.

Rape of the Lock) characterised i. 368.
Its verse admirable ii. 104.

Reading) chief talent of a fine reader
i. 428. Plaintive passions require a
slow pronunciation i. 460. *note.*
Rules for reading ii. 94, *&c.* compared with singing ii. 96.

Reality of external objects i. 88.

Reason) reasons to justify a favourite
opinion are always at hand, and
much relished i. 155.

Recitative ii. 101.

Refined pleasure i. 111.

Regularity) not so essential in great
objects as in small i. 214. not in a
small work so much as in one that
is extensive i. 214. How far to be
studied in architecture ii. 435. 455.
460. How far to be studied in a garden ii. 438. Regular line defined
ii. 521. Regular figure defined ii. 523.
Regularity proper and figurative
ii. 523.

Relations i. 18. Have an influence in
generating emotions and passions
i. 66, *&c.* Are the foundation of

fine arts as well as in morals corrupted by voluptuousness ii. 500. corrupted by love of riches ii. 500. Taste never naturally bad <570> or wrong ii. 503. Aberrations from a true taste in the fine arts ii. 497. 498.

Tautology) a blemish in writing ii. 359.

Telemachus) an epic poem ii. 370. *note.* Censured ii. 396. *note.*

Temples) of ancient and modern virtue in the gardens of Stow ii. 483.

Terence) censured i. 509, *&c.* ii. 425. 426.

Terror) arises sometimes to its utmost height instantaneously i. 117, *&c.* a silent passion i. 495. Objects that strike terror have a fine effect in poetry and painting ii. 362. The terror raised by tragedy explained ii. 377.

Theorem) general theorems agreeable i. 205.

Time) past time expressed as present i. 98, *&c.* Natural computation of time i. 165, *&c.* Time explained ii. 532. 533.

Titus Livius. *See* Livy.

Tone) of mind ii. 508.

Touch) in touching we feel an impression upon the organ of sense ii. 509.

Trachiniens) of Sophocles censured ii. 424.

Tragedy) the deepest tragedies are the most crowded i. 447. *note.* The later English tragedies censured i. 456. French tragedy censured i. 459. *note.* 486. The Greek tragedy accompanied with musical notes to ascertain the pronunciation ii. 96. Tragedy ch. 22. in what respect it differs from an epic poem ii. 370. distin-

guished into pathetic and moral ii. 372. its good effects ii. 374. compared with the epic as to the subjects proper for each ii. 375. how far it may borrow from history ii. 382. rule for dividing it into acts ii. 383. 384. double plot in it ii. 397. admits not violent action or supernatural events ii. 399. its origin ii. 412. Ancient tragedy a continued representation without interruption ii. 413. Constitution of the modern drama ii. 414.

Tragi-comedy ii. 399.

Trees) the best manner of placing them ii. 440. 441. 442.

Triangle) equilateral, its beauty i. 204.

Tribrachys ii. 178.

Trochaeus ii. 178.

Tropes ch. 20.

Ugliness) proper and figurative ii. 521.

Unbounded prospect) disagreeable i. 294. *note.* <571>

Uniformity of the operations of nature i. 325, *&c.* Uniformity apt to disgust by excess i. 204. Uniformity and variety ch. 9. conspicuous in the works of nature i. 330. The melody of the verse ought to be uniform where the things described are uniform ii. 141. Uniformity defined ii. 522.

Unity) the three unities ch. 23. of action ii. 405, *&c.* Unity of action in a picture ii. 410. of time and of place ii. 410, *&c.* Unities of time and of place not required in an epic poem ii. 411. Strictly observed in the Greek tragedy ii. 413. Unity of place in the ancient drama ii. 423. Unities of place and time ought to be

FINIS. <574>

Printed for J. Bell and W. Creech, Edinburgh;
G. Robinson and T. Cadell, London.

1. The Dictionary of Decisions of the Court of Session, from its first institution to the present time, 2 vols fol.

2. Decisions of the Court of Session from 1716 to 1730, folio, 10 s. bound.

3. Remarkable Decisions from 1730 to 1752, folio, 14 s. bound.

4. Select Decisions from 1752 to 1768, folio, 18 s. bound.

5. Historical Law-Tracts, 8vo, with additions, third edition, 6 s. bound.

6. Elucidations respecting the Common and Statute Law of Scotland, 8vo, 6 s. bound.

7. The Statute-Law of Scotland abridged, 2d edition, 8vo, 6 s. bound.

8. Essays on British Antiquities, 12mo, 2d edition, 2 s. 6 d. bound.

9. Sketches of the History of Man, 4 vols 8vo, 2d edit. 24 s. bound.

10. An Introduction to the Art of Thinking, 12mo, 3d edition, 3 s. bound.

11. Gentleman Farmer, being an attempt to improve Agriculture, by subjecting it to the test of rational principles, the second edition, with considerable additions, 8vo, 7 s.

12. Principles of Equity, 2 vols 8vo, 3d edition, 12 s. bound.

13. Essays on the Principles of Morality and Natural Religion, corrected and improved in a third edition. Several Essays added concerning the proof of a Deity, 5 s. bound.

14. Loose Hints upon Education, chiefly concerning the Culture of the Heart, 8vo, 2d edition, corrected and enlarged, 6 s. bound.

INDEX

Abdoulrahman, Moorish King of Spain, 189n

abstract or general terms: defined, 745–47; narration and description, 633–35; personification, 497, 540–42, 547–48; simile, use in, 497

abstract speculation, distaste of certain persons for, 26–27

acanthus leaves and Corinthian order, 715

accent in versification, 441; classical hexameter, 448–51; English blank verse, 481; English rhyme, 454, 470–73

action: custom and habit distinguished, 280; dignity of, 248; emotions and passions leading to, 38–40; external signs of emotions and passions, 301–2; language in drama and epic compositions required to be subservient to, 657–58; unity of action, 670–73, 678; violent action in drama, objections to, 666–67

active voice, 402, 461–63

Adam, Robert, xvi

Adam, William, 708n

Addison, Joseph: *The Campaign,* 455; *Cato,* 360, 515; causes of emotions and passions, 65; *The Drummer,* 331, 334; grandeur and sublimity, 160, 161n, 165n; Halifax, Earl of, as patron, 584n; Harrison, William, as

friend of, 347n; humorous writings, 255; Kames influenced by, xvi; Kit-Kat Club, member of, 76n; language used to express emotions and passions, 360; *A Letter from Italy,* 455, 473; "machinery" (appearances by supernatural beings), criticism of, 661–62; resemblance and dissimilitude, 209; rhyme, elevation of low subjects by, 489; *Rosamond,* 489–90; sentiments, 331, 334; signification, beauty of language with respect to, 394n; simile, 512, 515; versification, 455, 473, 489–90; violent action in drama, 667; wit, 265

Adelphi (Terence), 359

adjectives, 403, 404, 458–60

admiration: courageous action, produced by, 49–50; external signs of emotions and passions, 297–300, 298

adverbs, 403, 404, 460–61

Aeneid. See Virgil

Aeschylus: *Agamemnon,* 537; biographical information, 295n; *Choephori,* 295; dialogue, invention of, 675

Aesop, 650n

affection: defined, 741; habit of, 283–84. *See also* pleasure and pain

Africa, 160

Agamemnon (Aeschylus), 537

Agamemnon (Seneca), 339

genus, defined, 743

George III, dedication of *Elements of Criticism* to, 3–4

Georgics. See Virgil

Gerard, Alexander, xv, xvi, 171n

Gerusalemme Liberata. See Tasso, Torquato

Gibbs, James, 716n

Gilpin, William, xvii

Girard, G. (*French Grammar*), 389n

Gluck, Christoph Willibald, 50n

God's Revenge Against Punning (Arbuthnot), 417

Goethe, Johann Wolfgang von, 167n

good breeding and manners: anger, rough and blunt manners aligned to, 307n; external signs of emotions and passions, restraint in, 299, 307–8

good nature: dignity and, 247; external signs of emotions and passions, 296

Gothic style, 694, 701, 707–8, 721, 725

grace, 251–52

grammatical issues, 402–5. *See also* beauty of language, and specific grammatical elements, e.g., adverbs

grandeur and sublimity, 150–78; abstract and general terms, avoidance of, 170; ambition related to fondness for, 164–65; architecture, 686, 707, 709; beauty, relationship to, 144, 151–54; climax, 161, 171; coexistence of grandeur and terror, 94; defined, 151; dignity and meanness, 246; emotion of grandeur, 152; emotion of sublimity, 154; false sublime or bombast, 173–77; figurative sense of, 158–61; force and grandeur, 181; gardening, 686, 688, 690; heroic figures seldom disfigured by gross acts, 177–78; humbling object, artful introduction of, 171–72; limitations

of effect to what can be seen in one view, 161–63; littleness and lowness not necessarily disagreeable, 156–57; magnitude and elevation, 150–52; manner, rule for creating a grandeur of, 165–66; mind roused and animated without being stirred to, 163–64; painting, 169–70; poetic examples of, 166–69; poetic praise for, 154–56; reiterated impressions, importance of, 170–71; relationship between, 154, 158; rhyme, 488; risible objects never grand, 194; wit and ridicule not an agreeable mixture with grandeur, 213

gratitude, 49, 114, 130

Greek drama: origins and rules of, 674–75; pronunciation, notes for, 436

Greek hexameter. *See* classical hexameter

Greek language, 377n, 403, 404, 427

Greene, Maurice, 491n

Grenville, Sir Richard, 52n

grief and sorrow: causes of, 46–48; external signs of emotions and passions, 296, 298, 304; metaphor and allegory, 587–88; perceptions, opinions, and beliefs influenced by, 116; personification, 554; resemblance of emotions to their causes, 130; sentiments, proper representation of, 322; silence of immoderate passions, 348–49; simile, propriety of, 514–17

Guardian, The: signification, beauty of language with respect to, 389, 399, 409, 410, 416, 421, 424; simile, 512n

Guarini, Giovanni Battista (*Pastor Fido*): coexistent emotions and passions, 102–4; external signs of emotions and passions, 302–3; Handel's music for, 103n; hyperbole, 562–63;